Emory Symposia in Cognition 2

**Remembering reconsidered:
Ecological and traditional approaches
to the study of memory**

Remembering reconsidered: Ecological and traditional approaches to the study of memory

Edited by
ULRIC NEISSER
and
EUGENE WINOGRAD

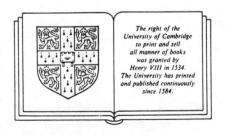

The right of the
University of Cambridge
to print and sell
all manner of books
was granted by
Henry VIII in 1534.
The University has printed
and published continuously
since 1584.

CAMBRIDGE UNIVERSITY PRESS

Cambridge
New York   Port Chester
Melbourne   Sydney

Published by the Press Syndicate of the University of Cambridge
The Pitt Building, Trumpington Street, Cambridge, CB2 1RP
40 West 20th Street, New York, NY 10011, USA
10 Stamford Road, Oakleigh, Melbourne 3166, Australia

© Cambridge University Press 1988

First published 1988
Reprinted 1990

Printed in the United States of America

Library of Congress Cataloging-in-Publication Data

Remembering reconsidered.
(Emory symposia in cognition ; 2)
Includes index.
1. Memory – Congresses.   I. Neisser, Ulric.
II. Winograd, Eugene.   III. Series.
BF371.R38   1988   153.1′2   87-27642

British Library Cataloging-in-Publication Data

Remembering reconsidered : ecological and
traditional approaches to the study of
memory. – (Emory symposia in cognition;2)
1. Memory
I. Neisser, Ulric   II. Winograd, Eugene
153.1′2   BF371

ISBN 0-521-33031-9 hardback

Contents

Preface

This is the second volume in the Emory Symposia in Cognition series. It was originally conceived in a seminar on memory that the two of us conducted together in the fall of 1984 – a seminar characterized, like all Cognition Project seminars, by a vigorous airing of many different points of view. Although we devoted a good deal of time and thought to the ecological approach (as is also typical of Cognition Project seminars), more traditional lines of research were not neglected. Indeed, we could not neglect them if we were to do justice to our topic. The study of memory has undergone a remarkable renaissance in the past few years; good ideas and important research have begun to appear from many different directions. There are new findings everywhere: in the naturalistic study of memory, in the laboratory study of basic processes, in development, in neuropsychology, in the understanding of clinical memory disorders. Although we could not do justice to all of those areas in the seminar (nor, alas, in this volume), we did our best to focus on good ideas wherever they might come from. A lot of those good ideas are in this book.

Although the primary goal of the seminar was to understand as much as we could about memory, it was clear that we were working toward a conference as well. The first Emory Cognition Project Conference – whose results have since been published by Cambridge University Press as *Concepts and Conceptual Development: Ecological and Intellectual Factors in Categorization* (1987) – was held that same fall, and we were pleased with its success. It, too, had grown out of a seminar held the year before. The way to get on top of critical areas in cognitive psychology, then, is as follows:

Begin by spending a semester or so on the area to be covered in a seminar, and try to figure out what is going on in it.
Identify the people who are doing the most interesting and important work in the area, whether from the ecological point of view or any other.
Persuade those people to come to a conference to present and discuss their work.

> Provide discussants at the conference who not only will take the speakers'
> views apart (as necessary) but also will show how they fit together.

We did all that; the result was the Second Emory Cognition Project
Conference, held October 10–12, 1985. Like the first conference, it was
an extraordinarily stimulating intellectual experience. Again, like the
first conference, it left us with a sense that our field of study was considerably more coherent than we had supposed. The two introductory chapters that follow this Preface (one by each of us) try to express that coherence; it is for the reader to judge whether or not we have succeeded.

If the understanding we gain at such a conference is to be shared with
(and tested by) the larger community of psychology and cognitive science, one more principle must be added to the foregoing list:

> Get all the conference participants to contribute chapters to a book based
> on the conference, and try to make sure that the book as a whole reflects
> the character and quality of the original meeting.

We think we have done that too – or, rather, it is the participants
themselves who have done it. Every contribution to the 1985 conference
has now become a chapter in this volume. Some of the chapters have
been substantially reworked (this is especially true of Brewer's chapter;
he had only preliminary data available at the time of the conference),
whereas others are almost unchanged. There are also three new chapters: our two introductory chapters plus Chapter 11 (on train-wreck
ballads) by Wallace and Rubin. David Rubin had described this work
with some preliminary data at an Emory Colloquium the previous
spring; it was so obviously an appropriate contribution that we did not
want to leave it out.

We are grateful to all our contributors, not only for their contributions
but also for their responsiveness to our suggestions and their patience
with our delays. We want to note, for the second time, what a pleasure it
is to work with Susan Milmoe and the Cambridge University Press. We
also want to express our appreciation to the Emory graduate students
who were so helpful in organizing the details of the conference, particularly JoNell Usher, Pamela Mink, Ira Hyman, Marion Eppler, and Eric
Bergman. Finally, we are grateful to Emory University for its continuing
support of the Cognition Project and its activities. In the last analysis, it is
the university that has made this book possible.

Ulric Neisser
Eugene Winograd

Contributors

HARRY P. BAHRICK is Jackson University Professor of Psychology at Ohio Wesleyan University.

CRAIG R. BARCLAY is Assistant Professor of Education and Human Development and Psychology at the University of Rochester.

LAWRENCE W. BARSALOU is Associate Professor of Psychology at the Georgia Institute of Technology.

WILLIAM F. BREWER is Professor of Psychology at the University of Illinois, Urbana-Champaign.

PEGGY A. DeCOOKE is a graduate student in psychology at the University of Pittsburgh.

ROBYN FIVUSH is Assistant Professor of Psychology at Emory University.

LARRY L. JACOBY is Professor of Psychology at McMaster University.

STEEN F. LARSEN is Associate Professor of Psychology at the University of Aarhus.

ROBERT N. McCAULEY is Assistant Professor of Philosophy at Emory University.

ULRIC NEISSER is Robert W. Woodruff Professor of Psychology at Emory University.

KATHERINE NELSON is Distinguished Professor of Psychology at the City University of New York.

ELIZABETH PHELPS is a graduate student in psychology at Princeton University.

DAVID C. RUBIN is Professor of Psychology at Duke University.

DONALD P. SPENCE is Professor of Psychiatry at Robert Wood Johnson Medical School, Piscataway, New Jersey.

WANDA T. WALLACE is Research Associate in Psychology at Duke University.

EUGENE WINOGRAD is Professor of Psychology at Emory University.

1

New vistas in the study of memory

ULRIC NEISSER

This book presents important new findings and new ideas about remembering: what people remember, why they remember it, and how we might best describe the processes involved. These issues have been considered before, most notably by Sir Frederick Bartlett in the 1932 book from which our title is derived. Arguing that standard laboratory methods did not do justice to what he called the subject's "effort after meaning," Bartlett introduced both new procedures (recall of meaningful stories) and new theoretical concepts (e.g., "schema") into the study of memory. Although the influence of his work was slow to develop at first, its importance is now widely acknowledged: Story recall has become a standard laboratory technique, and "schema" a standard theoretical idea. No longer revolutionary, Bartlett's insights have been effectively assimilated into the traditional psychology of memory.

In the mid-1970s I undertook a general critique of contemporary mental-model-oriented cognitive psychology, including the study of memory (see *Cognition and Reality* [Neisser, 1976]). In the hope of stimulating a serious reconsideration of the prevailing assumptions in memory research, I presented a paper sharply critical of traditional approaches at the Cardiff conference on "Practical Aspects of Memory" in 1978. After nearly a century of research, psychologists still knew almost nothing about recall of early childhood experiences, about memorizing songs and poems, about memory for places, faces, and names, about the fate of knowledge acquired in school, about oral history, about testimony, about prospective remembering, or even about individual differences. I summarized these omissions in a simple rule: "If X is an interesting or socially significant aspect of memory, then psychologists have hardly ever studied X" (Neisser, 1978, p. 4).

I developed the argument somewhat further in a book of readings called *Memory Observed: Remembering in Natural Contexts* (Neisser, 1982). The book presented some 40 examples of research from what I called "the low road" in memory research, to distinguish it from "the high road" of standard laboratory procedures. Following the high road had

1

not been fruitless: Valid empirical generalizations had been established, discoveries made, sophisticated models and theories proposed. Nevertheless, the overall result left much to be desired. The empirical generalizations were often rather obvious (e.g., the role of similarity in interference), the discoveries were intriguing but hard to intepret (e.g., the dependence of memory search time on the number of alternatives), and the models, which never applied outside of narrowly defined experimental contexts, were invariably soon disconfirmed. Although those who followed the low road had even fewer achievements to their credit, there was reason to believe that their route might open up new vistas. The principal goals of *Memory Observed* were to illustrate the possibilities of naturalistic memory research and encourage people to do more of it.

As things turned out, very little encouragement was needed. The past 10 years have witnessed a surprising surge of interest in the ecological approach to memory, and naturalistic studies have begun to appear in quantity. The principle that I enunciated in 1978 now almost applies in reverse: If X is an interesting or socially significant aspect of memory, some psychologist is probably trying to study it at this very moment! To some extent, this trend is part of a generally growing interest in the ecological approach to cognition, an approach that has implications ranging from the study of direct perception (Gibson, 1979) to concepts and conceptual development (Neisser, 1987). But that is only a small part of the story; most of those who are now engaged in naturalistic memory research came to it without any strong theoretical commitments. They have been primarily interested in the phenomena themselves—in autobiographical memory (Rubin, 1986), in school learning (Bahrick, 1984), in prospective memory and absentmindedness (Harris & Morris, 1984), in legal testimony (Wells & Loftus, 1984), in remembering events and places and people and whatever else there is to be remembered (Gruneberg, Morris, & Sykes, in press).

As always, success brings new responsibilities in its wake. Now that we have all these new facts, what are we to make of them? Are they adequately explained by principles derived from traditional theories of memory, or are entirely new concepts needed? If so, what are those concepts? It is no longer enough to denounce the old laboratory methods and call for more ecologically oriented studies; we have now to examine the findings of those studies and try to understand them. And in doing so we must not make the mistake of supposing that the "traditional" psychology of memory has simply been standing still, waiting for the ecological approach to come along. Since the mid-1970s, the laboratory-based study of remembering has undergone what amounts to a revolution of its own. Tulving's distinction between semantic and episodic memory, the postulation of "schemata" for everything from stories to selves, the research on scripts and event representations, the rush of new findings on memory development in children—all these are signs of renewed vigor and creativity in the field that I criticized so sharply a decade ago. In chapter 14 of this book, I try to interpret these new developments in ecological terms: In effect, they expand our definition of what kinds of real things exist to be remembered. Partly for that reason, I believe that future relations between ecological and traditional studies are more likely to be complementary than antagonistic. In any case, it seems that the time may be ripe for another reconsideration of remembering.

This book is the product of the second Emory Cognition Project Conference, held in Atlanta on October 10–12, 1985. Although the official focus of the conference was "Ecological Approaches to the Study of Memory," the invited speakers did not fit any single mold. Some of them had naturalistic findings to report, some had theoretical ideas to develop, and some had been doing laboratory research that was simply too important to ignore. Their presentations and interactions left us with a sense that a new psychology of memory is beginning to take shape—one that will eventually yield theoretically consistent interpretations of both laboratory paradigms and naturalistic phenomena. We do not have that psychology yet, but we are moving.

A brief overview of the chapters ahead may be helpful at this point. In chapter 2, my coeditor **Eugene Winograd** analyzes the convergence of ecological and traditional research findings in some detail, drawing not only on the work of contributors to this volume but also on other well-established phenomena. He notes that both research traditions are now concerned with issues of verifiability, that both have developed a new interest in the shape of the forgetting function, that both have recognized the critical importance of the distinctiveness of cues. Moreover, both can be considered as the logical successors of "functionalism"—a significant historical tradition that has consistently combined rejection of unnecessary mental hypothesis with an emphasis on adaptation and purpose.

In chapter 3, **William F. Brewer** reports a pair of extraordinary studies of memory for very ordinary events. His subjects carried "beepers" that went off randomly; whenever the beepers sounded, they wrote down where they were, what they were doing, and what they were thinking. Weeks or months later, Brewer tested their memories by recognition (Study 1) or cued recall (Study 2). His findings are rich and important. Memory for these unselected events was (predictably) poorer than in diary studies, in which subjects try to record "the most important event of the day," but forgetting proceeded very slowly, and there were almost *no* intrusions or false recalls. In the many instances when activity and thought were not closely coordinated, memory for the former was better than for the latter. Recall of actions depends most strongly on their uniqueness; recall of thoughts depends most strongly on their degree of excitement. Although many of these findings can be taken as confirmations of traditional principles, application of those principles to such data demands a detailed understanding of the actual lives of the subjects. Brewer is concerned with the theoretical interpretation of his results; for example, he takes the very low error rate to mean that memory is rather less "reconstructive" than he (and I!) used to believe. He also reports a new and interesting finding about the experience of remembering itself: Reports of vivid imagery at the time of test were associated with more complete recall. (But not necessarily with more *accurate* recall, it seems to me. In a study where subjects never make errors, it is logically impossible to establish correlations with accuracy.)

In the data reported by **Craig R. Barclay** and **Peggy A. DeCooke** (chapter 4), the to-be-remembered events were recorded by the subjects at the end of each day. The subsequent recognition tests included "foil" events that had not actually happened, but had been rewritten from the subjects' records. As might be expected on the basis of traditional principles, the probability of being deceived by such a foil depends on exactly what was changed in it and on the similarity between the altered item and the original. Because one of their subjects sustained a tragic personal loss during the time that the study was in progress, Barclay and DeCooke were also able to compare recall of a very important and stressful experience with memory for more mundane daily events. Overall, the stressful experience was remembered much better.

In a thoughtful commentary, **Robert N. McCauley** (chapter 5) discusses the notion of "memory for thoughts" in the light of modern philosophical concerns about reference and meaning. He also points to various difficulties of design and interpretation in the studies reported by Brewer and by Barclay and DeCooke. In a particularly interesting argument, McCauley disputes Brewer's claim that a low error rate is evidence against "reconstructive" theories of memory. Perhaps, he suggests, the subjects of the beeper experiments were just accurate in their reconstructions!

Larry L. Jacoby, who explicitly identifies himself as a functionalist, begins chapter 6 with a vigorous defense of traditional laboratory methods. He then shows in a series of ingenious experiments that past experiences that the subject does not recall—and cannot even identify as familiar—may nevertheless exert specific and long-lasting effects. This is not because structurally distinct memory systems are involved: Jacoby rejects structural hypotheses on principle. He suggests that the feeling of familiarity is itself the result of a process of attribution, vulnerable to error under certain conditions just as other attributions are. More generally, he notes that a detailed examination of the relation between encoding conditions and retrieval conditions often makes it unnecessary to postulate generalized mental representations, complex cognitive systems, and other hypothetical structures. Jacoby's reluctance to postulate mental structures in memory reminds me forcibly of James J. Gibson's approach to perception, though he obviously does not share Gibson's antipathy to traditional laboratory methods.

Harry P. Bahrick and **Elizabeth Phelps,** who also call themselves functionalists, present a new and elegant study of long-term semantic memory in chapter 7. Their study differs from Bahrick's earlier work on long-term retention (of Spanish learned at school, in Bahrick [1984]; of the layout of a town, in Bahrick [1983]; of high school classmates, in Bahrick, Bahrick, & Wittlinger [1975]) by introducing a specific experimental intervention. They begin by identifying items of information that the subject may once have known but now no longer remembers: bits of general knowledge, vocabulary words from a foreign language, and the names of pictured, once-famous individuals. Subjects are then given minimal "refresher" trials on some of this material (one correct trial per item). These refreshers have powerful effects, even on items that subjects did not think they knew at all when the experiment began. The relearning of such items is very much faster than the learning of entirely new (but comparable) material by control subjects. This is not only a novel finding but also an encouraging one: Evidently we all know a great deal more than we think we do. Much of that knowledge may not be difficult to reinstate with the procedures developed by Bahrick and Phelps.

In chapter 8, **Lawrence W. Barsalou** describes an approach to autobiographical memory that was originally stimulated by work in artificial intelligence (AI). He begins with a naturalistic study: People were simply asked to "tell me about events you were involved in this past summer." Surprisingly, their responses did not consist primarily of reports of specific events or occasions. Subjects usually recalled their summers in terms of generic (repeated) events, extended (noncontinuous) events, and comments. Barsalou considers these results in terms of various possible modes of mental organization – by events, by participants, by locations, and by times. A series of experiments with artificial materials then suggests that people can organize remembered experiences in a variety of different ways, with "global sequences of chronologically ordered extended events" being the most fundamental. Barsalou uses these findings as the basis of a rather elaborate theory: Autobiographical memory is structured in terms of "extended-event time lines" that are themselves hierarchically (perhaps spatially) organized. Remembered events involve sets of particular "exemplars" linked by various kinds of conceptual relations; generic mental representations also play an important role.

Barsalou's AI-oriented approach does not fit comfortably into either an ecological or a traditional memory niche, but his ability to address the issues raised by theorists of many different persuasions gives his work a special interest.

Although "cognition" and "cognitive development" are sometimes treated as separate fields of study, they are really just two ways of thinking about the same set of problems. In accord with this principle, about half the chapters in the first Emory Cognition Symposium (*Concepts and Conceptual Development* [Neisser, 1987]) were devoted to developmental issues. The third symposium volume (*What Young Children Remember and Why* [to be edited by Fivush & Hudson]) will deal entirely with the development of memory. In the present volume, however, there are only two developmental contributions: Nelson's chapter 9 and Fivush's subsequent commentary. **Katherine Nelson** offers nothing less than a functionally based account of the development of memory over the first few years of life – the most detailed and empirically justified such account that has yet been undertaken. As might be expected, she relies heavily on the large body of research on young children's memory that she and her collaborators have carried out so impressively in the last several years. In addition, she presents a set of new data based on the recorded presleep monologues of a single subject, Emily, who was 21 months old at the beginning of the study and 36 months at the end. Taken together, these findings allow Nelson to trace the early development of memory for events, as well as memory for scripts and routines, to examine the relations among remembering, fantasizing, and anticipating, and to speculate about the origins of genuinely autobiographical memory somewhat later in childhood.

Robyn Fivush's commentary in chapter 10 focuses on the role of memory in self-definition. Our notions of who we are depend heavily on what we remember about ourselves – not so much on specific past episodes, but on typical or extended sequences of events. Fivush finds striking structural similarities between Emily's later monologues and the responses of Barsalou's adult subjects recalling their summer vacations: Both are characterized by hierarchically organized routines in which summarized events are embedded. With age and development, the embedding events start to involve longer and longer time periods. Eventually they begin to form what amounts to an extended life history, and a genuinely autobiographical memory structure takes shape.

One of my own favorite examples of naturalistic research in memory is Albert Lord's study of ballad singers in Yugoslavia (Neisser, 1982, pp. 243–257). In chapter 11, **Wanda T. Wallace** and **David C. Rubin** report what amounts to a carefully controlled, quantitatively analyzed modern American replication of Lord's work. Their material is a folk ballad –

"The Wreck of the Old 97" – that is still sung in the hills on North Carolina. Wallace and Rubin used an elegant combination of field and laboratory techniques. They recorded the "Wreck" as it was actually sung by five different ballad singers, each on two different occasions; they also presented naive college-student subjects with various specially modified versions of the song and asked them to learn it. The data show in detail how various kinds of constraints – metric, poetic, and meaningful – interact to determine what is recalled. They summarize their findings as follows: "The memory for the ballad is not the exact song, nor is it a collection of words; rather, it is a collection of rules and constraints. . . . We have not only a schema for gist but also a schema for poetics, rhythm, imagery, and music. Together these schemata, and possibly others, constrain recall to the extent that it almost appears rote or verbatim." It seems to me that this work offers a striking example of the implications of ecological research for a domain – rote memory – that has usually been studied only in the laboratory.

Donald P. Spence, who writes about passive memories in chapter 12, is the author of *Narrative Truth and Historical Truth* (1982). Whereas that book was concerned primarily with recall during psychoanalysis, his chapter in this book deals (albeit speculatively) with several kinds of everyday memory experiences. In some situations a vivid memory may come to us unbidden, fleetingly, stimulated by some nearly unnoticed and often unreportable aspect of the "enabling context." Later on, such a memory may be incorporated into our recall of that context itself, lending it an air of fantasy and unreality. A related phenomenon is what Spence calls "repetitive remembering," where a particular memory comes to mind over and over again in a particular context, although it has no practical significance whatever. Spence suggests that repetitive memories often serve a defensive function, preventing us from remembering something that would be much less acceptable. He also notes that the "repetition" may be more apparent than real; repetitive memories may be especially subject to the systematic schema-based changes that Bartlett called to our attention long ago. Spence concludes with an example of one of his own memories, now some 15 years old, recalled on two different occasions. The second recall was far richer, more detailed, and more affect-laden than the first. Repetition can apparently lead to elaboration as easily as to schematization; it all depends, Spence believes, on the enabling context.

I have occasionally suggested (e.g., Neisser, 1985) that one way to begin a genuinely ecological approach to the study of memory would be with a preliminary list of the kinds of things that people actually remember. In chapter 13, **Steen F. Larsen** introduces a class of memoria that has been almost universally overlooked by theorists of memory, myself included: reported events of which we have only secondhand knowledge. This large category of memory includes events we have heard about from friends, read about in the newspaper, or watched on television. Such memories are neither "episodic" nor "semantic": Although not referenced to the self, they may be quite specific to a particular time and place. Larsen offers a detailed analysis of the characteristics of memory for reported events and contrasts it with memory of other kinds. For example, there is usually a dual structure that includes a "reception event" as well as the reported event itself. Sometimes the reception event can become a target for memory in its own right, as in Brown and Kulik's (1977) study of "flashbulb memories," but usually it is of little interest and soon forgotten. (This may be an individual-difference variable. I myself find it very hard to remember who told me things, even quite recently, but other people do not seem to have the same problem.) Larsen also notes that events as reported by the news media have a narrative structure of their own, quite different from the structure of more frequently studied memory materials such as stories or autobiographical episodes. How could we have failed to notice them for so long?

My own chapter 14 makes three more or less independent arguments. The first is an ecologically oriented analysis of what the traditionally oriented psychology of memory has accomplished in recent years. On this interpretation (not the only possible one, of course) the biggest single change has been the introduction of several new classes of "memoria" – things that people admittedly remember. Where psychologists used to study only memory for lists and list items, they now study memory for facts, stories, familiar routines, academic materials, geographical layouts, and personally experienced events – an enormous and highly significant change. Turning to the last of these categories, the second part of my chapter proposes a hierarchical analysis of the memoria of autobiographical memory itself. Real events always have a nested structure, with events of smaller scope embedded in more comprehensive ones. We apprehend, understand, and apparently remember events in just this way. I therefore suggest that the structure of autobiographical memory itself – the way the information is stored "in the head" – may be hierarchical in some corresponding sense. Finally, in a third section, I explore the (rather farfetched) conjecture that human autobiographical memory depends heavily on the mammalian spatial orienting system. The behavioral and neuropsychological parallels between the two systems are at least intriguing, and both seem to have similarly nested hierarchical structures.

In a final commentary (chapter 15), **David C. Rubin** is sharply critical of my second claim. To speak of "nested" structure in memory, he suggests, is to make a structure out of a process. It is one thing (and usually useful) to describe the environment at some appropriate level of analysis; it is another (and usually unfortunate) thing to copy that description into the mind. What people acquire as they journey through life are not structures but *skills:* capacities to act in certain adaptive ways. Skills may require stored information, but they do not require stored environment-mimicking structures.

I am grateful for Rubin's eloquent argument. Having argued for the primacy of skill over structure myself in other contexts (Spelke, Hirst, & Neisser, 1976; Neisser, 1983), I am not inclined to dispute it here. Admittedly I find it harder to dispense with structure where memory is concerned, but that is no reason not to try. Perhaps it would be better to say only this: If we want to think of the information in memory as having an intrinsic structure, that structure will turn out to be at least as complex as the hierarchies I have tried to describe. The issue is certainly still open. Indeed, a great many issues in the study of memory—ecological or traditional—are presently open; that is why this is a good time to reconsider them. The ecological and traditional approaches to memory are both making substantial progress, perhaps even in the same direction.

REFERENCES

Bahrick, H. P. (1983). The cognitive map of a city—50 years of learning and memory. In G. H. Bower (Ed.), *The psychology of learning and motivation: Advances in research and theory* (Vol. 17, pp. 125–163). New York: Academic Press.

   (1984). Semantic memory content in permastore: Fifty years of memory for Spanish learned in school. *Journal of Experimental Psychology: General, 113,* 1–29.

Bahrick, H. P., Bahrick, P. O., & Wittlinger, R. P. (1975). Fifty years of memories for names and faces: A cross-sectional approach. *Journal of Experimental Psychology: General, 104,* 54–75.

Bartlett, F. C. (1932). *Remembering.* Cambridge University Press.

Brown, R., & Kulik, J. (1977). Flashbulb memories. *Cognition, 5,* 73–99.

Gibson, J. J. (1979). *The ecological approach to visual perception.* Boston: Houghton Mifflin.

Gruneberg, M. M., Morris, P. E., & Sykes, R. N. (Eds.). (in press). *Practical aspects of memory* (Vol. 2). London: Academic Press.

Harris, J. E., & Morris, P. E. (1984). *Everyday memory, actions, and absent-mindedness.* New York: Academic Press.

Neisser, U. (1976). *Cognition and reality.* New York: W. H. Freeman.

   (1978). Memory: What are the important questions? In M. M. Gruneberg, P. E. Morris, & R. N. Sykes (Eds.), *Practical aspects of memory.* London: Academic Press.

   (1983). Toward a skillful psychology. In D. Rogers & J. A. Sloboda (Eds.), *The acquisition of symbolic skills.* New York: Plenum.

   (1985). The role of theory in the ecological study of memory: Comment on Bruce. *Journal of Experimental Psychology: General, 114,* 272–276.

(Ed.). (1982). *Memory observed: Remembering in natural contexts.* New York: W. H. Freeman.

(Ed.). (1987). *Concepts and conceptual development: Ecological and intellectual factors in categorization.* Cambridge University Press.

Rubin, D. C. (Ed.). (1986). *Autobiographical memory.* Cambridge University Press.

Spelke, E., Hirst, W., & Neisser, U. (1976). Skills of divided attention. *Cognition, 4,* 215–230.

Spence, D. P. (1982). *Narrative truth and historical truth: Meaning and interpretation in psychoanalysis.* New York: Norton.

Wells, G. L., & Loftus, E. F. (1984). *Eyewitness testimony.* Cambridge University Press.

2

Continuities between ecological and laboratory approaches to memory

EUGENE WINOGRAD

This conference on ecological and traditional approaches to memory was held in 1985, 100 years after the publication of Ebbinghaus's monograph (1885/1964) marking the beginnings of a science of memory. Although this happens to be a centennial coincidence rather than an observance, I want to emphasize some continuities between the tradition deriving from Ebbinghaus and more ecologically oriented research. There is a tendency to view the ecological approach to memory as contrasting sharply in both method and theory with the Ebbinghaus tradition. Indeed, some psychologists might see the research represented in this volume as exciting in direct proportion to the liberation it shows from the presumed dreariness and artificiality of the verbal learning tradition descending from Ebbinghaus. I argue here that this would be a mistake and, instead, suggest that there is much in common between laboratory studies of memory and the study of memory for events that did not occur in a psychology laboratory. Further, I believe that Ebbinghaus himself would have approved of most of what he would have heard at the conference.

Continuities across approaches

Verifiability

Ebbinghaus's most important methodological contribution to the scientific study of memory, in my opinion, is that he carefully controlled the conditions at encoding. In the Ebbinghaus tradition, the experimenter is present at the encoding and can therefore score for the accuracy of remembering later on. The problem of verifiability, as Brewer puts it, presents difficulties for the majority of studies of autobiographical memory. It is interesting to consider the research presented here with respect to verifiability.

Consider Jacoby and Bahrick first as the two researchers most firmly placed in the list-learning tradition. Indeed, both are proud to identify themselves as functionalists. In all of Jacoby's research, the subject is first

11

exposed to material under controlled conditions and then tested on it in a variety of ways. He is the only investigator represented here who never departs from this traditional method of studying memory. On the other hand, Bahrick and Phelps begin their research after the subjects have already learned the information on which they will be tested. Their experimental manipulation concerns the type of rehearsal used. Although not present at the encoding, Bahrick and Phelps are still able to score their subjects' answers to their questions for accuracy because of the shared nature of the cultural information requested. The experimenter can score whether or not the picture of a prominent athlete or entertainer is correctly named, or whether or not a Spanish noun is correctly translated, without assuming recall of a particular experience at which the experimenter was present. In short, Bahrick and Phelps are interested in semantic memory, not episodic memory. They can verify the correctness of the subject's knowledge, but not its source. Because they are concerned only with the current state of the knowledge, not knowing its source presents no problem.

If we ask whether or not any of the more ecologically oriented investigators represented here are concerned with verifiability, it may come as a surprise to observe for how many the answer is yes. Thus, Brewer ingeniously had a buzzer go off at unpredictable times as a signal for his subjects to record both their actions and thoughts at that time. The resulting record of activities and thoughts embedded in the daily lives of students provided the set of retrieval cues with which Brewer could ask the students about their past, as well as a record against which to score their memories for accuracy. The records kept in response to the buzzer's demands served Brewer in much the same way as word lists or stories serve the more traditional memory researcher, with the important difference, of course, being the rich ecological record of everyday events and thoughts that serve as the memoria in Brewer's work. Certainly Ebbinghaus would have been pleased.

In this respect, Barclay and DeCooke's methodology also incorporates verifiability. The major difference between their method and Brewer's is that their subjects did not record events until the end of each day. Barclay and DeCooke therefore test memory for those events memorable enough to be recallable at the end of the day in which they occurred. While Brewer discusses problems associated with sampling events in this way, remembering can still be checked against an earlier record. To a lesser extent, Nelson is able to gain some idea of the accuracy of her 2-year-old's musings by checking with Emily's parents about the events reported.

Special mention must be made of Wallace and Rubin, who are concerned not at all with verifiability or accuracy in their fine-grained

analyses of the consistencies between and within traditional ballad singers' versions of "The Wreck of the Old 97." The intertwined contributions of music and verse are demonstrated in Wallace and Rubin's
analysis of the oral tradition as memory demonstrated in performance.
Yet the same investigators shamelessly go on to present the results of
three experiments in which undergraduates were asked to listen to
either sung or spoken versions of the ballad in the psychology laboratory and then to recall the words. Wallace and Rubin, then, incorporate
controlled learning conditions when it suits them and, at other times,
performance by singers who learned the song years earlier under unknown conditions. Similarly, in his research on autobiographical memory, Barsalou presents data on remembering for personal events he
cannot verify, as well as for remembering artificial events learned in the
laboratory. These artificial events were constructed by Lancaster (1985)
to study the organization of recall for events constructed in line with
certain theoretical notions. Like Wallace and Rubin, Barsalou interprets
both sets of observations within a common theoretical framework. Neither set of data is privileged; both are ways of getting at how people
remember their own life histories. The same observation holds for
Wallace and Rubin, except that they are trying to account for remembering songs.

Forgetting

A strong methodological continuity between Ebbinghaus and the ecological research reported in this volume is to be found in the many forgetting
functions contained herein. There are five forgetting curves in Brewer's
chapter alone. In fact, forgetting functions seem as important to ecologically oriented memory researchers as they were to Ebbinghaus. One only
need point to recent work by Bahrick (1984a,b), Linton (1978), and
Wagenaar (1986) as illustrative of this strong preoccupation with the dura-
bility of memory. It has often been pointed out that the followers of Ebbinghaus were more interested in learning than in memory, as reflected in
their tendency to pay little attention to forgetting. It has been the students
of ecological memory who have renewed our interest in forgetting. In
particular, Bahrick, Bahrick, and Wittlinger (1975) have shown us that
memory for people with whom we went to high school remains steady for
about 35 years after graduation and that there is no forgetting of Spanish
language acquired in school if the information has survived for about 6
years (Bahrick, 1984a). Let me note that it is not Ebbinghaus's fault that
his particular function was reified as "the forgetting curve" for so long.
We now know that forgetting curves have many realizations.

A compelling continuity is to be found in Rubin's (1982) demonstration that the retention function for autobiographical memories, obtained using Crovitz and Schiffman's (1974) modification of Galton's cue-word method, is accurately described by Wickelgren's (1974) single-trace mathematical description. To the point, Wickelgren's function is based on laboratory data from list-learning tasks. Yet Rubin (1982) was able to show that autobiographical retention data fit neatly onto Wickelgren's plot. Further credibility is gained from Rubin's observation that only very early memories deviate from the function, confirming yet again the robustness of infantile amnesia.

Cue loading or distinctiveness

Another issue of concern to all students of memory is cue potency or efficiency. What kind of information about an event is most helpful in gaining access to the rest of the event? In the autobiographical memory literature, location, action, actor, and time are usually considered. Both Brewer and Barsalou are concerned with this problem. It is noteworthy that Brewer concludes that, other things being equal, distinctiveness can account for the varying levels of cue efficiency he finds for these different aspects of events. Distinctiveness is simply an inverse function of cue loading (the number of items associated to a given cue). Brewer points out that "infrequent locations and infrequent actions are by far the best predictors of later memory." By focusing on distinctiveness, we can avoid premature debates about the relative importance of location, activity, or person, when the differences among these types of cues in any situation may be due to differences in the numbers of events associated with each, rather than any intrinsic property they may possess. As Brewer points out, house painters carry out the same actions every working day, but in different locations. For them, location cues will be much more distinctive than action cues. For others, location will be overloaded, and actions more distinctive. Notions of distinctiveness, as Brewer notes, abound in theorizing about laboratory memory results. Specifically, Watkins and Watkins (1975) have presented an interpretation of some traditional interference phenomena in terms of cue loading, whereas the "fan effect" noted in many recent studies (Anderson, 1980, pp. 176–178) refers to the increase in retrieval time attributable to cue loading. The continuity between laboratory research on list learning and studies of autobiographical memory is very strong here.

Is memory constructive?

One issue separating the Ebbinghaus and Bartlett traditions has been the role of constructive processes in memory. The former group of researchers have emphasized the accuracy of memory, whereas the latter have found evidence that it is reconstructive (Alba and Hasher, 1983). Note that Neisser (1982) has attempted to deal with this split by suggesting that certain social conditions, such as performing and ritual, lead to verbatim reproduction, whereas other conditions are conducive to constructive recall. In this volume, Brewer, a careful scholar with great allegiance to Bartlett, points out that his subjects were overwhelmingly accurate in recalling their own daily lives; they rarely "recalled" something that actually had not occurred. Although the implications of this finding go deep (see McCauley's comments in this regard), my point here is that the accuracy of memory observed in a given situation is not a criterion for deciding whether or not the situation is close to real life. Again, this point is to be found in Neisser's discussion of verbatim recall (1982), but it gains in importance as evidence of highly accurate recall is found in autobiographical memory for everyday life.

Memorability of events

What kinds of events are memorable? Given that people remember some events better than others, can we find any common properties among those that they do remember? The traditional verbal learner had a lot to say about this question. Concreteness and word frequency come to mind immediately as factors determining word recall. Whereas the spirit of the inquiry is familiar to the student of the laboratory literature, Brewer's findings on this score are not. It turns out that, for action, memorability is associated with events of low frequency, but for thoughts, affect is a strong predictor. This, of course, is news, because nobody has compared memory for thoughts and actions before, to my knowledge.

Functionalism reconsidered

It is interesting to note that both Jacoby, in this volume, and Bahrick (1987) identify themselves as functionalists. In both cases, the contrast being drawn is between functionalism and structuralism, not between the functionalist verbal learning tradition of Ebbinghaus and an ecological approach. To both Jacoby and Bahrick, the important contrast is between a functionalist and a cognitive psychology of memory. Bahrick has said elsewhere, "By functional approaches I refer to theories that attempt to establish parsimonious relations between manipulated variables and memory performance, without necessarily attempting to reach conclusions about internal processing" (1987, pp. 389–90). Jacoby frames his chapter as a contrast between functionalism and structuralism, with the latter meant to represent contemporary cognitive theory of the information-processing kind, with its great emphasis on logogens, schemata, and other abstract cognitive structures. Jacoby perceives that structuralism can be made into a common enemy of both ecologically oriented students of memory and functionalists. In point of fact, the preferred theoretical language of a good many contributors to this volume, particularly those who have studied autobiographical memory (here I mean Barclay and DeCooke, Barsalou, Brewer, and Nelson), is modern cognitive. But Jacoby's point is well taken. The early functionalists had much in common with Neisser's notions of ecologically based research, as I show in the next section; and Bahrick's enormous body of research on memory for high school classmates (Bahrick et al., 1975), memory of professors for their former students (1984b), memory of alumni for the layout of Delaware, Ohio (1983), memory for Spanish studied in school many years earlier (1984a), and, in this volume, the effects of rehearsal on maintaining marginal knowledge is an extraordinary achievement. By itself, Bahrick's research goes a long way toward remediating the deficiencies in our knowledge about memory in everyday life pointed to by Neisser (1978). Yet Bahrick, as pointed out already, abjures cognitive explanations.

So, can one be an ecologically oriented memory researcher and still be a functionalist? The answer can only be "Of course." The ecological approach to memory does not derive its force from theory. Rather, its contributions have come from applying the empirical approach to natural phenomena of memory that have not been studied and, perhaps, would never be studied within existing laboratory paradigms. These remarks should not be taken to suggest that an ecological approach to memory can be successful in the absence of theory. Rather, it seems to me that the theoretical issues that will develop as a substantial body of knowledge based on broader observations develops will not be much different from the issues already familiar to us from the laboratory tradition. However, there is one difference to be noted, and that is a growing emphasis on the functions served by memory, or what is memory for? This approach is discussed next.

What is memory for?

In the previous section, functionalism was taken to mean the avoidance of postulating cognitive structures. Jacoby also emphasizes another fundamental aspect of early functionalism, that is, the importance of adaptation to the environment. In emphasizing what functions memory serves in the world, Jacoby invokes the early functionalists such as John Dewey. It is interesting that both Neisser (1978) and Bruce (1985) have called for a focus on the functions of memory in the service of an ecological approach.

The observant reader of Neisser's *Memory Observed* may notice that the sections of that anthology are labeled in functional terms – for example, "testifying," "performing," and "getting things done." Here, in chapter 6, Jacoby mentions two distinct functions of memory. The function of autobiographical memory, he points out, "is that it allows one to be aware of and communicate with others about one's personal past." One might add to this that in connecting present and past events, it provides us with a sense of continuity about our lives without which it would be hard to conceive of a sense of self. (See chapter 10 by Fivush for a fuller discussion of this point.) Jacoby is more interested in other functions of memory, however, as the following quotation shows: "Memory for the past serves the function of setting the stage for perception and the interpretation of later events." This notion of stage setting is similar to the "tuning" metaphor used by J. J. Gibson in accounting for how experience shapes perception. Indeed, the similarity between perception and memory is one of the dominant themes of Jacoby's work and is another example of how his approach shares a great deal with ecologically oriented psychologists, for whom perception has historically been a central concern.

Nelson emphasizes the adaptive function of memory in her analysis of 2-year-old Emily's nighttime musings and of infantile amnesia in general. Nelson's view of the earliest functions of memory is based on her observation that memory in very young children tends to be generic or scriptlike. In Tulving's (1983) terms, early memory is more like semantic memory than it is like episodic memory. Nelson sees this as adaptive because it helps the child develop expectations and behave effectively. The essential insight here is that memory development is about the future, not the past. Memory is future-oriented; it prepares the child to act in the world by encoding regularities. A consequence of this bias is that there is poor memory in later life for unique events occurring at this state of development, or infantile amnesia. This is a small price to pay for learning to be able to predict what will happen next. Here is a case where emphasis on the adaptive function of certain kinds of memory offers an intriguing new account of a very old problem.

Who is ecological depends on one's perspective

Let me point to a few phenomena addressed by Jacoby to highlight how difficult it is in practice to be able to say whether research of any kind, whether of naturalistic or laboratory origin, is ecologically valid. The point I wish to make is that it is much easier to say whether or not research is interesting or worthwhile than to classify it as being ecological or not. Jacoby discusses to what extent remembering requires awareness of the past, surely a fundamental question about memory. He suggests that awareness of the past is an inference or attribution that involves the present as much as the past. He uses nostalgia to make his point. Clearly, nostalgia is not part of what we encoded about the original event; we were not feeling nostalgic at the time the remembered experience occurred. Nostalgia has to do with the relationship between the present and the remembered past. This is hardly a trivial issue for the psychology of memory. Is it ecological?

Another illuminating aspect of Jacoby's work is his demonstration that the same encoding operations have opposite effects on perception and memory. This work was originally reported in 1983 and is shown in Table 6.3 of this volume. Accounting for such dissociations arising from the memory laboratory is a central topic in current theorizing. That many of these dissociations between active remembering and tasks that do not require awareness of the past, or explicit and implicit memory, are to be found in amnesics broadens the empirical base of memory dissociations and, perhaps, confers ecological validity on dissociations. It is always desirable that findings have a broad empirical base. But, even in amnesics, the dissociations have been found by studying performance with such artificial tasks as word fragment completion (Warrington & Weiskrantz, 1968) and reading mirror-reversed word triads (Cohen & Squire, 1980). One would be hard-pressed to draw a line where artificiality ends and ecological validity, or memory for "real" events, begins. My argument is that it would not be fruitful to do so, nor, may I add, do I see evidence that anyone is trying to. The findings reported by Jacoby are so interesting that one does not question their origin. They meet the one requirement for scientific research we all implicitly follow: Our understanding of memory is enhanced. Jacoby also points out to us why a person may no longer think a joke is funny, yet not remember having heard it before, how unintentional plagiarism is likely to occur, and why years of reading students essays may lead to a decline in our ability to spell.

The exciting work of Bahrick and Jacoby shows us how much progress there has been in the laboratory tradition. Their work does not seem to be dust-bowl empiricism, dreary verbal learning, or any of the terms often used to contrast whatever research is regarded as desirable with the perceived Ebbinghaus legacy. It would be a mistake to cast out this rich tradition on the basis of preconceptions. It is simply the case that within any research area, some research is more interesting than other research.

Conclusion

I have attempted to point out several important continuities between traditional laboratory research on memory and research more oriented to naturally occurring memory phenomena. The point of these efforts is, on the one hand, to indicate to strict Ebbinghausians the interesting findings that emerge when we broaden our observations and, on the other hand, to persuade ecologically oriented researchers that we do not have to start over in building a science of memory. The laboratory tradition is strong in method and rich in theory.

It needs to be pointed out that our discipline benefits when the ecologically oriented researcher finds out something the laboratory has not discovered, a well as when a principle of long standing is reaffirmed. In the first instance, there are obvious gains when we learn something new. In the case of replication, principles learned in the laboratory gain in generalizability.

REFERENCES

Alba, J. W., & Hasher, L. (1983). Is memory schematic? *Psychological Bulletin, 93*, 203–231.
Anderson, J. R. (1980). *Cognitive psychology and its implications*. San Francisco: Freeman.
Bahrick, H. P. (1983). The cognitive map of a city–50 years of learning and memory. In G. H. Bower (Ed.), *The psychology of learning and motivation: Advances in research and theory* (Vol. 17, pp. 125–163). New York: Academic Press.
  (1984a). Semantic memory content in permastore: Fifty years of memory for Spanish learned in school. *Journal of Experimental Psychology: General, 113*, 1–29.
  (1984b). Memory for people. In J. E. Harris & P. E. Morris (Eds.), *Everyday memory, actions and absent-mindedness* (pp. 19–34). London: Academic Press.
  (1987). Functional and cognitive memory theory: An overview of some key issues. In D. S. Gorfein & R. R. Hoffman (Eds.), *Memory and learning: The Ebbinghaus centennial conference* (pp. 387–95). Hillsdale, NJ: Erlbaum.
Bahrick, H. P., Bahrick, P. O., & Wittlinger, R. P. (1975). Fifty years of memory for names and faces: A cross-sectional approach. *Journal of Experimental Psychology: General, 104*, 54–75.
Bruce, D. (1985). The how and why of ecological memory. *Journal of Experimental Psychology: General, 114*, 78–90.
Cohen, N. J., & Squire, L. R. (1980). Preserved learning and retention of pattern-analyzing skill in amnesia: Dissociation of knowing how and knowing that. *Science, 210*, 207–210.
Crovitz, H. F., & Schiffman, H. (1974). Frequency of episodic memories as a function of their age. *Bulletin of the Psychonomic Society, 4*, 517–518.
Ebbinghaus, H. (1964). *Memory: A contribution to experimental psychology*. New York: Dover. (Original work published 1885.)
Jacoby, L. L. (1983). Remembering the data: Analyzing interactive processes in reading. *Journal of Verbal Learning and Verbal Behavior, 22*, 485–508.
Lancaster, J. S. (1985). *Experimental investigations of the organization of memory for events*. Unpublished doctoral dissertation, Emory University.

Linton, M. (1978). Real world memory after six years: An in vivo study of very long term memory. In M. M. Gruneberg, P. E. Morris & R. N. Sykes (Eds.), *Practical aspects of memory* (pp. 69–76). London: Academic Press.

Neisser, U. (1978). Memory: What are the important questions? In M. M. Gruneberg, P. E. Morris, & R. N. Sykes (Eds.), *Practical aspects of memory* (pp. 3–24). New York: Academic Press.

(1982). *Memory observed: Remembering in natural contexts.* San Francisco: Freeman.

Rubin, D. C. (1982). On the retention function for autobiographical memory. *Journal of Verbal Learning and Verbal Behavior, 21,* 21–38.

Tulving, E. (1983). *Elements of episodic memory.* New York: Oxford University Press.

Wagenaar, W. A. (1986). My memory: A study of autobiographical memory over six years. *Cognitive Psychology, 18,* 225–252.

Warrington, E. K., & Weiskrantz, L. (1968). A new method of testing long-term retention with special reference to amnesic patients. *Nature, 217,* 972–974.

Watkins, O. C., & Watkins, M. J. (1975). Buildup of proactive inhibition as a cue overload effect. *Journal of Experimental Psychology: Human Learning and Cognition, 104,* 442–452.

Wickelgren, W. A. (1974). Single-trace fragility theory of memory dynamics. *Memory & Cognition, 2,* 775–780.

3

Memory for randomly sampled autobiographical events

WILLIAM F. BREWER

This chapter describes two empirical studies of autobiographical memory that focused on the personal memory component of autobiographical memory. These experiments investigated the characteristics of randomly sampled events and of events that subjects selected to be memorable. The autobiographical memory data in these experiments were obtained from naive subjects, not from the experimenter. Both experiments were designed so that it would be possible to study memory for thoughts independently from memory for actions. The second experiment was designed to study cued recall of verifiable autobiographical memories, and in this experiment systematic reports were obtained of the subjects' phenomenal experiences during the recall process.

The data from these two experiments were used to address a wide range of issues in the study of autobiographical memory. Memory for random events was compared with memory for subject-selected events, and memory for thoughts was compared with memory for actions. A number of analyses were carried out to uncover the relationships between the characteristics of the original events and memory for these events after various time intervals. The cued-recall data were used to study the accuracy of autobiographical recall and to work out the relations between the contents of the events and memory for the events. An analysis was carried out to study the relative effectiveness of various forms of cues for the retrieval of information from autobiographical memory. The data from the phenomenal memory scales were used to explore the subjects' experiences during the recall process.

The relationships between the characteristics of the initial events and the memory data were explained with a theory that specifies the form of information in personal memory through an ecological analysis of the subjects' interactions with their physical and social environment. This analysis of the subjects' environment, in conjunction with a theory of "distinctive memory representations" and a "dual-process theory of repetition," was used to account for a number of basic findings, particularly the powerful effects of location and event frequency on autobiographical

21

memory. The qualitative analysis of the recall data was used to support a partly reconstructive theory of personal memory.

Definition of autobiographical memory

In a recent theoretical paper (Brewer, 1986) I defined autobiographical memory as memory for information related to the self. Within this larger class, four basic forms of autobiographical memory were defined in terms of frequency of experience and imaginal properties. The first two forms of autobiographical memory arise when an individual has been exposed to a single instance of an event:

(a) A *personal memory* is a recollection of a particular episode from an individual's past. Thus, for example, I recollect taking my overnight bag out of the trunk of Dick Neisser's car the day the Emory Cognition Project Conference was over. In my theoretical paper, this form of memory is described as typically being experienced as a "reliving" of the individual's phenomenal experience during the earlier episode. The recollection process almost always involves visual imagery and frequently includes occurent thoughts and felt affect. These memories are experienced as occurring at a specific time and location, where "specific time" is intended to indicate that the memory is experienced as having occurred at a unique time, not that the individual can assign an absolute date to the event. Personal memories are accompanied by a belief that the episode was personally experienced by the individual (thus the term "personal memory"). Finally, these memories typically are accompanied by a belief that they are a veridical record of the original event.

(b) In addition to personal memories, exposure to a particular episode can give rise to *autobiographical facts* or nonimage representations of information relating to the self. Brewer (1982) and Brewer and Pani (in preparation) have shown that in many forms of fact retrieval there is little reported imagery. For example, I know as a fact that I took a plane home from the Emory Conference, but I have no personal memory of walking onto the plane at the Atlanta airport. The other two forms of autobiographical memory described in the theoretical paper are postulated to result from exposure to events that are repeated with variation.

(c) A *generic personal memory* is a memory experience that seems to incorporate several repeated events. For example, I walked from my motel to the Emory campus several times during the conference. I no longer have a unique personal memory of a particular walk, but I have a generic memory of walking from a commercial area through a pleasant residential neighborhood, up a hill, and over a bridge onto the Emory campus. See Neisser's (1981) discussion of "repisodic memory" and Barsalou's (chapter 8) discussion of summarized events for somewhat similar constructs.

(d) With repetition of events, one accumulates a large body of generic nonimaginal autobiographical knowledge about one's self in the form of a *self-schema*. For example, I know that I go to conferences frequently and that I enjoy them. See Epstein (1973) and Markus (1980) for more general discussions of the self-schema.

For a more detailed discussion of the rationale behind this analysis of autobiographical memory, see Brewer and Pani (1983) and Brewer (1986). The experimental studies reported in this chapter were designed to study the characteristics of the personal memory component of autobiographical memory.

Methodology in the study of personal memory

Galton's breakfast questionnaire. The first empirical study of personal memory (Galton, 1880) occurred before the first standard laboratory experiment on memory (Ebbinghaus, 1885/1964); yet developing an appropriate methodology for the study of personal memory has proved to be very difficult. Galton's (1880) approach was to ask subjects to recall the appearance of their breakfast tables from that morning's breakfast. Thus, in the framework just outlined, Galton was studying the characteristics of a personal memory. His basic finding was that most of his subjects reported strong visual imagery in carrying out this personal memory task, although this is not how most secondary sources describe his findings (see Brewer & Schommer, in preparation, for an account of this issue).

The Crovitz technique. Galton also proposed a word technique to study human memory (1879a,b). In this technique, Galton read a word and then recorded whatever ideas the probe word elicited. Examination of Galton's papers and his data shows that this technique was designed to be a completely open-ended exploration of the contents of the mind and so does not properly qualify as a technique for studying personal memory. However, Crovitz and Schiffman (1974) modified the Galton technique so that it could be used to study personal memory. The crucial modification was to require that the subjects "think of a specific memory associated with each word" (Crovitz & Quina-Holland, 1976, p. 61). The development of the Crovitz technique for studying personal memory has recently given rise to an extensive literature (Robinson, 1976; Rubin, 1982; Rubin, Wetzler, & Nebes, 1986).

Nevertheless, there are several problems with this technique. First, even with the instructions to think of a specific memory, it is not clear if the obtained memories are actually unique episodes from the subject's past or if they are recalls of more generic information.

Second, it seems to me that the Crovitz technique does not allow enough experimental control over the subject's responses. One can easily modify the retrieval strategies used by subjects in this task. For example, Pillemer, Rhinehart, and White (1986) asked undergraduate subjects to give personal memories from their freshman year in college, and the subjects were able to do this with little trouble. Thus, one problem with the Crovitz technique is that the experimenter does not know what strategies the uninstructed subject is using, and, in fact, McCormak (1979) noted that some subjects in this task give responses restricted to particular portions of their lives.

A third problem with the Crovitz technique is that there probably are strong systematic differences between the sample of memories retrieved with this technique and the actual store of personal memories. In other words, the responses on the Crovitz technique may be biased in unknown ways through some form of availability heuristic (Tversky & Kahneman, 1973). This is, of course, an empirical issue. However, an anecdote reported by Hurlburt (1976) in the course of a thought-sampling experiment illustrates the possible problem. Hurlburt had subjects carry around a random alarm advice and then write down their thoughts in a notebook when the alarm went off. Hurlburt noted that "Two subjects during their individual debriefings naively told the experimenter that the sample was not representative of their usual thought patterns 'because I looked back over my notebook and there are no sex thoughts here; I know I spend 30 to 40% of my time thinking about sex, but the box never caught me!' " (p. 19). Hurlburt interpreted this observation as showing that "undergraduates don't think for extended periods about sex, but when they do, they remember it" (p. 19).

Finally, there is the problem of verifiability. As the Crovitz technique is typically used, there is no way to know how the personal memories obtained relate to the original experiences of the subjects. This analysis of techniques for studying personal memory suggests that we need methodologies with more experimental control over what is being studied. One solution to this problem is to provide the subject with a more restricted retrieval target (e.g., "times when you went to a museum and felt impatient") and then overtly study the retrieval strategies used by the subjects (cf. Reiser, 1983; Reiser, Black, & Kalamarides, 1986). Another solution is to gather information about specific autobiographical events and then use partial information from the initial event in a cued-recall procedure. This technique allows a comparison of the original experience and the subject's recall and is the procedure adopted in the present study.

The Linton technique. Linton (1975) developed a technique that solves a number of the problems posed by the Crovitz procedure. Linton carried out a heroic study of her own autobiographical memory. Each day over a 6-year period she selected several of the most memorable events of the day for later testing. This methodology has recently been adopted by several other researchers (Wagenaar, 1986; White, 1982).

However, it seems to me that the Linton technique also has several problems. The first problem is the use of the experimenter as subject. I do not have as strong feelings about this as many laboratory researchers might. In fact, before carrying out the present experiments, I ran myself in several extended pilot studies and then had several loyal graduate students try out the technique. However, as this area turns away from exploratory research and moves toward theory testing, it does seem safer not to have the experimenter be the only subject. A more important issue is the problem of item selection. The aspect of the Linton technique that involves selecting the most memorable event of the day corresponds to a verbal learning experiment in which a subject is given a list containing hundreds of words each day and at the end of each day is asked to select the one item that will be tested in later retention tests. This type of item selection does not seem to be an appropriate methodology for understanding the characteristics of personal memory. See Linton (1982, p. 82) and White (1982, p. 175) for similar criticisms of this approach. Thus, the experiments reported in this chapter have been designed to study the memory of randomly selected autobiographical events from the lives of undergraduate subjects.

Experimental studies of personal memory

Description of personal memory. In several treatments of the issue of autobiographical memory (Brewer, 1986; Brewer & Pani, 1983) I have given a rough characterization of the properties of personal memories. However, these descriptions were based on my introspections and extensive discussions of the issue by philosophers (e.g., Furlong, 1951; Locke, 1971; Russell, 1921). Clearly, these characterizations of personal memory are issues that require empirical study. Most of the recent studies of personal memory have been interested in the quantitative analysis of temporal ordering of events or in the study of forgetting curves and so do not provide much information on the qualitative characteristics of personal memories. However, some descriptive studies have been carried out. The original breakfast questionnaire study by Galton (1880) supports the imagistic properties of personal memories. Nigro and Neisser (1983) have presented data on visual point of view for personal memories suggesting that recent personal memories are experienced from the point of view of the initial experience, whereas older memories (e.g., memories from early childhood) show a higher percentage of personal memories that are experienced from the viewpoint of an observer.

Forgetting. The rate of forgetting for the recognition of written descriptions of self-selected autobiographical events appears to be quite slow. Linton (1978) and Wagenaar (1986) found little or no forgetting after 1 year; after 2 years, Linton reported approximately 89% correct, whereas Wagenaar reported approximately 96% correct. White (1982) showed a higher rate of forgetting, with approximately 60% correct after 1 year and 55% correct after 2 years. In comparing these forgetting rates, it should be noted that Linton and Wagenaar selected items to be the most memorable event of the day, whereas White used a less strict criterion. Obviously, we need data that will allow us to understand the forgetting rate for autobiographical memories and the degree to which it is related to event selection.

Event characteristics related to memory. White (1982) and Wagenaar (1986) reported correlations between rated characteristics of the initial autobiographical events and later memory. Both researchers found that the frequency of the initial event is significantly related to memory (with rare events recognized better). They both also found that events with high emotional content showed better memory, though White found that this relationship was not significant when he carried out a multiple regression on his data. This is clearly an area where more data are needed.

Theory of memory for types of autobiographical events. In addition to establishing the basic empirical relations between event attributes and memory, we also need to develop theoretical constructs that will allow us to explain these empirical relations.

Reconstruction in personal memory

Copy theories. In many of the early discussions of autobiographical memory there was a tendency to adopt a view that personal memories were veridical copies of the original experience. For example, the philosopher Furlong (1951) argued that personal memories were a representation of an individual's "whole state of mind of the past occasion" (p. 83). In their classic paper on "flashbulb" memories, Brown and Kulik (1977) proposed a "now print" mechanism that "indiscriminately preserves the scene" (p. 74). Although this view has been attractive to many researchers in autobiographical memory, there is currently little evidence to support it because most empirical studies in this area have not been designed in such a way that it is possible to verify the accuracy of the obtained personal memories.

Strong reconstructive theories. Recently there has been a powerful attack on the copy view of personal memories in favor of a strong reconstructive view (Barclay, 1986; Barclay & Wellman, 1986; Neisser, 1981, 1982). Perhaps the most extreme form of this position was outlined by Barclay (1986), who stated that "Memories for most everyday life events are therefore, transformed, distorted, or forgotten" (p. 89). The reconstructive position is based on several lines of evidence: A number of theorists have given anecdotal examples of errors in personal memory (e.g., Linton, 1975, p. 387; Neisser, 1982, p. 45). Neisser (1981) has shown that John Dean's recall of his conversations with Nixon during his Watergate testimony was accurate about the individuals' basic positions, but inaccurate with respect to exactly what was said during a given conversation. Barclay and Wellman (1986) had subjects record autobiographical events, tested the subjects after several months with actual events and foil events, and found that subjects made false recognition responses to the foils.

A partially reconstructive theory. The 1986 paper by Brewer argues against a strong form of the reconstructive view (yes, gentle reader, this is the same Brewer who wrote all those reconstructive memory papers). Although there is some evidence to support the reconstructive view of personal memory, it does not seem very compelling. First, it does not seem wise to put too much weight on anecdotal examples, and, in fact, Neisser's personal example of a nonveridical autobiographical memory (1982, p. 45) may not be as reconstructed as he thought it was (cf. Thompson & Cowan, 1986, and Neisser, 1986b). Second, the John Dean data (Neisser, 1981) seem more related to memory for conversations than to the issue of personal memory (see Brewer, 1986, pp. 42–43, for a discussion of this issue). Finally, the use of foils in the study of autobiographical memory (Barclay & Wellman, 1986) raises some difficult methodological issues. It seems clear that one could write foil items such that no subject would ever give a false recognition response (e.g., "I was climbing Mount Everest") or that one could make very subtle changes in an original item (e.g., "I put my right foot into the shoe") so that subjects would make a very large number of false recognition responses (see the discussion of methodology by Linton, 1975). Thus, it is hard to know how to interpret the finding that subjects make some false recognition responses.

Given the weakness of the evidence on both sides of the issue of the veridicality of personal memories, I have argued (Brewer, 1986) for a partially reconstructive view which proposes that "recent personal memories retain a relatively large amount of specific information from the original phenomenal experience (e.g., location, point of view) but that with time, or under strong schema-based processes, the original experience can be reconstructed to produce a new nonveridical personal memory that retains most of the phenomenal characteristics of other personal memories" (1986, p. 44). It seems obvious from the diversity of views on the veridicality issue that this is another aspect of the study of personal memories that needs additional research.

The experiments described in this chapter were designed to solve some of the methodological problems outlined earlier, to gather new data on the characteristics of personal memories, and to provide a theoretical account of the basic findings.

General methods

This section covers the general methods used in these experiments and the procedures that were common to both Experiments 1 and 2. The basic procedure was to have subjects carry a random-alarm mechanism and then record information about what was occurring each time the alarm went off.

Subjects

The experimental procedures were demanding; so an attempt was made to select very reliable and cooperative subjects. First, a large group of college students filled out a questionnaire that included questions designed to measure motivation (e.g., "Would you carry the beeper during an exam?" "Would you carry the beeper during a date?"). A small sample of individuals with high motivation and legible handwriting were asked to come in and fill out several example response cards. The final sample of subjects chosen for the experiment were those who showed a rapid grasp of the procedures, in addition to high motivation and legible handwriting. Subjects were paid for participating in the experiment.

Several aspects of the procedure were designed to safeguard the rights and privacy of the subjects. Subjects were given a complete description of the procedures before applying and were told not to fill out the application form if they thought they would have any problems with the experiment as described. From the beginning of the study each subject was assigned a code number, and all data were recorded in terms of the code number. The random-alarm mechanism was equipped with a switch that deactivated the alarm. Subjects were told to cut off the alarm at night and at any time when the signal might be inconvenient or embarrassing. If the alarm did happen to go off at a time that invaded the subjects' privacy, they were instructed to simply record "private" on the card. At the end of the study the subjects were asked to fill out an anonymous questionnaire asking their true feelings about the study and any problems that occurred. The privacy issues was apparently not a major problem. For example, one subject wrote "tell [future subjects] not to be afraid to take the beeper anywhere. People get a kick out of it. . ."

Random-alarm mechanism

The alarm (or "beeper") was a Divilbiss Electronics Adjustable Random Alarm Mechanism, model JD-IV-A. This device was designed for time sampling in work analysis (Divilbiss & Self, 1978). It is about the size of a pocket radio, weighs about 170 g, and emits a loud 2-kHz tone. The beeper can be set to go off on a random schedule with an adjustable mean rate. Pilot work suggested that using a rate in which the alarms occurred more often than once every two hours tended to become irritating for the individual carrying the device. When the subjects were in their rooms, they tended to keep the beeper out on some surface such as a desk or table. When they were away from home, they tended to keep it in a coat pocket or in a backpack.

Event sampling

The use of random sampling of events caused some minor problems. It is known that people are poor judges of randomness (Kahneman & Tversky, 1972), and our subjects' perceptions of the distribution of alarms add additional support to this finding. In an actual random distribution with an average of one alarm every two hours there will be many long periods with no alarm and a number of occasions when the alarm will go off twice in close succession. The data from the anonymous questionnaires showed that long periods without an alarm caused some of the subjects to become concerned because they thought the beeper was malfunctioning. In addition, a number of subjects said that the most irritating part of the experiment was when the beeper went off several times within a short time period.

The overall impression given by the anonymous questionnaire and by the actual events recorded by the subjects is one of honesty and cooperation. The sampled events included exams, romantic evenings, and highly emotional situations. However, it is also clear that the experimental procedures led to certain systematic sampling biases. On the anonymous questionnaire a number of subjects stated they had problems when the beeper went off while they were driving, at work, or in the process of leaving for class or for an appointment. Thus, it seems likely that events of this type are systematically undersampled. It also appears that subjects did not always turn on the random-alarm device the first thing in the morning. Finally, it is clear that the subjects occasionally exercised their right to turn off the alarm, which almost certainly resulted in a systematic undersampling of events such as parties, dates, and exams.

Response cards

When the random-alarm mechanism went off, the subject filled out a card with information about the event. The response cards (15.2 cm × 12.7 cm) requested that the subject report information such as time, location, actions, and thoughts, and then complete a number of rating scales. Subjects were told not to read the cards after filling them out and to try not to give the sampled events any special treatment. Subjects had extensive instruction in filling out the response cards before the experiment began, and after the first 3 days of the experiment they came in for an interview about any problems they were having with the experiment. During the interview, two of the subject's response cards were examined and discussed with the subject (the data from these cards were discarded).

The decision to use a procedure in which the subject wrote a description of the sampled event was based on several considerations. First, this was the only practical procedure that allowed the recording of the subject's thoughts. Second, this technique made possible the later verification of the subject's recalls. Finally, the work of Thompson (1982) suggests that writing down autobiographical events has little effect on memory for the events over long time intervals.

The decision to make a systematic distinction between thoughts and actions on the response cards was based on two pilot studies in which the author acted as subject. In the first of these studies my instructions to myself were "to record the event going on when the alarm sounded." However, I found myself unable to follow my own instructions. If the beeper went off while I was walking to work and planning an experiment, what was the event? Was it (a) walking by the Lincoln Avenue dorms, (b) deciding to use a between-subject design in the room schema study, or (c) both? Initially, I attempted to develop some arbitrary recording criteria to solve this problem, but eventually realized that my problem was that I was attempting to ignore the fundamental distinction between mind and body. My solution was to accept the distinction and systematically record both the physical actions and the mental phenomena (thoughts and emotions) occurring for each event. There is a certain irony in having all this happen to an experimenter/subject who has explicitly criticized cognitive psychology for failing to be sufficiently mentalistic (Brewer & Pani, 1983, pp. 4–5).

Acquisition and test procedures

In both experiments, data were acquired for a several-week period, and then tests were carried out on three occasions, one occurring immediately after the acquisition period and the other two spaced at longer periods. The several-week acquisition period allowed the examination of temporal-order phenomena during acquisition; the delayed testing allowed the examination of forgetting over time.

Experiment 1

The first experiment was designed (a) to show that the basic procedures for randomly sampling and recording autobiographical events would work, (b) to compare memory for randomly selected events with memory for "memorable" events, (c) to examine the forgetting curve and serial position curve for autobiographical events, (d) to compare memory for actions with memory for thoughts, and (e) to examine some of the characteristics of randomly sampled events and "memorable" events that are related to the memory for these events.

Method

Subjects

There were eight subjects in this experiment, selected from a group of 45 volunteers on the basis of their motivation to participate, legibility of handwriting, and ability to follow the instructions. All subjects were in the freshman year of college. Five subjects were female, and three were male. Each subject was paid a total of $50 in five installments.

Response cards

The response cards asked the subjects for the following types of information: (a) identification number; (b) time (day of the week, date, time); (c) location; (d) a summary sentence (thoughts and actions); (e) thoughts; (f) actions; (g) a rating of thought/action coordination; (h) a rating of thoughts on six scales; (i) a rating of actions on six scales.

Actions

The instructions for the action category stated: "Write down what you were doing just before the beeper went off. Try to give enough specific detail so that you would be able to distinguish it from similar events that might occur over a week's time. Include in your statement: what you were doing; who was with you; what objects were around you; body position; how dressed; the weather; etc."

In order to work out an appropriate methodology for recording naturally occurring actions, there are three characteristics of human actions that need to be considered: the action hierarchy, multiple actions, and action category versus action instance.

Action hierarchy. A number of writers have noted that human actions are hierarchical (Barker & Wright, 1955; Neisser, 1986a; Newtson, 1976; Reiser, Black, & Abelson, 1985). Thus, for a particular alarm, one of our subjects could have said: (a) "I was lifting my right leg"; (b) "I was walking along Green Street"; (c) "I was on my way to class"; (d) "I was obtaining a college degree." In practice, the action hierarchy did not cause much trouble because there appears to be a basic level for actions (Rosch, 1978), and our subjects typically described the actions with the basic level and then, because of our instructions, gave a little information from the level below the basic level. In the foregoing example, "I was on my way to class" seems to be at the basic level for the particular action. Subjects essentially never reported the information from very low in the hierarchy (e.g., lifting their right leg), nor information from a high level in the hierarchy (e.g., obtaining a college degree). Instead, a typical report would say: "I was on my way to Chem. I was on Green street in front of the Union. It was sunny and there was a guy in an Illini jacket right in front of me."

Multiple actions. Occasionally people carry out two different actions at the same moment in time (e.g., talking with someone while walking to class). There seem to be two possible solutions to this problem: The subject could fill out two record cards, one for each event, or the subject could be instructed to select only one action for recording. We chose the option of selecting one action. Subjects were told to fill out only one event card. If the card contained information on more than one action, the more central action was recorded for data analysis, and if the two actions seemed of roughly equal importance, the one the subject wrote first on the response card was selected.

Action instance and action category. In the early pilot studies, subjects were asked to rate actions on a scale of frequency of occurrence. This revealed a problem relating to treating an event as an instance or as a category. Suppose a student eats out frequently at fast-food restaurants, but the beeper goes off during the student's only visit to a local expensive French restaurant. How is this event to be rated? Is it a high-frequency event because the student frequently eats out, or is it a low-frequency event because the student rarely goes out to expensive restaurants? This problem was dealt with by making the distinction a systematic part of the experiment. Each event was rated in terms of frequency of the category and in terms of frequency of the instance. Thus, for an action such as the restaurant example, the subjects were instructed to give the action a high rating on Action Category Frequency but a low rating on Action Instance Frequency.

Action rating scales. After the subjects wrote down the action, they were asked to rate the action on a series of 7-point rating scales. The six scales were: (a) category infrequent/frequent; (b) instance infrequent/frequent; (c) unpleasant/ pleasant; (d) trivial/significant; (e) dull/exciting; (f) non-goal-directed/goal-directed. The instructions stated that the Significance scale was to be interpreted in terms of life goals. The Excitement scale was distinguished from the trivial/ significant scale by pointing out that winning a game of Space Invaders might be exciting, but it was trivial. The instructions for the Goal-Directedness scale stated that hurrying to class would be a relatively goal-directed action, whereas sitting on the grass watching the crowd go by would be a relatively non-goal-directed action.

Thoughts

The instructions to the subject for the thought category stated: "Write down what was going through your mind just before the beeper went off. Try to give enough specific detail so that you would be able to distinguish it from similar events occurring over a week's time." Examination of the response cards and the subjects' comments on the anonymous questionnaire suggested that subjects had little trouble distinguishing between thoughts and actions. Subjects were instructed to fill out the thoughts section of the response card first. This was based on pilot data showing that after a delay of only a few minutes there were already some problems in retrieving information about thoughts. Subjects were asked to rate the recorded thought on the same six rating scales that they used for actions.

Thought/action coordination. The final information requested on the response card was a rating, on a 7-point scale, of the overall event on a scale of thought/action coordination. This scale derived from the decision to systematically record both thoughts and actions for all events. Pilot work with events using the thought/action distinction suggested that events differed in the degree to which the actions and the thoughts were coordinated, and so subjects were asked to provide explicit information on this relationship for each event. The instructions to the subjects gave the example of "reading a book" (action) and "comprehending what is read" (thought) as an example of an event with high Coordination. The example of "reading a book" (action) and "thinking about a girlfriend" (thought) was given as an example of an event with low Coordination.

Memorable events

In addition to the events sampled by the random-alarm mechanism, each subject was asked to record at the end of each day "the most memorable event that

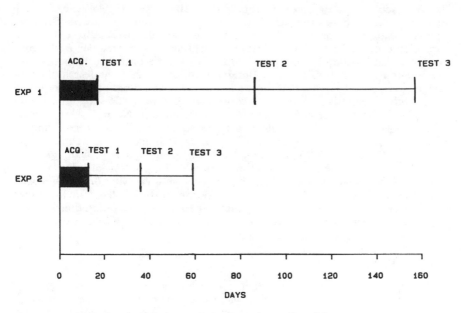

Figure 3.1. Acquisition and test intervals for Experiments 1 and 2.

occurred that day." These events were recorded on response cards using the same instructions and the same categories and scales as used for the randomly sampled events.

Acquisition

The subjects carried random-alarm mechanisms for an average of 17 days. The random-alarm devices were set to sample events at the rate of one event every 2 hours. The experiment was carried out so that Thanksgiving vacation occurred during the middle of the acquisition period. All of the subjects were first-semester freshmen; so for most of the subjects this vacation was their first return home as college students.

Test procedures

Test intervals. Each subject was tested three times: immediately after acquisition, at a mean of 69 days after the end of acquisition, and at a mean of 140 days after the end of acquisition. Thus, the average time from acquisition to test for an item in each of the three test sessions was 9 days, 78 days, and 149 days. See Figure 3.1 for an overview of the acquisition and test time intervals.

Item sampling. The items tested at each time interval were a random sample from the total items, stratified across the acquisition time interval. One-third of the total sample of items for a subject were tested at each of the three test sessions. The tested items included both the randomly sampled events and the memorable events.

Test procedure. Each subject's recognition memory for actions and thoughts was tested. The subject's response card was placed in a mask so that only the action description or the thought description was visible. After reading either the thought or the action description, the subject made recognition-memory judgments on a 7-point scale, where 1 was defined as "have no memory of the event," and 7 was defined as "certain that remember the event." Within a test session, the thoughts and actions from a particular response card were tested separately. Tests were designed so that the thought descriptions for events were tested first on half the trials and the action descriptions were tested first on the other trials. Within this constraint, the order of testing a particular thought description or action description was random. No foils were used in the recognition test. It is not clear, even in standard laboratory experiments, that it is necessary or even appropriate to use foils in a recognition-memory paradigm (Wallace, 1980). In the present experiment it is difficult to know what would constitute a "fair" foil (see Linton, 1975, pp. 394–395, but also see Barclay & Wellman, 1986). When the subjects were carrying out the recognition test, they were reading parts of response cards filled out in their own handwriting; therefore, it is obvious that our subjects were rating their current recognition memory for the events, not their belief about whether or not the events had actually ever occurred in their past.

Payment schedule

Subjects were paid a total of $50 in five installments of $10 each. The first payment was made during a meeting with the experimenter on the fourth day of acquisition. The second payment was made during a meeting with the experimenter during the 10th day of acquisition. An additional payment of $10 was made at the end of each of the three test sessions.

Results

Data presentation

The data obtained in the two experiments are complex, and so the results are presented and discussed in two stages. For each experiment the data are presented, and then there is a discussion that keeps fairly close to the data. Finally, in the general discussion at the end of the chapter, an attempt is made to bring together the results of both experiments and to draw out the larger theoretical implications.

The analyses for Experiment 1 are based on 563 randomly sampled autobiographical events (with a median of 63 items per subject, and a range of 39 to 130). There were 112 memorable events (with a median of 14 items per subject, and a range of 13 to 15).

Recognition-memory scales

Forgetting curves. The forgetting curves for *actions* for both memorable and random items are given in Figure 3.2. For the purpose of constructing these curves, a relatively conservative criterion of forgetting seemed desirable, so items that were given scores of 1 or 2 on the 7-point recognition-memory scale were considered to have been forgotten. Thus, the forgetting curves in Figure 3.2 are plotted in terms of the percentage of items with scores of 3 or greater on the recognition scale. The

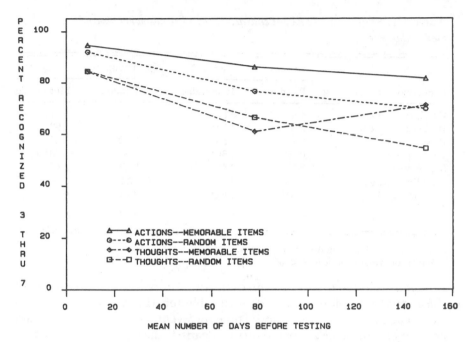

Figure 3.2. Experiment 1: Forgetting curves for recognition of actions and thoughts for both random and memorable items (recognition ratings > 2 scored as correct).

forgetting curves for *thoughts,* using the same dependent measure, are also given in Figure 3.2. All of the data, except those for memorable thoughts, show a relatively shallow forgetting curve.

Memory for thoughts versus actions. Memory for actions is better than memory for thoughts: (a) random events recognized: actions 79% versus thoughts 68%; (b) memorable events recognized: actions 87% versus thoughts 72%.

Memory for random versus selected events. Memory for the actions in memorable events is better than memory for the actions in randomly selected events (87% versus 79%), whereas the difference between the thoughts in memorable events and the thoughts in randomly selected events is smaller (72% versus 68%).

Event characteristics for memorable events

Self-selected items—means for event characteristics. One of the basic differences between this experiment and previous studies of autobiographical memory is that the core data in this study are randomly selected events, and the earlier studies used items selected by the experimenter/ subject to be memorable. The data just reported show that, at least for actions, subjects are capable of selecting items that are easier to remember, so it is of some interest to see how subject-selected events differ from

Table 3.1. *Experiment 1: Event characteristics of random events and memorable events*

Event characteristics	Actions		Thoughts	
	Random	Memorable	Random	Memorable
Category Frequency	4.48	3.50*	3.89	3.51
Instance Frequency	2.38	1.74*	2.14	1.92
Pleasantness	3.98	4.53*	3.82	4.47*
Extreme Affect	0.82	1.60*	0.92	1.78*
Significance	2.30	2.58	2.43	2.89*
Goal-Directedness	3.53	3.31	3.32	3.24
Excitement	3.54	4.64*	3.61	4.72*
Memory	4.80	5.83*	4.24	4.70

Note: Means are based on the subject means.
*Memorable versus random, $p < .05$.

randomly selected events in terms of the rated dimensions. Table 3.1 gives the means for random items and memorable items for the event characteristics that the subjects rated at the time the event was recorded. The data reported in this table are based on the means of the subject means, so that the results will not be distorted by the fact that some subjects contributed considerably more items than other subjects. The table includes data on one additional variable, Extreme Affect, which was derived from the ratings on the 7-point Pleasantness scale. The Pleasantness scale serves as an appropriate scale for testing hypotheses which postulate that positive items will show better memory than negative items (or the reverse). However, it does not provide an appropriate scale for testing the hypothesis that events associated with affect extremes, either positive or negative, will show better memory. Therefore, a new scale, Extreme Affect, was derived from the Pleasantness scale by taking the absolute value of deviations from the scale midpoint.

The results in Table 3.1 show that for the events selected by subjects to be more memorable, the *actions* show significantly lower Category and Instance Frequency scores and show significantly higher scores on the Pleasantness, Extreme Affect, and Excitement scales. The *thoughts* that occur during the memorable events show significantly higher scores on the Pleasantness, Extreme Affect, Significance, and Excitement scales.

Event characteristics and recognition memory

High memory items – means for event characteristics. A more direct way to investigate the attributes of autobiographical events that lead to superior memory is to examine the event characteristics of the events with the highest and lowest recognition scores. Table 3.2 gives the event attributes for those items showing very high memory scores for actions

Table 3.2. *Experiment 1: Event characteristics of actions and thoughts with high and low recognition-memory scores*

Event characteristics	Action memory		Thought memory	
	Low	High	Low	High
Actions				
Category Frequency	4.84	4.32*	4.70	4.44
Instance Frequency	2.60	2.25	2.44	2.33
Pleasantness	3.77	4.06	3.94	3.98
Extreme Affect	0.77	0.79	0.73	0.77
Significance	2.20	2.49*	2.35	2.47
Goal-Directedness	3.59	3.88	3.92	3.80
Excitement	3.35	3.79*	3.54	3.78
Thoughts				
Category Frequency	3.98	3.91	4.02	3.83
Instance Frequency	2.15	2.18	2.27	2.13
Pleasantness	3.62	3.88	3.78	3.96*
Extreme Affect	0.91	0.89	0.81	0.85
Significance	2.38	2.70	2.33	2.53*
Goal-Directedness	3.43	3.72	3.55	3.56
Excitement	3.46	3.82	3.51	3.89*
Thought memory	2.78	4.91*	—	—
Action memory	—	—	3.75	5.70*

Note: High memory = scores of 6 or 7 on recognition scale. Low memory = scores of 1 or 2 on recognition scale. Means and statistical analysis are based on the subject means.
*$p < .05$, high memory versus low memory.

(ratings of 6 or 7 on the memory scale) versus those showing very low memory scores (ratings of 1 or 2 on the memory scale). Table 3.2 also gives the event attributes for those items showing very high memory scores for thoughts (ratings of 6 or 7) versus very low memory scores (ratings of 1 or 2). Both of these tables are based on memory data obtained from the second and third test sessions only because many of the high scores obtained during the first test session are due merely to a recency effect, not to the attributes of the events themselves. The data reported in these tables are the means of the subject means. The data in this table demonstrate that events that show high recognition scores for *actions* are rated significantly lower on Action Category Frequency, and the actions are rated higher on the Excitement and Significance scales. The events that show high recognition-memory scores for *thoughts* have thoughts that are significantly higher on the Pleasantness, Significance, and Excitement scales.

Correlational results for event characteristics. The analyses reported earlier show that a number of the independent variables are associated with better memory for autobiographical thoughts and actions. Correlational techniques were also used to better understand these relations. Table 3.3 presents the intercorrelations of all of the item characteristics and the memory measures for the randomly sampled items. Examination of the intercorrelations of the characteristics of the autobiographical events provides some indication of the structure of events in the naturalistic setting of college life. The Category Frequency scale and the Instance Frequency scale show fairly high correlations, suggesting that it may not have been necessary to have the subjects make this distinction. The thought and action pairs associated with the randomly sampled events tend to receive similar ratings on a number of the variables: Category Frequency, Instance Frequency, Pleasantness, Extreme Affect, Significance, Goal-Directedness, and Excitement. There is a strong tendency for events high on the Excitement scale to receive high scores on the Pleasantness scale. Within the complex network of low correlations there is one moderately consistent pattern. The variables Significance, Goal-Directedness, and Coordination tend to intercorrelate, and this set of variables tends to be negatively correlated with Extreme Affect and Pleasantness. It seems to me that this pattern reflects the fact that these undergraduates rate events such as going to class and studying as high on Significance, Goal-Directedness, and Coordination, but low on Extreme Affect and Pleasantness, whereas they rate some recreational activities low on Significance, Goal-Directedness, and Coordination, but high on Extreme Affect and Pleasantness.

Correlational results – event characteristics and memory. The correlation matrix in Table 3.3 also shows the correlations of the event characteristics with the memory measures. *Action memory* is associated with low ratings on Action Instance Frequency and with high ratings on Extreme Affect for both actions and thoughts. *Thought memory* is associated with high ratings on Extreme Affect for actions and thoughts and with low ratings on Goal-Directedness for actions and thoughts and with low ratings on Action Significance.

General Linear Model – event characteristics and memory. Finally, in an attempt to reduce these complex patterns of findings, regression techniques were applied. The General Linear Model was used to see which event characteristics would predict action memory and which would predict thought memory, with test interval and subjects entered as factors in each case. As one would expect, the analyses show both subjects and delay intervals to be strongly related to the memory variables. The only additional significant variable ($p < .05$) for predicting *action memory* is Action Instance Frequency (negative sign), and the only additional significant variable for predicting *thought memory* is Thought Excitement.

Serial-position results. The subjects in this experiment carried their random-alarm devices for over 2 weeks; so it is possible to look at the serial-position curves for the two memory measures over this time

Table 3.3. Experiment 1: Intercorrelations of item characteristics and memory measures

	2	3	4	5	6	7	8	9	10	11	12	13	14	15	16	17
1. Act. Cat. Freq.	.58*	.02	−.05	.15	.02	−.01	.57*	.36*	−.00	.08	.13*	.06	−.03	−.06	−.05	−.05
2. Act. Inst. Freq.		.03	−.07	.19*	.05	−.04	.42*	.44*	.05	.06	.20*	.11*	.05	−.05	−.14*	.00
3. Act. Pleasant.			.03	−.16*	−.09*	.65*	−.00	.04	.58*	−.13*	−.15*	−.04	.47*	.04	.07	.04
4. Act. Extreme Af.				−.11*	−.10*	.05	−.03	−.05	−.08	.42*	−.11*	−.09*	−.03	.15*	.14*	.12*
5. Act. Signif.					.36*	.02	.23*	.26*	−.07	−.04	.78*	.41*	.08	.14*	−.06	−.09*
6. Act. Goal-Dir.						−.02	.08	.06	.02	−.06	.25*	.63*	.03	.18*	−.07	−.15*
7. Act. Excit.							.01	.06	.49*	−.07	.03	.05	.65*	.10*	.07	.01
8. Th. Cat. Freq.								.61*	.06	.15*	.28*	.19*	.13*	−.04	.02	−.04
9. Th. Inst. Freq.									.12*	.12*	.32*	.19*	.14*	−.02	.00	−.04
10. Th. Pleasant.										−.16*	−.06	.03	.61*	.03	.03	.06
11. Th. Extreme Af.											.09*	−.03	.06	.01	.11*	.13*
12. Th. Signif.												.48*	.16*	.04	−.02	−.04
13. Th. Goal-Dir.													.13*	.20*	−.06	−.11*
14. Th. Excit.														−.02	.01	.07
15. Coord.															.11*	.01
16. Act. memory																.45*
17. Th. memory																

*p < .05.

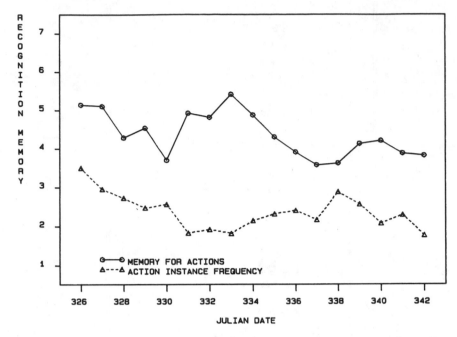

Figure 3.3. Experiment 1: Serial-position curves for recognition of actions and for Action Instance Frequency ratings (test sessions 2 and 3).

period. Figure 3.3 shows the serial-position curve for action memory. The serial-position curves are based on the data from the second and third test sessions because the overall high memory scores in the first test session tend to wash out the serial-position effects. In this figure the data on memory for actions show a classic primacy effect and a powerful "Thanksgiving effect." The Julian date 331 corresponds to the day before Thanksgiving, and on this day most of our subjects would have been traveling home for their first visit since they left for college. Most of the subjects spent Thanksgiving with their families (332) and then the next 2 days (333 and 334) visiting their high school friends and their families. Most came back to the university on Sunday (335) and began classes again on Monday (336). Clearly, our subjects' memories for the events that occurred during this vacation were much better than for the rest of the acquisition period and reached a peak the day after Thanksgiving. It is also possible to look at the serial-position curve for subjects' ratings of the characteristics of the events that occurred over the acquisition period. Examination of the serial-position curves for the scales that measure event characteristics show several that seem to be related to the serial-position curve for action memory. The variable that shows the strongest relation is Action Instance Frequency. This curve is also given in Figure 3.3, where it shows a nice *inverse* relation with the memory curve. Figure 3.4 displays the serial-position curve for thought memory.

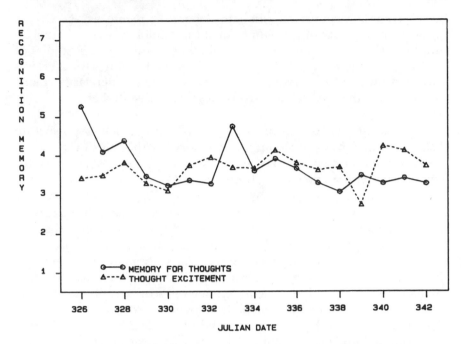

Figure 3.4. Experiment 1: Serial-position curves for recognition of thoughts and for Thought Excitement ratings (test sessions 2 and 3).

It shows a primacy effect and a somewhat weaker Thanksgiving effect. Examination of the serial-position curves for event characteristics related to memory for thoughts shows little consistent relation to the memory curve. The serial-position curve for the Thought Excitement scale is included in Figure 3.4 as an example.

Discussion

Methodology. The results of Experiment 1 demonstrate that it is possible to overcome a variety of methodological difficulties and carry out autobiographical memory studies with random sampling of autobiographical events. It is possible to develop techniques of recording autobiographical events and the characteristics of these events in ways that give lawful data. It is not necessary for the experimenter to be the subject in research on autobiographical memory.

Memorable events. The results indicate that autobiographical events selected by the subject to be memorable show higher recognition-memory scores than random events and that the memorable events are systematically different from the random events on a wide variety of dimensions.

Forgetting curves. The forgetting curves for randomly selected events show a relatively shallow slope, and the rate of forgetting seems to be relatively slow compared with many laboratory memory tasks. On the other hand, the rate of forgetting for these randomly selected autobiographical events seems to be more rapid than in other recent studies of autobiographical memory that have used selected events. However, it is hard to draw firm conclusions on these issues because there are so many differences in the methods and data analyses in these studies.

Thoughts versus actions. The results show that it is possible to distinguish memory for actions and memory for thoughts in studies of autobiographical memory. The memory data suggest that memory for actions is better than memory for thoughts.

Event characteristics. A number of different analyses were carried out to examine the characteristics of autobiographical events that are related to recognition-memory performance. These analyses found that a number of event characteristics were related to memory. Within this data there was a consistent pattern in which *actions* rated as occurring infrequently showed high recognition-memory scores, while *thoughts* that were rated as exciting showed high recognition scores. These results were also supported by the memory and rating data for the events that were sampled during our subjects' Thanksgiving vacations. The actions during this period tended to be of lower frequency than the usual events at the university, and the data displayed in the serial-position plot show better recognition memory for events during the vacation.

Metamemory. Finally, the data on events selected to be memorable show that these subjects have good metamemory skills. The events selected by these undergraduates to be memorable were recognized better than random events. The rated event characteristics for the selected events were remarkably similar to the randomly sampled events that actually showed high memory scores (cf. Tables 3.1 and 3.2). Both the subject-selected events and the events with high memory scores contained infrequently occurring actions and exciting thoughts.

Experiment 2

Method

The most important change in methodology from Experiment 1 to Experiment 2 was the shift to a cued-recall procedure for testing memory. This experiment also included an explicit assessment of the subject's phenomenal experience during recall. The acquisition and testing intervals were somewhat shorter in Experiment 2, and the response cards were modified to request more detailed information about affect. Subjects were not asked to record memorable events in this experiment.

Experiment 2 was designed (a) to study autobiographical memory with a cued-recall procedure, (b) to gather additional data on forgetting of autobiographical events and on the differences between memory for actions and memory for thoughts, (c) to gather additional data on the characteristics of randomly sampled events that are related to memory for the events, (d) to study the differential effectiveness of different types of information as cues for recall, (e) to study recall accuracy and to carry out a qualitative analysis of the recalled information in relation to the original event, (f) to relate the contents of the autobiographical events to memory for the events, and (g) to study the phenomenal experiences of the subjects during the recall process.

Subjects

There were 10 subjects in this experiment, selected from a group of 43 volunteers on the basis of their motivation to participate, legibility of handwriting, and ability to follow the instructions. The sample included 5 freshmen and 5 sophomores. There were 9 females and 1 male. Subjects were paid for participation in the experiment.

Response cards

The response cards asked the subjects for (a) identification number, (b) time (day of week, date, time), (c) location, (d) thoughts, (e) emotions, (f) actions, (g) thought/action coordination, (h) a rating of location on a frequency scale, (i) a rating of thoughts on four scales, (j) a rating of actions on four scales, and (k) a rating of emotions on six scales. Thus, the basic changes from Experiment 1 in the data gathered on the response card were the deletion of the summary sentence information and the addition of emotion information, emotion scales, and frequency information for location.

Location, thought, and action. Subjects were asked to write down location, thoughts, and actions as before. After they wrote down the location of the event, they were to rate the relative frequency of their experiences with the location on a 7-point rating scale, where 1 was defined as "infrequent" and 7 was defined as "frequent." In this experiment, thoughts and actions were each rated on four 7-point rating scales: category infrequent/frequent, instance infrequent/frequent, trivial/significant, and non-goal-directed/goal-directed.

Emotions. The instructions to the subject for the emotion category stated: "Write down what you were feeling just before the beeper went off, in one sentence. You may use any adjectives that you wish and are not confined to those listed in the adjacent scales." After the subjects wrote down the emotion information, they were asked to fill out six 7-point rating scales: (a) non-excited/excited; (b) non-happy/happy; (c) non-alert/alert; (d) non-anxious/anxious; (e) non-angry/angry; and (f) non-sad/sad. The overall instructions stated that "A rating of a '7' would indicate that you were feeling a particular emotion very strongly. A rating of '1' would indicate that you were not feeling that emotion at all." Finally, the instructions stated that we were defining "Excited as a positive feeling one would feel while riding a roller-coaster, and Anxious as a negative feeling that one would feel just before taking a final exam."

Acquisition

The subjects carried random-alarm mechanisms for an average of slightly over 13 days. The random-alarm devices were set to sample events at the rate of 0.64 events per hour. The experiment was carried out in the 2 weeks immediately preceding spring vacation.

Test procedures

Test intervals. Each subject was tested at three time intervals: immediately after acquisition, at a mean of 23 days after the end of acquisition, and at a mean of 46 days after the end of acquisition. Thus, the average time from acquisition to test for an item in each of the three test sessions was 7 days, 30 days, and 53 days. See Figure 3.1 for an overview of the acquisition and test time intervals.

Item sampling. The items tested at each time interval were a random sample from the total items, stratified across the acquisition time interval. One-third of the total sample of items was tested at each of the three test sessions.

Types of tests used

Cued recall. The subject's recall of the overall event was tested with a cued-recall technique. Five types of cues were used: Time; Location; Time and location; Thought; Action. Approximately one-fifth of the items were tested with each of the different types of retrieval cues. The cued-recall procedure was carried out by placing the response card to be tested in a mask so that only the appropriate cue information was visible. After reading the cue, the subject was asked to attempt to recall all of the remaining information about the experimental event. The subjects wrote their recalls on recall sheets that had places for the recall of time, location, thoughts, emotions, and actions. In addition to recalling the time, the subjects were asked to indicate the period during which the event occurred: the day/the night; a weekday/a weekend; the first half of the acquisition period/the last half of the acquisition period. In addition to recalling the emotions they were feeling just before the alarm sounded, the subjects were asked to fill out six 7-point emotion scales: Excited; Happy; Alert; Anxious; Angry; Sad.

Overall memory. After the subjects had completed writing their recalls, they were asked to fill out a 7-point scale giving a rating of their overall memory for the event. On this scale, 1 was defined as "have no memory of the event," and 7 was defined as "certain that remember the event."

Phenomenal experience scales. Immediately after completing the recall procedure and the Overall Memory scale, the subjects were asked to complete seven 7-point scales designed to measure their phenomenal experience during the recall process. The scales were intended to measure the following forms of mental experiences: visual, auditory, tactile, smell, taste, emotion, and thought. The instructions to the subject stated: "While you were recalling the information about the overall event above, to what extent were you reexperiencing (in your mind) each of the following." For the scale of Visual Phenomenal Experience, 1 was defined as "no reexperiencing of the particular visual experience"; 7 was defined as "complete reexperiencing of the particular visual experience." The instructions additionally stated that "by 'complete reexperiencing of the particular visual experience' we mean that you had a vivid visual image of the particular event during your recall of the item." The instructions for each of the other six scales were the same as those for the visual scale except that the word "visual" was replaced with the term relevant for the particular scale, that is, "auditory," "tactile," "smell," "taste," "emotional," and "thought."

Recognition scales. After carrying out the recall process, giving the rating on Overall Memory, and filling out the phenomenal experience scales for an item, the subjects' response cards were removed from the mask, and they were allowed to read the entire card. They were then asked to carry out a recognition-memory procedure for five aspects of information from the card: location, time, emotions, thoughts, and actions. The subjects indicated their recognition memory on a 7-point recognition-memory scale, where 1 was defined as "have no memory of the event," and 7 was defined as "certain that remember the event."

Payment schedule

Subjects were paid a total of $40 in four installments of $10 each. The first payment was made during a meeting with the experimenter early in the acquisition period. An additional payment of $10 was made at the end of each of the three test sessions.

Results

The analyses for Experiment 2 are based on 654 randomly sampled autobiographical events (with a median of 68 items per subject, and a range of 43 to 89). The data are presented in the following order: results based on (a) the recognition scales, (b) overall recall memory, (c) recall accuracy, (d) recall type, (e) recall content category, and (f) phenomenal experience scales.

Recognition scales

Forgetting curves. The forgetting curves for recognition of locations, times, emotions, thoughts, and actions are given in Figure 3.5. For the purposes of constructing this figure, a relatively conservative criterion of forgetting seemed desirable; so items that were given scores of 1 or 2 on the 7-point recognition-memory scales were considered to have been forgotten. Thus, the figure is plotted in terms of the percentage of items with scores of 3 or greater on the recognition-memory scales. The data show a very shallow forgetting curve. Recognition memory is fairly high, with some differences in recognition for the different aspects of the autobiographical events; the mean percentages in order of increas-

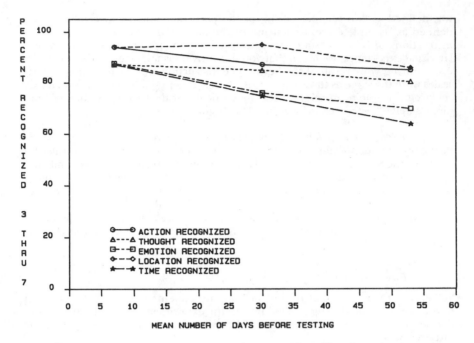

Figure 3.5. Experiment 2: Forgetting curves for recognition of locations, times, emotions, thoughts, and actions (recognition ratings > 2 scored as correct).

ing recognition memory are: time 75%, emotions 78%, thoughts 84%, actions 89%, and location 92%.

Serial-position curves. The subjects in this experiment carried the random-alarm devices for almost 2 weeks; so it is possible to plot the serial-position curves for the recognition scales. The data from this experiment were gathered in the 2 weeks immediately preceding spring vacation. Figure 3.6 gives the serial-position curves for recognition of actions and recognition of thoughts. Julian dates 59–60 and 66–67 were weekends. Overall, the serial-position effects are not very impressive. These two curves suggest a primacy and/or weekend effect, with another possible weekend effect on Julian date 66. The peak at the end may be due to the fact that the subjects were getting ready to leave for spring vacation, and there may also be a contribution due to recency because this plot includes data gathered in the first test session.

Overall memory

The results in the next section are based on the scale of Overall Memory, which was perhaps the best summary measure of memory for the overall

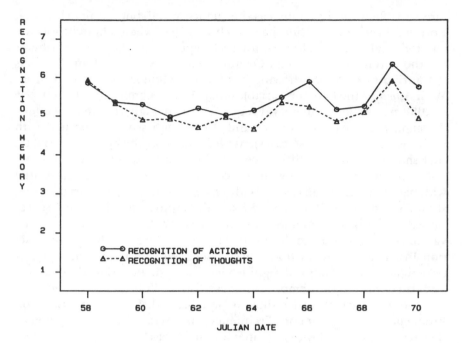

Figure 3.6. Experiment 2: Serial-position curves for recognition of actions and thoughts (data from all three test sessions).

event that was gathered in this study. The Overall Memory scores were obtained by asking subjects, immediately after finishing their recalls, to give a rating of their recall of the overall event on a 7-point scale, where 7 was defined as "certain that remember the event."

Cue type and memory ratings. There were extremely strong effects of cue type in memory for the events. The mean scores on Overall Memory given each cue type were as follows: Time 2.38, Location 2.51, Time and location 2.92, Thought 3.85, and Action 4.31. All of the differences in Overall Memory by cue type are significant ($p < .05$) except the differences between Time as a cue and Location as a cue and the difference between Location as a cue and joint Time and location as a cue.

Item characteristics for high and low memory by cue type. One way to explore the issue of what characteristics of autobiographical events lead to successful recall is to contrast those events that showed high memory performance with those that showed low memory performance. However, this analysis must be carried out separately for each type of recall cue because an interaction with this variable would be expected. For example, one might expect that Location Frequency would be an important variable when Location was the cue for recall, but it is not clear that Location Frequency should have such an effect when Thought was the cue for recall. Table 3.4 gives, for each type of cue, the event attributes for those items showing high Overall Memory (scores of 6 or 7) versus the attributes for those showing low Overall Memory (scores of 1 or 2). With *Action* as the cue, the variables that show a significant difference (p < .05) are Action Category Frequency (with high frequency better), Thought Significance, Excited, and Alert (high scores associated with high memory in all these cases). With *Location* as the cue, the variables that show a significant difference are Location Frequency, Action Category Frequency, and Action Instance Frequency (low scores associated with high memory in all cases). With *Thought* as the cue, the variables that show a significant difference are Excited, Happy, and Alert (high scores associated with high memory in all cases). With *Time* as the cue, the variables that show a significant difference are Location Frequency, Action Instance Frequency (low scores associated with high memory), Action Significance, Thought Significance, Excited, and Alert (high scores associated with high memory for these four). With *Time and location* as the cue, the variables that show a significant difference are Location Frequency, Action Category Frequency, and Action Instance Frequency (low scores associated with high memory in all cases).

Correlations of item characteristics and overall memory scores. The attributes of the autobiographical events that are associated with the Overall Memory scores were also examined with correlational procedures. Table 3.5 presents the correlations with Overall Memory of each of the event attribute measures. The pattern of correlations is in good agreement with data for high versus low Overall Memory that were presented in Table 3.4. An attempt was made to reduce the complex set of correlations by regression techniques. Within each cue type, the General Linear Model (GLM) was used to see which event variables would predict Overall Memory, with test interval and subjects also entered as factors. For each cue type, the variables that made a significant (p < .05) contribution in addition to test interval and subjects were as follows: (a) *Action cue:* Thought Instance Frequency, Thought Category Frequency (negative sign), Action Goal-Directedness; (b) *Location cue:* Location Frequency (negative sign); (c) *Thought cue:* Excited; (d) *Time cue:* Action Instance Frequency (negative sign); (e) *Time and location cue:* Location Frequency (negative sign) and Happy (negative sign).

Recall accuracy

For each of the 654 autobiographical events, the recalled information was compared with the original response cards, and recall accuracy was

Table 3.4. *Experiment 2: Event characteristics for events with high and low memory scores for each cue type*

Event characteristics	Cue types									
	Action		Location		Thought		Time		Time & loc.	
	Low	Hi	Low	Hi	Low	Hi	Low	Hi	Low	Hi
Loc. Freq.	5.1	5.2	6.3	2.5*	6.0	5.2	5.9	4.5*	6.1	3.1*
Act. Cat. Freq.	4.6	5.7*	5.4	4.4*	5.2	4.9	5.1	4.4	5.8	4.4*
Act. Inst. Freq.	2.9	2.0	2.8	1.7*	2.5	2.0	2.8	1.2*	3.2	1.9*
Act. Signif.	2.6	3.5	3.3	2.8	3.3	3.6	2.8	4.1*	3.5	3.2
Act. Goal-Dir.	3.7	4.9	4.5	4.1	4.5	4.6	4.3	4.6	5.1	4.6
Th. Cat. Freq.	4.3	4.6	4.5	4.1	4.2	4.4	4.0	4.4	4.6	3.4
Th. Inst. Freq.	1.8	2.7	2.5	1.7	2.5	2.0	2.0	1.1	2.4	2.0
Th. Signif.	2.2	3.9*	3.3	3.1	3.3	3.3	3.0	4.4*	3.5	3.0
Th. Goal-Dir.	3.1	4.0	3.6	3.4	3.4	3.9	3.4	3.0	3.9	2.8
Excited	3.0	4.1*	3.2	3.7	2.9	4.6*	2.8	4.5*	3.3	3.5
Happy	3.8	4.5	3.9	4.6	3.8	5.2*	3.7	4.6	4.1	4.1
Alert	3.6	5.0*	4.6	4.5	3.9	5.4*	4.0	5.5*	4.5	4.6
Anxious	2.6	3.0	2.7	2.7	2.4	2.4	2.9	2.3	2.6	2.9
Angry	1.5	1.6	1.7	1.4	1.2	1.3	1.6	1.8	1.6	1.6
Sad	2.1	1.6	2.0	1.2	1.7	1.6	1.9	2.0	1.8	1.6
Coord.	3.7	3.9	4.5	4.7	3.9	4.8	4.4	4.0	5.0	4.5
No. events	19	32	86	16	27	24	90	12	67	15

Note: High memory = scores of 6 or 7 on Overall Memory. Low memory = scores of 1 or 2 on Overall Memory.
*$p < .05$, high memory versus low memory.

Table 3.5. *Experiment 2: Correlations of event characteristics with overall memory for each cue type*

Event characteristics	Cue types				
	Action	Location	Thought	Time	Time & loc.
Loc. Freq.	− .04	− .71*	− .12	− .22*	− .50*
Act. Cat. Freq.	.22*	− .18*	.01	− .04	− .28*
Act. Inst. Freq.	− .21*	− .19*	− .11	− .18*	− .21*
Act. Signif.	.16	− .12	.05	.13	.09
Act. Goal-Dir.	.27*	− .08	.02	.03	− .14
Th. Cat. Freq.	.03	.13	.08	.07	− .19*
Th. Inst. Freq.	.08	− .17*	− .09	− .08	− .06
Th. Signif.	.32*	− .11	.00	.15	− .10
Th. Goal-Dir.	.17	− .04	.05	.00	− .11
Excited	.21*	.14	.34*	.24*	.00
Happy	.12	.16	.29*	.20*	− .02
Alert	.23*	− .10	.26*	.16	.01
Anxious	.09	.02	.06	− .09	.06
Angry	.07	− .03	.03	.07	.04
Sad	− .11	− .17*	− .01	− .01	.07
Coord.	.04	− .04	.13	− .03	− .10
No. events	118	137	127	140	132

$*p < .05.$

scored on a 3-point scale by the experimenter, where 1 was used for totally incorrect or omitted responses, 2 was used for responses that contained some correct information, even if this was possibly inferred information, and 3 was used for responses that were correct, fairly complete, and contained some episodic (noninferable) information.

Forgetting curves for recall accuracy by cue type. Figure 3.7 gives the forgetting curves for percentage recall of *actions* for each type of cue. For the purposes of this plot, responses given scores of 2 or 3 on the recall accuracy scale were considered to be correct recalls. Figure 3.8 gives the same information for recall of *thoughts,* and Figure 3.9, the information for recall of *locations.* As would be expected, the overall level of memory in recall is much lower than that for the recognition measures used in Experiment 1 or that for the recognition data from the present experiment displayed in Figure 3.5.

These figures show that as a type of information to be recalled (across cue types), location showed the best memory scores, actions next, and thoughts last. No recall accuracy scores were developed for emotions and time information because it was not clear how to make such scores comparable to the scores developed for location, actions, and thoughts.

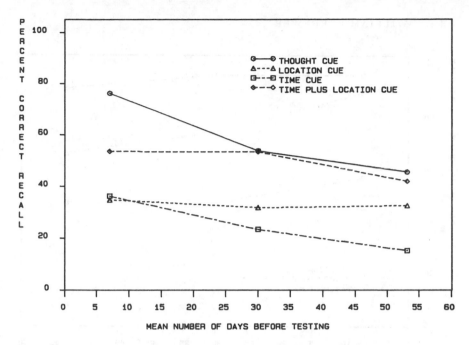

Figure 3.7. Experiment 2: Forgetting curves for recall of actions for Thought, Location, Time, and Time and location cues (recall accuracy > 1 scored as correct).

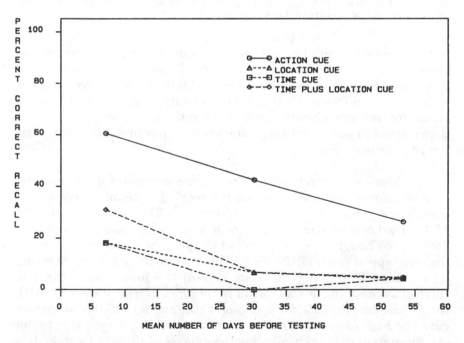

Figure 3.8. Experiment 2: Forgetting curves for recall of thoughts for Action, Location, Time, and Time and location cues (recall accuracy > 1 scored as correct).

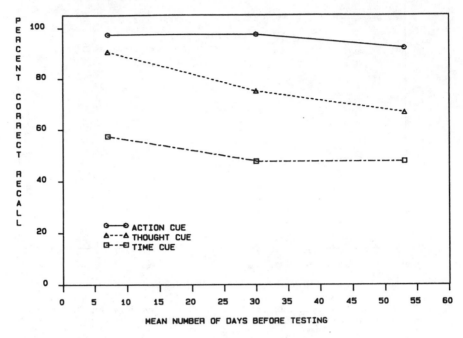

Figure 3.9. Experiment 2: Forgetting curves for recall of locations for Action, Thought, and Time cues (recall accuracy > 1 scored as correct).

The graphs for recall of actions and recall of thoughts show shallow forgetting curves. The graphs for recall of location show little or no forgetting, suggesting that the subjects' ability to give correct location information was frequently derived from location inferences. If location recalls are frequently based on inferences and not on true episodic recall, then one would not expect forgetting to occur over time, and this is what is seen in Figure 3.9.

Recall accuracy for each cue type. There are powerful effects of the type of information used as a cue for recall. For recall of *actions,* the overall rate of recall for each type of cue is (a) 25% for a Time cue, (b) 33% for a Location cue, (c) 49% for a Time and location cue, and (d) 58% for a Thought cue. For recall of *thoughts,* the overall rate of recall for each type of cue is (a) 7% for a Time cue, (b) 9% for a Location cue, (c) 14% for a Time and location cue, and (d) 42% for an Action cue. For recall of *locations,* the overall rate of recall for each type of cue is (a) 51% for a Time cue, (b) 76% for a Thought cue, and (c) 94% for an Action cue. The high scores for location recall are probably largely due to the effectiveness of the cues in allowing the subjects to infer the location. It is clear from these data that time information and location information are extremely poor cues for recall of actions or thoughts. Time and location together are only slightly better, whereas thoughts are relatively good cues for actions, and actions relatively good cues for thoughts.

Recall types

The analyses in the previous section focused on the issue of recall accuracy. The analyses in this section are based on a scoring of types of recall that attempts to capture a number of interesting relations between the initial events and their recalls based on a *qualitative* analysis of the events and their recalls. All recalls of actions and thoughts were classified by the experimenter into one of seven recall types: (a) omit, (b) wrong event, (c) wrong time slice, (d) overt error, (e) inference, (f) correct, and (g) correct with detail. This classification was carried out without knowledge of the event ratings. The criteria used to classify recalls into these categories were as follows:

Omit. An item was scored as an omit when the subject either wrote nothing down in the appropriate location of the recall sheet or wrote "don't know" in that location.

Wrong event. An item was scored as a wrong event when the recalled thought or action was simply a different thought or action from that on the response card. An example: [response card] "Sitting at a back table facing pin-ball machines. Coat on, leaning over with hand on backpack. Class around me, teacher at other end." [recall – Time cue] "Lying in bed."

Wrong time slice. An item was scored as a wrong time slice when the recalled thought or action seemed to be the correct event, but the subject appeared to be recalling a segment of the overall event that was slightly (seconds to minutes) offset in time from the particular event written down on the response card. An example: [response card] "P. and I were in Dad's car just in front of K.'s house and passing it. I noticed that his van wasn't home. We were heading for the car wash because Dad's car was filthy." [recall – Thought cue] "I was driving the car and P. was with me. We just passed K.'s house aways back." It is only possible to score an item in this category when the event has enough structure to allow the experimenter to judge that a probable recall of wrong time slice has occurred. Because most of the items scored as wrong events were probably recalls of events from the subjects' lives during the period of the experiment, they could also be thought of as retrievals from the wrong time interval, but with a much enlarged time scale from those scored in this category. Thoughts appear to have less temporally sustained structure, and so the wrong-time-slice category was used much less frequently for thoughts than for actions.

Overt error. An item was scored as an overt error when it appeared that the correct event had been recalled, but there was an overt contradiction between the information on the response card and the recall protocol. An example: [response card] "I was just reading chemistry on the review of atomic weights with isotopes. No one else is in the room. A few wet t-shirts and jeans are drying out on my bed." [recall – Thought cue] "I was studying chemistry and L. was at her desk."

Inference. An item was scored as an inference if it appeared to the experimenter that a subject could have written the recall using only the recall cue and generic knowledge about his or her life during the period of the experiment. In practice, an inference response was scored if the experimenter, after reading over all the subject's responses, judged that he could have written the recall given the cue without knowing what the initial response card contained. An example: [response card] "I am frying chicken for dinner. R. is here sitting at table. My boyfriend is lying on the couch watching Star Trek." [recall – Time and location cue] "I was probably cooking." The time was 10:28 a.m. on a Sunday, and the individual typically prepared a large dinner for her boyfriend on Sundays. This response was scored as an inference because the experimenter judged that the "recall" was totally derivable from generic knowledge of the subject's life during the experiment.

Correct. An item was scored as correct when the recall contained some correct information that did not seem to be inferable from the cue. An example: [response card] "I was sitting at my desk talking to Dad & Mom on the phone. I was telling them about running 2 miles. L. was at her desk studying. My 'Helter Skelter' book was laying in front of me." [recall – Time and location cue] "I was talking to Dad & Mom on the phone. L. was at her desk."

Correct with detail. An item was scored as correct with detail when the recall was correct as given and contained additional consistent detail. An example: [response card] "Walking home from Eisner's. I'm one house (B.'s house) from mine. Two birds are furiously chirping and fighting on a branch. Cold day. Old lady & dog just passed me by, cars and a girl who looks like C." [recall – Location cue] "Walking, carrying bag of groceries, just came back from Eisner. Bag was heavy – old lady & *white shaggy* (added detail) on leash just passed me. Girl across street who looks like C. Birds bickering on tree limb." This item was scored as correct with detail because the recall included additional consistent information about the dog.

The qualitative recall types have a complex relation with the recall accuracy score used in the previous section. All responses classified as *omits* and *wrong events* and some classified as *wrong time slice* were scored as 1 (totally incorrect) on the accuracy scale. All responses classified as *overt errors* and *inferences* and some classified as *wrong time slice* were scored as 2 (some correct information) on the accuracy scale. All responses classified as *correct with detail* and most classified as *correct* (depending on the overall amount of correct information) were scored as 3 (clearly correct) on the accuracy scale.

Frequency of recall types for actions. The number of action recalls falling into each of the seven recall categories was as follows (across cue types): 190 omit, 118 wrong event, 20 wrong time slice, 4 overt error, 70 inference, 109 correct, and 22 correct with detail. Thus, while there was a high percentage of errors overall, most of those errors were due to retrieving the wrong event or inferring the wrong event. There were very few overt errors.

Frequency of recall types for thoughts. The number of thought recalls falling into each of the seven recall categories was (across cue types): 325 omit, 94 wrong event, 7 wrong time slice, 0 overt error, 14 inference, 72 correct, and 1 correct with detail. Overall, this qualitative analysis is consistent with the earlier results in showing memory for thoughts to be poorer than memory for actions. In recalling thoughts, the most common response, by far, was to omit the information; there were many fewer inferences and no overt errors.

Recall types for actions by type of cue. A more detailed presentation of these data is given in Tables 3.6 and 3.7. Table 3.6 gives the percentage of each recall type for each type of cue for the recall of actions. The largest effects shown in this table are those due to the differential effectiveness of the cue types seen in the earlier analyses, with Thought acting as a fairly good cue, Time and location or Location acting as moderately successful cues, and Time serving as a very poor cue. In addition, it appears that with a Time cue there is an increase in the percentage of wrong events recalled, and with a joint Time and location cue there is an increase in the percentage of inferences.

Recall types for thought by type of cue. Table 3.7 presents the percentage of responses scored in each recall category for thought recalls. Here also there is a strong effect of cue type, with Action serving as a

Table 3.6. *Experiment 2: Percentage of each recall type for each type of cue for actions*

Cue types		Recall types						
		Corr. & d.	Corr.	Wrong t.	Error	Wrong e.	Inf.	Omit
Action	N = 0	—	—	—	—	—	—	—
Location	N = 136	5	18	4	0	16	7	50
Thought	N = 127	6	34	5	2	17	13	24
Time	N = 140	1	9	3	0	33	11	42
Time & loc.	N = 131	5	22	4	1	23	21	25

Table 3.7. *Experiment 2: Percentage of each recall type for each type of cue for thoughts*

Cue types		Recall types						
		Corr. & d.	Corr.	Wrong t.	Error	Wrong e.	Inf.	Omit
Action	N = 116	1	37	2	0	22	3	35
Location	N = 134	0	7	1	0	13	2	76
Thought	N = 0	—	—	—	—	—	—	—
Time	N = 135	0	5	0	0	18	2	75
Time & loc.	N = 128	0	10	2	0	21	3	63

relatively good cue for thought recall, and all of the other types of cues giving relatively few correct recalls. A moderate number of thought recalls were classified as wrong events, and they appear to be distributed relatively evenly across cue types. The rate of thought recalls classified as inferences is quite low, and the ones that occur do not appear to be associated with a particular type of cue.

Event characteristics for recall types for actions

The classification of thought and action recalls into the seven recall types makes possible a very interesting form of analysis. The items were subdivided by recall type, and then means were calculated for each of these types of items for each independent and each dependent variable in the study. The data for recall of actions are given in Table 3.8, and for recall of thoughts in Table 3.9. The data in both of these tables are collapsed

Table 3.8. *Experiment 2: Event characteristics and memory measures for recall types for actions*

Event characteristics	Recall types						
	Corr. & d.	Corr.	Wrong t.	Error	Wrong e.	Inf.	Omit
Loc. Freq.	3.7	4.4	4.1	5.0	5.4	5.7	6.0
Act. Cat. Freq.	4.7	4.8	5.2	5.5	5.4	5.4	5.3
Act. Inst. Freq.	2.0	2.4	2.3	2.8	2.7	3.2	2.8
Act. Signif.	3.9	3.1	3.3	3.3	2.9	3.2	3.1
Act. Goal-Dir.	4.6	4.7	3.8	5.0	4.4	4.6	4.4
Th. Cat. Freq.	4.2	4.1	4.2	5.0	4.2	4.5	4.4
Th. Inst. Freq.	1.9	1.9	2.3	1.8	2.5	2.6	2.2
Th. Signif.	3.8	3.1	2.6	3.0	3.2	3.5	3.0
Th. Goal-Dir.	3.4	3.9	3.1	3.3	3.7	3.8	3.3
Excited	4.1	3.6	4.1	2.5	3.2	2.9	3.0
Happy	4.1	4.3	4.9	3.8	4.0	3.8	3.9
Alert	5.6	4.7	4.7	4.0	4.2	3.9	4.3
Anxious	2.7	2.9	2.3	1.5	3.2	2.5	2.4
Angry	2.0	1.7	1.3	2.5	1.7	1.5	1.5
Sad	1.6	1.7	1.7	2.5	1.9	1.7	1.9
Coord.	4.2	4.7	4.3	4.5	4.6	4.6	4.5
Overall Mem.	6.0	4.5	4.9	3.8	3.1	2.7	1.3
Act. recall	3.0	2.7	1.7	2.0	1.0	2.0	1.0
Th. recall	2.1	1.6	1.3	1.0	1.0	1.1	1.0
PE Visual	6.3	4.8	5.3	3.3	3.4	3.3	1.4
PE Auditory	4.7	2.8	2.9	2.5	2.0	1.8	1.0
PE Tactile	4.1	2.9	3.7	2.3	2.0	1.6	1.1
PE Smell	2.6	1.7	2.3	1.0	1.5	1.3	1.1
PE Taste	2.5	1.6	2.1	1.0	1.5	1.2	1.0
PE Emotion	4.8	3.4	3.7	3.0	2.4	1.8	1.3
PE Thought	5.4	3.5	3.0	3.3	2.1	1.9	1.4
No. events	22	109	20	4	118	70	190

across cue type. This is a very rich set of data, and some important general trends can be noted.

Corrects and omits for actions. For the recall of actions (Table 3.8), a comparison of the items that were classified as correct ($N = 109$) with those classified as omits ($N = 190$) serves to set a framework in which the other recall types can be examined. The actions that were later to be recalled correctly were rated as having lower Location Frequency than those omitted (4.4 vs. 6.0); they were also lower on Action Category Frequency (4.8 vs. 5.3). These findings are similar to many of the analyses of event characteristics and memory that were reported earlier. One of the important dependent measures used in this experiment was the index of Overall Memory, which was obtained by asking the subjects, after they had completed their recalls, to rate their overall memory for the event on a 7-point scale. On this scale, the items later classified as correct by the experimenter had a mean of 4.5, and those omitted a mean of 1.3. This shows considerable agreement between the subjects' ratings of their overall recall performance and the experimenter's objective scoring of their recalls with respect to the original event card. On accuracy of recall (rated by the experimenter on a 1-to-3 scale), the *thoughts* associated with the action show a mean of 1.6 for correct action recalls and a mean of 1.0 for omitted action recalls.

Correct with detail. The class of action recalls classified as correct with detail ($N = 22$) could, technically speaking, be considered to be errors, because the recalls contain information not found in the description of the event on the original response card. However, I have chosen to consider these responses to be correct recalls, with the extra information identifying particularly rich memories for the event. The data in Table 3.8 for these items lends considerable support to this decision. On almost all independent and dependent variables these items behave as "hypercorrect" recalls. The events whose later recalls would be classified as correct with detail were originally rated lower on Location Frequency than the corrects (3.7 vs. 4.4), roughly equivalent on Action Category Frequency (4.7 vs. 4.8), and lower on Action Instance Frequency (2.0 vs. 2.4). The events classified as correct with detail also show higher means on the Alert scale (5.6 vs. 4.7) and on the Excited scale (4.1 vs. 3.6). On the scale of Overall Memory, the subjects rated their recalls of the items classified as correct with detail considerably higher than the corrects (6.0 vs. 4.5). The recall accuracy data show that the subjects were more likely to recall the thought associated with the action for the action recalls classified as correct with detail than for the corrects (2.1 vs. 1.6 on a scale that went from 1 to 3).

Wrong time slice. The action recalls classified as wrong time slice ($N = 20$) show a pattern of data on the event characteristics that is much like that of the correct recalls. For example, the scores of these events compared with the events scored correct were slightly lower on Location Frequency (4.1 vs. 4.4) and about the same on Action Instance Frequency (2.3 vs. 2.4). On the dependent measures of memory, these items show, if anything, a tendency toward higher memory scores than the items classified as correct (e.g., on Overall Memory the wrong-time-slice items showed a mean of 4.9, compared with 4.5 for the corrects). All of this suggests that from the point of view of the subjects, these items were much like correct recalls.

Overt errors. The class of action recalls classified as overt errors is very small ($N = 4$), but this class has important theoretical implications, and so it seems worth examining even with this limited sample. These items show a pattern of data somewhat in between the events that were recalled correctly and those that were omitted. For example, on Location Frequency, these items have a mean of 5.0, falling nicely between the corrects at 4.4 and the omits at 6.0. Similar results show up for the dependent measures. On the scale of Overall Memory, the recalls that were classified as overt errors have a mean of 3.8, whereas the recalls classified as corrects have a mean of 4.5, and the omits a mean of 1.3. This suggests that at the time of recall, the subjects were aware that the recalls that were later to be classified by the experimenter as overt errors were of somewhat inferior quality.

Wrong events. The set of action recalls classified as wrong events ($N = 118$) is much larger than that of those classified as overt errors and also shows a pattern of data that is intermediate between the items that were recalled correctly and those that were omitted, although with somewhat stronger similarities to the omits. The items classified as wrong events showed a mean score of 5.4 on Location Frequency, compared with 4.4 for the corrects and 6.0 for the omits. On Action Instance Frequency, they showed a mean of 2.7, compared with 2.4 for the corrects and 2.8 for the omits. On the measure of Overall Memory, these items showed a mean of 3.1, compared with 4.5 for the corrects and 1.3 for the omits.

Inferences. The action recalls that were classified as inferences ($N = 70$) show a pattern of data that is quite close to those classified as omits. These events have a mean score of 5.7 on Location Frequency, compared with 4.4 for corrects and 6.0 for omits. On Action Instance Frequency, they have an even higher score than the omits (3.2 vs. 2.8). This is consistent with the recalls of these items being classified as possible inferences rather than as true episodic recalls. On the measure of Overall Memory, the subjects rated the inference items well below the corrects; they have a mean of 2.7, compared with 4.5 for the corrects and 1.3 for the omits. The overall pattern of data for the inference items is most interesting. Technically speaking, these items were correct, but the subjects were clearly aware, at the time of recall, that what they wrote down was not of the same quality as what they wrote down for the items later classified by the experimenter as corrects.

Table 3.9. *Experiment 2: Event characteristics and memory measures for recall types for thoughts*

Event characteristics	Recall types						
	Corr. & d.	Corr.	Wrong t.	Error	Wrong e.	Inf.	Omit
Loc. Freq.	7.0	4.7	3.7	—	4.6	5.2	5.7
Act. Cat. Freq.	7.0	5.2	5.9	—	5.3	6.1	5.2
Act. Inst. Freq.	1.0	2.3	2.9	—	2.7	3.0	2.8
Act. Signif.	7.0	3.0	4.6	—	2.8	3.8	3.1
Act. Goal-Dir.	7.0	4.4	5.1	—	4.9	6.3	4.2
Th. Cat. Freq.	7.0	4.5	3.4	—	3.9	5.2	4.3
Th. Inst. Freq.	2.0	2.4	1.7	—	2.2	2.6	2.3
Th. Signif.	7.0	3.3	4.4	—	3.2	3.8	3.1
Th. Goal-Dir.	1.0	3.6	3.6	—	3.6	4.4	3.3
Excited	4.0	3.8	4.1	—	3.2	3.6	3.1
Happy	2.0	4.3	4.4	—	4.0	3.9	4.0
Alert	7.0	4.6	4.7	—	4.6	5.5	4.2
Anxious	1.0	3.0	2.1	—	3.1	3.9	2.4
Angry	7.0	1.6	1.0	—	1.8	1.3	1.6
Sad	1.0	1.9	1.3	—	1.8	1.6	1.8
Coord.	1.0	4.5	3.2	—	4.0	5.4	4.5
Overall Mem.	7.0	5.3	5.1	—	3.9	3.6	2.1
Act. recall	—	2.7	2.0	—	1.6	1.9	1.3
Th. recall	3.0	2.9	1.6	—	1.0	2.0	1.0
PE Visual	7.0	5.3	5.3	—	4.2	4.3	2.5
PE Auditory	7.0	3.5	3.1	—	2.7	3.4	1.6
PE Tactile	1.0	3.3	4.0	—	2.7	2.3	1.7
PE Smell	1.0	2.1	2.7	—	1.7	1.5	1.4
PE Taste	1.0	1.6	2.6	—	1.5	1.4	1.3
PE Emotion	7.0	4.3	5.0	—	3.4	2.1	1.6
PE Thought	7.0	4.5	3.6	—	2.8	2.4	1.2
No. events	1	72	7	0	94	14	325

Event characteristics for recall types for thoughts

The data on recall of thoughts that are given in Table 3.9 replicate many of the empirical relations just discussed for recall of actions; however, for most of the interesting recall types, there is much less information. There were no recalls of thoughts scored as overt errors. Seven recalls were scored as wrong time slice, and only one recall was scored as correct with detail. (The data for this single item are interesting and consistent, and so it is included in the table.) In comparing the items classified as *corrects* ($N = 72$) and those classified as *omits* ($N = 325$), there is a familiar pattern. The events that had thoughts that were scored as correct show lower Location Frequency scores (4.7 vs. 5.7) and a higher score on the Excited scale (3.8 vs. 3.1). For the action associated with a particular thought, the recall accuracy scores (1-to-3 scale) were 2.7 for corrects and 1.3 for omits. The *inference* ($N = 14$) items show a pattern similar to the omits. The items scored as inferences show even higher scores than the omits on Thought Instance Frequency (2.6 vs. 2.3), on Action Category Frequency (6.1 vs. 5.2), and on Action Instance Frequency (3.0 vs. 2.8). They show a higher score than the corrects on the Action Goal-Directedness scale (6.3 vs. 4.4), which is also consistent, because goal-directed activities tend to be routinized and thus allow inferences during recall. Finally, the subjects' ratings of these thought recalls on Overall Memory are consistent with the analysis of these recall categories outlined earlier. The mean scores for Overall Memory were as follows: correct with detail 7.0; correct 5.3; wrong time slice 5.1; wrong event 3.9; inference 3.6; omit 2.1.

Content categories

The use of the random-alarm devices to sample the autobiographical events for this study made available a (somewhat) random sample of the actions and thoughts of a group of undergraduate students. Thus, another way to look at these data is to examine the actual content of the recorded actions and thoughts and see how the contents of these actions and thoughts were related to recall. In order to carry out this analysis, an attempt was made to classify the actions and thoughts on the record card for each of the 654 sampled autobiographical events. Initially it was not at all clear how to develop an appropriate classification scheme for these content categories, but in order to carry out an analysis of content, some form of classification was necessary.

Content classification categories for actions. The content categories chosen for actions were roughly what one might label the actions if one saw them from a distance. Thus, "cooking" was one of the action categories, instead of the more general category of "housework" or the more specific category of "cooking eggs." Similarly, "attending a movie" was one of the action categories instead of the more general category of "going out" or the more specific category of "watching Star Wars." In retrospect, it appears that there was a tendency for the experimenter to subdivide frequent categories and collapse infrequent categories. Thus, reading was subdivided into "reading – academic" and "reading – nonacademic," but grocery shopping and clothing shopping were collapsed into the category "shopping." This systematic tendency in forming the classification categories should tend to *reduce* empirical relations based on category frequency. Each item was classified into a single category, and so it was necessary to deal with the problem of multiple actions (e.g., "studying" and "watching TV"). In general, an attempt was made to use the form of the subject's written description to resolve the issue. Thus, if the subject said "I was studying with the TV on," the item was classified as an instance of "studying." Thought content was not used to classify the actions (i.e., for the subject who said she was "studying with the TV on," the experimenter did not use the information from the thought responses to see if she said she was thinking about calculus or about the Donahue show). The thoughts were not used to help select the primary action in order to keep the classification of the action categories as independent as possible of the classification of the thought categories. Eventually each recorded action was classified into one of 43 unique action categories.

Content classification categories for thoughts. Although it was difficult to develop a satisfactory classification scheme for actions, it was even harder to classify thoughts. In general, an attempt was made to develop thought categories at about the same level of analysis as the action categories. This was fairly easy when the thoughts were about some action category (e.g., thinking about "cooking" or a "movie"). However, the thought categories covered a much wider range, so that there had to be categories for thinking about past events such as "high school," planning next week's "vacation," or worrying about "current events." Eventually each recorded thought was classified into one of 73 unique thought categories.

Sampled frequencies of actions. Table 3.10 gives the 20 most frequent actions and the 20 most frequent thoughts. The frequent actions are somewhat as one might expect. The three most frequent categories are college-related: academic writing, academic reading, and attending class. The ordinary activities of life such as walking, dressing, and eating are also very frequent. The frequency distribution of action categories is very J-shaped, with 60.6% of the total actions falling in the top 10 categories and 85.3% of the total actions falling in the top 20 categories.

Sampled frequencies of thoughts. The frequent thought categories are also somewhat as one might expect (if one takes a moment and considers what life is really like for an undergraduate). The most frequent thought category was thinking about individuals who were romantically involved with the subjects. The third most frequent thought category was thoughts about other types of friends. The second, fourth, and

Table 3.10. *Experiment 2: The 20 most frequent action and thought content categories*

Rank	Action category	Freq.	Thought category	Freq.
1	Writing–academic	60	Romantic friend	54
2	Reading–academic	54	Writing–acad. cont.	51
3	At lecture	49	Friend	47
4	Walking	43	Reading–acad. cont.	43
5	Dressing/grooming	38	Class content	30
6	Talking	38	Beeper	28
7	Studying	31	Organizing–acad.	27
8	Eating in	28	Plans–acad.	22
9	TV	28	Eating in	20
10	Beeper	27	Physical appear.	18
11	Phone	20	Blank mind	18
12	Reading–nonacad.	20	Plans–short range	15
13	Resting	17	Weight/health	13
14	Cooking	17	Misc.	12
15	Organizing–home	17	TV	12
16	Writing–nonacad.	17	Roommate	12
17	Waiting	15	Faculty/TA	12
18	Organizing–acad.	14	Cooking	11
19	At work	14	Physical discomf.	11
20	Eating out	11	Current issues	11

fifth most frequent thought categories were college-related: writing content, reading content, and class content.

Thought and action frequencies. Having both action and thought data on these subjects allows a rather interesting examination of the ecology of mental life among undergraduates. For some action categories there are relatively J-shaped distributions of co-occurring thoughts. Thus, for the action category of "writing–academic," 76.7% of the thoughts were about what was being written. However, for actions such as "walking" or "talking," the co-occurring thoughts ranged over a large number of different thought categories. For example, for the action category of "talking," the most frequent thought categories (romantic friend, reading content, family, academic plans) each made up only 8% of the total thoughts. Many readers of this chapter might be interested in the data on the category of "attending a college lecture." The distribution of thoughts here is intermediate, showing a moderate J shape. During a college lecture, 55.1% of the thoughts of these undergraduates were on the content of the lecture. The thoughts that were not on class content ranged over a number of content categories such as "romantic

Table 3.11. *Experiment 2: The 11 action content categories with the highest Overall Memory scores and the 11 action content categories with the lowest Overall Memory scores*

High categories	Means	Freq.	Low categories	Means	Freq.
Talking to fac./TA	7.0	1	Music – in	1.6	5
Card game	6.0	1	Organizing – home	1.9	17
Shopping	5.4	8	Resting	2.0	17
Movie	5.2	4	Studying	2.3	31
Drugs	5.0	1	Reading – acad.	2.5	54
Listening	5.0	11	Writing – acad.	2.5	60
Driving/riding	4.8	5	Eating in	2.5	28
Other/misc.	4.7	4	Sleeping	2.5	6
Using library	4.7	3	Organizing – acad.	2.6	14
Medical	4.7	3	Exam	2.7	3
Eating out	4.5	11	Bathroom	2.8	5

friend," "physical discomfort," "past TV programs," and "career plans." Although these results may hurt the feelings of many teachers, they were particularly sharp for me because several of these subjects were enrolled in one of my classes during the experiment. One response card shows that while I was lecturing mightily on psycholinguistics, one of the subjects was looking out the window planning her poster for a sorority meeting the next day!

Action categories with high and low memory scores. In order to examine the memory characteristics of the action and thought content categories, the mean score for Overall Memory for each category was obtained. Table 3.11 gives the 11 action categories with the highest scores on Overall Memory and the 11 action categories with the lowest scores on Overall Memory. The action categories that show high memory are associated with relatively unique events that are distinctive along a number of dimensions. Thus, the memorable categories include "talking with faculty," "eating out," and "taking drugs." The categories that show low memory scores are relatively amorphous actions such as "resting," "listening to music," and "sleeping" or extremely frequent actions such as "writing – academic," and "reading – academic."

The analysis of these data in terms of content categories provides a measure of empirically sampled event frequency. All of the previous analyses that have dealt with category frequency have used the subjects' subjectively judged frequencies of the categories. The present analysis allows an examination of the empirically sampled frequency. For actions,

Table 3.12. *Experiment 2: The 11 thought content categories with the highest Overall Memory scores and the 11 thought content categories with the lowest Overall Memory scores*

High categories	Means	Freq.	Low categories	Means	Freq.
Private	6.0	1	Weekend – past	1.0	1
Bureaucracy	6.0	1	Organizing – home	1.0	2
Animals	5.3	3	Emotions	1.3	3
Sex	5.0	1	Music – past	1.5	4
Play/theater	5.0	3	Acad. long-range pl.	2.0	7
Vacation plans	5.0	3	Party – past	2.0	1
Appointment plans	4.7	3	Writing – nonacad.	2.0	1
Shopping	4.5	4	Sleeping	2.2	5
Religion	4.4	7	Reading – acad. cont.	2.2	43
Weight/health	4.3	13	Organization plans	2.3	4
Family	4.3	10	Hunger/thirst	2.3	4

the correlation between Overall Memory and the empirically sampled frequency of actions is −.45. Thus, the general finding that infrequent events tend to be memorable holds for empirically sampled frequency also. This finding is particularly impressive when one takes into account the fact that the development of the action classification scheme was fairly arbitrary; yet to the degree that it separated classes that should have been combined or combined items that should have be separated, the obtained correlation is an underestimate of the true relation.

Thought categories with high and low memory scores. Table 3.12 gives the 11 thought categories with the highest scores on Overall Memory and the 11 thought categories with the lowest scores on Overall Memory. The thought categories that show high memorability tend to be categories with high affect, such as "thought labeled 'private'," "health/weight," and "sex" or categories with relatively distinctive thoughts such as "play/ theater," "animals," and "shopping." The thought categories that show low memory scores are somewhat harder to characterize. However, they appear to include a number of categories in which the thoughts might be considered to be diffuse or amorphous, such as "hunger/thirst," "sleeping," and "emotions."

Comparing the high and low categories for thoughts and for actions also supports another general finding in this study. Action frequency tends to have a strong effect on memory for actions, but frequency plays a smaller role in memory for thoughts. The correlation between empirically sampled frequency and Overall Memory for actions is −.45, whereas it is

Table 3.13. *Experiment 2: Percentages of phenomenal experience scores at each level for all events with scores of 7 on the Overall Memory scale*

Phenom. exp. types	Levels of phenomenal experience						
	1	2	3	4	5	6	7
Visual	0	0	0	0	0	36	64
Thought	6	9	3	9	9	20	46
Emotion	11	6	6	6	14	19	39
Auditory	8	6	11	17	14	8	36
Tactile	25	8	8	3	6	19	31
Smell	61	3	3	3	6	0	25
Taste	69	0	3	6	0	3	19

Note: Based on 36 events with Overall Memory scores of 7.

−.09 for thoughts. Another way to see this is to look at the median frequencies. For the 11 high memory *actions*, the median frequency is 4, whereas the median frequency for the 11 low memory actions is 17; for the *thought* categories the median frequency is 3 for the high memory thoughts, and 4 for the low memory thoughts. Overall, the analysis of the memory data in terms of the contents of the actions and thoughts provides another perspective on the data that tends to support the results reported earlier in this chapter.

Phenomenal experience

All of the analyses up to this point have been based on fairly traditional measures of recall and recognition. This section reports the results from the phenomenal experience scales. These scales were included in the study in keeping with my theoretical position that memory research should routinely examine subjects' phenomenal experiences during recall and because this type of data seems particularly important in the study of autobiographical memory. The phenomenal experience data were gathered after the completion of the recall of each item and the rating of that recall on Overall Memory. The subjects were asked to rate their phenomenal experience during the recall process on seven 7-point scales of mental "reexperiencing."

Phenomenal experience ratings for high memory items. Table 3.13 gives the distribution of each of the phenomenal experience scales for all event recalls that received the highest possible score (7) on the Overall Memory scale. The first point to note is that when subjects are confident of their

Table 3.14. *Experiment 2: Percentage of responses at each level of Visual Phenomenal Experience for each level of Overall Memory*

Overall Memory	Visual Phenomenal Experience							No. responses
	1	2	3	4	5	6	7	
7	0	0	0	0	0	36	64	(36)
6	2	3	0	0	19	40	37	(63)
5	3	0	5	15	39	29	10	(80)
4	2	6	16	35	24	8	8	(83)
3	9	12	27	29	17	3	4	(103)
2	29	33	22	10	6	1	0	(101)
1	91	4	2	2	1	0	1	(188)

memory on autobiographical memory tasks of this type, they give strong reports of phenomenal experience during the recall process. In fact, for every item receiving the highest possible Overall Memory score (i.e., "certain that remember the event"), the subjects rated their visual imagery as either a 6 or 7 on the 7-point scale, where 7 was defined as "complete reexperiencing of the particular visual experience." In addition to the high levels of reported visual imagery, the subjects reported fairly high levels of thought, motor, and auditory reexperiencing. They reported fewer incidents of tactile, smell, and taste reexperiencing. The distribution of responses on these last three scales is bimodal, with a moderate number of recalls showing the highest level of reexperiencing, whereas the majority show little or no reexperiencing. Presumably this distribution is due to the fact that many of the initial autobiographical events contained little experience in these more event-specific modalities.

Visual Phenomenal Experience for each level of memory. Given the strong degree of visual reexperiencing (visual imagery) found in the data presented in Table 3.13, the remaining analyses of the subjects' phenomenal experience will use the visual scale, even though this may well underestimate the total amount of imagery associated with the recall of a particular autobiographical event. Table 3.14 gives the distribution of Visual Phenomenal Experience ratings for each level of Overall Memory. Clearly, there is a strong relationship, with high levels of Visual Phenomenal Experience associated with high levels of Overall Memory. The data in Table 3.14 are collapsed across type of recall cue. The actual correlations between Visual Phenomenal Experience and Overall Memory, within recall cue, are as follows: Location cue .87, Thought cue .81, and Action cue .69.

Table 3.15. *Experiment 2: Percentage Visual Phenomenal Experience scores for response types for actions*

Response types	Visual Phenomenal Experience							No. responses
	1	2	3	4	5	6	7	
Correct with detail	0	0	0	5	14	32	50	(22)
Correct	5	6	12	18	22	23	15	(109)
Wrong time slice	5	0	5	15	30	15	30	(20)
Wrong event	25	16	12	19	8	13	7	(119)
Inference	17	17	20	19	20	4	3	(70)
Error	0	50	25	0	0	25	0	(4)
Omit	84	6	6	2	3	0	1	(190)

Note: The scores are based on the Visual Phenomenal Experience ratings during recall of the overall event for which the actions received the indicated classification.

Visual Phenomenal Experience and recall type for actions. In addition to the finding that subjects reported extremely high levels of visual reexperiencing during the recall of specific autobiographical events, these phenomenal experience scales can also be used to provide a deeper understanding of the memory process. In order to investigate this issue, an analysis was carried out for the Visual Phenomenal Experience scores associated with each of the qualitative types of recall discussed earlier. The results of this analysis for action recall types are given in Table 3.15. Most of the items scored as *correct* are rated toward the high end of the Visual Phenomenal Experience scale. As would be expected, most of the *omits* (84%) received the lowest possible Visual Phenomenal Experience score. Once again, the items scored as *correct with detail* act as "hypercorrect" items. For the recalls scored qualitatively as correct with detail, the subjects gave half of the items the very highest score on the Visual Phenomenal Experience scale, and no subject gave any of these recalls a score at the low end of the scale. The items classified as *wrong time slice* showed a distribution on the Visual Phenomenal Experience scale somewhat like that of the corrects. One might think that items classified as *wrong event* would show similar high rates of visual reexperiencing. However, in fact, the items classified as wrong events show a distribution of Visual Phenomenal Experience scores toward the low end of the scale. It appears that knowing what the subject's phenomenal experience is during the recall process may allow powerful predictions about the accuracy of the subject's recall. In this set of data, knowing that the subject rated the Visual Phenomenal Experience at the low end of the scale (1 to 3), it would have been possible to classify 50% of the wrong events as errors

Table 3.16. *Experiment 2: Percentage Visual Phenomenal Experience scores for response types for thoughts*

Response types	Visual Phenomenal Experience							No. responses
	1	2	3	4	5	6	7	
Correct with detail	0	0	0	0	0	0	100	(1)
Correct	3	3	10	13	15	32	25	(72)
Wrong time slice	0	0	0	29	43	0	29	(7)
Wrong event	10	11	18	15	19	17	11	(94)
Inference	7	7	14	14	43	7	7	(14)
Error	0	0	0	0	0	0	0	(0)
Omit	51	11	9	10	9	5	6	(325)

Note: The scores are based on the Visual Phenomenal Experience ratings during recall of the overall event for which the thought received the indicated classification.

without misclassifying a single one of the items scored correct with detail. The items classified as *inference* also show a very different pattern from the corrects. Few of these items received high Visual Phenomenal Experience scores, and there was a relatively even distribution across the middle and low end of the scale. These items showed considerably fewer high visual scores (6 and 7) compared with the corrects (7% vs. 38%) and relatively few very low scores (1) compared with the omits (17% vs. 84%). The subjects may have been experiencing weak visual images or perhaps generic (nonspecific) images during their recall of the items classified as inferences.

Visual Phenomenal Experience and recall type for thoughts. The data on the Visual Phenomenal Experience scale for thought recall types are given in Table 3.16. Note that the data displayed in this table are the Visual Phenomenal Experience ratings for recall of the *overall event* displayed in terms of the classification of the *thoughts*. The sample sizes for many of these recall categories are much smaller than those for the recall of actions, and so the distributions are not as stable. However, some of the basic features of the previous analysis are replicated. The *corrects* show a high proportion of Visual Phenomenal Experience scores at the high end of the scale; the *omits* show a high proportion at the low end of the scale. The *wrong events* show a relatively flat distribution of visual scores. The *inferences* show more scores in the middle of the Visual Phenomenal Experience scale, with a particularly large number of moderately high (5) scores. Data on the other personal memory scales and recall types can be found in Table 3.9.

Discussion

Methodology. The results of Experiment 2 show that the use of a cued-recall task in autobiographical memory research can provide a rich set of data that allows a wide array of analyses on a number of theoretically interesting issues.

Forgetting curves. The forgetting data for the recognition measure display a fairly high level of recognition memory, with a relatively shallow forgetting curve (Figure 3.5). The forgetting data for cued recall show, as one would expect, a lower level of memory performance, but these data also show a relatively shallow forgetting curve (Figures 3.7–3.9).

Cues and memory. The different types of cued recall led to strong differences in memory as measured by the Overall Memory scale. Action cues and Thought cues led to relatively high memory scores. Time and location, as a joint cue, led to intermediate levels of memory. Location cues led to low levels of memory, while Time cues led to the lowest memory scores.

There were similar strong differences in the effectiveness of cues in memory as measured by the recall accuracy scores. For the recall of *actions,* Thought cues were best, then joint Time and location cues; Location cues were next; and Time was the worst form of cue. For the recall of *thoughts,* Action was, by far, the best cue, and all the other cues were quite poor (none showed better than 14% accurate recalls). For the recall of *locations,* Action cues were very good, Thought cues were also good, and even Time was a fairly good cue.

Types of information and memory. There were also large differences in memory for the different types of information. *Actions* received the second highest scores on recognition memory and were the second best form of information recalled in terms of recall accuracy. *Thoughts* received the third best scores on both recognition memory and recall accuracy. *Locations* were the best recalled information in terms of recall accuracy. However, many of the "correct" recalls of location were almost certainly inferences (e.g., given an Action cue such as "I was studying French at my desk," the subject gives "my room" as the location recall). The argument that many of the correct recalls of location are inferences is supported by the finding that there is little or no forgetting of location information with Action or Time cues (Figure 3.9). Location also received the highest scores on the recognition-memory scale; however, it seems likely that these ratings are also inflated by a large inference component. *Emotions* received the next to lowest scores on the recognition-memory scale, and *time* received the lowest scores.

Cues versus types of information. In terms of retrieval value as a cue, the data are consistent in showing the following ranking (from best to worst cue): Action, Thought, Time and location, Location, and Time. In terms of a type of information in memory (as measured by overall memory and by recall accuracy), the equivalent ranking is as follows: location, action, thought, emotion, and time. It seems likely that the discrepancy for location information in these two rankings is at least partly due to a high number of location inferences scored as correct recalls on the recall accuracy scale.

Recall types. The qualitative analysis of the recalls gave a much more differentiated picture of what occurs in the recall of autobiographical information than has previous research. This analysis shows that for action recall, the most common response was to omit the item; recall of wrong events was the next most common, followed by correct recalls. Recalls that appeared to be inferences were next. There were modest numbers of recalls scored as correct with detail and recalls scored as wrong time slice. There were only four recalls scored as overt errors.

Event characteristics. In trying to understand what characteristics of autobiographical events lead to successful recall, it is probably best to focus on the results from the GLM analyses. Note that in this experiment, information on location frequency was obtained; so this information is available to play a role in these analyses. The results for the events with actions as cues are somewhat puzzling. For these items, higher Overall Memory scores are associated with events showing low thought frequency (instance), high thought frequency (category), and high goal-directedness. Good recall of events with time as a cue is associated with low-frequency actions. Good recall of events with a joint location and time cue or with location alone as a cue is associated with events with low-frequency locations. Good recall of events with thought as a cue is associated with highly exciting thoughts. Overall, these results replicate the findings of the first experiment fairly nicely (except for the items with actions as cues). Action frequency and exciting thoughts show up again in this experiment as important event characteristics, and location frequency appears to play a powerful role whenever location information is part of the recall cue.

Event characteristics of recall types. The qualitative analysis of the recall data made possible a very interesting analysis of event characteristics by recall type. The actions scored as *correct* were rated as having much lower action frequency and location frequency than the actions scored as omits. The actions scored as *wrong time slice* show a pattern of event characteristics very similar to the corrects; this is reasonable because this type of incorrect response had to be close enough to the original event for the experimenter to classify it as being the wrong moment of the correct event. The actions scored as *wrong events* show a pattern of event characteristics that is intermediate between the corrects and the omits. This result seems consistent with the intermediate status of these items in terms of the recall process. Apparently a number of these recalls were occasions when the event cue led to a personal memory, but not to the correct one. The actions scored as *inferences* show a pattern of event characteristics very similar to those scored as omits. These events were actually rated higher on action frequency than were the omits. Overall, it appears that for many of the events scored as inferences, the subjects were using the cue to recall generic information. They apparently did not retrieve a true episodic memory, and the low Overall Memory scores for these items suggest that the subjects were frequently aware that they were not "remembering the event." The small number of actions scored as *overt errors* show a pattern similar to the corrects, but with most scales showing shifts in the direction of the omits. These items received somewhat lower Overall Memory scores than the corrects, suggesting that the subjects had some awareness that there were problems with their recalls. The actions scored as *correct with detail* show a pattern of event characteristics that marks them as being more "correct" than the events scored as correct. This lends strong support to the view that these recalls reflected rich, complete memories.

Overall, the technique of examining the characteristics of the events that gave rise to the different recall types allowed an unusual bootstrap procedure in which the patterns of event characteristics support the qualitative recall classifications, and the qualitative classifications support the interpretations of the event characteristics.

Memory awareness. Examination of the Overall Memory scores for the different recall types also casts some light on the validity of these subjects' subjective ratings of their overall memory for autobiographical events. The subjects' mean memory ratings on the scale of Overall Memory for those recalls the experimenter later classified as correct with detail was 6.0; their memory rating for the omits was 1.3. These means span almost the full range of the 7-point Overall Memory scale. Clearly, these subjects' subjective memory ratings were in strong agreement with the experimenter's independent objective scoring of their written recalls.

Content categories. The analysis of the sampled events into content categories makes it possible to gain a richer understanding of what types of recalls were behind the more abstract analyses of rated event characteristics. For actions, the events that showed the highest Overall Memory scores were relatively unique actions, often in unique locations, such as talking to a faculty member or going to the doctor. The events that showed the lowest Overall Memory scores were repeated actions, such as reading texts and doing homework, and relatively unstructured actions, such as resting or listening to music. The importance of the repetition of actions and locations shows up nicely with the eating events. The set of items classified as "eating out" is one of the content categories that showed high memory; the set of items classified as "eating in" is one of the content categories that showed low memory scores.

Phenomenal experience. The data from the phenomenal experience scales provide some descriptive evidence on the conscious mental experiences during the process of recall of autobiographical memories. The core finding is that *every* event receiving the highest possible Overall Memory score also received a Visual Phenomenal Experience rating in one of the two highest categories. Clearly, when individuals recall an autobiographical event with a high degree of confidence, they also experience visual imagery.

Phenomenal experience and recall type. The analysis of the Visual Phenomenal Experience scores for the different recall types gives some insight into the recall process. The recalls scored correct show strong visual imagery. The items scored correct with detail show even higher imagery (82% of these items fall in the two highest visual imagery categories). Thus, in terms of experienced imagery, as with most other analyses, the items scored as correct with detail behave as hypercorrect items. The recalls classified as wrong time slice show Visual Phenomenal Experience scores that are very similar to the items classified as correct, suggesting that from the point of view of the subjects, these items were experienced as correct recalls. The items classified as wrong events show a relatively flat distribution of Visual Phenomenal Experience scores. It seems possible that items in this category are a mixture of recalls that were just nonepisodic guesses (low visual imagery), whereas others were "true" retrievals of the wrong events (high visual imagery). The recalls classified as inferences show a distribution of Visual Phenomenal Experience scores across the middle and the low end of the scale. These items are, technically speaking, all correct; yet there are very few Visual Phenomenal Experience scores at the high end of the scale (only 7% in the two highest categories, compared with 82% for the correct-with-detail items). On the other hand, there are also very few items in the lowest imagery category, compared with the omits. It would appear that the subjects giving recalls that were later scored as inferences were experiencing weak visual images or perhaps generic (nonspecific) images that they rated at the low end of the scale.

General discussion

This section brings together the findings from the two experiments and points out some of the implications of the data for the larger theoretical issues in the study of autobiographical memory.

Information in personal memory

Elsewhere (Brewer, 1986) I argued that personal memories have the appearance of a reliving of the original autobiographical event. To the degree that this is a correct description, a personal memory should almost always contain information about the perceived physical environment of the individual (location, actions, people) and typically should also contain nonobservable information about the individual's thoughts and feelings.

Many researchers (e.g., Linton, 1975) have stated that time is somehow a crucial part of the information in a personal memory because this form of memory is a part of autobiographical memory. It is not clear how the time information is to be represented, but a number of investigators in the laboratory study of memory have suggested that memory representations may contain time tags (Anisfeld & Knapp, 1968, p. 177; Yntema & Trask, 1963, p. 70). However, given the analysis outlined in Brewer (1986), most examples of personal memory would not contain information about the absolute time of the event. Many personal memories would contain information about the time of day (e.g., walking home in the dark), but only if the event itself is time-tagged (e.g., a birthday party) will it contain information about the actual date of the event. The data from the experiments reported here support the analysis of personal memory content given in Brewer (1986). The results of these experiments show that location, action, and thought information received relatively high memory scores, whereas time information received the lowest scores.

Barclay and Wellman (1986, p. 100) raised another issue about time information. They presented data showing that subjects are not very accurate in assigning absolute dates to autobiographical events and concluded that because the memories do not contain an absolute date, they cannot be true episodic memories as defined by Tulving (1972). However, I have argued (Brewer, 1986, p. 34) that experiencing a personal memory as occurring at a *unique time* and location is logically independent of the ability of the individual to assign an *absolute date* to the unique experience. Overall, the treatment of personal memory in Brewer (1986) and the present data suggest that personal memories typically contain information about actions, location, people, and thoughts, but contain only limited information about time.

Distinctive-representation hypothesis

In order to account for the data in the experiments reported here, it seems necessary to hypothesize that recall of information is directly related to the distinctiveness of the mental representation. This position is implicitly a core component of many forms of memory theory and has been made explicit by a number of researchers (Craik & Jacoby, 1979; Gibson, 1940; Norman & Bobrow, 1979).

In the experiments reported here, the data on event characteristics show that infrequent locations and infrequent actions are by far the best predictors of later memory. This seems best accounted for by assuming that rare locations and rare actions give rise to personal memories with relatively distinctive mental representations. Some types of information in personal memories may be more distinctive than other types; this may give a partial account for the data in Experiment 2 showing that the scores for recognition accuracy were as follows: location 92%, actions 89%, thoughts 84%, emotions 78%, and time 75%. However, the distinctiveness of a particular form of information is relative to the overall structure of the individual's life. Thus, if one lives a life in which one carries out the same actions in a different location each day (house painter?), the distinctiveness of location information should increase, whereas that of actions should decrease. The distinctive-representation hypothesis also gives a good account of the Thanksgiving effect in the serial-position curves for Experiment 1. The autobiographical events occurring during these undergraduates' first trips home as college freshmen are quite likely to be distinctive, compared with the ordinary events of the weeks before and after. Finally, an examination of the types of autobiographical events (Tables 3.11 and 3.12) that show high memory scores and those that show low memory scores lends support to the distinctive-representation position. It seems highly likely that eating out at a particular restaurant with someone or going to talk to a faculty member gives rise to a more distinctive representation than sitting at a desk reading one more chapter of a French text or solving one more set of calculus problems. Thus, the distinctive-representation hypothesis can account for many of the basic findings in these experiments. However, it is clear that we need an independent, theory-based characterization of what constitutes a distinctive representation.

Dual-process theory of repetition

In order to account for how certain representations become distinctive and others become nondistinctive, a number of theorists in the area of memory have proposed that repetition increases the strength of semantic information, while decreasing the strength of episodic information (Bower, 1974, p. 2; Brewer & Pani, 1983, p. 20; Hintzman, 1978, p. 374). This position does not have a consistent name; however, I shall call it the "dual-process theory of repetition" and use that name to indicate a theory that is neutral with respect to mechanism (e.g., interference vs. decay).

Several theorists have recently applied the dual-process theory of repetition to autobiographical memory (Brewer, 1986, p. 45; Linton, 1982, p. 79). In my 1986 paper I suggested that "repetition of events leads to the development of generic personal memories at the expense of the individual personal memories that were repeated" (p. 45). The dual-process theory of repetition can thus account for the consistent result in these experiments that personal memories for infrequent events and locations is good, whereas memory for repeated events and locations is poor.

The present data provide little insight into the mechanism that underlies the repetition effect. However, one might argue that repetition produces a large number of similar representations, and so any particular one is not distinctive.

Relations of cues to personal memory representations

The hypothesis that distinctive mental representations lead to good memory performance can be extended to the cues used to retrieve personal memories. Thus, a recall cue can be expected to lead to successful retrieval of a personal memory to the degree that the cue forms a distinctive path to the memory representation. The means from Experiment 2 on the effectiveness of cues (for the Overall Memory measure) were as follows: Action 4.3, Thought 3.9, Time and location 2.9, Location 2.5, and Time 2.4. If the hypothesis of distinctive retrieval cues is correct, these data suggest that the cues show considerable differences in distinctiveness and that the degree of distinctiveness is in the order of the means reported earlier. A possible explanation of these differences in terms of the structure of these subjects' lives is given in the next section.

The ecology of the environment and the structure of memory

Neisser (1985, 1986a) has recently argued for the development of a Gibsonian approach to human memory. As part of this approach, Neisser proposes that we need a more serious analysis of the environment and its relation to various memory phenomena. It seems to me that this approach can be used to give an account of many important aspects of personal memory.

A reading of the 654 autobiographical event cards suggests that the experienced environment for these undergraduates takes the following form: They carry out a variety of actions in locations, often with other people around, and they have a variety of thoughts and feelings while carrying out the actions. They experience one location (their rooms) with enormous frequency, have moderate exposure to a number of other locations (e.g., classrooms), and infrequent exposure to a range of other locations (e.g., a particular restaurant). They carry out a wide range of very different actions, some fairly frequently (e.g., reading academic material, dressing), others relatively infrequently (e.g., using the library, going to the doctor). There are certain people they see frequently; however, they engage in a variety of actions with respect to these individuals. They experience a range of thoughts, but for some thoughts there is little or no relation to the concurrent actions and location (e.g., thinking about an upcoming fraternity party during a lecture). There appear to be a limited number of emotions that reoccur in association with particular events and thoughts. Finally, each event occurs at a unique absolute time (but, as discussed earlier, it appears that this information is not typically stored directly in personal memory).

These different aspects of the environment are tied together in a web of relations determined by the structure of the individual's activities within this environment. Thus, because a variety of different actions often occur in the same location, a frequent location will be a poor predictor of a particular action, but a particular action will be a good predictor of a frequent location. However, an infrequent location will probably be a good predictor of a particular action or thought. A frequent person will be a poor predictor of a particular action, but a particular action may be a good predictor of a frequent person. A wide variety of thoughts will occur in frequent locations, so a frequent location will not be a good predictor of a particular thought; and because a particular thought is only moderately related to location, a particular thought will be only a moderate predictor of a particular location. For coordinated action/thoughts, a particular action should be a relatively good predictor of a particular thought, and a particular thought a relatively good predictor of a particular action; but for uncoordinated action/thoughts, actions and thoughts should be less successful predictors of each other. Although absolute dates do not reoccur (e.g., November 27, 1980), generic time does (e.g., Tuesdays at 10:00 a.m.), and generic time is frequently associated with recurring actions (e.g., physics lectures occur Tuesdays at 10:00). Thus, *if* absolute date were stored in personal memory, it would be a good predictor of all other information, but because it does not typically appear to be stored, absolute time should be a poor predictor of all other types of specific information. Generic time will be a good predictor of generic actions and generic locations, but a relatively poor predictor of infrequent actions and locations. Infrequent locations, actions, people, and thoughts will tend to cooccur and be related (e.g., standing next to a tour guide on top of the Sears Tower in Chicago looking for the University of Chicago and thinking about the site of the first nuclear chain reaction); so they should predict each other well.

This analysis of the environment of college undergraduates plus the distinctive-memory-representation hypothesis and the dual-process theory of repetition can be used to generate much of the data from these experiments. It explains why both location and time serve as poor cues for recall, whereas thoughts serve as moderate cues, and actions serve as excellent cues. It also explains why action frequency and location frequency are event characteristics that are strongly associated with memory. However, it also predicts that thought frequency should show at least a moderate association with memory, and the present data tend not to support this prediction.

Memory and emotion

A number of researchers have stated that emotion plays a large role in autobiographical memory (Brown & Kulik, 1977; Thomson, 1930; Waters & Leeper, 1936). The recent studies of White (1982) and Wagenaar (1986) found that measures of emotionality correlated with recognition of personal memories. Previous studies of autobiographical memory have used the overall event as the unit to be studied. The separation of thoughts and actions in the present study strongly suggests that the primary effect of emotional variables is on memory for thought, not on memory for actions. There is a consistent trend in the results of these experiments for affective variables (particularly, "exciting" thought) to predict memory for thoughts.

It is not clear that the account of autobiographical memory developed in this chapter so far can account for these findings. First, it appears that memory for affect as a content is not the crucial variable, because the analysis of thought content categories showed that thoughts about emotions or about feelings of hunger and thirst showed particularly low memory scores. This is consistent with an argument that the emotions per se show a limited range of distinctiveness (e.g., How many uniquely different feelings of anger are there?). Thus, the impact of affect on memory must be as it is associated with or "colors" a given thought. There are several possible hypotheses about how affect might have an impact on personal memory. One could hypothesize that high affect is associated with events that have distinctive memory representations on other dimensions (e.g., frequency). The problem with this hypothesis is that the pattern of correlations among the characteristics of the autobiographical events in this study and the regression analyses do not support this position. However, it should be noted that the randomly selected events in this study are relatively dull, whereas the more dramatic events (e.g., the Kennedy assassination) studied in the investigation of "flashbulb memories" (Brown & Kulik, 1977; Winograd & Killinger, 1983; Yarmey & Bull, 1978) might show such a relation. Another approach to this problem would be to argue that the addition of affect to a memory representation increases its distinctiveness and thus its accessibility in memory. This hypothesis would include the affect phenomena within the general framework used earlier to account for the results of these experiments. Finally, one might hypothesize that (strong) affect has some direct impact on the strength of the memory representation (cf. Brown & Kulik, 1977). The present data do not discriminate between the last two hypotheses.

Reconstruction

The data from Experiment 2 that relate the recalls to the actual recorded events make possible a direct examination of the recent arguments that personal memories are strongly reconstructed (Barclay, 1986; Barclay & Wellman, 1986; Neisser, 1981, 1982). In the cued-recall task there were 531 occasions when subjects wrote responses in attempting to recall either a thought or an action. Of these responses, 50% were in error. This finding looks as if it might support the strong reconstructive view, but a closer analysis of the data suggests otherwise. Of the total errors, 90% were classified as either wrong event or wrong time slice, and these categories of responses would seem best explained as retrieval errors, not reconstructions. Another 8.5% of the errors were responses classified as correct with detail. Technically speaking, these were errors, because the written response contained consistent information that was not on the initial event card. However, the analysis of these recalls in terms of the characteristics of the initial events lends considerable support to the view that these were items that showed very strong memory and that the subjects were simply writing down additional information from the very rich memory representations. Thus, of the total set of wrong responses, only 1.5% were true errors in which the subject recalled information that was in conflict with the information written down on the original response card. Clearly, the data from this study do not support Barclay's (1986) strong reconstructive position. In this set of data it appears that the subjects' recalls are quite accurate when compared with the event that had been experienced earlier.

Given the theoretical importance of the overt errors, it seems worthwhile to examine them in more detail. There were only four responses classified as overt errors. The four overt errors were the following:

1. [response card] "I was making a pizza, J. at my right making an XL pepperoni . . . S. laughing at my left." [recall] "working & making pizza. S. at right."
2. [response card] "Walking from the dorm on our way to Giordano's. We were talking about the fact that it wasn't snowing anymore." [recall] "Walking across Garner parking lot on the way to Giordano's w/B., D., S., G. It's snowing."
3. [response card] "I'm in an Adv class lecture listening to my teacher lecture about Maslow's hierarchy of needs – wearing jeans, sweater & pink striped shirt. Not sitting next to D. whom I usually sit next to." [recall] "I was next to D. taking notes on lecture."
4. [response card] "I was just reading chemistry on the review of atomic weights with isotopes. No one else is in the room. A few wet t-shirts and jeans are drying out on my bed." [recall] "I was studying chemistry and L. was at her desk."

These "reconstructive" errors are not very dramatic, and, in fact, a more liberal scoring criterion might well have classified several as time-slice errors, because it is possible that the initial event changed (e.g., in event 2, it was snowing and stopped). Items 2 and 3 are particularly interesting because they contain negative statements. Statements of this kind are frequently used to point out a schema-inconsistent fact in writing (cf. Brewer & Treyens, 1981, p. 224). Thus, it seems likely that these two items *were* reconstructed to become schema-consistent (cf. Brewer & Nakamura, 1984).

It seems to me that the general accuracy of these recalls may be due to two factors. First, as suggested in Brewer (1986), those aspects of the personal memories (specific visual perceptual information) that correspond to the surface structure of linguistic material may have a much slower rate of forgetting than do their linguistic counterparts. Second, given the routinized nature of everyday life revealed in the subjects' response cards, many schema-based reconstructions would tend to give correct responses, not errors. Overall, the data from these experiments are consistent with the partial reconstructive view proposed in Brewer (1986), which stated that "recent (days to weeks) personal memories are, in fact, reasonably accurate copies of the individual's original phenomenal experience" (p. 43).

Random items versus items selected to be memorable

Previous studies of memory for personal events have used items selected by the experimenter to be memorable (Linton, 1975; Wagenaar, 1986; White, 1982). The data of Experiment 1 show that there are strong systematic differences in the characteristics of events selected to be memorable, when compared with random events, and that recognition-memory data show similar strong differences. In criticizing the use of selected items, Linton (1982) notes that her sample of items "is silent on whole sets of activities that comprise the warp and woof of my existence. One could scarcely know that I teach, or spend many hours each day in academic activities" (p. 82). During the debriefing session, one of the subjects in Experiment 1 commented on the differences between the randomly sampled items and the memorable items, noting that for memorable items "I found it difficult to record thoughts and actions because often times my most memorable event was quite complex — involving many detailed thoughts and actions." All of this evidence strongly suggests that randomly sampled items are to be preferred to selected items, unless there is a theoretical motivation for some other form of event sampling.

Forgetting of personal memories

The previous studies of autobiographical memory have shown remarkably little forgetting of personal memories when recognition memory was tested. Linton (1978) and Wagenaar (1986) appeared to find less than 1% of their items forgotten after 1 year, whereas White (1982), who used less selected items, found about 40% of his items forgotten after 1 year.

The randomly selected personal memories in the present study show much more rapid forgetting. In Experiment 1, after only 5 months, recognition measures show about 30% of the actions forgotten and about 46% of the thoughts forgotten. In Experiment 2, the cued-recall measures show that after slightly less than 2 months (in the condition with the most effective cue), about 54% of the actions are forgotten, and about 74% of the thoughts are forgotten (where a forgotten item is defined as a recall that was "totally incorrect or omitted").

The results of Experiment 1, using recognition memory, show that events selected to be memorable are forgotten less rapidly than random items (only 18% of the memorable actions were forgotten at 5 months).

Thus, it is clear that part of the very low rate of forgetting in the previous studies was due to event selection. However, there may also be contributions due to some repeated item testing in the other studies and to the use of the experimenter as subject. Even though the work of Thompson (1982) suggests that writing down events has little effect on later recall, it seems to me that there must be some memory advantage produced by writing down an autobiographical event; if this is so, then the data from the earlier studies and from the present study probably underestimate the true rate of forgetting of personal memories. In the present experiments and in the earlier studies, the forgetting curves tend to be fairly flat. However, none of these studies investigated the very early portion of the forgetting curve (i.e., the first week); until data on that portion of the forgetting curve are obtained, it is not clear what the overall shape of the forgetting curve will be for personal memories.

Although much of this section has been devoted to showing that the rate of forgetting of personal memories is more rapid than earlier work would suggest, one should not lose sight of fact that this type of memory is still quite impressive when compared with memory in many laboratory tasks. In Experiment 1, recognition memory for both random and memorable actions was quite high in the first test session (after an average retention interval of 9 days).

Personal memories over the life span

In order to relate the results of the present study to memory over much longer periods of time, it is interesting to compare the present results with those of Smith (1952). In this overlooked but extraordinary study, Madorah Smith attempted, at age 63, to carry out a recall of her whole life. She retrieved 6,263 memories, and for certain periods of her life she was able to verify the events recalled with information in diaries that she kept. Her data analysis is somewhat difficult to follow, but, in essence, she provided information on the characteristics of three types of events: (a) her clearest memories, (b) ordinary memories, and (c) forgotten items (items recorded in her diaries, but not retrieved during her recall sessions). She then examined the event characteristics associated with each of these recall types. For the three recall types, the percentages of novel memories (memory for unique events) were: clearest 38%, ordinary 16.5%, and forgotten 1.7%, whereas the percentages of memories with extreme affect were: clearest 58%, ordinary 12%, and forgotten 0.4%. These findings for the recall of an individual's total stock of recallable personal memories are thus in close agreement with the results from the much shorter time periods of the present study.

Actions versus thoughts

Previous studies have tended to treat the autobiographical event as the unit of analysis. In the present study, a systematic attempt was made to distinguish between the actions and the thoughts that occurred during a given autobiographical event. The data relating the characteristics of actions and thoughts to memory show consistent systematic differences between the two forms of information; this provides empirical support for the decision to distinguish between these two forms of information.

The data from both experiments show that memory for actions is better than memory for thoughts in recognition-memory tasks and in recall tasks. In both of these experiments there are consistent differences, for actions and for thoughts, in which event characteristics best predict memory. High memory for actions is associated with autobiographical events of low frequency, whereas high memory for thoughts is associated with autobiographical events that are exciting.

Metamemory

Several aspects of the present experiments allow an examination of the degree to which naive undergraduates have knowledge about the functioning of their own autobiographical memories. In Experiment 1, subjects were asked to select the most memorable event of the day, and the data for these events were compared with randomly sampled events. The subjects did show considerably better memory for the items they selected, and comparison of the selected items with the random items on event characteristics shows a pattern that is almost identical with the pattern shown when well-remembered randomly sampled items were compared with poorly remembered randomly sampled items.

Memory awareness

Data on the subjects' awareness of the accuracy of their recalls can be found in the analysis of recall types in the cued-recall data of Experiment 2. After completing their recalls for each item, the subjects gave the item a rating on Overall Memory. Later the experimenter compared each recall with the original event and made a qualitative classification of each recall. When the results from the subjects' ratings are compared with the experimenter's classifications, it is clear that the subjects have good insight into the quality of their memories.

First, the subjects' ratings on the Overall Memory scale are quite accurate in distinguishing a complete and accurate memory from a memory failure. The recalls of actions that the experimenter classified as correct with detail received a mean score of 6.0 on the Overall Memory scale, whereas the recalls classified as omits received a mean score of 1.3 on this scale. The subjects' ratings on the Overall Memory scale were also capable of showing more subtle differences, as reflected by the ratings on this scale for the other types of recalls. The Overall Memory scores for the action items the experimenter scored as correct was 4.5. Those that were classified as wrong events had Overall Memory scores of 3.1; those classified as inferences had Overall Memory scores of 2.7. Taken together, these data show that naive individuals have considerable awareness about the accuracy of recalls from the personal memory system.

However, it is not clear if this relationship holds over longer time intervals. There have been several anecdotal reports in the autobiographical memory literature of individuals who appear to have had strong personal memories that were later found to be inaccurate. It seems likely that these individuals would have given these inaccurate memories a high rating on an Overall Memory scale and thus would be showing a breakdown between memory awareness and memory accuracy. If we are to gain a deeper understanding of these issues, we need systematic studies that access recognition memory, memory awareness, memory imagery, and accuracy of recall in autobiographical memory over long time intervals.

The phenomenal properties of personal memories

Brewer and Pani (1983) have argued that memory researchers should treat the phenomenal aspects of memory tasks as data to be studied, just like any other form of data. In 1986 I gave a theoretical description of personal memories which states that they "appear to be a 'reliving' of the individual's phenomenal experience during that earlier moment. The contents almost always include reports of visual imagery" (1986, p. 34). The results of the image-rating data from Experiment 2 provide powerful support for this claim. For the items with the highest Overall Memory scores (a 7 on a 1-to-7 scale) the subjects gave *every item* a rating of 6 or 7 on the 7-point Visual Phenomenal Experience scale, where 7 was defined as "complete reexperiencing of the particular visual experience."

The data on visual-imagery experiences during recall also add to the understanding of the recall process in autobiographical memory. The items classified as correct with detail show very high levels of visual imagery. This is consistent with laboratory memory studies that have found a positive relation between the accuracy of recall of an item and the degree of visual imagery reported for the item (Sheehan & Neisser,

1969). The recall errors scored as wrong time slice show Visual Phenomenal Experience scores similar to those classifed as correct, suggesting that the subjects' experiences for these two types of items were similar. On the other hand, the recall errors scored as wrong event show a relatively flat distribution of Visual Phenomenal Experience scores that is quite different from that shown by the correct recalls. The recalls that were scored as inferences are, technically speaking, correct, and yet they show a distribution of Visual Phenomenal Experience scores toward the middle and low end of the scale, suggesting that the subjects were experiencing either weak visual images or generic visual images. Clearly, there is much to be gained from gathering and understanding data about the subject's phenomenal experience during the recall process.

Conclusions

The results of these two experiments on memory for randomly sampled autobiographical events lead to the following conclusions:

1. It is possible to study randomly sampled autobiographical events in naive subjects. The use of a cued-recall technique allows the recalls to be verified against the originally experienced events.

2. The results of Experiment 1 show that events selected to be memorable (as used in most previous studies of autobiographical memory) have higher recognition-memory scores than randomly sampled items, and the memorable items show systematic differences from the random items on a number of theoretically important dimensions.

3. The forgetting curves for randomly selected autobiographical events show considerably more forgetting than those obtained in previous studies with selected events. Nevertheless, recognition memory remains relatively high (70% recognition of actions at 5 months in Experiment 1). The forgetting curves for autobiographical memory tested with cued recall show much more forgetting (only 46% correct recall of actions at 2 months with the best cue type in Experiment 2).

4. Across both experiments, the characteristics of events that show the most consistent association with good memory performance are rare actions and rare locations.

5. There are systematic differences in autobiographical memory for thoughts versus actions. Thoughts show lower memory performance than actions on both recognition-memory tasks and cued-recall tasks. The characteristics of thoughts associated with memory performance are different than those for actions. Thoughts that were rated as exciting show consistently better memory performance.

6. The data from Experiment 2 show that actions and thoughts serve as relatively good cues for recall. Time and location as a joint cue led to

intermediate levels of recall. Location alone was a poor cue, and time was the least effective cue of all.

7. By contrasting autobiographical recalls with the original autobiographical events it is possible to develop a qualitative classification of recall types. The resulting recall types show a variety of interesting characteristics. Recalls that contain added consistent details behave as hypercorrect items along a number of dimensions. For example, they come from events showing lower location and action frequencies than do the correct recalls. Recalls that appear to be from the right event but wrong time slice show characteristics very similar to correct recalls. Recalls of completely wrong events show characteristics intermediate between correct recalls and omits. Recalls that appear to be inferences show characteristics similar to omits. Recalls that appear to have been of the correct event, but that contain an overt inconsistency with the original event record, show characteristics somewhat like the correct recalls, but with a consistent tendency in the direction of the omits.

8. The technique of examining the event characteristics of the qualitatively classified recall types is a powerful form of data analysis. This bootstrap procedure allows one to use the pattern of event characteristics to support the qualitative recall classifications and the qualitative recall classifications to support the analysis of the event characteristics.

9. Analysis of the initial autobiographical actions and thoughts in terms of their content shows that actions with unique content (e.g., talking with a faculty member) have high memory scores, whereas repeated actions (e.g., studying chemistry) and diffuse actions (e.g., resting) have low memory scores.

10. The measures of phenomenal experience during recall show that autobiographical recalls with high memory confidence are virtually always accompanied by high visual imagery. Accurate recalls are also associated with high visual imagery. The different recall types also show systematic differences in visual imagery. Correct recalls show high visual imagery, whereas correct recalls with added details show even higher visual-imagery scores. Recalls of the apparently correct event, but of the wrong moment, show high visual imagery. Recalls of the wrong event have a wide range of imagery scores. Recalls that appear to be inferences have a range of visual imagery, with few very low scores and few very high scores.

11. The subjects' abilities to successfully select events that are more memorable than randomly selected events show that naive subjects have good knowledge about their own autobiographical memory (i.e., good metamemory skills).

12. The data from these experiments and my earlier theoretical analysis of personal memory (Brewer, 1986) suggest that personal memory

typically contains information about actions, location, and thoughts, but rarely about absolute time.

13. The qualitative analysis of autobiographical recalls found few overt recall errors and thus supports a partly reconstructive view of autobiographical memory (Brewer, 1986), which suggests that recent personal memories are reasonably accurate copies of the individual's original phenomenal experiences.

14. Much of the data in these two experiments can be accounted for by the hypothesis that recall of information in autobiographical memory is directly related to the distinctiveness of the representation.

15. The impact of frequency in autobiographical memory can be explained by the dual-process theory of repetition, which asserts that with repetition, semantic information increases in strength, and episodic information decreases in strength.

16. Finally, the differential effectiveness of cues in the recall of autobiographical memory can be accounted for by an ecological analysis of the experienced environment of subjects in this experiment. Thus, the fact that for each of these subjects many different actions typically occurred in the same location (their room) predicts that actions should be a good cue for location information, but that location should be a poor cue for specific action information.

NOTE

First, I want to thank the 18 undergraduates who were willing to let me see random samples of their lives for several weeks so that we could better understand the workings of autobiographical memory. I would like to thank Paula Schwanenflugel and Rich Newel for help in carrying out some of the early phases of this research, and I would like to thank Ed Lichtenstein and John Pani for help with some of the initial data analyses. This chapter was much improved by comments on the original draft by Bob McCauley, Glenn Nakamura, Dick Neisser, Brian Ross, Tricia Tenpenny, and Gene Winograd. I also owe Dick Neisser a debt for prodding me to get my ecological study into print. Most of all, however, I want to thank Ellen Brewer for her extraordinary efforts in the final data analysis. This chapter, in its present form, simply could not have been written without her steady hand on the SAS package. Finally, I would like to thank the University of Illinois Research Board for having the imagination to fund this unconventional line of research.

REFERENCES

Anisfeld, M., & Knapp, M. (1968). Association, synonymity, and directionality in false recognition. *Journal of Experimental Psychology, 77,* 171–179.
Barclay, C. R. (1986). Schematization of autobiographical memory. In D. C.

Rubin (Ed.), *Autobiographical memory* (pp. 82–99). Cambridge University Press.

Barclay, C. R., & Wellman, H. M. (1986). Accuracies and inaccuracies in autobiographical memories. *Journal of Memory and Language, 25*, 93–103.

Barker, R. G., & Wright, H. F. (1955). *Midwest and its children*. Evanston, IL: Row, Peterson.

Bower, G. H. (1974). Selective facilitation and interference in retention of prose. *Journal of Educational Psychology, 66*, 1–8.

Brewer, W. F. (1982). Personal memory, generic memory, and skill: A reanalysis of the episodic-semantic distinction. *Proceedings of the Fourth Annual Conference of the Cognitive Science Society* (pp. 112–113).

(1986). What is autobiographical memory? In D. C. Rubin (Ed.), *Autobiographical memory* (pp. 25–49). Cambridge University Press.

Brewer, W. F., & Nakamura, G. V. (1984). The nature and functions of schemas. In R. S. Wyer & T. K. Srull (Eds.), *Handbook of social cognition* (Vol. 1, pp. 119–160). Hillsdale, NJ: Erlbaum.

Brewer, W. F., & Pani, J. R. (1983). The structure of human memory. In G. H. Bower (Ed.), *The psychology of learning and motivation: Advances in research and theory* (Vol. 17, pp. 1–38). New York: Academic Press.

(in preparation). Phenomenal reports during the recall process.

Brewer, W. F., & Schommer, M. (in preparation). Imagery reports during memory retrieval: Galton's breakfast questionnaire revisited.

Brewer, W. F., & Treyens, J. C. (1981). Role of schemata in memory for places. *Cognitive Psychology, 13*, 207–230.

Brown, R., & Kulik, J. (1977). Flashbulb memories. *Cognition, 5*, 73–99.

Craik, F. I. M., & Jacoby, L. L. (1979). Elaboration and distinctiveness in episodic memory. In L.-G. Nilsson (Ed.), *Perspectives on memory research* (pp. 145–166). Hillsdale, NJ: Erlbaum.

Crovitz, H. F., & Quina-Holland, K. (1976). Proportion of episodic memories from early childhood by years of age. *Bulletin of the Psychonomic Society, 7*, 61–62.

Crovitz, H. F., & Schiffman, H. (1974). Frequency of episodic memories as a function of their age. *Bulletin of the Psychonomic Society, 4*, 517–518.

Divilbiss, J. L., & Self, P. C. (1978). Work analysis by random sampling. *Bulletin of the Medical Library Association, 66*, 19–23.

Ebbinghaus, H. (1964). *Memory*. New York: Dover. (Original work published 1885).

Epstein, S. (1973). The self-concept revisited, or a theory of a theory. *American Psychologist, 28*, 404–416.

Furlong, E. J. (1951). *A study in memory*. London: Thomas Nelson.

Galton, F. (1879a). Psychometric experiments. *Brain, 2*, 149–162.

(1879b). Psychometric facts. *The Nineteenth Century, 5*, 425–433.

(1880). Statistics of mental imagery. *Mind, 5*, 301–318.

Gibson, E. J. (1940). A systematic application of the concepts of generalization and differentiation to verbal learning. *Psychological Review, 47*, 196–229.

Hintzman, D. L. (1978). *The psychology of learning and memory*. San Francisco: Freeman.

Hurlburt, R. T. (1976). *Self-observation and self-control*. Unpublished doctoral dissertation, University of South Dakota.

Kahneman, D., & Tversky, A. (1972). Subjective probability: A judgment of representativeness. *Cognitive Psychology, 3*, 430–454.

Linton, M. (1975). Memory for real-world events. In D. A. Norman & D. E. Rumelhart (Eds.), *Explorations in cognition* (pp. 376–404). San Francisco: Freeman.

(1978) Real world memory after six years: An *in vivo* study of very long term memory. In M. M. Gruneberg, P. E. Morris, & R. N. Sykes (Eds.), *Practical aspects of memory* (pp. 69–76). London: Academic Press.

(1982). Transformations of memory in everyday life. In U. Neisser (Ed.), *Memory observed: Remembering in natural contexts* (pp. 77–91). San Francisco: Freeman.

Locke, D. (1971). *Memory*. Garden City, NY: Anchor.

McCormak, P. D. (1979). Autobiographical memory in the aged. *Canadian Journal of Psychology, 33,* 118–124.

Markus, H. (1980). The self in thought and memory. In D. M. Wegner & R. R. Vallacher (Eds.), *The self in social psychology* (pp. 102–130). New York: Oxford University Press.

Neisser, U. (1981). John Dean's memory: A case study. *Cognition, 9,* 1–22.

(1982). Snapshots or benchmarks? In U. Neisser (Ed.), *Memory observed: Remembering in natural contexts* (pp. 43–48). San Francisco: Freeman.

(1985). The role of theory in the ecological study of memory: Comment on Bruce. *Journal of Experimental Psychology: General, 114,* 272–276.

(1986a). Nested structure in autobiographical memory. In D. C. Rubin (Ed.), *Autobiographical memory* (pp. 71–81). Cambridge University Press.

(1986b). Remembering Pearl Harbor: Reply to Thompson and Cowan. *Cognition, 23,* 285–286.

Newtson, D. (1976). Foundations of attribution: The perception of ongoing behavior. In J. H. Harvey, W. J. Ickes, & R. F. Kidd (Eds.), *New directions in attribution research* (Vol. 1). Hillsdale, NJ: Erlbaum.

Nigro, G., & Neisser, U. (1983). Point of view in personal memories. *Cognitive Psychology, 15,* 467–482.

Norman, D. A., & Bobrow, D. G. (1979). Descriptions: An intermediate stage in memory retrieval. *Cognitive Psychology, 11,* 107–123.

Pillemer, D. B., Rhinehart, E. D., & White, S. H. (1986). Memories of life transitions: The first year in college. *Human Learning, 5,* 109–123.

Reiser, B. J. (1983). *Contexts and indices in autobiographical memory.* Cognitive Science Technical Report No. 24, Yale University.

Reiser, B. J., Black, J. B., & Abelson, R. P. (1985). Knowledge structures in organization and retrieval of autobiographical memories. *Cognitive Psychology, 17,* 89–137.

Reiser, B. J., Black, J. B., & Kalamarides, P. (1986). Strategic memory search processes. In D. C. Rubin (Ed.), *Autobiographical memory* (pp. 100–121). Cambridge University Press.

Robinson, J. A. (1976). Sampling autobiographical memory. *Cognitive Psychology, 8,* 578–595.

Rosch, E. (1978). Principles of categorization. In E. Rosch & B. B. Lloyd (Eds.), *Cognition and categorization* (pp. 27–48). Hillsdale, NJ: Erlbaum.

Rubin, D. C. (1982). On the retention function for autobiographical memory. *Journal of Verbal Learning and Verbal Behavior, 21,* 21–38.

Rubin, D. C., Wetzler, S. E., & Nebes, R. D. (1986). Autobiographical memory across the lifespan. In D. C. Rubin (Ed.), *Autobiographical memory* (pp. 202–221). Cambridge University Press.

Russell, B. (1921). *The analysis of mind.* London: Allen & Unwin.

Sheehan, P. W., & Neisser, U. (1969). Some variables affecting the vividness of imagery in recall. *British Journal of Psychology, 60,* 71–80.

Smith, M. E. (1952). Childhood memories compared with those of adult life. *Journal of Genetic Psychology, 80,* 151–182.

Thompson, C. P. (1982). Memory for unique personal events: The roommate study. *Memory & Cognition, 10,* 324–332.

Thompson, C. P., & Cowan, T. (1986). Flashbulb memories: A nicer interpretation of a Neisser recollection. *Cognition, 22,* 199–200.

Thomson, R. H. (1930). An experimental study of memory as influenced by feeling tone. *Journal of Experimental Psychology, 13,* 462–468.

Tulving, E. (1972). Episodic and semantic memory. In E. Tulving & W. Donaldson (Eds.), *Organization of memory* (pp. 381–403). New York: Academic Press.

Tversky, A., & Kahneman, D. (1973). Availability: A heuristic for judging frequency and probability. *Cognitive Psychology, 5,* 207–232.

Wagenaar, W. A. (1986). My memory: A study of autobiographical memory over six years. *Cognitive Psychology, 18,* 225–252.

Wallace, W. P. (1980). On the use of distractors for testing recognition memory. *Psychological Bulletin, 88,* 696–704.

Waters, R. H., & Leeper, R. (1936). The relation of affective tone to the retention of experiences of daily life. *Journal of Experimental Psychology, 19,* 203–215.

White, R. T. (1982). Memory for personal events. *Human Learning, 1,* 171–183.

Winograd, E., & Killinger, W. A., Jr. (1983). Relating age at encoding in early childhood to adult recall: Development of flashbulb memories. *Journal of Experimental Psychology: General, 112,* 413–422.

Yarmey, A. D., & Bull, M. P., III (1978). Where were you when President Kennedy was assassinated? *Bulletin of the Psychonomic Society, 11,* 133–135.

Yntema, D. B., & Trask, F. P. (1963). Recall as a search process. *Journal of Verbal Learning and Verbal Behavior, 2,* 65–74.

4

Ordinary everyday memories: Some of the things of which selves are made

CRAIG R. BARCLAY AND PEGGY A. DeCOOKE

This chapter is organized in three major sections. A brief review of our previous research is presented first. Next, new findings regarding the nature of self-selected events and memory for those events are reported. This section is based on the diaries of four women who kept written records of memorable daily events. Two recognition-memory posttests were given following 2 weeks of record keeping. On each posttest, original records were presented for verification, together with foil items. Foils derived from the participants' actual records were designed to show that the meaning of daily events is preserved in personal memories. This section includes an ethnographic-type description of self-selected daily events and activities. The accidental and tragic death of the parent of one of these women unfortunately occurred during data collection. Because she and another participant were both keeping records at the time of the accident, we were able to investigate the impact of a highly significant life experience on memory for everyday events in a controlled case study.

Introduction

The content of much human cognition is represented as a rich collection of autobiographical memories. Certainly, some of these memories are of formative life experiences, although many more appear as insignificant happenings. If these seemingly unimportant, ordinary everyday memories are considered alone, or isolated from the mosaic of one's personal recollections, they may be interpreted as trivial fragments of the past, but in the context, flow, and rhythm of daily life they become the fabric of a self-knowledge system.

Two propositions guided the research reported here. The first is that self-knowledge is in large part a by-product of what we do, think, and feel every day. The complexity of behavior and thought reflects the complexity of an imposing and changing environment (Simon, 1969). We engage in purposeful activities in a practical sense – because we have

91

to–experiencing an objective world, eventually coming to act on that world, not just reacting to it (Davydov, Zinchenko, & Talyzina, 1983; Leont'ev, 1981). The second proposition is that most autobiographical memories have distinct semantic qualities representing, in schematic form, the consequences of varied life experiences (Linton, 1986; Neisser, 1981, 1987). Autobiographical memories are not wholly episodic, but on many occasions they may appear to be (Hudson, 1986; Tulving, 1972). They often are independent of temporal and spatial constraints and perhaps are organized at different levels of abstraction (Linton, 1986). Autobiographical recollections are not necessarily accurate, nor should they be; they are, however, mostly congruent with one's self-knowledge, life themes, or sense of self (Barclay, 1986; Csikszentmihalyi & Beattie, 1979; Erikson, 1968; Markus, 1977).

On this view, many literary critics consider written autobiography as a genre separate from fiction and nonfiction in that any autobiography must convey the author's intention that the life portrayed is the life actually lived (Gusdorf, 1956; Howarth, 1974; Olney, 1980; Renza, 1977). Authors tell the truth about their lives. An author presents a self-portrait that has integrity, even though the facts, situations, and contexts may not mirror actual life experiences. Howarth (1974), for example, writes:

Inevitably, readers will ask if such a character [author] is "true." Certainly, he is not "true to life," since he tells a censored account, epitomizing himself, like Raphael and Michelangelo, admitting no facts that fail to support his central thesis: Gibbon excludes his childhood; Bunyan and Adams omit their marriages. This censorship may savor of insincerity, but it also serves an orator's purposes as he converts the surviving details into meaningful allegory. Malcolm X writes exhaustively on the art of designing a perfect "conk"–a straightened hairdo that represents his bankrupt racial pride. The details are not literal history but figural narration. They give us selected aspects of a larger allegory, representing the Afro-American "experience" through the manipulative power of art. (p. 93)

An allegorical strategy conveniently summarizes the meanings of many different, but conceptually related, life experiences. As with allegory, autobiographical memory often is a *constructive* and *reconstructive* process used to condense everyday memories of events and activities, extracting those features that embrace and maintain meaning in one's self-knowledge system (Bartlett, 1932; Freud, 1899/1950; Linton, 1982; Neisser, 1981). In turn, seemingly unconnected episodic recollections become allegorical in that particular events can be remembered and used as instances of generalized life experiences to convey one's sense of self to an audience.

If autobiographical memories serve an allegorical purpose, then knowing about the kinds of experiences people find memorable from their daily lives could be informative about how personal histories are acquired and structured. Through following individuals longitudinally, we can also examine how memory for everyday events changes with the occurrence of repetitious episodes and unique, personally significant events. Comparing verifiable accounts of self-selected memorable happenings with memory for those events makes it possible to chart the acquisition of self-referenced allegory, the nature of information stored in an autobiographical memory system and variables that influence the acquisition process, and the form of self-knowledge representation. Questions of interest here include the following: What kinds of experiences do people report as memorable from their daily lives? What do people remember about such self-selected activities—how accurate are their memories, how "truthful" are these memories in the sense of being consistent with the meaning of the reported events? And what factors affect memory for everyday events and activities?

Previous research

The specific aim of our initial work (Barclay & Wellman, 1986) was to examine the accuracy of everyday autobiographical memories. Some evidence supported the claim that such memories remained highly accurate for years (e.g., flashbulb memories), whereas intuition and other data suggested that many self-referenced memories (e.g., going to eat at a favorite restaurant) were forgotten or easily confused as people experienced the same kinds of events repeatedly. Anecdotal reports suggested further that even seemingly vivid personal memories sometimes were error-prone (Linton, 1975; Neisser, 1982).

Many personal experiences are also consistent with the view that autobiographical memories are accurate. We typically believe without question that past life events are remembered as they actually happened. Often there are no motives or means for checking our recollections. However, much of one's past probably is forgotten or inaccessible at the time of recall. Because what we remember seems to be logically consistent with what should have happened, we tend to accept our memories as if they were accurate.

Barclay and Wellman (1986) proposed that competing views of memory accuracy needed to be evaluated by comparing veridical records of actual events with memory for those events. A recognition-memory paradigm was used in which actual records were presented along with foil items—that is, records of nonevents. Foil items were used to separate true memory for autobiographical information from the tendency to identify all presented items as original records; such a response bias would lead to an overestimation of, as well as overconfidence in, the accuracy of one's personal recollections.

Two types of foils were presented on recognition tests, along with original records. One foil type consisted of transformations of original-event records in which either (a) reported descriptive details were changed (foil-description items) or (b) the person's evaluations or reactions to events were modified (foil-evaluation items). Records of non-events not reported by any of the subjects were used as the other foil type (other-foil items).

Six graduate students were recruited who kept diary-type records of three self-selected memorable events per day, 5 days per week (excluding weekends), for 4 consecutive months. Data collection was followed by five delayed-memory tests given over a 2.5-year period. Three subjects completed the entire study.

In data collection, all participants were encouraged to use a simplified record-keeping procedure that included recording an event, a context in which the event occurred, and a reaction. A reaction to an event could be either an emotional response or a physical response or both. How an event was defined was subjectively determined (cf. Linton, 1986). An illustrative example follows:

I was walking to the grocery to pick up a few things for dinner [context] when this squirrel ran out in front of me [event]. It scared me [emotional reaction]; fortunately, I did not step on the thing, but I did kick at it [physical reaction].

Subjects were told to record events as they occurred or at the end of each day. Every participant chose the latter tactic, and subsequently they were instructed to review the day's events and record those they thought most memorable.

The five recognition-memory posttests followed data collection at delay intervals of 1–3, 4–6, 7–9, 10–12, and 30–31 months. Each test consisted of 45 items: 18 duplicates of original records, 9 foil evaluations, 9 foil descriptions, and 9 other foils. Testing required subjects to accept or reject each item as an exact reproduction of an original record and then rate how confident they were that they had made the correct choice.

The results of primary interest here indicated that subjects had a strong response bias toward falsely recognizing many foils as actual events. Specifically, subjects (a) falsely accepted foil items manufactured from their original records about 50% of the time and (b) falsely identified other-foil items as their own at a 23% error rate. Performance on original records remained high (approximately 94% correct acceptance of original items) through the 10–12-month delayed posttest, declining to 79% correct after 2.5 years. Overall confidence ratings remained high throughout the study and did not decline significantly with decreasing accuracy—subjects were more sure of their memory accuracy than they should have been.

Most of the inaccuracies and accuracies in the kinds of everyday autobiographical memories studied here appeared to result from a reconstructive memory process (Bartlett, 1932). Memory errors may mirror contrived information consistent with what one expects to have occurred in the past or information imported from related activities; the correct identification of actual memories could also result from the same kinds of expectations. Expectations are learned, and perhaps represented as self-schemata or self-scripts acquired through a schematization process (Freud, 1914/1960; Markus, 1977; Nelson, Fivush, Hudson, & Lucariello, 1983; Piaget & Inhelder, 1973; Shank & Ableson, 1977; Slackman & Nelson, 1984). Schematization theoretically accounts for the formation of generalized knowledge structures (e.g., generalized event representations) representing the consequences of one's actions and procedures for controlling future actions (Neisser, 1976; Piaget & Inhelder, 1973; Schank & Ableson, 1977).

We reasoned that differences in the magnitudes of the reported false alarm effects (false alarm rates for foil-evaluation, foil-description, and other foil items were .50, .48, and .23, respectively, after a 1-year delay) were due to how conceptually similar foils were to events that actually occurred—a subjective perception of similarity acquired through schematization. Other foil items were least similar, because they were someone else's records; the false alarm rate was the lowest for these items. Foil-description and foil-evaluation items were next in similarity, because they were rewrites of the subjects' actual records; they were near replications of original records. The false alarm rates were higher on these items than for other-foil items.

Eight independent raters subsequently judged the degree of semantic relatedness between all of the foil-description and foil-evaluation items and their corresponding original records from the first four recognition tests. A 7-point scale was used: 1 indicated "not semantically different" and 7 indicated "very semantically different." The mean semantic difference rating was *less* for items falsely identified as originals (3.35) than for items correctly rejected as nonevents (4.02). False alarm rates rose as these foils became more alike in meaning to original records.

In a follow-up analysis, Barclay (1986) argued that the false alarm rates on foil-evaluation and foil-description items should also covary with time, because schematization is a process that presumably changes the mental representational form of memorable events. Furthermore, because semantic relatedness affects recognition-memory accuracy, false alarm rates for foil items high in conceptual similarity to the originals from which they were written should be elevated at shorter delay intervals relative to foils

Table 4.1. *Semantic similarity by delay interaction expressed as false alarm rates*

Semantic similarity	Delay (months)			
	1–3	4–6	7–9	10–12
High	.36	.68	.61	.70
Low	.21	.31	.40	.73

low in similarity. A similarity by delay-interval interaction was found in comparison of the upper and lower thirds of the semantic-difference rating distributions (foil-evaluation and foil-description ratings were combined, because the patterns of results were the same for both). The data are presented in Table 4.1, where it is seen that at short delays (1–3 months) the false alarm rate for high-similarity foils was greater than that for low-similarity items. As the delay interval lengthened to 4–6 months, the false alarm rate for high-similarity items differentially increased relative to that found for low-similarity items. At the 7–9 month delay interval, high-similarity items were again falsely recognized as originals at a higher rate than low-similarity items; by 10–12 months, however, no differences were evident between high- and low-similarity foils.

The mosaic of findings from our previous research, including the particular false alarm patterns on foil items and the semantic-similarity effect in the Barclay and Wellman (1986) study and the interaction of semantic similarity with temporal delay (Barclay, 1986), is consistent with the proposition that many, if not all, autobiographical recollections are reconstructions of life experiences. A reconstruction process contributes not only to veridical memories of our past but also to memory errors and inflated beliefs about the accuracy of autobiographical knowledge.

These findings are limited, however, in at least two important ways. First, semantic-similarity ratings were post hoc analyses done to explain differential false alarm rates over foil types. It may be that the false alarm patterns reflect a systematic bias in the way the foil-evaluation and foil-description items were manufactured. No attempts were made to scale or control how different in meaning foil-evaluation and foil-description items were from original records. Second, not only were the meanings of events affected by manipulating evaluative and descriptive components of original records, but also the subjects' writing styles may have been noticeably altered. If a word was included in a rewritten foil that was never used by a subject, then that item might be rejected without thoughtful consideration. Likewise, similar word usage and phrasing in a foil could make the foil unusually difficult to detect, because we know that surface structure is quickly forgotten, at least on certain laboratory-type tasks (Sachs, 1967). For personalized diary records, though, it is not yet known whether or not the manner in which some event is written affects one's memory for that event. It seems reasonable to argue that one's writing style, like the brush strokes of the artist, can be used to detect the authenticity of an artifact, especially if the person making the judgment created the object being judged. How a person phrases an event description, together with the intended meaning of the written record, could provide subtle and indelible marks of the individual. Accordingly, semantic and stylistic changes could have been confounded in our previous work, even though foils were constructed carefully with no blatant or obvious style differences. Therefore, in the design of the research reported next, foils manufactured from the original records were explicitly written with obvious semantic or syntactic changes.

Memory for the meaning of daily events and activities

Rationale

The purposes of this study were to offer a detailed description of the kinds of events people report as memorable daily happenings, because no such description is currently available in the literature, and to explore more fully than in our previous work the question of accuracy in autobiographical memories. Based on the results of the Barclay and Wellman (1986) study, it seemed that a likely dimension underlying reconstructive memory errors and accuracy was the subjective meaning of self-selected daily events. Because our previous work had not been designed to examine this hypothesis directly, the question remained whether or not we could create foil items from original diary records that people would correctly reject most of the time and others that would be accepted incorrectly at high rates without manufacturing foils with totally implausible modifications. Our approach was similar to that used in our previous research, except here we purposefully constructed foil items so as to capture the "end points" of the presumed semantic-similarity dimension. Those end points were represented by foil items in which (a) the meanings of original records were changed through negation and (b) meaning was not changed, but the stylistic form of the records was modified.

Method

Diary records were collected from four female adults ranging in age from approximately 23 to 36 years ($X = 27.5$). Three of the women were graduate students, and one was a nonacademic professional. They had comparable educational levels and family backgrounds. One subject was married, two had at least one significant other, and one was unattached at the time. We intended to gather records from six individuals, divided in two successive data-collection waves of three subjects each.[1] Unfortunately, attrition claimed one subject in wave one because of a death in her family. For this reason, her diary records were analyzed separately and are reported later. It was eventually decided to recruit two subjects for each wave.

Data collection consisted in subjects recording and rating five events or activities per day for 14 consecutive days. The record-keeping format used by Barclay and Wellman (1986) (i.e., records should include a context, event description, and reaction) was again used here. Subjects were told that we were especially interested in the content of the events and activities they found most memorable from their daily lives; also, they were told not to sacrifice content to meet the recommended format parameters. Specific instructions stressed the keeping of memorable events: "this means that of all the things you do each day, select the five most memorable – even if you think something is not worth reporting, in the context of all things that happened that day, it may be one of the most memorable."

Once a record was written, the subjects were instructed to rate it on eight subjective dimensions: memorability, personal significance, frequency of occurrence, typicality, satisfaction, surprise, similarity to other events and activities engaged in, and emotionality. Each symmetrical 7-point scale was labeled "neither" at the midpoint, and, in order from there outward, "somewhat," "quite," and "very." These dimensions were selected to reflect the subject's perceptions of the kinds of events self-selected as memorable (Csikszentmihalyi, Larson, & Prescott, 1977; Larson & Csikszentmihalyi, 1983). In addition, after data collection and testing were completed, subjects sorted all of their own records into event or activity categories so that records within a category were conceptually related, and different categories were independent.

Subjects were instructed to place their completed records in an envelope. Records were gathered from subjects at the end of every day, or morning of the next day, as a means of reducing rehearsal.

Subjects in wave one kept records from November 26 through December 9, 1984; wave-two subjects recorded their memories from January 21 through February 3, 1985. Two recognition-memory posttests followed data collection for each wave. Posttest 1 was given 1 day following the last data-collection day (a 1–14-day delay interval); Posttest 2 was given approximately 1 month later (32–45-day delay). Records selected for each posttest were drawn from the entire data-collection period.

Table 4.2. *Sample items for MDSS and MSSD foils*

MDSS		MSSD	
Original	Foil	Original	Foil
—— rode her bike through the park while I ran . . . I ran until I had to stop to get her out of the snow, walk her bike up a hill, etc. We were out an hour – it was beautiful out. Again it made me think how much I've enjoyed the city.	—— rode her bike through the park while I ran . . . I ran until I had to stop to get her out of the snow, walk her bike up a hill etc. We were out an hour – it was a mess out. Again it made me think how hard it is to adjust to the city.	—— practiced her concerto this morning in preparation for tryouts for All-City Orchestra – she listened to her new Suzuki accompaniment tape. She made it! She was so proud of herself – I'm glad she had that success. Now I hope she sticks with it.	I was so happy that —— made the All-City Orchestra. She practiced the concerto using the new Suzuki tape. She was very pleased with her success; so was I. I hope she will continue her music.

A 40-item recognition test was given at each posttest. Records used for Posttest 1 were selected without replacement; consequently, items on Posttest 2 were new. Ten original items and 30 foils were included on each posttest. Ten foils were constructed by changing the meaning of original records while preserving the subject's writing style – Meaning Different, Style Same (MDSS); because the meaning of original records was negated here, these foils were comparable in type to the low-similarity items reported by Barclay (1986). Ten other originals were rewritten so that the meaning was largely unchanged (thus creating high-similarity items), but the writing style varied – Meaning Same, Style Different (MSSD). Illustrations of these foil types are given in Table 4.2. The ten remaining items were other foils, that is, records from a person not participating in this study.

The subject's task on each posttest was to rate test items using a 6-point scale (Graesser, 1981; Graesser, Woll, Kowalski, & Smith, 1980): 1 – *"positive* the record *is not* my recorded memory"; 2 – *"fairly sure . . . is not . . . ,"*; 3 – *"uncertain,* but *guess . . . is not . . ."*; 4 – *"uncertain,* but *guess . . . is . . ."*; 5 – *"fairly sure . . . is . . ."*; 6 – *"positive . . . is . . . ."* Foil items were scored as "false alarms" if rated 4–6; correct rejections were 1–3 ratings. Original items rated 4–6 were scored as "hits," and "misses" were 1–3 ratings.

Written instructions emphasized that the task was to identify items that were *exact duplicates* of reported events or activities and to reject all others as nonevents. Each test item was typed on a separate 5- × 8-in. index card. The cards were ordered randomly and self-presented, one at a time, at the subject's own pace. Subjects were not permitted to alter their ratings once the next item in the deck was being considered. Individual testing took approximately 15 min.

Results

The results are presented in two parts. First, descriptive data are reported, followed by the recognition-memory results.

Description of everyday events and activities. The available records are discribed in three ways. First, group (N = 4) data are presented: Event frequencies at each rating level (1–7) were calculated and reported separately for each subjective dimension rated. Average ratings for these dimensions were then found. Second, typical and atypical events and activities were identified in reference to subjects' own ratings of memorability, personal significance,and so forth. Third, after Posttest 2, subjects were asked to sort their own records "into groups or categories on the basis of some aspect of meaning." Once these categories were determined, a representative record was selected at random from the categories with the highest and lowest event frequencies. The reason for having subjects sort their records into categories was to explore possible sources of individual differences and similarities in subjective interpretations of everyday events.

Event frequencies. Nearly complete data were available; of the 280 records written, 272 were rated. Event frequencies falling at the various rating levels for the different subjective dimensions are given in Table 4.3. Here it is seen that the majority of reported events where not seen as unusual or unexpected. A slight positive skew was found for memorability, personal significance, frequency, and surprise – fewer records were rated 6–7 than 1–2. Consequently, there were fewer events seen as highly memorable, personally significant, frequently occurring, and unexpected than easily forgotten, somewhat irrelevant, rare, and surprising. Slight negative skewness indicated relatively high frequencies for typicality, satisfaction, similarity, and emotion; thus, more events were judged routine, satisfying to engage in, similar to other events experienced, and exciting than unique, unfulfilling, dissimilar to other daily activities, or boring.

Average ratings (and standard deviations [SD]) for the dimensions were as follows: memorability 3.77 (.84), personal significance 3.77 (.49), frequency 3.58 (.84), typicality 4.08 (.72), satisfaction 4.36 (.59), surprise

Table 4.3. *Frequencies of events at each rating level on eight subjective dimensions (N = 4)*

Dimension	Rating[a]						
	1	2	3	4	5	6	7
Memorability	48	47	33	25	57	36	26
Personal significance	42	31	29	59	66	31	14
Frequency	70	31	34	21	58	38	20
Typicality	45	19	33	46	62	33	34
Satisfaction	26	23	26	59	51	55	26
Surprise	37	32	64	58	34	29	18
Similarity	28	19	37	49	61	48	30
Emotionality	17	7	11	76	76	57	18

[a]Memorability (1 – easily forgotten, 7 – memorable), Personal significance (1 – irrelevant, 7 – significant), Frequency (1 – infrequent, 7 – frequent), Typicality (1 – unique, 7 – routine), Satisfaction (1 – unfulfilling, 7 – satisfactory), Suprise (1 – expected, 7 – suprising), Similarity (1 – not similar, 7 – similar), Emotionality (1 – boring, 7 – exciting).

3.66 (.64), similarity 4.32 (.69), and emotion 4.64 (.44). These results show that events tended to be rated just below the middle scale point on half of the eight dimensions. The grand mean for all scales was 4.02.

One interesting finding was that the mean memorability rating was 3.77, even though subjects were instructed to report the most memorable daily events. It may be that the subjects decided not to comply with those instructions because of the personal nature of some activities (still, some records were very self-disclosing) or because most everyday events simply were not seen as that memorable. We suspect the latter is true. Almost all subjects in this and previous studies stated that formerly they had thought of their lives as really interesting until they had to keep records of what they did every day! Memorability ratings could also indicate an awareness of whether or not a detailed recounting of an event was possible, especially because subjects knew they would be tested later (Flavell & Wellman, 1977).

Most memorable daily events and activities were not perceived as being loaded with personal significance or very surprising. They were generally expected, fairly typical, and similar to what occurred every day, but recurring somewhat infrequently. Subjects did feel that their daily activities were somewhat satisfying and exciting (either positive or negative); this could reflect the fact that all of the participants were involved in chosen career and family activities.

The mean ratings tell the same story as the frequency data in Table 4.3. The majority of daily events and activities were routine and not very

Table 4.4. *Typical and atypical items for each subject*

Subject	Typical	Atypical
A	Went for a bike ride since it is such a nice day. Went through Frick Park and Schenley Park where there is hardly any traffic. Good enjoyable ride which covered about 18 miles. I thought I was out of shape but it comes back quickly if there is adequate motivation. One of my favorite activities, especially when in present state of mind. (4, 4, 3, 3, 6, 3, 4, 5)	This was a bit awkward deciding who was going to go home with who! I realized ____ had already made a statement but it is real hard for me to drink with ____ and not touch ____ or even look at ____ in a way that ____ wouldn't be offended. What happened was I decided I want ____ and I don't want *too* much emotional control over me so there was no alternative but to leave with ____. ____ drove everyone home and it was really nice that ____ dropped ____ off first. I can't help but wonder what ____, ____ and ____ think 'cause usually I go to ____'s. ____ is a really cool person. We went back to the house and listened to music, drank and had a great time. Well finally time to get some precious sleep! (6, 7, 1, 1, 7, 2, 6, 7)
B	Met ____ for lunch. ____ was shocked about ____ losing the job – they used to date. We talked about it for a while. ____ wanted to hear about our ____ ____ program. Since ____ runs the ____ ____ program – I've regularly talked with ____ about ours – ____'s not a planner and gives good practical feedback. Besides ____'s a neat person – I don't now why all these single people don't get together. Also made me feel good that I had kept my resolve to take a lunch break. (3, 4, 5, 5, 5, 3, 5, 5)	____left for ____ today. ____ stopped back to kiss me and talk a minute. . . . sometimes I really marvel at how strong our affection is after so many years. (6, 6, 2, 2, 7, 6, 2, 6)
C	____called to ask about the procedure at the test service (Office of Measurement and Evaluation). We talked about other things too – all to do with school (almost). (5, 4, 3, 4, 6, 4, 6, 4)	I went out to dinner at ____ to celebrate my birthday. I was expecting 10 people at the *most*, but it ended up being more like 20. People gave me presents too; it wasn't quite what I'd expected (not at all). ____ had taken over the arrangements because I hate arranging things. We stayed for over 4 hours. I'd planned on going up the Incline, but it was too cold so nobody wanted to go. I felt very good about

Table 4.4. *(cont.)*

Subject	Typical	Atypical
		the whole thing; it was fun and relaxing at the same time. It did get a bit manic, but not out of control. (7, 6, 1, 1, 7, 6, 1, 7)
D	Took ____ out for lunch after church. We went to ____ at ____'s suggestion. I haven't been to one since ____ ____. (3, 4, 3, 3, 4, 4, 4, 4)	Went over to ____ to confront the janitor who removed the crate from my office. He says he threw the crate out – thought it was trash! I can't believe this. He doesn't even care *or* see the seriousness of this. I think he took it home. That crate was very nice – his story doesn't wash. (7, 5, 1, 1, 1, 7, 1, 7)

Note: Typical examples were selected so that the mean deviation around each subject's average subjective ratings was minimized; atypical examples were selected so that the mean deviation was maximized. Numbers in parentheses following each record are the subject's ratings for the record's memorability, personal significance, frequency, typicality, satisfaction, surprise, similarity, and emotional arousal, respectively. Subjects B and C had two atypical records; the one presented here was randomly selected.

memorable. Nonetheless, they did give a sense of personal fulfillment. Our subjects, while engaging in many mundane activities, appeared generally to enjoy their daily lives.

Typicality. Typical and atypical events are presented for each subject in Table 4.4. Typicality was characterized in terms of the subjective ratings and determined by locating the subjects' unique records that minimized and maximized mean deviation scores. That is, the average rating on each dimension was calculated for each subject. Next, this mean was subtracted from the rating given to each record on that dimension, and the absolute value taken. The resultant deviation scores were then summed over dimensions for each record and divided by the number of dimensions rated for that record. The record with the smallest mean deviation was taken as the typical event or activity; the one with the largest deviation as atypical.

Typical records identified by this procedure were most similar to the subjects' prototypic events or activities – the hypothetical records with ratings equal to the mean ratings on each dimension. Not surprisingly, the typical records in Table 4.4. are accounts of ordinary daily activities like those portrayed earlier. Compared with the group means given in the preceding section, the record with the greatest deviation was written by Subject C. Ratings of satisfaction and similarity contributed most to the deviation; both rated high relative to the group means. The record with the smallest deviation was reported by Subject D.

Another perspective taken on these individual differences, and one helpful in understanding similarities and differences among subjects' perceptions of everyday events, was to examine the dimensions contributing most to typicality. Deviations between mean ratings on each dimension and corresponding ratings of the typical and atypical records shown in Table 4.4 were calculated. For typical records, the two dimensions with the smallest deviations were similarity(+)[2] and emotion(+) for Subject A, memorability(+) and similarity(+) for Subject B, personal significance(−) and frequency(−) for Subject C, and typicality(−) and satisfaction (+) for Subject D. It is seen that different subjective dimensions and valences correspond to the typical record of each subject (except Similarity for Subjects A & B). Indeed, there are similarities in the nature of the written records, but idiosyncrasies echo how different people evaluate ordinary life events. Such differences may be grounded in the diversity of experiences making up these individuals' personal histories. Accumulated past experiences are likely frames of reference to use when one makes judgments about the meaning of particular everyday happenings.

The atypical records (Table 4.4) were most deviant from each subject's ideal statistical prototype. Across all subjects, atypical events were rated very emotional ($X = 6.75$) and memorable ($X = 6.5$), quite personally significant ($X = 6.0$) and satisfying ($X = 5.5$), somewhat surprising ($X = 5.25$) and dissimilar ($X = 2.5$) to other events encountered, very unique ($X = 1.25$), and infrequent ($X = 1.25$). The most atypical event was reported by Subject D.

An examination of individual subject ratings indicated that the two dimensions contributing most to atypicality were personal significance(+) and typicality(−) for Subject A, memorability(+) and satisfaction(+) for Subject B, typicality(−) and similarity(−) for Subject C, and memorability(+) and satisfaction(−) for Subject D. Unlike typical events, atypical happenings shared more common dimensions across subjects. It may be that events seen as out of the ordinary tap shared knowledge (as culturally relevant expectations) about what features constitute an unusual daily experience. It appears that there is less agreement among people about what qualifies as typical as opposed to an atypical life event.

Event categories. Event categories were determined by having subjects sort their own records into meaningful groups. The aim was to explore possible organizational structures for reported events. People might

Table 4.5. *Individual-subject descriptive data on event categories and records in event categories*

Subject	No. of event categories	Records in event categories		
		Mean	Median	Range (SD)[a]
A	10	7	6.5	1–16 (5.35)
B	3	23.3	29	5–36 (16.26)
C	6	11.67	6.5	4–33 (11.4)
D	13	5.39	4.52	2–16 (3.91)

[a]Standard deviations given in parentheses.

structure their activities according to personalized schemata. Such schemata could serve a continuity function, providing tacit connections among events that superficially appear as unrelated to the naive observer.

Subjects sorted their records a few weeks following the second posttest. Complete record sets were available for all subjects. Essential components of the sorting instructions were as follows:

These are all the records you kept. I want you to read them carefully and then sort them into groups or categories on the basis of some aspect or meaning . . . decide which records are alike in some respect and put them together in the same group. The aspects of meaning you select are entirely up to you. After sorting all of the records, I want you to describe each category; put a label or short description on each of your categories . . . put those events you cannot possibly categorize into either a "Unique" or "Miscellaneous" group . . . do not use these categories if at all possible . . . use as few categories as you can, but as many as it takes to group the records.

An added restriction was to place the records in mutually exclusive and exhaustive categories so that the records in a given category were more similar to each other in meaning than to those in other categories (Kruskal & Wish, 1978).

Subjects reported having little difficulty completing this task, which took each of them approximately 30 min. Further, all subjects but one were able to sort their records into clearly identifiable and nonoverlapping categories. Six records were placed in a "Unique events" category by Subject D.

Individual-subject data are summarized in Table 4.5, which shows that the number of categories created ranged from 3 to 13 ($X = 8.0$, SD = 4.39). The mean number of records per category ranged from 7 to 23.3. The group average was 8.75 (SD = 8.96). Inspection of the medians indicated markedly uneven distributions for two subjects: Subject B, with three categories, sorted five records into one category and 36 into another; Subject C placed four records in each of two categories, and 33 in a third category. Hence, one important source of individual variation was the degree of differentiation among events – the more fine-grained the analysis, the more categories needed, with fewer records per grouping. Subject B, for example, formed a category, with 29 records, labeled "Events/activities about which I felt negative, angry, or remorseful," whereas Subject D labeled a category with two records as "Events related to my drive home and back during the bad storm." Also, none of the subjects created exactly the same categories, in spite of the fact that they shared similar environments and presumably common experiences.

Two related topics were evident in all of the subjects' records. These synthesizing topics were "People" and "Work/school." Neither topic was formulated by the subjects. Nevertheless, they represent a higher-order level of organization. Although "People" and "Work/school" were less differentiating among events than the subjects' groupings, they allowed us to classify the majority of all the records.

An independent judge used the category labels given by Subjects A, C, and D to sort records by topic. Subject B's records were sorted on an event-by-event basis because her chosen category descriptions in themselves did not include the topics of interest. Between 65% and 81% of each subject's records were associated with either "People" or "Work/school." Three subjects (A, B, & D) reported more events involving people (49–63%) than work or school (16–26%); the opposite was found for Subject C, with 33 records categorized as "Assignments/research (school)," and only 12 events dealing in some way with people.

Once the sorting task was completed, an example was selected randomly from the categories with the most frequent and infrequent numbers of records. These records are presented in Table 4.6 for each subject by category.

Frequency of occurrence within categories was chosen as another means of describing daily events. How often a particular kind of activity occurs and is reported as memorable could inform us about the types of materials used to construct self-knowledge. Our belief is that the perceived nature of everyday events determines what self-referenced information eventually gets stored in memory. That different people share similar social environments could lead to commonality in certain aspects of self-knowledge, and individual differences might be found to the extent that people develop unique personal histories.

One hypothesis is that frequently occurring events are schematized whereby typical event features are abstracted and condensed. Memory for those repetitious experiences is thus driven more by generic knowledge than by some direct-access mechanism – repeated encounters of similar kinds blend, and the details of any single event may be forgotten or considered exemplary of recurring episodes (Barclay, 1986; Brewer,

1986; Linton, 1986; Slackman & Nelson, 1984). Infrequent events may be more readily forgotten than repeated events (because of decay or interference; cf. Kinsbourne & George, 1974; Shepard, 1967), or recollected with apparent vividness, as with flashbulb memories (Brown & Kulik, 1977; Rubin & Kozin, 1984). Therefore, an event that occurs with a high frequency may be recalled *less* precisely (i.e., more errors in memory for actual details than with a remembered low-frequency event). Plausible, but inaccurate, information may be imported for a high-frequency event through elaborations consistent with the person's general knowledge of the kind of details likely to be associated with that happening (Graesser, Gordon & Sawyer, 1979; Graesser et al., 1980).

Limited indirect evidence consistent with these notions was gleaned from the subjective rating and category data. Memorability and frequency ratings were negatively correlated ($r = -.31, p < .001$). Records rated as more memorable were also seen as occurring less often, whereas events judged as frequently recurring were seen as less memorable. Moreover, events classified as "Frequent" (Table 4.6) on the basis of category membership were not rated as memorable ($X = 3.61$) as events occurring less frequently ($X = 4.16$).[3] These data, though not showing an actual correlation between memorability and frequency, suggest that these subjects at least believed in this hypothesized relationship.

Considering the evidence reported on event categories, it appears that subjects organized their records into meaningful groups without difficulty. The wide variations in categories formed and numbers of events per group possibly reflected differences in life histories. The meaning of daily events may be derived by linking those happenings to evolving life themes, and valid category membership cannot be determined without privileged knowledge of those themes (Csikszentmihalyi & Beattie, 1979; Neisser, 1987). Individual differences arose because different levels of analyses were used in creating categories. Most relatively memorable events involved other people and work or school – especially people for most subjects. These topics could easily change depending on the kinds of activities engaged in. Activities can certainly reflect occupation, age, or time of the year records are kept. In addition, events reported more often were viewed as less memorable than infrequent occurrences.

Recognition-memory results. Recognition data for individual subjects are given in Table 4.7. The dependent variable was number of items correct at delay intervals of 1–14 and 32–45 days separated by item type. Correct responses were hits for originals and rejections of foils. Subjects identified their own original records with nearly perfect accuracy at both delay intervals. Only Subject C missed a single original item on the first posttest. A similar ceiling effect was found for the rejection of other-foil items. Subjects A and D were 100% correct on

Table 4.6. *Examples of frequent and infrequent items by category for each subject*

Subject	Frequent			Infrequent		
	Category	F		Category	F	
A	Time with my lovers	16	——— and I cooked a really good breakfast, the works. It was nice 'cause I hardly ever get a real breakfast – bacon, eggs, mushrooms, bagels, and juice. I definitely made some good choices last night, but hopefully I won't have such cognitive dissonance next time.	Visit with kids at nursery school	1	I just went to the ——— Nursery School where I used to work. ——— was to type my paper so I had to drop it off. I enjoyed seeing some of the kids that are still up there. Kids get so excited when they haven't seen you for a while. It was fun to visit.
B	Events/activities which made me feel good-positive	36	I took ——— to pick up a friend in band – and to school – they were boarding buses to go downtown to march and play. I enjoy watching ——— interact with other people – she's extremely perceptive, still a little unsure of herself but, I think, finally finding a niche for herself at ——— Except for the fact that we are holding out on Guess Jeans, she seems to be adjusting.	Events/activities about which I was neutral	5	Wanted to run this morning but ——— needed a ride to school with her poster board . . . I was partly relieved to have an excuse – it's so difficult to get out in the cold to run. Still it makes me "feel" better, healthier. Try for tomorrow.

C	33	Assignments/research (school)	I gave up on my statistics assignment and can't get past 1a) and I've tried everything except lighting a candle. It is very frustrating. I've been trying to get something reasonable on paper.
	4	Family	I read a letter from my dad. It was really a good letter – very funny. He told me a couple of cold weather stories and encouraged me to insulate the windows with shrink plastic. He doesn't know that our landlord has taken care of it. I felt good; I look forward to his letters every week. They are rarely dull and always well thought-out.

D	16	Events that involve having to deal with annoying people who I want something from and therefore, can't say what I'd really like to, i.e., people in positions of authority who shouldn't be: 4 classes
		
		  1. Parking
		  2. _____ people
		  3. Bank
		  4. Maintenance
			Burned out decorator light bulb in the bathroom, called rental agency to replace it. The receptionist tried to tell me it was my responsibility. I asked when they had changed their policy – they had always replaced specialty bulbs before. She got rather flustered. And then said they would be out to fix it. _____'s people can be so annoying. I won't be surprised at all if they show up with the wrong bulb, although I explained the type needed.

	2	Weather-related. All concerned with the extreme cold this winter.	Got up. Figured weather would be bad and didn't want to be late for _____ meeting with _____. Heard the weather report and temp. Decided meeting wasn't all that important and that it would be safer to stay home.

Note: For subjects A, C, and D there was more than one infrequent category; thus, a representative example was selected randomly.

Table 4.7. *Individual-subject data (number correct) by item type and delay interval*

| Subject | Delay (days) | Item type | | | |
		O	MSSD	MDSS	OF
A	1–14	10	5	9	10
	32–45	10	1	8	10
B	1–14	10	2	8	8
	32–45	10	3	9	7
C	1–14	9	1	10	10
	32–45	10	0	7	9
D	1–14	10	0	9	10
	32–45	10	2	9	10

Note: Maximum possible score was 10; O – Originals; MSSD – Meaning Same, Style Different; MDSS – Meaning Different, Style Same; OF – Other-Foil.

both posttests. Subject B falsely recognized two other-foil items at the 1–14-day delay interval, and three after 32–45 days; Subject C erred only once on Posttest 2. The relatively high false alarm rate for Subject B could reflect the fact that her environment more closely resembled that of the person whose records were used as other-foil items than did the environments of the other subjects. People obviously can recognize events from their own lives and separate those events from what happens in another person's life – at least to the extent that there is no overlap in particular life experiences.

The performances on original and other-foil items replicate our earlier findings (Barclay & Wellman, 1986). However, these results must still be interpreted in the context of performance on MDSS and MSSD items – foils designed specifically to examine the nature of memory for self-referenced information. Subjects responded with high accuracy in rejecting MDSS items (86% correct rejections) – foils with the meaning changed – as nonevents. But all subjects also incorrectly accepted MSSD foils as original records at a high rate (82% false alarms); they had great difficulty distinguishing stylistically changed items from original records if meaning was held constant. The fact that there was little variance in the correct rejection of MDSS items – those designed to be low in semantic similarity to original records – clearly shows that meaning plays a key role in recognition memory of everyday life events, as it does in the accurate and inaccurate recognition of other types of stimuli. In comparison with the false alarm rates recorded by Barclay and Wellman (1986), it seems that the MDSS items used here were less semantically similar to original records than were the foil-evaluation and foil-description items used in that earlier work.

The apparent discrepancy between false alarm rates on MDSS (approximately .14) and foil-evaluation and foil-description items reported by Barclay and Wellman (1986) merits two additional comments. First, the posttest delay intervals between record keeping and testing were shorter in the present experiment than in the Barclay and Wellman (1986) study; thus, the lower false alarm rates found here may simply reflect less forgetting than that previously reported. Second, MDSS items were manufactured (a) to be as different from originals in meaning as possible (yet plausible) as an index of the limits of the semantic-similarity dimension and (b) to address the possible criticism that the false alarm effects reported by Barclay and Wellman (1986) were artifactual. In a sense, the results from the present study, together with those from our previous work, represent an ordinary scale of semantic similarity: (high similarity) – MSSD > foil evaluation and foil-description items > MDSS > other-foil items – (low similarity).

An Item Type (4: original, MDSS, MSSD, other-foil) × Delay (2: 1–14-, 32–45-day delay intervals) χ^2 test on the average frequencies of correct responses was significant, $\chi^2_{(7)} = 47.60$, $p < .01$.[4] The decomposition of this overall effect revealed a reliable difference among item types, $\chi^2_{(3)} = 44.40$, $p < .01$, and no delay effect or interaction between delay and item type. The largest single χ^2 was for MSSD items. Other statistical tests using signal-detection procedures (Grier, 1971) were consistent with these χ^2 analyses. A $d' = 2.65$ indicated subjects could distinguish among item types, although a powerful response bias was also found, $B'' = -.93$.

These results show that semantic properties of everyday autobiographical events are cognitively represented – a finding similar to that reported by Sachs (1967) for impersonal stimulus materials. The actual phrasing of an event description in an original account was not remembered and did not predict the subjects' ability to differentiate MSSD foils from actual records. Performance patterns on MSSD items suggest that people do remember the events that have occurred in their lives, but forget how those events were actually reported. This effect, of course, may reflect more memory for diary entries than event memory. Memory for everyday life events is not necessarily reproductive in nature; if it were, our subjects would have correctly rejected MSSD items more frequently than they did. It is nonetheless a bit surprising that subjects did not detect the syntactic changes in their writing styles on MSSD items.[5] The complementary findings associated with MDSS items lend the stronger support to the view that event memory often is driven by access to self-knowledge used to derive the subjective interpretation of past life happenings. If that were not the case, then subjects should have falsely recognized MDSS foils at a higher rate (or at chance levels), because the meanings of the test items themselves could be taken as the intended meanings of original records.

A semantic-similarity effect – increasing congruence in meaning between foils and original records leads to higher false recognition rates – is evident in these new results if it is assumed that MDSS items marked the low-similarity end of the semantic-similarity dimension, and MSSD items the high-similarity end. The bias exposed by signal-detection analyses suggests that subjective familiarity with different item types was an important factor in overall performance (Locksley, Stangor, Hepburn, Grosovsky, & Hochstrasser, 1984; Mandler, 1980). Such a bias, along with the capability to accurately identify original records, may be driven by learned expectations consolidated as self-schemata (Barclay, 1986; Markus, 1977). Self-schemata, acquired through varied experiences with many different, but often routine, daily events, function to set likelihood parameters for estimating the acceptability of some "event" as one's own memory.

There was no indication of schematization over the 45-day delay interval, nor was there any effort made to systematically vary fine gradations of semantic similarity to expose such a process. We suspect further that this delay interval was too short to find either increased error rates on foil items, especially on MDSS items, or forgetting of originals. Manipulating meaning and style produced ceiling and floor effects, respectively, on both posttests, perhaps masking potential changes in memory for everyday events. Errors might increase on MDSS items with extended delays, but no performance differences on MSSD items would be expected, nor could they be detected using our methodology. People would probably forget even more about how they phrased records as time passed. Because the false recognition rates on MSSD items and correct rejections of MDSS foils were so high, it is conceivable that many sematic aspects of everyday events are coded in memory at the time records are written, or shortly thereafter. Meaningful event characteristics may be used then to mediate reconstructive memory at the time of testing (Bransford & Franks, 1971). Determining when and how meaning is assimilated and determining possible mechanisms underlying the encoding and retrieval of self-referenced information await future research (Loftus & Loftus, 1980; Tulving & Pearlstone, 1966).

Significant life episodes and memory for everyday events and activities: A controlled case study

Rationale

Central to the study of memory is an analysis of elements that influence what information and how much information is remembered (Bransford, 1979; Glass, Holyoak, & Santa, 1979; Neisser, 1976). How information is processed at encoding and retrieval and what ocurs before, during, and after acquisition are two important elements (Atkinson & Shiffrin, 1968; Bartlett, 1932; Craik & Lockhart, 1972; Morris, Bransford, & Franks, 1977). The quality of information elaboration (Anderson & Reder, 1978; Bransford, Franks, Morris, & Stein, 1978; Craik & Tulving, 1975) and interference (Postman & Underwood, 1973; Tulving & Psotka, 1971; Underwood, 1957) influence both the amount and kind of information remembered. Memory accuracy improves with semantically congruent elaborations, at least to the extent that such elaborations make target information distinct and relevant, and common incidents of interference in retention result from information being processed before (proactive) and after (retroactive) the acquisition of to-be-remembered material. A traumatic episode may also interfere with access to information stored prior to its occurrence, as in systematized amnesia, or may disrupt memory for information available at the time of the experience and for material processed before and after the trauma, for example, anterograde amnesia (Loftus & Burns, 1981; Nemiah, 1979).

Less dramatic instances of elaboration and interference in ordinary memory are experienced throughout almost everyone's life. Unremarkable, yet traumatic, experiences such as witnessing an accident or coping with illness, death, or dying do not usually elicit pathological states such as hysterical amnesia. Just the opposite is true in many cases: traumatic events may be recollected with apparent vividness and detail (Baddeley & Wilson, 1986; Brown & Kulik, 1977; Butters & Cermak, 1986; Kihlstrom & Evans, 1979; Loftus, 1979; Neisser, 1981; Rubin & Kozin, 1984).

Widely, if not universally, encountered life-cycle traumas could affect memory for everyday events, because mental upset tends to be stressful and constrains attention to a narrow information domain for some extended time period. Although considerable basic and clinical research has demonstrated the influence of elaboration and interference on memory, there are no studies, to our knowledge, exploring the impact of unexpected traumatic experiences on memory for everyday events in which accurate records of events were available before and during the traumatic episode. The extent to which such traumas interfere with memory, or enrich and enhance memory through elaboration, is an open question. In this controlled case study, verifiable daily records were collected from a person whose mother died of an accident during data gathering. Because this person was a subject in the first data-collection wave, a matched control subject was available who recorded events over the same time period, but did not experience trauma.[6] This chance occurrence afforded an opportunity to study everyday memory in the flow of personally significant and emotionally charged life-cycle changes (Bronfenbrenner, 1979).

Method

Records from these two subjects were used to construct a cued-recall test given approximately 85 days after data collection was completed. Subject T, who experienced the trauma, wrote 35 records before abandoning record keeping. Records 1–14 were of experiences resembling those described in detail earlier. Record 15 recounted the phone conversation informing her that her mother had had a serious accident and was hospitalized. All but 2 of the remaining 20 records were of events concerned with the hospitalization, treatment, and health status of her mother. The control subject (NT = no trauma) recorded a complete set of 70 records; only the first 35 were used for cued recall, thereby maintaining a comparable delay interval in regard to T.

Nine records were selected at random from those written before T received word of her mother's accident and 10 were selected after that time. Record 15 was included purposefully to complete the test-item pool. For NT, 20 items were selected randomly from the 35 available records, with the restriction that chosen items corresponded temporally to those sampled for T. Memory cues were derived from the event portion of the record (Tables 4.8 and 4.9). These cues were presented at testing without regard for the chronological order in which original records were written.

T and NT were tested individually within 4 days of each other. Testing lasted 30–45 min, and each subject was told she would be given cues taken from her own records to aid recall. No foil cues were used. Instructions stressed recalling as much information as possible and indicating when no more material could be remembered. The cues and the subject's elicited recall were both given orally and tape-recorded.

The tape recordings were transcribed, and independent judges rated the amount of gist, elaboration, and exactness recalled. Comparative judgments were made between original written records and the transcribed verbal protocols. Eight different judges (16 total) scored each subject's 20 protocols using 7-point scales to rate each dimension (gist, elaboration, exactness). The essential aspects of the judges' task were to decide the extent to which each protocol (a) captured the gist, theme, or fundamental meaning written about (7–high gist similarity), (b) elaborated on the original information, given the elaborations were consistent with the meaning of the original record (7–high in amount of elaboration), and (c) replicated exactly, in words used, and word and sentence order, the written record (7−exact duplicate). Ratings were averaged over judges for each of the three dimensions and separately by record. A total memory score (TMS) for each record was then calculated by summing the averaged ratings for gist, elaboration, and exactness. T and NT also rated their own protocols for the same dimensions. Correlations between the judges' ratings of gist, elboration, exactness, and the TMS and those done by T (gist = .85, elaboration = .86, exactness = .89, TMS = .92) and NT (.78, .70, .70, .70, respectively) were all positive and significant ($p < .01$, for all).

Results

TMSs were used to identify typical and atypical recall protocols. Minimum (typical) and maximum (atypical) mean deviations were found between individual-record TMSs and the grand mean (over all records) TMS. Typical and atypical records were located for T, both before and after being told about her mother's accident; for NT, a single example of each protocol type was found. Record 15 was not included in these calculations. T's unique records are shown in Table 4.8, and NT's in Table 4.9. Original records are shown for comparison. All cued-recall analyses were doine using the verbal protocol ratings. Statistical comparisons were not made between written and verbal recalls.

T's subjective ratings for record 15 revealed the shock of being told about the accident. The event was rated highly memorable (7) and personally significant (7), very infrequently occurring (1), unique (1), and unfulfilling (1), but somewhat expected (5), because her mother had a history of less serious accidents, although this particular incident was dissimilar (1) to others in the past, and highly emotional (7).

Comparisons were made of correlations between the grand mean TMSs and the overall mean subjective ratings of the nine events written before the initial trauma with those (10 records) recorded afterward. The only significant relationship uncovered for items written before the trauma was between frequency and memory for Subject T ($r = -.70, p < .05$). Recall was poorer for items rated high in perceived frequency than for those rated low. After the trauma, T's actual recall correlated with memorability ($r = .87, p < .01$), personal significance ($r = .87, p < .01$), frequency ($r = -.70, p < .05$), typicality ($r = -.62, p < .05$), and similarity ($r = -.73, p < .05$). In contrast to earlier recorded events, episodes associated with the trauma were rated higher in memorability (4.22 before vs. 5.60 after), personal significance (3.22 vs. 5.60), and emotionality (4.00 vs. 5.60) and lower in frequency (3.44 vs. 2.20), surprise (3.33 vs. 3.10), and similarity (4.22 vs. 1.90), and five of these dimensions were reliably associated with later recall in anticipated direction. NT's recall

Table 4.8. *Typical and atypical items for subject T occurring before and after experiencing a traumatic episode*

Item	Events/activities occurring *before* traumatic episode		Events/activities occurring *after* traumatic episode	
	Typical	Atypical	Typical	Atypical
Original	The pants I ordered from Spiegal finally arrived after being back-ordered for a month. They were 9/10 tall and way too big. I guess I really have lost weight. They forgot to enclose a return label so I had to call them for the return address as well as order a new pair – bothersome and disappointed.	Talked to —— about a Spring teaching slot as well as the Summer slot. Had to re-point out that I have no support over the summer – he'd forgotten again. He gave me the evening —— section. Will give me the opportunity to teach a new course.	Finally got to talk to —— alone. I'm glad she's —— been with Dad and —— and ——. Apparently the damage is much worse than Dad would indicate or admit but still not sure.	Talked to Dad – He's been at the hospital pretty much all day. While Mom's far from safe, things are looking up. The Dr.'s are keeping her drugged (paralyzed) and she's on total life support. They'll start bringing her out and letting her systems take over for short periods of time on Saturday. She may not be on her own totally for as long as another 2 weeks. Pupils are reactive and she looks better. There's hope.
Recall	[cue: "Pants you ordered from Spiegal."] Oh. That was so frustrating. To finally get those. I had ordered them because I was going to that New Year's Eve party at ——'s, and I couldn't afford to get a new sweater this year; so I decided, well I'd just get a new pair of pants to wear with the old sweater that I had, that I hadn't worn for a couple of years. And, I ordered a size 9 tall; and when I got them, they came . . . you probably could	[cue: "Talking to —— about Spring teaching."] Oh. Teaching lists came out and —— for—got again that I don't have support over the summer. That the —— grant doesn't go through the summer and, he had only put me down for teaching one course in the Summer term, so, I went to put in a request as early as possible, that I have something else to teach as well, so I could eat over the summer. At first he didn't remember that I was, . . .	[cue: "Finally got to talk to ——."] OK. That was, I think, later in the day after I got to the hospital, and really found out the seriousness of the situation; realized that my father had kind of selectively been hearing all the positive aspects and kind of magnifying those, such as, we're not sure, she has a 50/50 chance for survival, she could even end up coming through this with very, very little impairment, when what was really going on was	[cue: "Your dad called after he had been at the hospital all day."] Is that on Thursday? ["Yes."] OK. He sounded almost exhausted. He explained what they have been doing with my mother, that they had her on, as he put it, some paralyzing drug that stopped her body functions and everything was being handled by machines. And, that all of the signs that they had seen that day were positive. Her pupils were responsive, she was fairly

have fit at least two of me in them. There were . . . I have never put on a pair of pants that were so long; and it wasn't just the legs . . . it, like they came up to here [pulls hands up to neck to show how long the pants were] and moved independently of my body, so I had to pack them up and send them back, ["Do you remember anything else?"] I remember thinking, "Maybe I can alter them," and decided, we're talking basic reconstruction here. (5.13, 4.50, 3.13)

only had that one course. And I got one of those looks like, "Are you after more money, or why are you asking this?" And, I had to remind him that the _____ grant doesn't support the students over the summer. So then he was, like, 'Oh, fine, what do you want to teach?" You know, "I have these courses open, and when do you want to teach?" He basically gave me my pick out of what was available. So, I got a section of _____ which is something that I've been interested in teaching for a while. (6.13, 5.38, 5.25)

that she never stood a chance from the start. And, things were very serious, and it was through talking to _____ that I finally got a sense of what was going on; and could weed through what my father had said and what she had said, and the nurse — we had either just talked to the nurse, yeah, I think we had just talked to the nurse that had been with my mother all week, and _____ filled in the details. And, just kind of remember getting this really cold feeling inside; kind of realizing it was just a matter of waiting, and that there wasn't any hope and that, I think — at the same time both of us realizing — that the biggest task was gonna be kind of to prepare Dad for what was going to happen because he seemed to be ignoring all of the negative aspects of the situation. I think we were standing right outside the ICU unit in a little kind of area. They have two sets of doors that you have to go through, and we were standing between those doors — so, it was private and very quiet. And that's all I remember. (4.75, 6.00, 3.13)

stabilized; and they were even talking about taking her off of the drug for short periods, within 24 to 48 hours, something like that, to let her own body start taking over; and he really, at that point, thought that she was going to make it; and that everything was going to be OK. And, was just so happy, and so relieved, and I remember at the same time we, I just said look, this is the third time she has done this to herself. It's obvious that this is not in her control, no matter how much she claims it is, and we're going to have to do something. And we talked a little bit about trying to get her into some sort of a program like at _____. Hospital; to take care of this because, at this rate she was going to kill herself with this. But, the whole conversation was upbeat, he was extremely hopeful, and things were really looking good, and I can remember getting off the phone and just, not being able to work because I was really happy at that point too. (6.13, 6.38, 4.75)

Note: Numbers in parentheses are average ratings for gist, elaboration, and exactness, respectively.

Table 4.9. *Typical and atypical items for Subject NT*

Item	Typical	Atypical
Original	Woke up very early after a very restless night – replaying the movie "Testament" over and over . . . seems so possible. I sometimes wish I had the capacity to be oblivious to the threats "out there." I felt depressed about my sense of powerlessness.	I was supposed to have lunch with ___ ___, who I enjoy. But due to the long morning in ___ and the gnawing guilt about my backlog of work awaiting me, I decided not to take the time for lunch. However, when I called to cancel, ___ had already gone to lunch so I was able to make it appear that he had forgotten. He called and we rescheduled. I resolved to take time for people I enjoy.
Recall	[cue: "Woke up early from a restless night."] I probably said I . . . got up, did laundry or read . . . ["Can you remember anything else?"] Oh! I remember. It was the night after we watched the movie about the nuclear disaster . . . and how I couldn't sleep the whole night . . . 'cause I kept dreaming about it, and thinking about it, and I woke up early after that . . . still uneasy about it . . . realizing what a real possibility it was. (4.13, 4.88, 2.75)	[cue: "You were supposed to have lunch with ___ ___."] I was supposed to have lunch with ___ . . . and I had so much to do that I was, was going to call him and make up an excuse for not being able to come, and when I called, he had already gone out to lunch so he had forgotten, and I was relieved 'cause I didn't have to make up an excuse and could make it look like it was his fault . . . , he had forgotten . . . but that's when I made my resolve . . . I think . . . to, to take more time to do things like that . . . and not always to feel I didn't have time to do anything. . . . (6.50, 2.63, 6.00)

Note: Numbers in parentheses are average ratings for gist, elaboration, and exactness, respectively.

Table 4.10. *Average scores for gist, elaboration, and exactness for subjects T and NT before and after T's traumatic episode*

	T		NT	
Measure	Before	After	Before	After
Gist	4.01	4.82	4.24	4.05
Elaboration	4.57	5.49	4.17	3.83
Exactness	3.08	3.38	3.33	3.21

Note: Nine records "before," and 11 "after."

did not correlate significantly with any of her subjective ratings. It may be that certain life events must reach some personally defined importance threshold before self-assessed event characteristics become predictive of memory.

Now consider the judges' memory ratings indexed by gist, elaboration, and exactness. These data are summarized in Table 4.10. Examination of the three measures for T and NT shows little difference in memory for everyday events and activities written prior to T's traumatic experience. The subjects were comparable in how much they remembered; therefore, there was no indication of interference or amnesia associated with this particular traumatic event. Also, NT actually remembered a little less information about events recorded relatively recently than more remotely occuring incidents. Further, the rated degree of exactness was the lowest of all measures for both subjects, supporting the view that relative to gist, many details of everyday happenings are forgotten. Of most interest are the uniform changes from before to after experiencing an upsetting event seen in all measures of T's memory. Significant increases were found in the amount of gist [$t(158) = -2.44, p < .02$] and elaboration [$t(158) = -2.77, p < .01$], whereas exactness improved only slightly. Again, exactness was low relative to the amounts of gist and elaboration in recall. Events carrying great personal and emotional significance appeared to capture T's attention instead of blocking access to memories for comparatively trivial past experiences. Significant events, such as the death of a parent, may function as temporal markers, segmenting one's life into subjectively determined and conceptually distinct modules.

Altogether, these results indicate that the meaning of events makes up a large portion of one's everyday autobiographical memories; otherwise, fewer elaborations and amount of gist would have been recalled along with more precise recollections. Ordinary traumatic experiences do not necessarily interfere with recollections of daily events occurring before the upset. Memory for events surrounding the episode are enhanced. This enhancement could be due to the mental effort and concentration allocated to such experiences. These experiences seemingly benchmark one's personal history (Neisser, 1982). In the case study reported here, that benchmark links T's own life history with that of her family. She shared the experience of her mother's accident and eventual death with her family and through that experience wove her own history with that of a larger social unit. Personally upsetting events are surely richer in content than repetitious daily happenings. They usually involve novel experiences, perhaps forcing one to reflectively process novel and unfamiliar information in situations loaded with emotion and uncertainty— all of the ingredients needed to produce cognitive disequilibration and promote cognitive change.

Conclusion

Most everyday events and activities are fairly mundane. They are typically routine happenings, not seen as especially memorable, although they are perceived as relatively self-fulfilling. And yet, ordinary everyday events may yield up much of the raw materials from which self-knowledge systems are constructed and reconstructed. The recognition data reported here were consistent with this view. Although recognition memory for routine daily events was excellent, such accuracy must be interpreted together with inaccuracy in memory for nonevents similar in meaning to what one expects to have occurred in the past. In the context of false recognitions of nonevents, performance on original records overestimates true memory accuracy. One's beliefs in the accuracy of one's own autobiographical memories may reflect the fact that the information remembered is the only information available to remember at the time of retrieval. Accounting for both accuracies and inaccuracies in memory for autobiographical material leads to the notion that much event knowledge is represented schematically, not necessarily in a form isomorphic with actual happenings. Thus, the apparent memory accuracy found for original items and foils in which the meanings of events were changed, and the inaccuracies found for items in which meaning was held constant but writing style was varied reflect performances driven by the same underlying cognitive structure. That structure is knowledge about what events and activities are likely occurrences given accumulated life experiences—a kind of self-schemata and contemporary ego perspective (Greenwald, 1980; Markus, 1977; Nigro & Neisser, 1983).

People grouped their own memories into conceptually distinct and coherent categories of meaningfully related events. It is very unlikely that outside observers could retrieve those same categories unless the observers and subjects shared identical social and interpersonal environments (cf. Nisbett & Ross, 1980; Nisbett & Wilson, 1977). The point is that much autobiographical information is privileged, and seemingly isolated events in a person's life make sense only because those happenings fit into a broader framework of self-knowledge. Cohesiveness in this framework, like a sense of self (Erikson, 1968), comes about through knowledge of one's own life history (Linton, 1986; Neisser, 1987, 1986). This historical aspect should make some self-knowledge privileged, fostering individual differences in autobiographical memories.

Authenticity judgments about test items as original records were based largely on semantic properties. This ability once more demonstrates access to self-knowledge. Imagine, for instance, someone else taking the same recognition tests as one of these subjects, even if the two persons have had similar life experiences. The gist of routine everyday events and activities presumably is stored as generic schemata and is used to reconstruct plausible past experiences or make likelihood estimates about the originality of proposed remote events. People certainly did not remember exactly how they reported events. Recognition memory for the syntactic form of the records was much worse than that for the meaning, even after a short delay (cf. Brewer, 1986). These results complement other work showing that accuracies and inaccuracies in autobiographical memories result from judgments about what could or should have happened in one's life (Barclay & Wellman, 1986), not necessarily from direct access to event representations isomorphic with the way in which events actually occurred. As in literary autobiography, the person's integrity is maintained in self-recollections (Mandel, 1972). It is unimportant for one's memories to reproduce the past as long as truth is maintained. It is in this way that autobiographical memories can serve an allegorical purpose (Howarth, 1974).

Memory for events constituting a traumatic episode was enhanced compared with what was remembered about less significant events, even though memory for the exact wording of original records was relatively poor. Elaborations in recall could indicate more and semantically richer processing of mentally upsetting material. The trauma did not interfere with memory for events occurring either before or during the episode. The trauma was an especially salient happening, richly encoded and elaborated in recall.

Although our current analyses are at the event level, surely events make up larger self-defined conceptual structures, such as self-scripts, extendures, or life themes (Csikszentmihalyi & Beattie, 1979; Linton, 1986). These structures may be, as Neisser (1986) and Linton (1986) suggest, nested such that events at a molecular level are composed of elements and specific details that sum to form molar units such as life themes. These themes could then be organized around a sense of self (Erikson, 1968; Greenwald, 1980).

In sum, this chapter reflects our attempts to conduct ecological studies of everyday autobiographical memories (Bruce, 1985; Neisser, 1978, 1985). We approached the task by describing the material to be remembered: self-selected and naturally occurring daily events and activities. Factors thought relevant to how such material might be coded in memory were manipulated. Our hope was to discover what the real environment offers as memorable events and activities and how individuals recollect those happenings. We assumed that most autobiographical memories were by-products of purposeful activities and practical experiences and that these memories were the raw materials out of which one constructs a sense of self.

NOTES

1 Two waves were run because of the time-consuming nature of collecting records daily from the subjects and writing foil items.
2 A plus sign indicates a rating above the subject's mean for that dimension; a minus sign indicates a rating below the mean.
3 In order to increase the number of infrequently occurring events considered, event categories with eight or fewer records were analyzed in addition to those presented in Table 4.6.
4 These analyses were done only as rough approximations of type I errors, because the frequencies were nonindependent and so few subjects were tested.
5 It might be argued that the MSSD effect arose because subjects did not understand the test instructions; i.e., they did not know that items with stylistic changes should be rejected as nonevents. Two subjects, however, after reading the instructions, asked the experimenter if "exact duplicate" meant writing style as well as gist – the answer was yes. These subjects performed no differently than the subjects not given this information directly.
6 The person experiencing the trauma eventually withdrew from the first-wave data collection, but was included again in the second wave.

REFERENCES

Anderson, J. R., & Reder, L. M. (1978). An elaborative processing explanation of depth of processing. In L. S. Cermak & F. I. M. Craik (Eds.), *Levels of processing and human memory* (pp. 385–403)., Hillsdale, NJ: Erlbaum.
Atkinson, R. C., & Shiffrin, R. M. (1968). Human memory: A proposed system and its control processes. In K. W. Spence & J. T. Spence (Eds.), *The psychology of learning and motivation: Advances in research and theory* (Vol. 2, pp. 89–195). New York: Academic Press.
Baddeley, A., & Wilson, B. (1986). Amnesia, autobiographical memory, and confabulation. In D. C. Rubin (Ed.), *Autobiographical memory* (pp. 225–252). Cambridge University Press.
Barclay, C. R. (1986). Schematization of autobiographical memory. In D. C. Rubin (Ed.), *Autobiographical memory* (pp. 82–99). Cambridge University Press.
Barclay, C. R., & Wellman, H. M. (1986). Accuracies and inaccuracies in autobiographical memories. *Journal of Memory and Language, 25*, 93–103.
Bartlett, F. C. (1932). *Remembering: A study in experimental and social psychology.* Cambridge University Press.
Bransford, J. D. (1979). *Human cognition: Learning, understanding and remembering.* Belmont, CA: Wadsworth.
Bransford, J. D., & Franks, J. J. (1971). The abstraction of linguistic ideas. *Cognitive Psychology, 2*, 331–350.
Bransford, J. D., Franks, J. J., Morris, C. D., & Stein, B. S. (1978). Some general constraints on learning and memory research. In L. S. Cermak & F. I. M. Craik (Eds.), *Levels of processing and human memory* (pp. 331–354). Hillsdale, NJ: Erlbaum.

Brewer, W.(1986). What is autobiographical memory? In D. C. Rubin (Ed.), *Autobiographical memory* (pp. 25–49). Cambridge University Press.

Bronfenbrenner, U. (1979). *The ecology of human development: Experiments by nature and design.* Cambridge, MA: Harvard University Press.

Brown, R., & Kulik, J. (1977). Flashbulb memories. *Cognition, 5*, 73–99.

Bruce, D. (1985). The how and why of ecological memory. *Journal of Experimental Psychology: General, 114*, 78–90.

Butters, N., & Cermak, L. S. (1986). A case study of the forgetting of autobiographical knowledge: Implications for the study of retrograde amnesia. In D. C. Rubin (Ed.), *Autobiographical memory* (pp. 253–272). Cambridge University Press.

Craik, F. I. M., & Lockhart, R. S. (1972). Levels of processing: A framework for memory research. *Journal of Verbal Learning and Verbal Behavior, 11*, 671–684.

Craik, F. I. M., & Tulving, E. (1975). Depth of processing and the retention of words in episodic memory. *Journal of Experimental Psychology: General, 104*, 268–294.

Csikszentmihalyi, M., & Beattie, O. V. (1979). Life themes: A theoretical and empirical exploration of their origins and effects. *Journal of Humanistic Psychology, 19*, 45–63.

Csikszentmihalyi, M., Larson, R., & Prescott, S. (1977). The ecology of adolescent activity and experience. *Journal of Youth and Adolescence, 6*, 281–294.

Davydov, V. V., Zinchenko, V. P., & Talyzina, N. F. (1983). The problem of activity in the works of A. N. Leont'ev. *Soviet Psychology, 21*, 31–41.

Erikson, E. H. (1968). *Identity: Youth and crisis.* New York: Norton.

Flavell, J. H., & Wellman, H. M. (1977). Metamemory. In R. V. Kail & J. W. Hagen (Eds.), *Perspectives on the development of memory and cognition* (pp. 3–33). Hillsdale, NJ: Erlbaum.

Freud, S. (1960). *The psychopathology of everyday life.* New York: Norton. (Original work published 1914).

    (1950). Screen memories. *Collected papers* (Vol. 5). London: Hogarth Press. (Original work published 1899).

Glass, A. L., Holyoak, K. J., & Santa, J. L. (1979). *Cognition.* Reading, MA: Addison-Wesley.

Graesser, A. C. (1981). *Prose comprehension beyond the word.* New York: Springer-Verlag.

Graesser, A. C., Gordon, S. E., & Sawyer, J. D. (1979). Recognition memory for typical and atypical actions in scripted activities: Tests of a Script Pointer + Tag hypothesis. *Journal of Verbal Learning and Verbal Behavior, 18*, 319–332.

Graesser, A. C., Woll, S. B., Kowalski, D. J., & Smith, D. A. (1980). Memory for typical and atypical actions in scripted activities. *Journal of Experimental Psychology: Human Learning and Memory, 6*, 503–515.

Greenwald, A. G. (1980). The totalitarian ego: Fabrication and revision of personal history. *American Psychologist, 35*, 603–618.

Grier, J. (1971). Nonparametric indexes for sensitivity and bias: Computing formulas. *Psychological Bulletin, 75*, 424–429.

Gusdorf, G. (1956). Conditions and limits of autobiography. In G. Reichenkron & E. Haase (Eds.), *Formen der Selbstdarstellung: Analekten zu einer geschichte des literarischen Selbstportraits.* Berlin: Dunker & Humblot. (Reprinted in Olney, 1980).

Howarth, W. L. (1974). Some principles of autobiography. *New Literary History, 5*, 363–381. (Reprinted in Olney, 1980).

Hudson, J. (1986). Memories are made of this: General event knowledge and the development of autobiographical memory. In K. Nelson (Ed.), *Event knowledge: Structure and function in development* (pp. 97–118). Hillsdale, NJ: Erlbaum.

Kihlstrom, J. F., & Evans, F. J. (Eds.). (1979). *Functional disorders of memory.* Hillsdale, NJ: Erlbaum.

Kinsbourne, M., & George, J. (1974). The mechanism of the word-frequency effect on recognition memory. *Journal of Verbal Learning and Verbal Behavior, 13*, 63–69.

Kruskal, J. B., & Wish, M. (1978). *Multidimensional scaling.* Beverly Hills: Sage Press.

Larson, R., & Csikszentmihalyi, M. (1983). The experience sampling method. In H. T. Reis (Ed.), *Naturalistic approaches to studying sound interaction* (pp. 41–56). San Francisco: Jossey-Bass.

Leont'ev, A. N. (1981). *Problems of the development of the mind.* Moscow: Progress Publishers.

Linton, M. (1975). Memory for real-world events. In D. A. Norman & D. E. Rumelhart (Eds.), *Explorations in cognition* (pp. 376–404). San Francisco: Freeman.

   (1982). Transformations of memory in everyday life. In U. Neisser (Ed.), *Memory observed: Remembering in natural contexts* (pp. 77–91). San Francisco: Freeman.

   (1986). Ways of searching and the contents of memory. In D. C. Rubin (Ed.), *Autobiographical memory* (pp. 50–67). Cambridge University Press.

Locksley, A., Stangor, C., Hepburn, C., Grosovsky, E., & Hochstrasser, M. (1984). The ambiguity of recognition memory tests of schema theory. *Cognitive Psychology, 16*, 421–448.

Loftus, E. F. (1979). The malleability of human memory. *American Scientist, 67*, 312–320.

Loftus, E. F., & Burns, T. E. (1981). *Mental shock.* Paper presented at the 22nd annual meeting of the Psychonomic Society, Philadelphia.

Loftus, E. F., & Loftus, G. R. (1980). On the permanence of stored information in the brain. *American Psychologist, 35*, 409–420.

Mandel, B. J. (1980). Full of life now. In J. Olney (Ed.), *Autobiography: Essays theoretical and critical* (pp. 49–72). Princeton, NJ: Princeton University Press.

Mandler, G. (1980). Recognizing: The judgment of previous occurrence. *Psychological Review, 87*, 252–271.

Markus, H. (1977). Self-schemata and processing information about the self. *Journal of Personality and Social Psychology, 35*, 63–78.

Morris, C. O., Bransford, J. D., & Franks, J. J. (1977). Levels of processing versus transfer appropriate processing. *Journal of Verbal Learning and Verbal Behavior, 16*, 519–533.

Neisser, U. (1976). *Cognition and reality.* San Francisco: Freeman.

   (1978). Memory: What are the important questions? In M. M. Gruneberg, P. Morris, & R. H. Sykes (Eds.), *Practical aspects of memory* (pp. 3–25). New York: Academic Press.

   (1981). John Dean's memory: A case study. *Cognition, 9*, 1–22.

   (Ed.). (1982). *Memory observed: Remembering in natural contexts.* San Francisco: Freeman.

   (1985). The role of theory in the ecological study of memory: Comment on Bruce. *Journal of Experimental Psychology: General, 114*, 272–276.

(1986). Nested structure in autobiographical memory. In D. C. Rubin (Ed.), *Autobiographical memory* (pp. 71–81). Cambridge University Press.

(1987). From direct perception to conceptual structure. In U. Neisser (Ed), *Concepts reconsidered: The ecological and intellectual cases of categorization* (pp. 11–24). Cambridge University Press.

Nelson, K., Fivush, R., Hudson, J., & Lucariello, J. (1983). Scripts and the development of memory. In J. A. Meacham (Ed.), *Contributions to human development* (Vol. 9, pp. 52–70). New York: S. Karger.

Nemiah, J. C. (1979). Dissociative amnesia: A clinical and theoretical reconsideration. In J. F. Kihlstrom & F. J. Evans (Eds.), *Functional disorders of memory* (pp. 303–323). Hillsdale, NJ: Erlbaum.

Nigro, G., & Neisser, U. (1983). Point of view in personal memories. *Cognitive Psychology, 15,* 467–482.

Nisbett, R., & Ross, L. (1980). *Human inference: Strategies and shortcomings of social judgment.* Englewood Cliffs, NJ: Prentice-Hall.

Nisbett, R. E., & Wilson, T. D. (1977). Telling more than we can know: Verbal reports on mental processes. *Psychological Review, 84,* 231–259.

Olney, J. (Ed.). (1980). *Autobiography: Essays theoretical and critical.* Princeton, NJ: Princeton University Press.

Piaget, J., & Inhelder, B. (1973). *Memory and intelligence.* New York: Basic Books.

Postman, L., & Underwood, B. J. (1973). Critical issues in interference theory. *Memory & Cognition, 1,* 19–40.

Renza, L. A. (1977). The veto of the imagination: A theory of autobiography. *New Literary History, 9,* 1–26. (Reprinted in Olney, 1980).

Rubin, D. C., & Kozin, M. (1984). Vivid memories. *Cognition, 16,* 81–95.

Sachs, J. S. (1967). Recognition memory for syntactic and semantic aspects of connected discourse. *Perception and Psychophysics, 2,* 437–442.

Schank, R. C., & Abelson, R. (1977). *Scripts, plans, goals, and understanding.* Hillsdale, NJ: Erlbaum.

Shepard, R. (1967). Recognition memory for words, sentences, and pictures. *Journal of Verbal Learning and Verbal Behavior, 6,* 156–163.

Simon, H. A. (1969). *The sciences of the artificial.* Cambridge, MA: MIT Press.

Slackman, E., & Nelson, K. (1984). Acquisition of unfamiliar script and story form by young children. *Child Development, 55,* 329–340.

Tulving, E. (1972). Episodic and semantic memory. In E. Tulving & W. Donaldson (Eds.), *Organization of memory* (pp. 381–403). New York: Academic Press.

Tulving, E., & Pearlstone, Z. (1966). Availability versus accessibility of information in memory for words. *Journal of Verbal Learning and Verbal Behavior, 5,* 381–391.

Tulving, E., & Psotka, J. (1971). Retroactive inhibition in free recall: Inaccessibility of information available in the memory store. *Journal of Experimental Psychology, 87,* 1–8.

Underwood, B. J. (1957). Interference and forgetting. *Psychological Review, 64,* 49–60.

5

Walking in our own footsteps: Autobiographical memory and reconstruction

ROBERT N. McCAULEY

One of the fundamental issues guiding work on autobiographical memory in recent years concerns the role of higher-order cognitive structures in these recollections. Presumably, the influence of such structures is a matter of degree, depending on such variables as the delay between the remembered event and the memory, the cues available at the time of recollection, and the character of the materials remembered. Boldly or timidly advanced, views that attribute a role to such structures require that at least some features of some autobiographical memories involve not the retrieval of mental copies of the original experiences but rather reconstructions based largely on our general knowledge of related everyday affairs. The teeth in this reconstructionist position show when its partisans employ it to explain even those memories that seem to subjects as if they *did* involve nothing more than the direct retrieval of mental copies.

Until quite recently, Craig Barclay and William Brewer both have defended relatively strong versions of the reconstructionist view of autobiographical memory. Now, apparently, only Barclay does. Both Brewer's chapter and Barclay and DeCooke's chapter respond to challenges to the sort of schema-based approach to mnemonic reconstruction that they have championed in the past. Barclay and DeCooke aim to improve on the previous research in order to offer additional evidence in support of this position. Brewer, by contrast, continues a recent trend toward a more moderate-sounding position (Brewer, 1986). In chapter 3 he is willing only to endorse a "partially reconstructive theory" of autobiographical memory that he contrasts with "strong reconstructive theories" of the sort that Barclay and DeCooke continue to advocate (Brewer, 1986).

Brewer has offered various reasons for his theoretical shift. Initially in chapter 3 he indicates that reservations about evidential and methodological issues motivate his moderation. He holds that too much of the evidence for the reconstructionist position is either anecdotal or concerned with matters (e.g., memory for conversations) that Brewer maintains are not central to the study of autobiographical memory.

126

Brewer raises questions about the use of foils in recognition tests of subjects' autobiographical memories. He argues that the construction of foils for recognition tasks in the examination of autobiographical memory is a very tricky business—for example, in Barclay and Wellman (1986). (Of course, this methodological problem is one of the concerns that Barclay and DeCooke's chapter attempts to address.) It is no problem to construct foils that subjects would reject without hesitation. Unfortunately, though, it is comparably easy to construct foils that involve only minor differences from original records, so that subjects incorrectly recognize large numbers of such foils (as Barclay and DeCooke's chapter ably illustrates). Brewer fears, no doubt, that this would surreptitiously enhance the appearance that autobiographical memories are frequently inaccurate and that they are therefore also frequently reconstructed.

The organization of this chapter is simple enough. In the first section, I discuss Brewer's chapter 3, and in the following section, Barclay and DeCooke's chapter 4. Although the more moderate rhetoric of Brewer's partially reconstructive position is preferable, on consideration of several matters in the final section—

1. the role of inference in autobiogrpahical memory (discussed in the first section),
2. the range of possible views about what constitutes reconstruction in autobiographical memory,
3. the role of cues and foils in the experiments' designs, and
4. the stringency of the criteria that these experiments employ in deciding about the accuracy of their subjects' responses—

these studies do not so obviously support either the strong or the partially reconstructive view of autobiographical memory nearly as clearly as they may seem to initially. In particular, Brewer's study may neither examine "the recent arguments that personal memories are strongly reconstructed" (chapter 3, p. 79) nor clarify the role in autobiographical memory of higher-order cognitive structures nearly as unequivocally as he might have hoped. Both studies, though, provide a wealth of further insights about autobiographical memory, and Brewer's chapter, in particular, constitutes an important beginning in controlled empirical research on the difficult and relatively unexamined topic of memory for thoughts.

Coordination, inference, and memory for thoughts: Comments on Brewer

This section explores two rather general questions about Brewer's chapter 3. The first, treated briefly, concerns the logical problems presented by any request for descriptions of events, actions, and thoughts. The second concerns the role of inference in Brewer's findings on memory for both thoughts and actions.

Brewer clearly recognizes the difficulties that accompany having subjects provide written accounts of randomly sampled events, especially of what they were doing and thinking at the time. The following are just *some* of the logical complications that come to mind:

1. It is a truism that events submit to an infinite number of possible descriptions.
2. Standardized principles for the individuation of events do not exist.
3. Events can have both extremely complex internal structures and comparably complex external relations.
4. Some events are either spatially discontinuous or temporally discontinuous or both. (On items 3 and 4, see Neisser, 1986.)
5. Events can contain multiple actions and thoughts.
6. Items 1–4 are all equally true of actions.
7. Items 1–3 are also equally true of thoughts, and, like events, thoughts may be temporally discontinuous as well.
8. Many thoughts are like actions in a number of respects—for example, when we make decisions.

Brewer discusses items 2 and 3 (as they pertain to actions) under the titles "action hierarchy" and "action instance and action category," respectively, and item 5 under the title "multiple actions." Overall, Brewer's treatment of these issues is commendable both for its candor (e.g., he explicitly admits having no satisfactory solution for the problem of multiple actions) and for its attempt to render the problem of the role of action categories and their instances in autobiographical memory empirically tractable. Although the information that Brewer collected from subjects about both action categories and instances generally showed fairly high correlations, making the distinction was worthwhile in order to learn the fact and because it was action instance frequency that showed the most systematic relation to serial position in subjects' memory for actions in Experiment 1 (see Figure 3.3). It is regrettable (though completely understandable) that Brewer could not address more of the complications listed earlier.

Perhaps the most interesting and most important contribution of Brewer's research concerns his discussion of memory for thoughts and of thoughts as memory cues. The extent of the information he has gathered on these topics is virtually unprecedented. In light of both the complexities these topics raise and the relative scarcity of research on them, it is all the more remarkable that Brewer's experiments yielded systematic results. The remainder of this section includes a brief discussion of some of those special problems with memory for thoughts as a way of introducing a discussion of the implications of the coordination of thoughts and actions for Brewer's results and for his account of the role of inference in autobiographical memory.

Intuitively, memory for thoughts seems to be a more complicated matter than memory for actions. This has a lot to do with all of the traditional problems surrounding analyses of mental goings-on. Thoughts, even quite complex ones, can be fleeting or discontinuous. On the other hand, frequently no *single* moment marks the point at which we have had a particular thought. This only adds to the intrinsic difficulties that surround the individuation and and identification of thoughts.

Much, if not most, of the time our thoughts are propositional. But they need not be. Often our thoughts seem to involve a good deal of visual imagery – for example, in our daydreams and flights of fancy. Does recall of our thoughts require that we reexperience them in the same modality? To remember a thought in propositional form, must we recall the precise proposition, or merely one that has the same meaning? But, of course, the latter possibility raises the exceedingly thorny problem of how we ascertain the meanings of the propositions that we mentally entertain.

No problems have preoccupied 20th-century philosophy more than those that are raised by the so-called referential opacity of the intentional contexts that the propositional attitudes engender. The major issue concerns the fact that most common psychological verbs (such as "believe," "hope," "regret," "remember," etc.) that express attitudes toward propositions produce contexts in which the substitution of coextensive terms for those in the original proposition does not guarantee the preservation of the truth value of the overall psychological claim, even though the new proposition's truth value is the same as that of the original. So, for example, although it may be true that John believes that Davies is the author of *Fifth Business*, it could still be false that he believes that the author of *The Rebel Angels* is the author of *Fifth Business*, even though Davies *is* the author of *The Rebel Angels*. (Note that the epistemic honor we typically associate with the term "remember," as opposed to "believe," should carry no weight in an argument about reconstruction in memory.) The problem, in short, is that we lack a convincing semantics of these psychological states. Without one, there is little hope of justifying any but the most demanding standards in the assessment of memories for thoughts occurring in propositional form – standards that would require the recollection of the precise sentential form of the proposition implicated in the original episode.

It is impossible to remember a thought without rethinking it. The sorts of considerations raised in the previous paragraphs are just some of those that suggest that it is not especially clear how we know when a rethinking is and when it is not also a remembering. Brewer points out in chapter 3 that his thought categories included "categories for *thinking* about past events" (emphasis added). Is it a necessary condition for the remembering of a thought that it result from a conscious search and that the mental experience in question have the appropriate subjective feel, namely that of remembering? Furthermore, often it is only the most loose of associative connections with the current state of the environment that occasions these rethinkings. Is it the absence of an obvious tie to the immediate surroundings that is the crucial evidence that the episodes in question are also rememberings? That hardly seems sufficient.

Brewer distinguishes correct recall of our personal past from inference about it. Because most autobiographical memory does not seem to concern memory for propositions, previous worries about propositional memory surely matter less here. But in the absence of propositions, the notion of "inference" that Brewer employs is also much less clear. The arrangement of Brewer's categories for his data in the tables for Experiment 2 in conjunction with his comments about visual imagery seems to indicate that the lack of detailed visual imagery is at least as important as the *possibility* of drawing inferences to his discussions of his inference category. He also repeatedly suggests that the amount and quality of the visual imagery that accompanies some autobiographical recollection will basically prove proportional to its accuracy (as assessed both by Brewer's independent scoring system and by the subjects' own ratings of their overall memory). Brewer claims that "it appears that knowing what the subject's phenomenal experience is during the recall process may allow powerful predictions about the accuracy of the subject's recall" (p. 68). If we can reexperience the episode in the mind's eye when we are removed in space and time from its actual occurrence, then, presumably, this is the sort of rethinking in autobiographical contexts that is also a genuine remembering and not some inferential ersatz.

But some obvious problems arise. First, the bearing of phenomenal reexperience on autobiographical memories for thoughts is unclear at best – certainly, for the large number of thoughts we have that do not seem to involve *any* sensory or phenomenal features and are thoroughly unrelated to our current activities and surroundings. Second, and more important for what is to come in the remainder of this section, what is to count as inference here? Does it follow from the fact that a mental experience (e.g., a recollection) has prominent phenomenal properties that neither the experience as a whole nor any of its phenomenal properties have arisen on the basis of inference? Can our *reexperiencings of the phenomenal properties of events* result from inferential processes?

To give the issue more focus, it might be better to ask about the features that distingush nondemonstrative inference from cued recall in autobiographical memory. If they do not know the information available to the subject (especially idiosyncratic information about the subject that may be available to the subject only and that may serve as the basis of inferences that the experimenter would never guess), how can experimenters definitively decide about the status of subjects' responses on this count? Brewer's findings suggest that knowledge of subjects' "visual phenomenal experience" and of their ratings of their overall memory, that is, their perceptions of the accuracy of their various particular memories, may be the key (regardless of the actual accuracy of the memories in question). The questions in the following paragraphs are not intended to obliterate Brewer's suggestion, but rather to point to a systematic feature of his analysis that bears directly on the issue of reconstruction in autobiographical memory.

First, Brewer does not provide the entire picture with respect to the question of accuracy. Brewer's various comments about his subjects' visual phenomenal experience and the accuracy of their responses, their assessments of their overall memory, and his arrangement of his response types in Tables 3.8 and 3.9 all suggest that the responses he calls "inferences" are not very accurate. Yet his general discussion of that category of response types indicates that they were always accurate or at least nearly so! Simply from the fact that we may later draw inferences in thinking about our pasts, nothing follows about the inaccuracy of the conclusions that we arrive at. Brewer never denies this, but neither does he discuss or resolve the problem it presents for his analysis (e.g., the claim on p. 69 concerning the relation of measures of subjects' phenomenal experiences and the accuracy of their responses).

Brewer's data on visual phenomenal experience in Table 3.14 demonstrate the overwhelming relationship between this variable and subjects' ratings of their overall memory. However, the ability to use the data in the two subsequent tables (Tables 4.15 and 4.16, which deal with the relationship of visual phenomenal experience for response types for actions and for thoughts, respectively) to distinguish inferences and correct recalls is less marked. Brewer does not explore the underlying relation of his subjects' measures of overall memory and of their visual phenomenal experience to one another. The two may seem to correlate so well simply because his subjects may be employing the same theory that Brewer entertains in assessing mnemonic accuracy.

If, as it seems for a large part of our knowledge about ourselves, we can move freely between "phenomenal" and propositional representations, then the view that visual reexperience of an event could not result from inferential processes, because the "conclusion" of the "inference" in question was not entertained propositionally, is a somewhat misleading position to adopt. Presumably, Brewer accepts the crucial assumption that it is the antecedent of the previous conditional claim. If he does not, then he certainly is operating with an unusual notion of "inference." Because many personal memories involve visual reexperience, it does not follow that they cannot result from inferential processes, unless, of course, such ready "translations" between these two mental modalities are impossible. However, they do not seem to be impossible! Unless some experience is wholly unlike any other (whatever *that* might mean), not only are we able to imagine something about what our "phenomenal experience" might be like exclusively from some description of that experience, but we often do so automatically. (This is an important part of the reason why reading the novel is almost always a more enriching experience than seeing the movie.) This ability is not affected by the fact that the description may be the conclusion of some inference (demonstrative or not). In short, subjects' phenomenal experience in memory often may result from their use of inference.

Where this may matter most for Brewer's findings is with those events his subjects remembered where thoughts and actions were coordinated. People often can remember both their thoughts and actions better if the two are coordinated with one another. If they have access to one, frequently they can infer the other, especially if the action is one that requires some concentration. Often we *must* think about what we are doing, and we know most of the sorts of things we do that require such coordination. Many features of Brewer's data suggest that such relationships between thoughts and actions had a prominent role in his subjects' performances. If subjects employed their knowledge of these relationships *inferentially*, then Brewer may have underestimated the amount of inference going on and overestimated the divergence of "correct" recalls and inferentially based responses.

The findings in Experiment 1 are consistent with this proposal. Brewer notes in his discussion of Experiment 1 that coordination intercorrelates significantly with the significance of thoughts and actions and the goal-directedness of actions. It also significantly intercorrelates with memory for actions. It is the findings in Experiment 2, though, that seem to support this view outright. Brewer repeatedly emphasizes that in Experiment 2, cue types showed extremely strong effects in memory for the events and that action cues and thought cues were consistently the two best cues overall and *the best cues for one another* (see Tables 3.6 and 3.7 and Figures 3.7–3.9). Brewer also highlights the fact that actions were the *only* cues that were much good at all in aiding subjects' recall of thoughts. Furthermore, Brewer points out that "for some action categories there are relatively J-shaped distributions of cooccurring thoughts," which result, presumably, from the need for coordinating the actions and thoughts in question. In illustrating this phenomenon, Brewer employs his *most frequent* action category, namely, "writing – academic" (Table 3.10). Finally, Brewer also states that "on accuracy of recall . . . the thoughts associated with the action show a mean of 1.6 for correct action recalls and a mean of 1.0 for omitted action recalls." It seems that for any event, the correct recall of actions was strongly related with the correct recall of thoughts.

Brewer discusses the effectiveness of these cues in terms of "the distinctive path to the memory representation" that they constitute, and he proposes to explain their relative distinctiveness in terms of "the structure of these subjects' lives" (p. 58). But in the case of thought and action cues especially (but not exclusively), the question is whether or not subjects proceed down that path to their memory representation by inferential means more often than Brewer seems to allow. Of course, this bears directly on the amount of reconstruction that goes on in autobiographical memory. An underestimate of inferentially based responses, presumably, produces an underestimate of reconstruction.

Events, schemata, and constructions: Comments on Barclay and DeCooke

At the conclusion of their review of previous research, Barclay and DeCooke state that Barclay's earlier work (Barclay & Wellman, 1986, in particular) suffered from a confound of semantic and stylistic considerations in the construction of foil records for recognition tests. Consequently, it remained unclear whether it was semantic (as opposed to stylistic) similarities between authentic records and foils that persuaded subjects to identify so many of the foils as their own. Barclay and DeCooke designed the central study of chapter 4 precisely to address this methodological shortcoming in that earlier research.

This section opens with a pair of comments about the design of that study, the second of which concerns these more sophisticated attempts to construct foils. Subsequent comments in this section explore more theoretical issues that Barclay and DeCooke's discussion of schemata raises.

The assumption in Barclay and DeCooke's chapter 4, in Brewer's Experiment 1, and in other research on autobiographical memory that subjects can at the end of a given day (let alone during the moments immediately following some event) reliably assess which events will prove the most memorable of that day means that these studies will miss factors that sometimes can have an important effect on the contents of autobiographical memory and, consequently, miss the dynamics underlying some of our salient personal memories. The events from our past that we work the hardest at remembering are not infrequently a function of our subsequent aims and purposes. Furthermore, what determines those aims and purposes depends in part on the course of subsequent events. In fact, *how* and *what* we remember about an event often are functions of new information and new theories (broadly speaking) that we acquire *after the fact*—indeed, sometimes a *long time* after the fact. For example, learning much later that somebody is a committed Marxist, a devout Catholic, or a doctrinaire Freudian may highlight any number of details *in memory* about our previous interactions with that person and render those details salient not only in all future interactions but also in all subsequent recollections of past interactions. This is not to suggest that these considerations are overwhelming, but only that they are relevant. (The data in both chapters do not indicate that they played a significant role.) Still, what proves "most memorable" sometimes depends on both our aims and purposes in calling events to mind and the new information that we have at our disposal that informs those aims and purposes (McCauley, 1984).

Barclay and DeCooke have improved on the design of Barclay and Wellman (1986) in certain respects. In contrast to the study by Barclay and Wellman (1986), where foils could be perfectly consistent with the original records, here the semantically discrepant foils involve outright inconsistencies, whereas stylistically variant foils do not. (Note, however, that the apparent deletion of material in the stylistically variant foils in this study still involves *semantic* differences from the original records to which they are related.) The semantically discrepant foils in this study (i.e., the "Meaning Different, Style Same" foils) are, then, an improvement over the "foil description" items from Barclay and Wellman (1986). However, they and the other-foil items in this study share a problem with the "foil other" items of Barclay and Wellman (1986). Because defensible foils must be *plausible* fabrications, and because many of the experimental materials seem to have involved *relatively routine* events in subjects' lives, in neither study can they with complete confidence count as incorrect recognitions the subjects' false positive responses to at least some of these descriptions. Both the data reported in Table 4.3 (on the memorability, typicality, and "similarity" of the events in question) and Barclay and DeCooke's summary comment that, their instructions notwithstanding, most of the events on which their subjects reported "simply were not seen as that memorable" are evidence that routine events were not rare among their experimental materials. In such routine cases, the fact that the experimenters' records did not indicate that the subjects had such experiences does not guarantee that the subjects had, in fact, not had experiences on other occasions sufficiently similar to the foils to justify their responses. This is just one of the problems with the experimental control of foils for which there is no easy solution.

This is no problem whatsoever, though, if the assumption throughout both studies was that the subjects' task was either to recognize that they had made a record of the particular event in question or to recognize *their particular records of the events* (as opposed to the events those records documented). Unfortunately, the design of Barclay and DeCooke's study in which the *style and syntax of the records* was a crucial variable suggests that what they were actually tapping was something closer to rote linguistic skill rather than autobiographical memory in general or personal memory in particular. (For a discussion of these categories, see Brewer, 1986.)

Other problems with their construction of foil items for recognition tests support this view. For example, Barclay and DeCooke found that "recognition memory for the syntactic form of the records was much worse than that for the meaning [of those records], *even after a short delay*" (p. 121, emphasis added). The differences in style in the "Meaning Same, Style Different" example supplied in Table 4.2 involve shifts in sentence order, deletion of some material, and alternative lexical items. However, as previously noted, it is not obvious that the deletion of material constitutes a primarily stylistic alteration so much as a semantic one. Also, the general syntactic forms of the sentences are the same, and the lexical alternatives are terms of comparably high frequency. So, again, it is unclear how much such minor revisions in the style of subjects' records of events test their memory for those *events* in contrast to their memory for rather minor syntactic and lexical details of their *specific records of the events*.

Sometimes Barclay and DeCooke seem to appreciate this point, and sometimes not. For example, although they concede that the results of their research "may reflect more memory for diary entries than event memory" (also see Barclay, 1986, pp. 91–92), they also instructed subjects "to identify items that were *exact duplicates* of reported events or activities" – in contrast to exact duplicates of *their reports of* reported events. This infelicity is obviously inconsequential (see chapter 4, note 5), but it does seem symptomatic of an important tension in the interpretation of this research.

Barclay and DeCooke's results clearly indicate that personal memory is not the same thing as rote linguistic skill. It is much less obvious that they have revealed very much about either the processes or the representations that underlie the bulk of our personal memories. Their suggestion that they have turns on an argument that employs a largely irrelevant assumption that also, as it stands, may well be false. After acknowledging that laboratory research has consistently shown that subjects remember extremely little about the surface structure of their verbal reports, Barclay and DeCooke state in chapter 4 that for personalized diary records . . . it is not yet known whether or not the manner in which some event is written affects one's memory for that event. . . . One's writing style, like the brush strokes of the artist, can be used to detect the authenticity of the artifact, especially if the person making the judgment created the object being judged. (p. 97)

These considerations are largely irrelevant, because even if memory for precise details of written reports is a legitimate part of autobiographical memory, it is probably not a prominent one. Most people write about their lives infrequently, at most, and rarely is it the precise syntactic or stylistic details of such written records that are crucial. In addition, though, their claim is empirically suspect. If they confined their research to professional writers' recognition of their written records, then the analogy with artists would make more sense. The point is that typically only *experts* reliably judge matters of this sort. Although people usually have little difficulty identifying their own handwriting, most neither employ obviously distinct prose styles nor qualify as experts at recognizing them, even if they do employ them. The assumption that most subjects are especially suited to make such judgments is dubious and, minimally, requires support.

Pending that support, it seems that Barclay and DeCooke have not shown why false alarms (motivated by minor stylistic differences) in recognition tests for subjects' *reports about events* are sufficient to justify broader conclusions about either the processes or the forms of representation in autobiographical memory. This consideration – as well as

1. their recogntion that subjects may not have been completely forthcoming about their most memorable events,
2. the proposal, advanced earlier, that subjects may not have very good grounds for assessing an event's memorability when they reflect back on it quite soon after the fact, and
3. the suggestion that the events studied may not be "the most memorable events of our days" –

raises the question of how directly Barclay and DeCooke's results pertain to what Brewer (1986) calls "personal memory" (at least). Brewer describes personal memories in terms of "a partial reliving of the original experience that is typically accompanied by "strong visual imagery" (Brewer, 1986, p. 30).

Although Barclay and DeCooke have little to say about imagery, their claim that "autobiographical memories are not wholly episodic, but on many occasions they may appear to be" (p. 92) would seem to indicate that they intend to address many of the phenomena that fall under Brewer's notion of personal memory. In contrast to Brewer, who has talked of partially reliving the original experience, Barclay and DeCooke are inclined to account for whatever accuracies their subjects demonstrated in terms of their *reconstruction* of past events in memory—reconstructions that are "mostly congruent with . . . self-knowledge, life themes, or sense of self" (p. 92). Schemata generally and "self-schemata" in particular provide the fundamental framework for their proposal. They claim that "schematization theoretically accounts for the formation of generalized knowledge structures" (p. 95; see also Barclay, 1986, p. 83). This is important because Barclay and DeCooke suggest that their results lend support to a reconstructive view of autobiographical memory and to an account of that reconstruction in terms of schemata. In addition to addressing that question, in part, the remainder of this section includes three additional questions about various claims Barclay and DeCooke make in behalf of schemata.

1. The first set of questions serves only as a reminder (because these are questions that have been nearly universally postponed in the literature of experimental psychology). All proponents of schemata face the problem of explaining their *origins*. Barclay and DeCooke construe these cognitive structures as the results of constructive processes. Schemata are built from the bottom up, and their construction exemplifies an "allegorical strategy [that] conveniently summarizes the meanings of many different, but conceptually related, life experiences" (p. 92; see also Brewer, 1986, p. 31). However, obvious questions arise. How does this process of construction come about? What guides it? What are the bases of the allegorical and conceptual relations that organize events under the appropriate schemata?

These are standard problems with all schema-based approaches to cognition. In discussions of autobiographical memory, though, they assume a special poignancy. Discussions of *autobiographical* memory that rely on assumptions about our "sense of self," "self-knowledge systems," "life themes," "self-scripts," "self-schemata," and "contemporary ego perspectives" in order to specify the underlying organization of events in autobiographical memory arguably risk begging the crucial question. Empirical evidence of the influence of such structures that will not involve very small circles logically is necessary to prevent that suspicion (Brewer, 1986, p. 34).

2. As Barclay and DeCooke note in chapter 4, it would seem to follow from an emphasis on schematization that the categories into which subjects classified their records would be intimately involved with the schemata that inform them. Would not these schemata be the single most important factor in subjects' underlying organization of events? But, of course, if so, why did subjects employ such widely varying numbers of categories (and widely different categories) in this task, especially given the apparent similarities of their lives? Generally, this point concerns the evidential relations between these categories and the operative schemata.

If schemata are as cognitively prominent as so many theorists have alleged, would not this sort of task have been tailor-made to exhibit that fact?

3. The final question concerns the processes employed in autobiographical recollection. Barclay and DeCooke (p. 92) emphasize that autobiographical memory "often is a *constructive* and *reconstructive* process." Two comments are in order. First, neither of these notions is the same as either Brewer's notion of partially reliving the original experience or the classical notion of *retrieving* a memory trace. On Barclay and DeCooke's view, this constructive and reconstructive process condenses the vast amount of details about particular experiences into abstract schemata of types of events and activities. Both the frequency of an event type and the delay between the event and the memory of it are generally proportional to the probability that generic knowledge of events (captured in schemata) plays a role in their recollection (Barclay, 1986, p. 89). Consequently, as Barclay and DeCooke suggest, subjects remember high-frequency event types less precisely and less accurately, especially as delays increase. (Brewer's data also support this contention.)

The second comment concerns the fact that it is not completely clear how "reconstructive" exclusively schema-driven recollections are. Such memories, by definition, do not involve attention to the details of any particular episode. They may involve plausible *constructions* that result from consultation with the available schemata, but they certainly do not appear to involve the reconstruction of the particular event in question. Presumably, it is precisely on such grounds that Barclay maintains that "memories for most everyday life events are, therefore, transformed, distorted, or forgotten" (Barclay, 1986, p. 89).

Arguably, the notion that most autobiographical memories are *constructed* makes sense of subjects' poor performance in distinguishing their actual reports of events from stylistically variant foils that had the same meaning, and this is the hypothesis that Barclay and DeCooke seem to adopt. However, the fact that in *most* situations (not just those involving autobiographical memory) people do not usually remember the linguistic details of either their utterances or their prose seems a more straightforward account.

A reconstruction of the debate about reconstruction

The overall goal of this chapter is to evaluate how the findings in these studies bear on the debate about the role of reconstruction in autobiographical memory. Unfortunately, once we sort through the role of foils in their designs, the criteria employed in each study to gauge subjects' performances, and their respective views of reconstruction, it is difficult to ascertain how much their findings clearly support one view over the other, especially because the authors of both chapters see their results as corroborating their respective positions. In light of some of Brewer's general theoretical comments, it is also unclear how much of the difference between these two views is substantive rather than rhetorical.

That they differ rhetorically is beyond question. Brewer defends what he calls "a partly reconstructive view of autobiographical memory" that holds, among other things, that "recent personal memories are reasonably accurate copies of the individual's original phenomenal experiences" (p. 87). In contrast, Barclay and DeCooke hold that "accuracies and inaccuracies in autobiographical memories result from judgments about what could or should have happened in one's life" (p. 121) and that "in memory for autobiographical material . . . much event knowledge is represented schematically, not necessarily in a form isomorphic with actual happenings" (p. 120). Of course, these differences are not the sorts of things that readily lend themselves to exact measure. Still, it is clear that strong reconstructive values should predict more reconstruction and errors in autobiographical memory than less strong views. Consequently, it is in Barclay and DeCooke's interest to downplay the general accuracy of peoples' recollections, and in Brewer's interest to emphasize it.

The sorts of events examined in each of these studies certainly *did* contribute to the force of these researchers' tests of their hypotheses about the level of subjects' reconstructions in autobiographical memory. Barclay and DeCooke studied events deemed "most memorable," which, contrary to their "strategic" interest, should have aided subjects' memory, whereas in his Experiment 2 Brewer looked exclusively at randomly sampled events that, contrary to his "strategic" interest, should have depressed subjects' performances. The results of Brewer's Experiment 1 indicate that these two forms of data collection have a genuine influence on subjects' performances. Still, Barclay and DeCooke admit that "most everyday events simply were not seen as that memorable" (p. 101) and report that subjects rated nearly a fifth of the events in question as "very easily forgotten" (Table 4.3).

Otherwise, though, at least relative to one another, the designs and analyses of these two studies tended to bias either the results or the descriptions of the results in the direction of their respective favored hypotheses. One of the most obvious differences in the designs was Barclay and DeCooke's use of foils and Brewer's failure to use foils.

Brewer's method of assessing the accuracy of subjects' recollections (exclusively according to what Barclay and DeCooke would term "semantic" criteria) is appropriate in the study of autobiographical memory. (This is in contrast to Barclay and DeCooke's concerns with quite specific linguistic features of subjects' written reports.) Still, the *complete* absence of foils in Brewer's designs (which is a function of the special character of the experimental materials he chose to use) inevitably limits the strength of the conclusions that Brewer's recognition data might seem to suggest.

Brewer's random data collection notwithstanding, his subjects seemed to possess only slightly less startling autobiographical memory than did subjects from previous studies. Brewer points out that though his subjects' performances seem comparable to those in other studies, his methods and materials differ so much from those of previous studies that, ultimately, it is difficult to compare them. Surely, the two most important differences were that most of the events Brewer's subjects had to remember were *randomly selected* rather than self-selected and that Brewer's data included subjects' performances on memories for *thoughts*. Still, these two considerations notwithstanding, in both experiments Brewer's subjects seemed to demonstrate a remarkable ability to recognize their reports as their own, even after a considerable delay in Experiment 1 (see Figures 3.2 and 3.5). As Brewer says in describing his recognition data from both of his experiments, as well as the recall data from Experiment 2, the forgetting curves are quite "shallow." The questions that arise concern what roles (if any) the absence of foils and the presence of subjects' original reports *in their own handwriting* had in inflating these results.

Brewer's concerns about the construction of foils in previous research are appropriate. Nonetheless, from the fact that it is difficult both to construct foils and to interpret their impact on subjects' performances, it does not follow that the project should be abandoned. Questioning Barclay and DeCooke's success in ascertaining the proper criteria for forging interesting foils and, consequently, their success in *actually* forging them does not require rejecting their general goal of attempting to construct adequate foils.

Brewer cites Wallace (1980) in support of his position. What Wallace shows, in short, is that subjects' performances on tests of recognition memory yield recognition failures whether or not the design employs distractors. Wallace also argues that unless the use of distractors is considerable and involves frequent presentations or the distractors themselves are especially similar to the target items, little evidence exists that they have a substantial effect on subjects' responses; that is, commonly, the level of recognition failures is only slightly higher than it would be if the experiments had not used distractors at all. However, in not a single study that Wallace cites did subjects' performances on recognition tests without distractors fall below those on tests with distractors. (Because an effect is not substantial does not mean that it is not significant.)

Wallace's arguments do seem largely to exonerate Brewer's foil-free designs, at least for the data that were collected randomly. However, two further problems remain. First, in light of Brewer's claim that "recent personal memories are reasonably accurate copies of the individual's original phenomenal experiences," he should have observed nearly perfect responses on his recognition tests of recent events. He does indicate that subjects' performances were good, but without a clearer statement of his own position it is unclear what would count as *good enough* in the absence of foils.

It is another feature of Brewer's design, though, that made it virtually impossible for him to construct foils of any sort – adequate or not – and only compounds the problems with interpreting his results as they bear on both the question of reconstruction in autobiographical memory and the question of the value of foils in the design of studies of recognition memory. In both the recognition and the cued-recall phases of his experiments, Brewer presented subjects with *their own handwritten reports* of the events, memory for the contents of which Brewer was testing. Brewer twice mentions the possible aid to memory that writing down a description of an event may have on memory for that event, but he virtually ignores concerns about the influence of subsequently seeing what they have written down on subjects' memory for the events and on their assessments of their memory for the events. At least three consequences of the decision to use subjects' own handwritten reports may have affected Brewer's results. In all three cases the possible effects surely would have been to enhance subjects' performances on the memory tests.

First, the design needlessly permitted the possibility of subjects confusing either recognition of and assessment of recognition of the record or recall of and assessment of recall of the act of recording with memory for and assessment of memory for the recorded event to be remembered. If either of these confusions arose, then Brewer is incorrect in claiming that it follows from the fact that his subjects "were reading parts of response cards filled out in their own handwriting" that "it is obvious that [they] were rating their current recognition memory for the events" (p. 34). Second, in the cued recall phase of Experiment 2 the appearance of the script (including such things as the style of the handwriting, the type of writing instrument employed, and the color of ink) could provide clues about the event to be remembered. Third, in both the overall memory assessment in Experiment 2 and in the recognition phases of both experiments, the mere familiarity of the writing *guaranteed* that subjects' recognized the *records* as their own. As Brewer notes in his discussion of Experiment 1 it is obvious that his subjects were not rating their "belief about whether or not the event had actually ever occurred in the past" when they judged their recognition memory after the fact (p. 34). The point here is not that Brewer's design included no foils, but that subjects were immediately aware that *there could be no foils*. Even if they thought that the experimenter might want to "trick" them, they knew that he could not. (Surely, it is not out of the question to suspect that seeing their own handwritten records has a different effect on subjects than do assurances from an experimenter that no distractors have been included among the test items.)

The question is whether or not the opportunity to see their own handwritten records illicitly enhanced either subjects' apparent memory or their actual memory for the events as well as their confidence ratings about their memory. Typing out the records would have eliminated these possible problems and would fulfill a necessary constraint on the construction of any adequate written foils.

Although Barclay and DeCooke did use foils, their criterion for evaluating their subjects' responses similarly guaranteed that their subjects would perform less impressively. They required subjects to recognize virtually *all of the linguistic details* of their records in the "Meaning Same, Style Different" condition. Their findings add to the ample body of research that indicates that under normal circumstances people do not remember the syntactic and lexical details of their comments or others' comments. Remember Neisser's report (1981) on John Dean's performance. Instead, they are much more likely to remember the gist of such comments. But, of course, *that* is the source of the problem with constructing adequate foils. On the one hand, if foils involve substantial alterations in meaning from the descriptions of the original events, then they may be easily unmasked. On the other hand, if they employ quite minor differences in meaning, the foils may not differ enough semantically. The fear, of course, is that all the action turns on the construction of the foils. However, given Brewer's emphasis on "the individual's original phenomenal experiences," it would seem that the sort of inconsistency about phenomenal details between original descriptions and foils in Barclay and DeCooke's "Meaning Different, Style Same" condition (as exemplified in their Table 4.2) is not a bad start.

Brewer's criteria for evaluating his subjects' responses tend to magnify the appearance that they performed quite well (and hence were less likely to have reconstructed their memories). His forgetting curves were "shallow," in part because of his decision to use his "relatively conservative criterion of forgetting" in his reports on his subjects' recognition-memory scales. Brewer claims that this conservative criterion "seemed desirable," but he gives no reasons for this claim, and from the standpoint of a concern with rigorously testing his hypothesis, its desirability is a matter of some dispute. Similarly, in his ratings of recall accuracy in Experiment 2, Brewer's criteria seem comparably friendly to his position.

Sometimes Brewer seems to want it both ways. In his description of recall types, he states, for instance, that "while *there was a high percentage of errors overall*, most of those errors were due to *retrieving* the wrong event or inferring the wrong event. *There were very few overt errors*" (p. 55, emphasis added). It is not surprising, though, that in his attack on the strongly reconstructive view, Brewer ultimately emphasizes the accuracy of his subjects' performances. Certainly, his decision not to count "wrong event" items as "true errors" (because they seem to involve *retrieval* errors only) sharpens this impression. On the basis of this and similar decisions, he finds that only 1.5% of the errors were "true errors."

It is unlikely that advocates of the strong reconstructive view would be impressed by this analysis. Too much seems to turn on how "true errors" are defined. Furthermore, Brewer's implicit distinction between errors of reconstruction and errors of retrieval is question-begging in this context. Presumably, advocates of the strong reconstructive view would be inclined to reject that distinction. Barclay and DeCooke emphasize that autobiographical memory results from "a *constructive* and *reconstructive* process." If so-called retrieval errors are neither errors of construction nor errors of reconstruction, then how much *stronger* than Brewer's view is Barclay and DeCooke's view of "construction and reconstruction" in autobiographical memory? Not unreasonably, a strong reconstructivist is likely to count any errors as true errors. So, of the 531 responses reported in Brewer's Tables 3.8 and 3.9 that were not "omits," the strong reconstructivist is likely to count at least 216 (40.6%) as true errors.

However, errors are not the only relevant items in an attempt to ascertain the extent of reconstruction in autobiographical memory. The issue is how much reconstruction is going on, not how much incorrect reconstruction is going on. Brewer reports that another 15.8% (84) of the items involved inference, which is surely a reconstructive process as well. So, using Brewer's account of things alone, the strong reconstructivist can make a plausible case that at least 56.4% (300 of 531) of the memories reported involve reconstruction. Furthermore, if the argument in the second section about the role of inference in memory for coordinated actions and thoughts has any force at all, then Brewer may well have *underestimated* the number of his subjects' responses that involved inference and hence reconstruction.

Brewer's own comments (p. 80) about the accuracy of his subjects' responses complicate things even more! He attributes their *accuracy* to the fact that his subjects reported largely about routine events where "many schema-based reconstructions would tend to give correct responses, not errors." So it seems that Brewer is willing to account for *many of his subjects' accurate recollections* in terms of (schema-based) reconstructions. On the other hand, Barclay and DeCooke concede that they have shown only that people forget how they reported events. They have not provided convincing evidence that people forget the events reported! They state that "performance patterns on MSSD items suggest that people do remember the events that have occurred in their lives, but forget how those events were actually reported" (p. 111).

In the light of these considerations, and on the assumption that Barclay and DeCooke do not insist that *every* memory is a schema-based reconstruction, that is, that at least some nonnegligible percentage of our memories involves mnemonic processes that are more direct (in some sense), it is not overwhelmingly obvious how much the strong and the partial reconstructive positions, ultimately, differ.

NOTE

I wish to thank Gene Winograd and Dick Neisser for their comments on an earlier draft of this chapter. I also wish to express my gratitude to the Emory University Research Committee and Emory College for their support of this research.

REFERENCES

Barclay, C. R. (1986). Schematization of autobiographical memory. In D. Rubin (Ed.), *Autobiographical memory* (pp. 82–99). Cambridge University Press.

Barclay, C. R., & Wellman, H. M. (1986). Accuracies and inaccuracies in autobiographical memories. *Journal of Memory and Language, 25,* 93–103.

Brewer, W. F. (1986). What is autobiographical memory? In D. Rubin (Ed.), *Autobiographical memory* (pp. 25–49). Cambridge University Press.

McCauley, R. N. (1984). Inference and temporal coding in episodic memory. *Behavioral and Brain Sciences, 7,* 246–247.

Neisser, U. (1981). John Dean's memory: A case study. *Cognition, 9,* 1–22.

    (1986). Nested structure in autobiographical memory. In D. Rubin (Ed.), *Autobiographical memory* (pp. 71–81). Cambridge University Press.

Wallace, W. (1980). On the use of distractors for testing recognition memory. *Psychological Bulletin, 88,* 696–704.

6

Memory observed and memory unobserved

LARRY L. JACOBY

In his book *Memory Observed* (1982), Neisser claimed that almost all interesting questions about memory have been ignored by experimental psychologists. The conference that is documented by this book was meant to help remedy this situation by launching an ecological approach to memory research. Contributors were invited to attend the conference because their research was considered ecologically valid. When I received my invitation, I viewed this with some misgivings, because I identify with the "establishment" memory researchers who apparently have done uninteresting work. Also, my research addresses different issues and, perhaps, is less clearly ecologically valid than is the research other contributors are reporting here. However, I gained some comfort by noting at least a superficial similarity between the ecological approach to memory research and the approach advocated by functionalists such as Dewey (1910). The approaches agree in their claim that the functions of memory must be viewed as allowing adaptation of an organism to its environment and in their preference for talking in terms of processes or mental operations rather than in terms of mental structures. Most of the research of the early functionalists would seem to meet Neisser's criteria for ecological validity, although they conducted their research in the laboratory as well as in natural contexts. The advantage that I gain by noting these similarities is that the functionalists provide an excellent example of the coordination of laboratory research and ecological concerns. Not only did they avoid the excesses later shown by the behaviorists, but their approach was so loosely organized that I have no problem fitting in.

I begin by briefly contrasting questions about memory that have motivated my research with those highlighted by Neisser. Next, I provide an example to illustrate differences between the "structuralist" view of memory that has dominated cognitive psychology for the past several years and the functionalist view that has guided my research. I then give an overview of my recent research to further illustrate the types of questions that I think are important to ask about memory and its functions.

145

In *Memory Observed,* Neisser emphasized the importance of studying remembering in natural contexts. The majority of the papers that he chose as satisfying his criteria can be described as investigations of autobiographical memory, that is, investigations of factors influencing the ability of people to recall or recognize events from their own past. The topic of autobiographical memory was also the dominant theme of our conference. The function of memory that is highlighted by investigations of this sort is that it allows one to be aware of and communicate with others about one's personal past. Although memory clearly does serve this function, it also serves other functions that are equally important but are not accompanied by awareness of the past.

The most dramatic examples of unaware uses of memory come from experiments revealing functions of memory that are preserved by amnesics. Very dense amnesia is the most striking symptom of the Korsakoff syndrome. My favorite example of memory preserved by a Korsakoff patient comes from a story told by Bruce Whittlesea. Before coming to McMaster University as a graduate student, Bruce encountered a Korsakoff patient while working in a hospital. The patient seemed unable to remember anything from his recent past. Bruce saw this as an ideal opportunity for a man with a limited repertoire of jokes. He reasoned that it should be possible to repeatedly tell the same joke to the patient and get a laugh every time. The first time he told his joke he was reinforced by the patient's laughing. When he told the same joke a day or so later, the patient did claim not to have heard the joke before. However, rather than laughing, the patient told Bruce that the joke was just "dumb," not funny. The patient's memory was apparently sufficient to allow him to anticipate the punch line, spoiling the joke, although he was unable to recall or recognize the joke as one that he had previously been told. A book edited by Squire and Butters (1984) includes several chapters that provide reviews of more formal experiments that reveal functions of memory that are preserved by amnesics.

These unobserved or unaware uses of memory are also evident in the performance of normals. Let me give a commonplace example as an attempt to show the pervasiveness of effects of this sort. Our choice of words during a conversation often seems to be influenced by the particular words used by others involved in the same conversation. At a meeting of a grant-selection committee that I recently attended, one member of the committee described a proposal as being "trite." Later in the same meeting, another member of the committee, discussing a different proposal, described the applicant as proposing to use "trite and true" procedures. This substitution of "trite" for "tried" was clearly unintended by the speaker. He was unaware of the substitution until it was signaled by the laughter of other members of the committee. Similar to the dissociation shown by amnesics, memory for the prior encounter with the word influenced later performance, with the use of memory being unaccompanied by either awareness of the past or intent. I shall later review research to show that memory for a prior presentation of an item can also influence its later perception and interpretation and that these effects can be independent of a person's ability to recognize the item as having been previously presented.

A popular account of dissociations of this sort is to claim that unaware uses of memory rely on a memory store separate from that used in performance on tests of autobiographical memory. Tulving (1983) has claimed that performance on tests of recognition memory or recall relies on episodic memory, whereas unaware uses of memory rely on semantic memory or some third memory system. Cohen and Squire (1980) also assume that two memory stores or types of representation are involved, but they identify aware uses of memory with declarative memory, and unaware uses with procedural memory. As an alternative, I have emphasized differences in the retrieval requirements of tasks and also stressed the importance of encoding–retrieval interactions. Arguments against the proposal of separate memory stores have been presented at length elsewhere (Jacoby & Brooks, 1984; McKoon, Ratcliff, & Dell, 1986). Rather than repeat all of those arguments here, I use an example from the history of psychology to illustrate two different sets of assumptions about the functions served by memory for particular prior events. Although the example deals with judgments of weight, the alternative sets of assumptions correspond to those that have been used to describe the relationship between aware and unaware uses of memory.

Marbe was a member of the Würzburg school and was interested in judgments of weight. By the structuralist account that was dominant at the time, differences in weight were judged by forming an image of a first weight that was lifted, forming an image of a second weight that was lifted, and then comparing the images to decide which of the two weights was the heavier. Marbe noted that when he judged weights, he had no awareness of comparing images; rather, the judgment of heavier or lighter seemed to be immediate when the second weight was lifted. This observation led to discussions of "imageless thought" and "determining tendencies" (Schultz, 1981, pp. 81–83). An account that is consistent with those notions appeals to differences in the adjustment of the musculature required to lift a weight. Consider a simpler case where the musculature is adjusted to support an object placed in the hand, and the first object is then replaced by a second object without the musculature being readjusted. If the second object is heavier, the hand will go down, whereas if it is lighter, the hand will go up. The "immediate" judgment of weight may rely on an assessment of adjust-

Table 6.1. *Structuralist versus functionalist views of cognition*

Structuralist view
Perceiving relies on abstract representations and fixed procedures
Events have transsituational identity
Judgments are analytic: memory attributes

Functionalist view
Memory for prior episodes contributes to perception
Emphasis on retrieval
Events lack transsituational identity
Judgments are nonanalytic: memory attributions

ment to the local environment, that is, assessment of preparation to support the second object.

The assumptions that differentiate the two descriptions of judging weights are outlined in Table 6.1. An important difference between the two views is in their assumptions about the relationship between perception and memory for particular prior events. By the structuralist account, perceiving utilizes fixed procedures and abstract representations of prior experience that do not reflect memory for particular prior events. The fixed procedure that is used to assign a weight to an object is little influenced by context and does not reflect memory for any particular object that was previously lifted. Any influence of experience on perception is by means of abstract representations that record prior experience in a summarized form. These abstract representations may specify the general relationship between size, apparent density, and weight and may even represent the "typical" weight of objects of a given class. However, memory for particular events is stored separately from the fixed procedures and abstract representations used by perception and can be accessed only after an object has been perceived. The result of the use of fixed procedures and stable abstract representations is that the weight of an object has transsituational identity. Judgments of weight are analytic, because the transsituational identity of weight allows it to be treated as an attribute that is separable from other attributes of an object.

The alternative view is more functionalist in orientation and emphasizes rapid adaptation to local circumstances. By the functionalist view, memory for a particular prior event can influence later perception. Rather than perception and the use of memory for particular prior events being separate acts, memory for particular events contributes to later perception. When judging weights, the specific memory of the first weight is retrieved and used as a context for interpretation or as a basis for dealing with the second weight. I say "retrieved" because there is no reason to think of these effects as being short-term. As an example of a relatively long-term influence of a particular prior experience on the later judgment of weight, consider a person in a bar who drinks half a bottle of beer prior to being called away. If, during his absence, a full or an empty bottle is substituted for the half-finished one, the result when he returns and lifts the bottle will be an immediate double take. The person is prepared to pick up the beer that he left in that context, not some "generic" bottle of beer. Preliminary processing of an event and the context in which it occurs serve as cues for retrieval of memory for relevant prior events, and those memories are then used to aid perception and interpretation of the later event. By this view, events lack transsituational identity because there is no fixed set of procedures used for their perception or interpretation. Also, judgments are nonanalytic in that a definitionally relevant attribute has not been abstracted and so cannot be used as a basis for an analytic decision. Continuing the example of judging weights, a change in the situation produces a global effect in performance, and that effect is then attributed to some source. The falling of the hand when the second weight is placed in it might commonly be attributed to the second weight being heavier than the first weight, but other factors such as fatigue can also contribute to the change in hand position. The basis used for the judgment of weight is not sufficient to separate the effects of a change in weight from those of other factors producing the same effect in performance.

The structuralist account clearly does adequately describe the way that some judgments are made. At the extreme, scales can be used to judge weights—a fixed procedure for assessing weight that will produce a value that has transsituational identity and that can serve as an analytic basis for a decision. However, it seems likely that the functionalist account better describes the way that judgments are commonly made. What is at issue here, of course, is not just the judgment of weights but the more general relationship between perception and memory for prior episodes. My claim is that memory for episodes not only is accessed after an event is perceived but also contributes to the earliest phases of perception and interpretation of an event.

The structuralist view has dominated cognitive theorizing. Perception is said to rely on abstract representations such as schemata and logogens (Friedman, 1979; Morton, 1979) that serve to represent extensive prior experience in a summarized form and that do not preserve the details of any particular event. Also, it is common to claim that performance on a test of recognition memory results from a person encoding an item and then searching through memory for a match (e.g., Glass & Holyoak, 1986), implying that the use of memory for particular prior experiences is a separate act that follows that of perception. By this dominant view, a particular event can have a substantial influence on perception only by means of "priming" some abstract representation. Morton (1979), for example, proposed that a prior presentation of a word can serve to temporarily prime its corresponding logogen, resulting in a temporary reduction in the amount of information that must be collected before the subject can decide that the particular word has occurred. A great deal of additional experience is typically required to produce more permanent effects in perception. Effects of that sort require an amount and type of additional experience that is sufficient to have a substantial impact on the abstract representation that summarizes earlier experience. A single presentation of a word, for example, would not be expected to have a long-lasting influence on its later perception.

The functionalist view shares assumptions with the "exemplar" or "instances" account of concept learning advanced by Brooks (1978, 1986), Medin (Medin & Schaffer, 1978; Medin & Smith, 1984), and Hintzman (1986) and is, in some ways, similar to the "remembering operations" approach proposed by Kolers (Kolers & Roediger, 1984). The functionalist view is also similar to notions proposed by Kahneman and Miller (1986) in their argument that an event recruits or retrieves its own norms. By these accounts, variability in performance across situations reflects the differential contribution of memories for particular instances of a concept or type of event and is greater than could be produced by the use of fixed procedures. Kahneman and Miller, for example, use variability in judgments across situations to argue that an event is compared to a very local norm or set of alternatives, rather than invariably being compared to some global norm. Also, the role given memory by the functionalist view is similar to that described by Dewey (1910) and to the "stage-setting" metaphor used by Bransford, McCarrell, Franks, and Nitsch (1977). Memory for the past serves the function of setting the stage for perception and the interpretation of later events.

This stage-setting function of memory for a prior event is not necessarily accompanied by awareness of the past. What is the basis for awareness of the past? The "priming" account of effects of prior experience does not consider the question of awareness. By other accounts (e.g., Tulving, 1983), awareness of the past, as measured by performance on a test of recall or recognition memory, depends on events being represented in and retrieved from a particular memory store such as episodic memory. However, that solution does not seem satisfactory. If the functionalist view is correct, memory for a particular prior event, episodic memory, can be accessed and influence later perception without being accompanied by awareness of the past. Also, as noted by James (1892), awareness of the past necessarily requires an inference about the relationship between the past and the present. "Pastness" involves the present as much as the past and so cannot simply be retrieved as an attribute from some memory store. The feeling of nostalgia serves as an example. Nostalgia cannot be retrieved from memory, because one was not feeling nostalgic when one had the original experience. Rather, nostalgia must rely on an inference about the relationship between the past and the present.

When awareness of the past is treated as relying on an inference, the existence of unaware functions of memory is less surprising. Judgments of "pastness" may be similar to the nonanalytic judgments of weight described earlier. A global change in performance may be detected and then attributed to prior experience. Details of the test situation would be important for eliciting an attribution and for determining the particular attribution that is made (Harvey & Weary, 1984). Similar to the dissociation of effects of prior experience in perception and performance on a test of recall or recognition memory, change can be detected but not correctly attributed. A commonplace example is the detection of a change in appearance when an acquaintance shaves off his beard, followed by a failure to identify the particular aspect that has been changed. The change in appearance is commonly misattributed to some characteristic other than the beard having been changed. The functionalist view allows the effects of prior experience to be misattributed to some other source.

Treating awareness of the past in this way also allows one to predict a variable relationship between performances on different types of tests by considering differences in verification processes. A prior encounter with a fact, for example, might make that fact come to mind more readily regardless of whether the test is one of general knowledge or one of memory. This influence on availability may be used as a basis for responding for either type of test (Kahneman & Tversky, 1973), producing similar effects in performance. The effects of prior experience on performances on the two types of tests could be very different, however, if the persons being tested engage in substantial additional processing to verify their answers prior to responding. The processing done to verify that a fact is true can differ substantially from that done to verify that one remembers a particular prior encounter with a fact. Differences in the nature and extent of verification processes, then, are factors that determine the relationship between effects of prior experience on performances of difference types of tests.

Empirical issues

In the following sections, I use the contrast between the structuralist and the functionalist views of memory to examine empirical issues and to show the value of the functionalist view. In a first section, research is reviewed to show that, in line with the functionalist approach, memory for a particular prior event can influence later problem solving and perception. Also, it is shown that these effects in cognitive and perceptual tasks can be independent of recognition-memory performance. Similar to amnesics, normals can use memory for a particular prior experience to aid perception and interpretation of later events without any accompanying awareness of the past. In a second major section, I consider the bases for awareness of the past. It is argued that an attribution process, similar to that described in the context of judgments of weights, can serve as a basis for memory judgments.

Persistent effects of memory for a prior experience

The first issue examined is that of analyzing repetition effects in investigations of recall or recognition memory. By the structuralist view, encoding of an item remains stable across its repetitions, allowing some abstract form of the item to be represented in memory. Repetition serves to lower the threshold of this abstract representation or to "strengthen" the association between the abstract representation of the item and those of other items or the context. By the functionalist view, in contrast, memory for a prior encounter with an item influences its later processing. The encoding of an item is not expected to remain stable across its repetitions, but rather is expected to change in ways that reflect memory for its prior presentations.

Solving versus remembering: Analyzing repetition effects. Suppose you are asked to find the sum of 37 + 15. Immediately after giving an answer, you are again asked to find the sum of the same two numbers. Although the same answer is given when the question is repeated, the processing required to arrive at that answer will differ radically across the two encounters. On the first encounter, you undoubtedly went through the process of addition to obtain the sum; on the second encounter, the sum is readily available and can be given without going back through the operations of adding the numbers. The use of memory for a prior encounter with a problem when the problem is repeated is not necessarily intentional and can be very difficult to avoid. The difficulty of avoiding memory is probably the rationale for the commonly prescribed procedure of checking an addition by adding the numbers in reverse order rather than simply adding them again in the same order. If added in the same order, the influence of memory for the prior encounter is sufficient to make it likely that errors will be repeated. Also, these effects of memory can be long-term, dependent on accessibility of the memory for the prior encounter when the problem is repeated. Concerns such as these point toward the functionalist view of interpreting repetition effects. Rather than some fixed set of procedures being invariably applied to solve a problem and strengthened by their use, memory for a prior encounter with a problem influences its later processing.

This example of addition served as the basis for a series of experiments designed to analyze the effect of repetition on memory (Cuddy & Jacoby, 1982; Jacoby, 1978). Rather than addition problems, however, subjects in those experiments solved problems similar to those encountered in a crossword puzzle. A cue word was presented along with a few letters and a series of blanks representing the missing letters of a word that was related to the cue word (e.g., lawyer, c_u_t). The subject's task was to report the word that could be produced by filling the blanks ("court" in this example). In some instances, the cue, along with the solution word, was presented to be read prior to the presentation of the puzzle. The influence of reading the solution on the later solving of the puzzle was assessed by giving an unexpected test of cued recall in the final phase of each experiment. For the final test, the cue word from each of the puzzles (e.g., lawyer) was given as a cue for recall of the solution words. Akin to the example of repeating an additional problem, preceding a problem with the presentation of its solution was meant to reduce the amount of processing required to obtain the solution. This reduction in processing was expected to produce a decrease in the probability of the solution word being recalled on the final test. A similar claim that the means by which a solution is obtained will influence subsequent retention performance was used by Bruner (1966) to recommend "discovery" learning as compared with "reception" learning. The suggestion is that working through a problem to its solution enhances memory, as compared with a situation where the solution is made easily accessible by means of its prior presentation.

Data from an experiment reported by Cuddy and Jacoby (1982) show that preceding a problem by presentation of its solution does influence the way that the problem is solved. In that experiment, the sequence of events was manipulated by presenting the cue, accompanied by the solution word, to be read either prior to presentation of the problem to be solved (Read–Construct) or after subjects had already constructed a solution for the problem (Construct–Read). Factorially combined with this manipulation, presentations of the problem and its solution either immediately followed one another (zero-spacing) or were separated by 20 intervening events that were a mix of other problems presented to be solved and other cue–solution pairs presented to be read. Memory for the encounter with the solution can trivialize solving of the problem only when that encounter precedes the problem (Read–Construct), not when

Table 6.2. *Mean probability of correct cued recall*

Condition	Spacing	
	0	20
Read–Construct (R–C)	.30	.54
Construct–Read (C–R)	.61	.69

it follows the problem (Construct–Read). Even in the Read–Construct condition, an influence on problem solving would require that memory for the previously read solution be accessible when the problem requiring the solution is presented. The manipulation of spacing was meant to influence this accessibility. Differences in later cued recall were expected to reflect the influence of the sequence of events on their processing.

The probability of final cued recall of the solution words, for each of the combinations of conditions, is shown in Table 6.2. The disadvantage in cued recall of the Read–Construct condition as compared with the Construct–Read condition provides evidence that memory for a previously read solution does influence later problem solving. This disadvantage was largest when memory for the previously read solution was made readily accessible by presenting the solution to be read immediately prior to the problem requiring the solution (zero-spacing). The effect of spacing in the Read–Construct condition was more pronounced than that in the Construct–Read condition and can be interpreted as being due to memory for the solution becoming less accessible as spacing was increased. This decrease in accessibility had the effect of increasing the amount of processing required to construct a solution to a problem, and, thereby, enhanced later cued recall. However, even at the greater spacing, later cued-recall performance in the Read–Construct condition was still poorer than that in the Construct–Read condition. Memory for the prior reading of a solution still influenced later problem solving even when the two events were widely spaced. Varying the spacing of repetitions corresponds to a manipulation of retention interval and is only one of several means of varying the accessibility of memory for a prior presentation. Other experiments in the same series showed that factors such as similarity of repetitions, the type of intervening material, and cue effectiveness also influenced the processing of repetitions through their effects on accessibility.

The reduction in final cued recall that came from reading a solution to a problem prior to its presentation could be described as being a "generation" effect (Slamecka & Graf, 1978). Similar to arguments made by

Bruner (1966), the notion is that generating a solution to a problem produces *better* memory than does reading a solution. Results that are described later, however, show that the advantage in retention performance produced by generating an item can be reversed when a different type of retention test is used. Generating an item does not produce better memory than does reading an item, but rather produces a difference in what is remembered. For retrieval, the similarity of the retrieval cues and the encoded trace is important, making it necessary to consider encoding and retrieval jointly rather than in isolation (Tulving & Thomson, 1973). In a similar vein, Kolers (1979) emphasized the importance of processing by speaking of remembering operations rather than of memory traces. He stressed the uniqueness of the way an item is treated in a processing episode and argued that good transfer depends on the similarity of the specific operations required at test and those that were applied earlier. These micro encoding–retrieval interactions make transfer performance, cued-recall performance in the foregoing experiment, extremely useful for analyzing changes in processing that are produced by repetition of an item.

The finding that memory for a particular prior event can influence the processing of a later event is important for theories of learning and those of problem solving. For learning, retention performance is typically plotted against the number of repetitions of an item. However, an objective repetition of an item may not result in a full repetition of the processing of that item. In line with the functionalist view, memory for a particular prior presentation of an item can result in a qualitative change in its later processing. These qualitative changes in processing limit the opportunity for any "strengthening" effect of repetition. Any strengthening effect should be expected to be limited to processing that is repeated across presentations of an item (Jacoby, Hartz, & Evans, 1978). The commonly observed effects of spacing repetitions in list-learning experiments (Melton, 1967) may, in part, reflect the influence of memory for a prior presentation of an item on its later processing.

For theories of problem solving, much effort has been directed toward specifying fixed procedures or algorithms that people invariably apply to solve a class of problems. Even if fixed procedures of this sort do exist, they may be used only for the first encounter with a problem in a particular context. Returning to the example of addition, the procedures for adding a set of numbers is not likely to be applied when memory for a prior encounter with the problem, including its solution, is readily accessible. A recent experiment by Brooks and Allen (Brooks, 1986) provides support for this argument. In their experiment, people were given a rule to be used to categorize stimuli. Despite knowledge of this adequate explicit rule, experience with prior instances facilitated later categorization of old and new similar instances. Subjects used memory for previously encountered instances as analogies for categorizing later-presented instances, rather than totally relying on the rule.

The use of memory for a particular prior experience to solve a later problem is not necessarily accompanied by awareness of the relevant prior experience. The prior presentation of solution words often seems to make it easier to "see" the solution when the corresponding word fragment is presented. That is, the effect sometimes seems perceptual in nature. Experiments that are described later (Jacoby & Dallas, 1981; Jacoby & Witherspoon, 1982) show that effects in perception can be independent of recognition-memory performance. Also, Tulving, Schachter, and Stark (1982) used a fragment-completion task and found effects of prior experience that were independent of recognition-memory performance. Although effects in fragment-completion performance are often similar to those in perceptual identification, we have preferred the perceptual identification task because it seems to better isolate effects in perception from those in problem solving. The rationale underlying experiments using the perceptual identification task, however, is the same as described for the "solving-versus-remembering" experiments. Measures of transfer are used to assess the effects of manipulations meant to influence the prior processing of an item, as well as to show that memory for a particular prior encounter with an item can influence its later processing.

Retrieving the past in perception of the present. In collaboration with colleagues, I have carried out a large number of experiments to examine the influence of a prior presentation of a word on its later perceptual identification and to assess the relationship between that effect and performance on a test of recognition memory. A few studies are described here to show that, in line with the functionalist view, memory for a particular prior presentation of a word does influence its later perception and that those effects in perception can be independent of recognition-memory performance (see Jacoby & Brooks, 1984, and Jacoby & Witherspoon, 1982, for more extensive reviews). Others (e.g., Kolers, 1976; Roediger & Blaxton, 1986) have used different tasks but have observed dissociations in performance that are similar to those that are described here.

Typically, subjects in our experiments were presented with words under various study conditions and were then given two types of tests. One test was a standard yes/no recognition-memory test in which words previously presented in the study phase of the experiment, old words, were intermixed with new words, and the task was to pick out the previously studied words. The second type of test was a perceptual identification test. For that test, old and new words were intermixed, and each word was flashed for a very brief duration, such as 35 msec, followed by the presentation of a visual mask. The task was to identify words by reading them aloud; the probability of identification served as the dependent variable. An advantage in perceptual identification for old words over new words provides evidence of an influence of memory for a prior presentation of a word on its later perception. However, note that for an effect of this sort it is not logically necessary that old words be recognized as having been previously presented. For the perceptual identification task, subjects are asked only to report the word that has been presented without reference to whether it is an old word or a new one.

Memory for a prior presentation of a word can have a large and long-lasting influence on its later perception. A single prior presentation of a low-frequency word is sometimes sufficient to double its later probability of identification and greatly diminishes the influence of frequency of words in the natural language on their perceptual identification. Jacoby and Dallas (1981, Exp. 3) found that the probability of identifying a new low-frequency word was .37, whereas that of identifying an old low-frequency word was .73. The probability of identifying old low-frequency words was comparable to that of identifying new high-frequency words (.68) and not a great deal smaller than the probability of identifying old high-frequency words (.84). This effect of a prior presentation of a word lasts for at least 5 days (Jacoby, 1983a). Effects also remain when a word is read as one of an extremely long list of words. P. M. Merikle (personal communication) presented a list of 500 words to be read and found as large an effect in later identification as observed when only 100 words had been read. The motivation for Merikle's experiment was that studies of perception often use a fixed vocabulary of words and repeat those words under different viewing conditions across sessions. The common assumption has been that these repetitions do not influence performance, because perception relies on fixed procedures that do not reflect long-term memory for any particular prior encounter with a word. Merikle had hoped to show that this assumption was justified when the vocabulary of words was large. His finding of effects with a list of 500 words provides no comfort for those ignoring repetition effects.

These effects in perception are relatively specific to the details of the prior presentation of a word. The effect of prior presentation is largely modality-specific. Although reading a word greatly enhances its later identification, hearing the word (Jacoby & Dallas, 1981; Morton, 1979) or producing the word as a name for a picture (Winnick & Daniels, 1970) has little influence on visual perceptual identification. Effects are partially specific to the visual details of a presented word. Reading a word in lowercase letters rather than uppercase letters does more to enhance performance when the word is later presented in lowercase letters for the test of perceptual identification. However, words read in uppercase letters are still more likely to be identified than are new words (Jacoby & Hayman, 1987). The effects are also partly specific to the list context, in that the advantage in identification of old words over new words is larger when the majority of the tested words are old (Jacoby, 1983a).

Consistent with the functionalist view, it seems safe to conclude that effects in perception can reflect the retrieval of memory for a particular prior encounter with an item. The effect of a prior presentation of a word on its later identification cannot be easily accounted for by claiming that the prior presentation served to "prime" some abstract representation of the word. The effects are too long-lasting and too specific to the details of the prior presentation of the word to be described as being due to priming (Jacoby & Brooks, 1984). Also, perceptual identification of nonwords can be enhanced by their prior presentation (Feustel, Shiffrin, & Salasoo, 1983; Jacoby & Witherspoon, 1982). Effects for these non-words clearly cannot be explained as due to priming, because no abstract representation of the nonword existed in memory to be primed prior to its presentation in the experiment.

Perceiving and remembering: Encoding–retrieval interactions. Although long-lasting and relatively specific to the details of the prior presentation of a word, these effects in perception can be independent of recognition-memory performance. The levels-of-processing manipulation that has large effects in recognition-memory performance (Craik & Lockhart, 1972) does not influence perceptual identification. Superficial processing of a word required to answer a question about its constituent letters does as much to enhance later identification of the word as does the "deeper" processing that is required to answer a question about the meaning of the word (Jacoby & Dallas, 1981). Also, words that are not recognized as being old can gain as much in identification performance from their prior presentation as do words that are recognized as being old. However, this relatioship between identification and recognition-memory performance is a modifiable one. Greater dependence between effects in identification and recognition-memory performance is found when the stimulus materials are nonwords rather than words (Johnston, Dark, & Jacoby, 1985; Witherspoon, 1984).

I have argued that the modifiable relationship between effects in perception and recognition-memory performance is better accounted for in terms of encoding–retrieval interactions rather than by proposing separate memory stores. The argument is that effects in perception can reflect memory for a different type of prior processing than does recognition-memory performance; so independence in performance on the two types of tests will sometimes be observed. However, under other

Table 6.3. *Probability of a correct response*

	No context	Context	Generate	New
Recognition	.56	.72	.78	—
Perceptual identification	.82	.75	.67	.60

conditions, performance on the two types of tests can rely on the same form of prior processing, and so dependence in performance will be observed. An encoding–retrieval interaction involving performance on the different types of tests was observed by Jacoby (1983b). Variations in the amounts of data-driven versus conceptually driven processing of a word during its prior presentation had effects in later identification that were opposite to those observed for recognition memory.

In that experiment, a word was presented to be read either with no context (xxxx, cold) or in the context of its antonym (hot, cold) or was not presented to be read but was generated from its antonym as a cue (hot, ???). As shown in Table 6.3, later perceptual identification of the target word (cold), presented individually, was highest when the word had previously been read without context, next highest when the word had been read in context, and poorest when the word had previously been generated but not read. An opposite ordering of conditions was found when a recognition memory rather than a perceptual identification test was given. Presumably, conceptually driven processing of target words was dominant when they were generated in the first phase of the experiment, whereas data-driven processing was dominant when words were read in isolation. As commonly claimed (e.g., McClelland & Rumelhart, 1981), a mix of data-driven and conceptually driven processing was used to read a word in context. In agreement with prior research, recognition memory improves from increases in "deeper," conceptually driven processing, the processing of meaning (Craik & Lockhart, 1972). Effects in perceptual identification are reliant on prior processing, as are those in recognition memory. For perception of words presented in isolation, however, it is the extent of data-driven processing rather than that of conceptually driven processing that is the important determinant of later performance.

This encoding–retrieval interaction encourages the comparison of effects in perceptual identification with those in recognition memory as a means of analyzing reading in terms of differences in data-driven versus conceptually driven processing. The interaction also shows that the "generation" effect commonly observed in studies of recall or recognition memory (Slamecka & Graf, 1978) is reversed when a test of perceptual identification is used to measure retention. Reading a word has a larger effect in later identification than does generating the word; so generating does not produce better memory than does reading. Rather, it is the compatibility of the type of prior processing and that required by the retention test that is the important determinant of performance.

Roediger and Blaxton (1986) note that most experiments showing a dissociation between performances on different types of memory tests have used only two tests. They argue that the disadvantage of a design of this sort is that it does not allow one to compare effects in the performance of tests that supposedly rely on the same memory system. They also point out that there has been a confounding in most prior experiments such that the task chosen to tap episodic memory (recall or recognition memory) is likely to reflect prior conceptually driven processing, whereas that chosen to tap semantic memory (perceptual identification or fragment completion) is likely to reflect prior data-driven processing. Given this confounding, one cannot distinguish the memory-systems approach to explaining dissociations from an explanation in terms of encoding–retrieval interactions.

To remove the confounding, Blaxton (1985) varied the episodic-versus-semantic nature of tasks orthogonally with the type of processing the tasks required. Free recall was considered a conceptually driven episodic-memory test. The data-driven episodic test was cued recall with words that were graphemically similar to the target words being given as cues (e.g., CHOPPER for COPPER). Subjects were instructed to ignore the meanings of the cues and to recall words from the study list that looked like the cues. The data-driven semantic task was fragment completion. Subjects were simply told to give the first word that they could think of that would complete the fragment. The conceptually driven semantic test was a test of general knowledge. For both the fragment-completion test and the general-knowledge test, the correct answer for half the questions was a previously studied word, and for half it was not. Subjects in Blaxton's (1985) Experiment 1 studied a list of words under conditions analogous to those used to vary conceptually driven and data-driven processing in my experiments (Jacoby, 1983b). Words were read out of context, were read in the context of a semantic associate, or were generated given the semantic associate as a cue. In the second phase of the experiment, subjects were given one of the four different tests described earlier.

If the memory-systems approach to explaining dissociations is accurate, the patterns of results in the two episodic tasks (free recall and cued recall with graphemic cues) should be similar, and different from that in the two semantic tasks (fragment completion and general knowledge). In contrast, if it is the type of processing that is required by a task that is important, encoding–retrieval interactions, the patterns of effects in the two data-driven tasks (fragment completion and cued recall with graphemic cues) should be similar, and different from that in the two conceptually driven tasks (free recall and general knowledge). The data support the account in terms of encoding–retrieval interactions. Generated items produced better performance than those read without context in both the free-recall and general-knowledge tests. The pattern of results was reversed for tasks that rely on prior data-driven processing–the fragment completion and cued recall with graphemic cues. For those tasks, reading a word out of context produced better performance than did generating the word. Performance on words that had been read in context was generally intermediate between the levels of performance produced by the other two study conditions.

These results can be used to argue that dissociation in the performance of different types of memory tests is due to encoding–retrieval interactions rather than the involvement of separate memory systems. It was the type of prior processing most relevant to a task, not the episodic-versus-semantic nature of the task, that determined the pattern of results. If the account of dissociations in terms of separate memory systems is to be maintained, it must be explained why tasks that supposedly tap the same memory system can produce such radically different patterns of results. By concentrating on the type of information used by a task, in contrast, highly modifiable relations among tasks are predicted. The variable relationship between performance on episodic and semantic tasks produced by using words versus nonwords as stimuli can also be understood in terms of encoding–retrieval interactions. Perceptual identification of words can reflect prior data-driven processing, whereas recognition memory of words can reflect prior conceptually driven processing; so independence in performance on the two types of test can be observed. Recognition memory of nonwords, however, cannot rely on prior conceptually driven processing, because nonwords have no meaning. The finding of dependence between perceptual identification and recognition-memory performance when nonwords are used as stimuli (Johnston et al., 1985; Witherspoon, 1984), then, is likely due to performance on both types of tests relying on memory for prior data-driven processing. That is, there is not a one-to-one mapping between the type of retention test and the type of prior processing that is most compatible with the test. Depending on the materials and other details of the situation, recognition-memory performance can rely on either prior conceptually driven processing or prior data-driven processing. Performance on a perceptual identification test also probably can rely on either of the two types of prior processing. The testing of an item out of context results in prior data-driven processing being most relevant. However, if the context in which an item had been studied was re-presented at the time of test, prior conceptually driven processing would be expected to be important for perceptual identification performance.

Memory attributes versus memory attributions

Encoding–retrieval interactions are sometimes responsible for the dissociation in performances on different types of tests. However, to fully understand the relationship between aware and unaware uses of memory, it is necessary to more closely examine the basis for awareness of remembering. My argument that recognition-memory performance can rely on either memory for prior data-driven processing or that for prior conceptually driven processing is similar to an argument made by Mandler (1980). He suggests that the familiarity of the appearance of an item can serve as a basis for a fast-acting judgment process, whereas the use of interitem associations or meaning is a slower process that requires "memory search" for judgments of recognition memory (cf. Atkinson & Juola, 1974). I have tried to better specify the feeling of familarity by relating it to effects in performance and by treating the feeling of familiarity as involving an attribution process. The feeling of familiarity is seen as arising from a nonanalytic judgment process that is typically fast but does not isolate attributes that are definitionally relevant to the task. Analytic judgments are often slower and involve more deliberate reflective processes and serve as a more sure basis for judgments by isolating attributes that are definitionally relevant. As discussed later, the distinction between nonanalytic and analytic judgments is widely applicable, rather than being restricted to judgments of recognition memory.

Judgments of familiarity may be similar to the nonanalytic judgments of weight described earlier in that some global difference in performance is noted and then attributed to a source. Awareness of remembering, then, would involve an attribution process that is similar to the process involved in using the availability heuristic to estimate probabilities (Kahneman & Tversky, 1973). When using the availability heuristic, a person infers that a class of events is a probable one if an instance of that class is highly available (i.e., it can be readily brought to mind). For awareness of remembering, fluency in performing a task, like availability, can serve as a basis for application of a heuristic. That is, subjective familiarity or awareness of remembering a particular event resembles probability in being a dimension that can be judged by application of a heuristic. If an item is fluently perceived or interpreted, it will be judged as having been previously presented. Subjects taking a recognition-memory test, for example, often claim that the old items "jump out" at them and that they are basing their recognition-memory judgments on this difference in perception. The use of this fluency heuristic often will produce accurate recognition-memory performance, because a prior presentation of an item does enhance its later perception. Akin to the nonanalytic judgments of weight, however, this basis for recognition-memory judgments is error-prone because of the existence of other factors that have the same effects in global performance as does a prior presentation of an item. Although judgments commonly rely on non-analytic, attribution processes, more sure analytic bases for judgments are sometimes available to a subject and will be used when the situation demands a high level of accuracy.

Several advantages can be gained by treating familiarity as an attribution rather than as an inherent characteristic of some memory system, such as episodic memory (Tulving, 1983), that is supposed to be responsible for recognition-memory performance. As argued in conjunction with the example of nostalgia, awareness of remembering involves the present as much as the past; so it cannot simply rely on the retrieval of some memory attribute. Also, feelings of familiarity do not invariably arise when we encounter previously experienced people, events, or objects. We do not experience a feeling of familiarity when we encounter a colleague at work, but would experience such a feeling and would be aware of recognizing the colleague if we encountered him in an unexpected location. The feeling of familiarity seems to rely on a discrepancy reaction of some sort or on a direct question about recognition that calls for an attribution to be made. Indeed, it would be incredibly disruptive if a subjective feeling of familiarity intruded every time we encountered a previously experienced person, location, object, or event.

Treating familiarity as an attribution also has the advantage of allowing for variability in the relation between effects in performance and a subject's attributions. In the example of nonanalytic judgments of weight, it was argued that effects in performance are sometimes misattributed to a change in weight, although some other factor is the true source of the effects. Effects in performance due to factors other than recent prior experience will also sometimes give rise to feelings of subjective familiarity. The higher probability of a false recognition of a high-frequency word than of a low-frequency word can be seen as due to subjects mistakenly attributing the performance effects of frequency in the language to prior study. By a structuralist view, errors of this sort have been taken as evidence that people base their memory reports on general knowledge or schemata, even when they are asked to report on their memory for a particular prior episode. By an attribution view, however, not only can the general be mistaken for the specific, but also the specific can be mistaken for the general. That is, memory for a particular prior experience can influence perceptual performance or the interpretation of an event, and these effects can be mistakenly attributed to the operation of more general knowledge. When nonanalytic bases for judgments are used, people may be unable to discriminate the feeling of familiarity that is due to a particular encounter with an item from the feeling of familiarity that is due to more general knowledge. The effects of prior experience can be misattributed to "knowing," to a wild guess, to a feeling of intuition, or even to a difference in the physical stimulus. Experiments described in later sections provide evidence that these sources of effects in performance are sometimes confused.

Sources of fame: Becoming famous overnight. Is Sebastian Weisdorf famous? Most people will immediately respond "no" and support their decision by stating that the name is not a familiar one, claiming never to have encountered the name. If a name is familiar, in contrast, people may be willing to judge that the name is a famous one even if they cannot recall anything that the named person did to become famous. Judgments based on familiarity may be nonanalytic in that people are unable to discriminate between the general familiarity of a name that is due to its being a famous one and the "situational" familiarity that results from previously reading the name in the experimental setting. The familiarity used as a basis for judgments of fame, then, would not be discriminable from that used as a basis for judgments of recognition memory. For each of the two types of tests, however, there is a more sure analytic basis for judgments. The more analytic basis for judgments of fame is to judge a name to be famous only if one can recall what the named person did to become famous. For recognition memory, recall of the details surrounding the study encounter with an item would provide a more analytic basis for judgments than would familiarity. An experiment done in my laboratory examined the effect of a prior presentation of a name on later judgments of its fame.

In the first phase of that experiment, a list of nonfamous names was presented to be read. Subjects were informed that all of the names were nonfamous ones and were told that the intent of the experiment was to examine the effects of factors thought to influence the pronunciation of names. In a second phase of the experiment, these old nonfamous names were mixed with new nonfamous names and new famous names to be presented for judgments of fame. The famous names in this list were selected to be only "moderately" famous. The names were ones that a group of undergraduates judged to be famous, although the majority of the people in the group were unable to recall what the named person did to become famous. Examples of the famous and the nonfamous

Table 6.4. *Examples of names used*

Famous	Nonfamous
Arthur Rubenstein	Joseph Pacenti
Anne Hathaway	Sandra Brophy
Thomas Hobbes	Larry Jacoby
Marsha Mason	Adrian Marr
Helmut Schmidt	Sebastian Weisdorf

Table 6.5. *Probability of being judged famous*

	Type of name		
		Nonfamous	
	Famous	Old	New
Immediate	.64	.12	.21
Delayed	.55	.16	.08

names used in the experiment are presented in Table 6.4. Note that for judgments of fame, if subjects recognized a name as one read in the first phase of the experiment, they could be sure that the name was nonfamous, because they were informed that all of those names were nonfamous ones. Recognition memory, then, could be used to "discount" any familiarity of a name gained by its having previously been read in the experimental context. As an attempt to manipulate the probability of recognition memory, the test requiring judgments of fame either immediately followed the reading of the list of nonfamous names or was delayed for 24 hours.

The probability of judging a name as being famous is displayed in Table 6.5 for each combination of conditions. On the immediate test, old nonfamous names were less likely to be judged famous than were new nonfamous names. On the delayed test, however, the pattern of results was reversed. Some of the old nonfamous names had become famous overnight, whereas the new nonfamous names were less likely to be judged famous on the delayed test than on the immediate test. Effects in reaction times mirrored those in the probability of a judgment of fame. Judgments that a name was nonfamous were more rapid on the immediate test for old nonfamous names, but slower on the delayed test for old nonfamous than for new nonfamous names.

The increase across retention interval in the probability of judging an old nonfamous name to be famous is similar to the sleeper effect observed in studies of social psychology (e.g., Cook, Gruder, Hennigan, & Flay, 1979; Hovland, Lumsdaine, & Sheffield, 1949). In those experiments, it was found that a communication from a low-reliability source had little impact on attitude change measured immediately after the communication, but did result in attitude change when the test was delayed. Hovland et al. (1949) suggested that on an immediate test the content of the communication is discounted because of its low-reliability source being readily retrieved. Across time, the content of the communication continues to be remembered, but its discounting becomes less possible because of forgetting of the source of the communication. Similarly, the increase across time in the probability of judging old nonfamous names to be famous presumably was due to subjects becoming less able to recognize the nonfamous names as having been previously presented and, thereby, being less able to discount the familiarity of those names when judging fame. These effects of familiarity in judgments of fame are similar to effects observed in experiments requiring subjects to answer questions (Glucksberg & McCloskey, 1981; Kolers & Palef, 1976). The results of those experiments show that lack of familiarity with the topic of a question can be a basis for a fast "no" or "don't know" response. For present purposes, the important point is that there is a basis for recognition memory of a name that can be inaccessible even when the name continues to be familiar. People are unable to discriminate the general familiarity of famous names from the situational familiarity produced by previously reading the name in the experimental context. Similar to effects observed in perceptual identification and other tasks, memory for the particular prior presentation of an item influenced judgments of fame, although people were unable to recognize the item as having been previously presented. Indeed, a failure to recognize an item as having been previously presented was a precondition for the effects observed in judgments of fame.

It may be argued that the results of this experiment only show that the content of an experience can be remembered separately from the context in which that experience took place (Tulving, 1983). That is, prior presentation of a nonfamous name may result in a semantic memory for the name that is separate from the episodic memory that preserves information about the particular prior encounter with the name and that is necessary for recognition memory. The issue here is the same as that encountered when considering the effects of a prior presentation of an item on its later perceptual identification. The specificity of effects is important. If it is semantic memory that is involved, effects should not be specific to the details of the prior presentation of a name. For example, changing modality between the prior presentation of a name and its later presentation for the judgment of fame should have no effect. In contrast, finding an effect of changing modality would show that the "semantic" memory representation of a previously encountered nonfamous name is not totally general, but rather is modality-specific. Also relevant here is the question about the relationship between memory for context and that for the content of an experience. Although memory for the two may sometimes be separable, as claimed by Tulving, it seems likely that the content of an experience often is not separable from the context of that experience. For example, the meaning of a sentence is sometimes not separable from the speaker of the sentence and the context in which it was spoken. The importance of this issue is discussed more extensively by Jacoby and Brooks (1984).

If it is memory for a particular prior experience that is important, increasing the similarity between the conditions of study and those of test may aid retrieval and produce effects that are not accompanied by recognition memory. An example of unintentional plagiarism can serve to illustrate this possibility. Many of us have had the experience of presenting an idea to a colleague only to have the colleague thoroughly reject the idea. In a later conversation, however, the colleague may reintroduce the rejected idea and claim it as being an insight this colleague has recently had. The retrieval of memory for the prior conversation that is required for an unintentional act of plagiarism may rely on relatively specific cues. Nature may be so "perverse" as to make it likely that one will present a stolen idea as being one's own to the very person from whom one stole it. The physical cues offered by one's appearance and the content of a current conversation may be similar to those present during the prior conversation and serve as excellent cues for retrieval. This retrieval of an idea from the prior conversation, however, is not necessarily accompanied by awareness of the past and can be mistaken for a new insight.

Analytic versus nonanalytic judgments: When analysis fails. Familiarity does not specify its source; so nonanalytic judgments are prone to error. For judgments of fame, however, errors can be avoided by using the more sure analytic strategy of judging a name to be famous only if one can recall what the named person did to become famous. In the experiment that was just described, subjects in the delayed-test condition were generally less willing to call a name famous than were subjects in the immediate-test condition. Presumably, subjects receiving the delayed test were aware of their confusion of the general familiarity and the situational familiarity of names, and they partially protected themselves against that confusion by relying more heavily on the analytic basis for judgments of fame. The difference between the probabilities of famous names and new nonfamous names being judged famous was actually slightly higher in the delayed-test condition than in the immediate-test condition. This increase in discrimination between the two types of names can be taken as evidence of a qualitative shift from reliance on the nonanalytic toward reliance on the more sure analytic basis for judgments. We have observed a similar, but larger, effect in other experiments that have also tampered with the validity of familiarity as a basis for judgments by presenting nonfamous names to be read prior to requiring judgments of fame.

Reducing the validity of familiarity by means of prior presentation of "foils" can result in improved accuracy when an analytic basis is available as an alternative to the nonanalytic basis for judgments. In many domains, however, there may be no analytic basis for judgments that can be relied on when the validity of nonanalytic judgments is made doubtful. In those domains, reducing a person's faith in the accuracy of nonanalytic judgments can have dramatic effects. Consider the "self-consciousness" that one sometimes feels in social situations. If we are made to doubt the effectiveness of our "natural" style of interaction with others, an attempt to be analytic often fails. There seems to be no set of rules for social interactions nor an analytic basis for social judgments that can be universally applied and that will always produce satisfactory results. Removing faith in nonanalytic judgments can result in a general loss of confidence and inaction, rather than increasing the accuracy of judgments.

We have observed effects of this sort in the task of spelling words. In a first phase of those experiments, a list of words that was presented to be read included some words that were misspelled. Subjects were required to spell those words as well as new words in a second phase of the experiments. Reading a misspelled version of a word slowed later correct spelling of the word and also increased the probability of an error in spelling. When asked to judge the spelling of a word, people often claim that they are reliant on the word "looking" right. A prior encounter with a misspelled version of a word may serve to lower confidence in this basis for judgments by making words sometimes look right for the wrong reason. Similar to the findings in judgments of fame, subjects are unable to discriminate between the familiarity produced by a prior presentation of a misspelled word and the familiarity that is due to a word being correctly spelled.

The most dramatic results were produced not by the subjects in the experiments, but rather by my technician, Ann Hollingshead, who collected the data for those experiments. Whereas subjects read the misspelled versions of words only once in an experiment, she had much more extensive experience with the misspellings. She claims that this extensive experience has had the effect of generally reducing her confidence in her spelling and also has produced an increase in her spelling errors. Prior to working in my lab, Ann was an executive secretary and had a great deal of pride in the accuracy of her spelling. Her claim of a general deterioration in her spelling performance seems sufficiently well justified to make us hesitant to do further experiments of that sort. Any effects in her spelling performance, however, probably pale in comparison with those effects in our own spelling performance produced by repeatedly encountering misspelled words when reading students' essays. Ann also collected the data for the "fame" experiments and now sometimes mistakes the nonfamous names used in those experiments for famous ones. The use of an analytic basis for judgments of fame to correct these errors, however, is more convenient than is continually looking up words in the dictionary to check their spelling.

A recent experiment done by Begg, Armour, and Kerr (1985) has shown that a prior presentation of a statement to be read can increase people's later willingness to judge that the statement is true, and this influence on belief can be independent of subjects' ability to recognize the statement as one that was previously read. The material used in those experiments was a list of "trivia," isolated facts whose validity cannot be checked by examining their consistency with other known facts. The impossibility of this analytic basis for judgments makes people totally reliant on the familiarity of a statement to judge its truth. Zajonc (1980) found affective judgments to be influenced by previous presentations of an item, although subjects were unable to recognize the item as having been previously presented. He concluded that there is an affective system, separate from the cognitive system, that is responsible for recognition memory. The stimuli employed by Zajonc were typically meaningless and originally affectively neutral; so subjects had no alternative to using familiarity as a nonanalytic basis for judgments about affect.

Memory for a prior presentation of an item can influence performance on a wide variety of tasks. By the attribution view, the influence of a memory for a prior presentation of an item on its later perception and interpretation can be attributed to any of a number of sources dependent on the details of the test situation, including the question that is asked. People can be misled to claim that a statement is true, a name is famous, a misspelled word is correctly spelled, an old idea is a new insight, and so forth. The effects in fluency of perception and interpretation that serve as a basis for these nonanalytic judgments are the same as those that can be attributed to familiarity and that can serve as a basis for recognition-memory decisions.

These effects of memory for a prior experience can be largely independent of recognition-memory performance, however, because recognition-memory decisions can have a basis that is more analytic than are judgments of familiarity. Rather than relying on familiarity, people can refuse to claim that they recognize an item as having been encountered in a particular context unless they can retrieve details of that prior encounter. In a similar vein, Lockhart (1984) considered how a present thought or image comes to be accepted as a valid account of past experience. Following Baldwin (1920), he suggests that memories can be validated by checking them against the physical world, comparing them to the memory claims of others, or they can be validated internally by checking them against other memories and known facts. Validation of these sorts, however, is likely to be expensive in terms of time and attention. We may often bypass validation of memory and rely instead on familiarity as a nonanalytic judgment.

Memory for the past in subjective experience of the present. Effects of memory for a particular prior experience can also appear to subjects as being perceptual in nature. That this is true became evident in our experiments investigating the influence of a prior presentation of a word on its later perceptual identification. Several subjects in those experiments told us that some words were obviously more easily identified than were other words because they stayed on the screen longer. As it turns out, the words thought to stay on the screen longer often were words that had been previously read in the experimental setting. Witherspoon and Allan (1985) did experiments that were similar to our earlier experiments, but required judgments of the duration of presentation. They found that words that had been previously read were judged as staying on the screen longer than were new words. Subjects apparently attribute the influence of a prior presentation of a word on its later identification to a difference in the physical stimulus.

A recent experiment done in collaboration with Lorraine Allan and Linda Larwill reveals a similar effect in judgments of the loudness of noise. In that experiment, subjects heard a list of sentences that they were instructed to remember for a later test. These old sentences were then mixed with new sentences and presented against a background of white noise that varied in loudness. The task was to judge the loudness of the noise, using a 5-point scale. The results of that experiment are shown in Table 6.6. Increasing the loudness of white noise produced an increase in judged loudness for both old sentences and new sentences. At all levels, however, the noise accompanying old sentences was judged as being less loud than was that accompanying new sentences. Memory for the prior presentation of a sentence served to enhance its later perception through noise, and this influence on perception had the subjective effect of making the noise seem less loud. Effects of this sort are very compelling when one sits through the experiments. Indeed, my own

Table 6.6. *Mean noise judgments*

Noise levels	Sentence type	
	Old	New
Soft	1.86	2.16
Medium	2.54	3.01
Loud	3.38	3.78

judgments show the effects even when I try to guard against them. There is no impression that an inference is being drawn. Rather, the noise accompanying old sentences simply does not seem as loud.

These effects of memory for a prior experience in judgments of physical dimensions are similar to effects considered by Bruner (1957) in his discussion of perceptual readiness. Investigations of perceptual readiness, however, were typically designed to examine the influence of general needs or concepts and used differences in accuracy of perception as evidence of differences in perceptual readiness. Effects can be obtained that are much more specific to memory for a particular prior experience than are those effects considered by Bruner. Also, similar to the example of an effect in judgments of weight used to illustrate the functionalist approach, memory for a particular prior experience can influence the perceived duration, loudness, and, perhaps, other dimensions of a physical stimulus.

Summary and conclusions

The functionalist view of cognition has considerable heuristic value. By a structuralist view, cognition relies on fixed procedures that are invariably applied across a wide range of contexts. Those fixed procedures do not preserve memory for any particular prior experience; so the use of memory for specific events necessarily follows perception, concept utilization, and other cognitive activities that rely on general knowledge or fixed procedures. Counter to the structuralist view, however, there is evidence that memory for a prior encounter with an item does influence its later perception. These effects in perception are too specific and too long-lasting to be explained as due to the temporary "priming" of some general, abstract representation. Consistent with the functionalist view, memory for a particular prior experience can be retrieved and then contribute to the earliest phases of perception and interpretation of a later event.

Also, repetition does not, as the structuralist view would have it, only serve to strengthen or to lower the threshold of some abstract representation. Rather, when an item is repeated, memory for a prior encounter with the item can be retrieved and can influence its later processing. Effects of this sort are important for understanding the influence of repetition on memory performance and are also important for theories of problem solving. Even if there is some general set of procedures or an algorithm that can be used to solve a particular class of problems, those procedures are unlikely to be invariably used to deal with repetitions of a problem, and also may not be used to solve problems that are similar to previously encountered problems. As in the examples involving arithmetic and the completion of word fragments, gaining a solution to a problem may rely on retrieval of memory for a prior encounter with the problem, or similar problems, rather than relying on the application of some general set of procedures. The structuralist view emphasizes the general by proposing abstract representations of knowledge; so it is poorly prepared to account for the rapid adaptation of processing to local circumstances that is commonly observed.

Memory for a prior encounter with an item, then, can be retrieved and can serve to set the stage for later perception or interpretation of the item. This stage-setting function of memory can be independent of recognition memory or recall of the item as having been previously presented. Amnesics reveal evidence of memory for a particular prior experience in their performance of a variety of tasks, although they are unaware of any memory for the prior experience. Normals also show effects of a particular prior experience in their perception and interpretation of later events, and those effects are sometimes independent of recognition-memory or recall performance. Dissociations of this sort can be due to encoding–retrieval interactions. Effects in perceptual identification, for example, can rely on prior data-driven processing, whereas recognition-memory performance can rely on prior conceptually driven processing, producing a dissociation in performance of the two types of tasks. The compatibility of prior processing with that demanded by a test is a more important determinant of the relationship between performances on different types of tasks than is the "episodic" versus "semantic" nature of the tasks. The emphasis on encoding–retrieval interactions also has the advantage of predicting variable relations among tasks.

Awareness of the past seems so commonplace as not to require an explanation until unaware functions of memory are noted. Prior research has been aimed at the importance of metamemory (e.g., Brown, 1975), awareness of how memory operates, and reality monitoring (Johnson & Raye, 1981), the ability to discriminate between memory for real events and that for imagined events. However, the more fundamental question about the basis for awareness of the past has been largely ignored by researchers. Following James (1892) and others, I have claimed that awareness of the past necessarily relies on an inference about the relationship between the past and present and so cannot be viewed as relying on an "attribute" that is retrieved from memory. Similar to the example of judging weights, familiarity is seem as being a nonanalytic judgment that involves a global effect in performance being noted and then attributed to a source. The feeling of familiarity that is produced by memory for a prior presentation of an item has the same nonanalytic basis as do feelings of knowing, intuition, changes in affect, or even apparent changes in the physical stimulus, resulting in confusions among these sources. For some domains, however, there is also a surer, more analytic basis for judgments. Awareness of a particular past event, for example, can sometimes rely on validation by others or can be checked against other memories or the physical world. Manipulations that reduce a person's confidence in a nonanalytic basis for judgments can either increase the accuracy of judgments or produce a general deterioration in performance dependent on the availability of a more analytic basis for judgments.

Do we need a revolution that results in an ecological approach to memory research? The work on autobiographical memory is fascinating. However, the goal of some of that work seems to be to specify *the* structure of autobiographical memory. Against the chances of success for these attempts, reports on the past are likely to be influenced by situational factors such as the particular person we are talking to, the question that is asked, our estimate of the person's prior knowledge, whether or not the person has asked the same question previously, and so forth. That is, encoding–retrieval interactions are likely to be so important as to make it impossible to talk about the structure of autobiographical memory independent of the test of retention that is being used. Although I agree that it is important to study memory in natural contexts, the types of questions that are being asked do not seem radically different from those asked by more "traditional" investigators of memory. There is also the problem of specifying the basis for awareness of the past. It may be tempting to "solve" this problem by proposing that there is an autobiographical memory that is separate from other types of memory and that is responsible for awareness of the past. I have already discussed difficulties for an account of this sort. Also, identifying an ecological approach to memory with autobiographical memory ignores that many of the important functions of memory are not accompanied by awareness of the past.

I am not a great fan of revolutions or of separate memory systems. My main complaint against both is that they run the risk of imposing artificial boundaries that obscure the relationships among different "areas." It is the similarity of effects in perception, concept learning, social cognition, and memory that I find to be exciting. For each of these areas, there is evidence that performance is less stable across situations than would be predicted by the invariable application of fixed procedures or by total reliance on abstract representations of prior experience. People are impressive in their ability to rapidly adapt their processing and judgments to local circumstances. Revolutions are designed to sever us from the past by providing "new" directions. My bias is that we should pay more attention to the older research and theorizing about memory, not less attention. Also, given that the use of memory for the past without awareness is commonplace, I hesitate to claim that any approach is revolutionary.

REFERENCES

Atkinson, R. C., & Juola, J. F. (1974). Search and decision processes in recognition memory. In D. H. Krantz, R. C. Atkinson, R. D. Luce, & P. Suppes (Eds.), *Contemporary developments in mathematical psychology (Vol. 1). Learning, memory and thinking* (pp. 243–293). San Francisco: Freeman.

Baldwin, J. M. (1920). *Mental development in the child and the race.* (3rd ed.) New York: Macmillan.

Begg, I., Armour, V., & Kerr, T. (1985). On believing what we remember. *Canadian Journal of Behavioural Science, 17,* 199–214.

Blaxton, T. A. (1985). *Investigating dissociations among memory measures: Support for a transfer appropriate processing framework.* Unpublished Ph.D. thesis, Purdue University.

Bransford, J. D., McCarrell, N. S., Franks, J. J., & Nitsch, K. E. (1977). Toward unexplaining memory. In R. Shaw & J. Bransford (Eds.), *Perceiving, acting, and knowing* (pp. 431–466). Hillsdale, NJ: Erlbaum.

Brooks, L. R. (1978). Non-analytic concept formation and memory for instances. In E. Rosch & B. Lloyd (Eds.). *Cognition and categorization* (pp. 169–211). Hillsdale, NJ: Erlbaum.

  (1987). Decentralized control of categorization: The role of prior processing episodes. In U. Neisser (Ed.), *Categories reconsidered: The ecological and intellectual bases of categories* (pp. 141–174). Cambridge University Press.

Brown, A. L. (1975). The development of memory: Knowing, knowing about knowing, and knowing how to know. In H. W. Reese (Ed.), *Advances in child development and behavior* (Vol. 10, pp. 104–152). New York: Academic Press.

Bruner, J. S. (1957). On perceptual readiness. *Psychological Review, 64,* 123–152.

  (1966). Some elements of discovery. In L. S. Shulman & E. R. Kiesler (Eds.), *Learning by discovery.* Chicago: Rand McNally.

Cohen, N. J., & Squire, L. R. (1980). Preserved learning and retention of pattern-analyzing skill in amnesia: Dissociation of knowing how and knowing that. *Science, 210,* 207–210.

Cook, T. D., Gruder, C. L., Hennigan, K. M., & Flay, B. R. (1979). History of the sleeper effect: Some logical pitfalls in accepting the null hypothesis. *Psychological Bulletin, 86,* 662–679.

Craik, F. I. M., & Lockhart, R. S. (1972). Levels of processing: A framework for memory research. *Journal of Verbal Learning and Verbal Behavior, 11,* 671–684.

Cuddy, L. J., & Jacoby, L. L. (1982). When forgetting helps memory: An analysis of repetition effects. *Journal of Verbal Learning and Verbal Behavior, 21,* 451–467.

Dewey, J. (1910). *How we think.* Boston: Heath.

Feustel, T. C., Shiffrin, R. M., & Salasoo, A. (1983). Episodic and lexical contributions to the repetition effect in word identification. *Journal of Experimental Psychology: General, 112,* 309–338.

Friedman, A. (1979). Framing pictures: The role of knowledge in automatized encoding and memory for gist. *Journal of Experimental Psychology: General, 108,* 316–355.

Glass, A. L., & Holyoak, K. J. (1986). *Cognition* (2nd ed.). New York: Random House.

Glucksberg, S., & McCloskey, M. (1981). Decisions about ignorance: Knowing that you don't know. *Journal of Experimental Psychology: Human Learning and Memory, 7,* 311–325.

Harvey, J. H., & Weary, G. (1984). Current issues in attribution theory and research. *Annual Review of Psychology, 35,* 427–459.

Hintzman, D. L. (1986). "Schema abstraction" in a multiple-trace memory model. *Psychological Review, 93,* 411–428.

Hovland, C. I., Lumsdaine, A. A., & Sheffield, F. D. (1949). *Experiments on mass communication.* Princeton, NJ: Princeton University Press.

Jacoby, L. L. (1978). On interpreting the effects of repetition: Solving a problem versus remembering a solution. *Journal of Verbal Learning and Verbal Behavior, 17,* 649–667.

(1983a). Perceptual enhancement: Persistent effects of an experience. *Journal of Experimental Psychology: Learning, Memory, and Cognition, 9,* 21–38.

(1983b). Remembering the data: Analyzing interactive processes in reading. *Journal of Verbal Learning and Verbal Behavior, 22,* 485–508.

Jacoby, L. L., Bartz, W. H., & Evans, J. D. (1978). A functional approach to levels of processing. *Journal of Experimental Psychology: Human Learning and Memory, 4,* 331–346.

Jacoby, L. L., & Brooks, L. R. (1984). Nonanalytic cognition: Memory, perception and concept learning. In G. H. Bower (Ed.), *The psychology of learning and motivation: Advances in research and theory* (Vol. 18, pp. 1–47). New York: Academic Press.

Jacoby, L. L., & Dallas, M. (1981). On the relationship between autobiographical memory and perceptual learning. *Journal of Experimental Psychology: General, 3,* 306–340.

Jacoby, L. L., & Hayman, G. A. (1987). Specific visual transfer in word identification. *Journal of Experimental Psychology: Learning, Memory, and Cognition, 13,* 456–463.

Jacoby, L. L., & Witherspoon, D. (1982). Remembering without awareness. *Canadian Journal of Psychology, 36,* 300–324.

James, W. (1892). *Psychology.* London: Macmillan.

Johnson, M. K., & Raye, C. L. (1981). Reality monitoring. *Psychological Review, 88,* 67–85.

Johnston, W. A., Dark, V., & Jacoby, L. L. (1985). Perceptual fluency and recognition judgments. *Journal of Experimental Psychology: Learning, Memory, and Cognition, 11,* 3–11.

Kahneman, D., & Miller, D. T. (1986). Norm theory: Comparing reality to its alternatives. *Psychological Review, 93*, 136–153.

Kahneman, D., & Tversky, A. (1973). On the psychology of prediction. *Psychological Review, 80*, 237–251.

Kolers, P. A. (1976). Reading a year later. *Journal of Experimental Psychology: Human Learning and Memory, 2*, 554–565.

——— (1979). A pattern-analyzing basis of recognition. In L. S. Cermak & F. I. M. Craik (Eds.), *Levels of processing in human memory* (pp. 363–384). Hillsdale, NJ: Erlbaum.

Kolers, P. A., & Palef, S. R. (1976). Knowing not. *Memory and Cognition, 4*, 553–558.

Kolers, P. A., & Roediger, H. L. (1984). Procedures of mind. *Journal of Verbal Learning and Verbal Behavior, 23*, 425–449.

Lockhart, R. S. (1984). What do infants remember? In M. Moscovitch (Ed.), *Infant memory* (pp. 131–143). New York: Plenum.

McClelland, J. L., & Rumelhart, D. E. (1981). An interactive activation model of context effects in letter perception: Part I. An account of basic findings. *Psychological Review, 88*, 375–407.

McKoon, G., Ratcliff, R., & Dell, G. S. (1986). A critical evaluation of the semantic-episodic distinction. *Journal of Experimental Psychology: Learning, Memory, and Cognition, 12*, 295–306.

Mandler, G. (1980). Recognizing: The judgment of previous occurrence. *Psychological Review, 87*, 252–271.

Medin, D. L., & Schaffer, M. M. (1978). Context theory of classification learning. *Psychological Review, 85*, 207–238.

Medin, D. L., & Smith, E. E. (1984). Concepts and concept formation. *Annual Review of Psychology, 35*, 113–138.

Melton, A. W. (1967). Repetition and retrieval from memory. *Science, 158*, 532.

Morton, J. (1979). Facilitation in word recognition: Experiments causing change in the logogen model. In P. A. Kolers, M. E. Wrolstal, & H. Bonma (Eds.), *Processing of visible language* (Vol. 1, pp. 259–268). New York: Plenum.

Neisser, U. (1982). *Memory observed.* San Francisco: Freeman.

Roediger, H. L., & Blaxton, T. A. (1986). Retrieval modes produce dissociations in memory for surface information. In D. S. Gorfein and R. R. Hoffman (Eds.), *Memory and cognitive processes: The Ebbinghaus centennial conference.* Hillsdale, NJ: Erlbaum.

Schultz, D. (1981). *A history of modern psychology* (3rd ed.). New York: Academic Press.

Slamecka, N. J., & Graf, P. (1978). The generation effect: Delineation of a phenomenon. *Journal of Experimental Psychology: Human Learning and Memory, 4*, 592–604.

Squire, L. R., & Butters, N. (Eds.). (1984). *Neuropsychology of memory.* New York: Guilford Press.

Tulving, E. (1983). *Elements of episodic memory.* London: Oxford University Press.

Tulving, E., Schacter, D. L., & Stark, H. A. (1982). Printing effects in word-fragment completion are independent of recognition memory. *Journal of Experimental Psychology: Learning, Memory, and Cognition, 8*, 336–342.

Tulving, E., & Thomson, D. M. (1973). Encoding specificity and retrieval processes in episodic memory. *Psychological Review, 80*, 352–373.

Winnick, W. A., & Daniels, S. A. (1970). Two kinds of response priming in tachistoscopic recognition. *Journal of Experimental Psychology, 84*, 74–81.

Witherspoon, D. (1984). *The relationship between perceptual identification and recognition memory.* Unpublished Ph.D. thesis, McMaster University.
Witherspoon, D., & Allan, L. G. (1985). The effects of a prior presentation on temporal judgments in a perceptual identification task. *Memory & Cognition, 13,* 101–111.
Zajonc, R. B. (1980). Feeling and thinking: Preferences need no inferences. *American Psychologist, 35,* 151–175.

7

The maintenance of marginal knowledge

HARRY P. BAHRICK AND ELIZABETH PHELPS

The view that memory research should relate directly to real-life problems has received much support during the past decade. The new ecological emphasis is evident in the titles of recent books (Harris & Morris, 1984; Poon, in press), including this volume, and in the materials, situations, and procedures selected for study by many investigators. However, the new ecological emphasis has yielded uneven benefits because it has focused on autobiographical event memory and on short time periods. In contrast, long-term retention of semantic-memory content continues to be neglected.

The failure to investigate lifetime retention of semantic content leaves memory research largely irrelevant to education. A primary goal of education is to establish and preserve knowledge, and relevant memory research must explore retention of knowledge systems over long periods of time. Findings based on event memory or limited to short intervals are comparatively trivial. This problem has been discussed by Neisser (1982), who has sharply criticized psychologists for neglecting research concerned with the long-term retention of academic content.

Psychologists recognized long ago that the scientific study of learning ought to produce benefits to education. The relation of psychology to education can be viewed as comparable to the relation of biological science to medicine, or the relation of genetics and botany to agriculture. To be sure, societies grew crops, treated the ill, and educated their youth long before scientists began to investigate the principles involved in these essential enterprises, but the advances in biological and agricultural sciences during the last 200 years have led to dramatic improvements in the way medicine and farming are practiced. The psychological impact on education came later; it has been modest in comparison, but it is by no means negligible. Herbart, Thorndike, Skinner, and others were concerned with classroom learning, and their contributions have made a difference. Empirical evidence against the assumption of broad transfer of training helped to change the curriculum from its classical content to a functional content, more closely tied to the knowledge and skills needed

178

in adjusting to life. Skinnerian programs and the Keller methods are examples of more recent contributions. In contrast to these contributions of learning research, it seems to us that memory research has failed to yield benefits to education, primarily because of the previously discussed exclusive emphasis on episodic content and on short time periods (Bahrick, in press).

Education can profit from memory research if we examine the retention of semantic content over long time periods, and this can happen only as we perfect methods suitable for dealing with this type of content. Boring (1954) stated long ago that the history of psychological science is a history of methodological improvisation. New content areas become amenable to exploration as methods suitable for the empirical study of that content are improvised. The development of the various areas of research from psychophysics to intelligence testing and information processing illustrates this principle of the primacy of methodological innovations, and memory research is no exception.

Our research strategy is based on this principle; we have concentrated on developing methods that permit the examination of semantic-memory content over extended periods of time. An additional metatheoretical consideration that has guided our efforts assigns high priority to obtaining a suitable data base and to establishing functional relations among major independent and dependent variables. In contrast, we have given lower priority to the testing of specific cognitive hypotheses regarding the nature of the representation, the encoding, the transformation, or the retrieval of knowledge. We have deferred, for example, questions as to whether memory is predominantly schematic or associative, constructive or replicative in favor of establishing independent retention functions for various types of semantic-memory content. Our emphasis on a functional approach versus a cognitive approach to theory (Bahrick, 1987) reflects the belief that the available methods for answering cognitive questions are overextended, and as a result the questions frequently turn out to be intractable.

The present investigation extends earlier efforts to develop suitable methods for the study of long-term retention of knowledge. Previous research has taken two approaches: A cross-sectional adjustment method was used to investigate the acquisition and maintenance of complex knowledge systems over the entire life span, under ecologically realistic conditions (Bahrick, 1983, 1984; Bahrick, Bahrick, & Wittlinger, 1975). This method has yielded normative data and significant conclusions regarding permastore memory content. Work now in progress will establish the extent to which these earlier conclusions can be generalized. A disadvantage of this method is that it does not permit the manipulation of independent variables, and it therefore does not lend itself easily to the testing of specific hypotheses.

The second approach is longitudinal and laboratory-based. It involves successive relearning of the same material over extended time periods (Bahrick, 1979). This method permits manipulation of the conditions of acquisition and rehearsal, but it limits the amount of memory content under investigation to that which can be acquired within the time available in a few laboratory sessions.

The method adapted for the present investigation bridges the two earlier methods. Marginal semantic content, acquired over extended time periods in naturalistic settings, was identified and rehearsed in the laboratory. The concept of "marginal knowledge" is critical to this approach; it refers to knowledge the individual once acquired, but can no longer demonstrate on a test of recall. The purpose of the investigation is to establish the effects of various forms of rehearsals on recall of the marginal content several weeks later. This approach combines the use of naturalistically acquired knowledge with the laboratory manipulation of rehearsals. The combination makes it possible to deal with content acquired over very long time periods and to explore the effects of specific rehearsal activities experimentally. The significance of this approach to the concerns of educators is obvious. Much of the knowledge acquired in schools is partially, but not completely, forgotten. Very little is known about the effects of various types and amounts of periodic rehearsal needed to reactivate such knowledge. Investigations that identify marginal knowledge and establish general principles regarding the long-term maintenance of such knowledge will enhance understanding of memory and promote the effectiveness of education.

Method

Design

Three areas of knowledge were selected to include a variety of memory content. These areas deal with (a) general information (GEN), (b) vocabulary of a previously learned foreign language (VOC), and (c) recall of names of well-known individuals cued by presenting their portraits (PIC). To identify marginal information, a preliminary test for each knowledge area was administered. On each test the participants were presented with 100 questions and were required to write down any answers they were able to recall. Questions for which they failed to recall the correct answer were rated on a feeling-of-knowing scale (FOK). On this scale, subjects indicated their confidence of being able to identify the correct answer on a multiple-choice test. Questions correctly answered by each participant were discarded, and the FOK-rated questions in each knowledge area were assigned to one of four treatment conditions (three experimental treatments and one control or no-treatment condition) in such a way that the distribution of FOK ratings across treatment conditions was matched. The treatment conditions were (1) a forced multiple-choice test, with knowledge of the correct answer given immediately after each response, (2) a series of alternating test and presentation trials continuing to a criterion of the first correctly recalled response to each question, (3) a combination of (1) and (2), that is, a forced-choice recognition test followed by relearning trials, and (4) a control or no-treatment condition to provide a baseline for evaluating the effects of the other treatments. Thirty days after the knowledge tests were first administered, the same tests were readministered to determine the effects of the treatments on recall.

Subjects

Twenty-eight male and female undergraduates at Ohio Wesleyan University participated in the original study. Ten additional undergraduates were recruited for a control condition after the main results had been analyzed. Some of the participants fulfilled one option of a course requirement in introductory psychology; others were paid. With the exception of the control subjects, individuals were eligible to participate only if they had the equivalent of at least 1 year of high school instruction in French or Spanish, but were not enrolled in a French or Spanish language course at the time of testing.

Knowledge tests

Each of the three tests consisted of 100 questions. The tests were assembled on the basis of pilot data. The goal was to identify large amounts of marginal knowledge. Thus, the tests needed to be of an appropriate difficulty level, that is, a level that would not be so easy that individuals could recall most of the correct answers, nor so difficult that participants would answer only a few questions correctly and rate the remaining ones low on the FOK scale. The pilot study yielded questions for which the probability of correct answers ranged from approximately .1 to .5 for the population of students from which the participants were recruited.

The VOC tests were prepared in French and Spanish, and participants were given the test appropriate to their previous language training. Individual words were selected from college textbooks and from Julliand and Rodrigues (1964). Cognates of English words were avoided, and the selected words included nouns, the infinitive forms of verbs, and adjectives. Participants were instructed to write down the English meaning of each word they could recall. If they were unable to recall the English meaning, they were instructed to circle one of the numbers from 1 to 7 printed next to each word on an answer sheet. The circled number was to reflect the degree to which they were confident that they would be able to identify the corresponding English word on a multiple-choice recognition test. The number 1 was to be circled if they were completely confident, and the number 7 if the word was completely unfamiliar and their answer on a multiple-choice test would be a pure guess.

The GEN test consisted of general-knowledge questions to which the correct answer was the name of a person. Several of the questions listed by Nelson and Narens (1980) were included. Most of the remaining questions called for the names of authors, scientists, discoverers, and so forth. The test was assembled on the basis of pilot data using the same selection criteria as in the VOC test.

In the PIC test, subjects were presented with portraits of well-known individuals. The portraits were assembled from a variety of sources; they ranged in size from 5 × 8 cm to 10 × 15 cm; some were black and white, and others were in color. Portraits of individuals currently in the news were excluded in order to reduce the likelihood of uncontrolled access to the material during the retention interval. The individuals portrayed included government leaders, authors, and scholars, but the majority were entertainers and athletes prominent during the preceding decade. Pilot data indicated that these portraits were most likely to yield the desired high familiarity ratings. An effort was made to choose only those portraits that gave an easily identifiable likeness, so that familiarity with the appearance of the individual portrayed, rather than familiarity with the particular portrait, was the major determinant of a correct response. The portraits were attached to consecutively numbered index cards, and participants were tested by going through the cards in a predetermined, arbitrary sequence at a rate determined by the subject. Participants marked their answer sheets in the same manner as for the other two tests. The three knowledge tests were administered to subjects in an arbitrary sequence during a single session that lasted approximately 40 to 60 min.

Assignment of questions to treatment conditions

The tests were scored, and only those participants who obtained more than 20, but fewer than 60, correct answers on at least two of the three tests were retained in the investigation. Four individuals whose performances exceeded or fell short of these limits were eliminated. This constraint was imposed in order to obtained a sufficient amount of marginal material in each knowledge area for each individual. As a result, it was possible to train all individuals who continued in the study in at least two of the three knowledge areas.

The FOK-rated questions of each participant on each test were then assigned to the four treatment conditions (including the control condition), so that near equality of FOK ratings among the conditions was achieved. Questions rated 1 were assigned by systematic alternation among the four conditions until the pool of these questions was exhausted. Questions rated 2 were then assigned, and so forth, until the largest possible number of questions divisible by 4 had been assigned, and differences in the mean FOK ratings of questions assigned to the four treatments were minimal.

Construction and administration of recognition tests

Two of the four treatment conditions involved recognition testing, and individual recognition tests were assembled for each participant consisting of the questions assigned to these two conditions. Each recognition question offered the correct answer and four foils. For the VOC test, the foils were words of the same category (noun, adjective, etc.) as the correct answer; for the GEN test, the foils were names of prominent individuals, usually in the same profession as the individual named in the correct answer; for the PIC test, the foils were names of individuals of the same sex and generally the same profession as those shown in the portraits. The alternative names were written below the portraits. Some care was taken to avoid using foil names of individuals who were better known than the individuals portrayed in order to limit the possibility that subjects would select correct answers by eliminating readily identifiable foils. Participants were shown the correct answer immediately after responding to each test question.

The recognition tests were administered 1 day after the knowledge tests; the three tests were given in an arbitrary sequence, and subjects worked at their own pace.

The relearning treatment

Relearning sessions were administered 2 or 3 days after the knowledge tests. Half of the material to be relearned had been included in the prior recognition session (recognition followed by relearning treatment); the other half had not been tested previously (relearning-only treatment). Items to be relearned were first presented in the form of a test trial. The test trial consisted of presenting the questions (portraits) individually on index cards and requesting the appropriate answer. Subjects were given 5 sec to generate the correct answer. Correctly answered questions were removed, and the remaining questions were retained for a subsequent presentation trial. The presentation trial consisted of a 2-sec exposure to each question (portrait) paired with its correct answer in an arbitrary sequence. Each of the paired associates was presented on an index card. For the PIC test, the correct name of the individual portrayed was written on an index card presented together with the portrait. Immediately following the presentation trial, a new test trial was administered, using a new arbitrary sequence of items. The alternating series of test and presentation trials continued, with the removal of correctly answered test items until all remaining items were answered correctly on a given test trial. The number of presentation trials required to obtain a correct answer was recorded for each item. The sequence of retaining the three knowledge areas was arbitrary.

PIC control group

An additional group of 10 participants was trained under a control condition. The decision to obtain these data was made after results from the main study had been analyzed and it had become apparent that additional information would be useful in interpreting results. The test given to this group paralleled the PIC test, but it involved portraits of individuals unfamiliar to the participants. The 100 portraits were comparable in size to those used for the PIC test, and the individuals portrayed were chosen to be comparable in regard to race, sex, and age to the individuals portrayed in the PIC test. One hundred names selected randomly from a telephone directory were assigned to the portraits in such a way that the name was appropriate to the sex of the individual portrayed, and in a few instances to the ethnic origin (e.g., Arab, Indian) of the individual. Control subjects were told to view the 100 portraits and to assign FOK ratings. In most instances these were ratings of 7, but other ratings were obtained when the participants believed they would be able to guess the names of the individuals portrayed in a multiple-choice test. Sixty of the portraits were then arbitrarily selected for training, and the same procedures were followed as described for the PIC test. Some of the foils on the recognition test were names assigned to other portraits; other foils were names not previously used; this paralleled the procedure used with the PIC test.

Results and discussion

FOK predictions of recognition success

Table 7.1 reports the percentages of correct recognition for items in each of the three areas of knowledge as a function of their FOK ratings. The table is based on only one-half of all items selected for training, because the other half were not tested for recognition. However, the

Table 7.1. *Probability of correct recognition as a function of FOK rating*

Knowledge type	FOK rating						
	1	2	3	4	5	6	7
VOC	.78	.58	.61	.59	.53	.56	.48
GEN	.84	.61	.67	.65	.45	.42	.46
PIC	.89	.67	.64	.56	.65	.51	.42

results can be generalized to all test items, because the assignment of items to recognition-test conditions was unbiased.

It is apparent that participants were able to predict their success on recognition tests with fair accuracy, and this finding agrees generally with those reported by Hart (1965) and by Nelson, Gerler, and Narens (1984). FOK ratings of 1 yield significantly ($p < .01$) higher recognition performance than lower ratings. However, the discriminatory power of the lower ratings is poor, and for this reason ratings of 2 to 4, and of 5 to 7, were pooled for subsequent analyses. This result agrees with Nelson's (1984) conclusion that a 3-point scale reveals most of the available metamemory information.

An important conclusion drawn from Table 7.1 is that participants grossly underestimated their knowledge. The probability of a correct answer was more than twice the probability of obtaining a correct response by chance, even for questions rated 7 on the FOK scale. Apparently, individuals were able to bring knowledge to bear on many answers, even if they predicted that their answers would be mere guesses. Similar underestimation of knowledge has been reported by Gruneberg and Monks (1974) and to a lesser extent by Hart (1965).

The high scores on the recognition tests confirm that the procedures used succeeded in identifying marginal knowledge. A portion of that knowledge is marginal in the sense that the subjects had a strong feeling of knowing, and this feeling was validated by high performance on the test. Another portion is evidenced through high recognition-test performance, but it was not anticipated on the basis of FOK ratings. Apparently, subjects are not aware of that knowledge until the information is presented to them on a recognition test.

This study had the goal of establishing the effects of various rehearsal treatments on the long-term maintenance of marginal knowledge. To achieve this goal, it was necessary to compare the results with the effects of the same treatments on nonmarginal information, that is, information that was newly acquired and had not benefited from prior exposures. It was expected that this baseline comparison would be available within the

Table 7.2. *Mean number of learning trials as a function of FOK rating*

Knowledge type	FOK rating		
	1	2–4	5–7
For all questions			
VOC	1.63	2.02	1.90
GEN	1.56	1.90	2.31
PIC	1.74	1.97	2.11
PIC control			3.86
For questions answered correctly on the recognition test			
VOC	1.05	1.46	1.53
GEN	1.23	1.45	1.41
PIC	1.41	1.47	1.55
PIC control			3.03
For questions failed on the recognition test			
VOC	2.00	2.12	2.29
GEN	1.69	1.95	2.43
PIC	1.83	2.33	2.28
PIC control			3.80
For questions not tested for recognition			
VOC	1.94	2.34	1.99
GEN	1.77	2.17	2.52
PIC	1.99	2.15	2.33
PIC control			4.12

study by contrasting the long-term retention of information rated high on the FOK scale with the retention of information rated low on the FOK scale. However, the results shown in Table 7.1 made it clear that this comparison would not provide an appropriate baseline, because individuals seriously underestimated the amount of knowledge they had. Apparently, some of the answers to questions in every FOK category benefited from marginal knowledge. The PIC control group described earlier was added for the purpose of providing additional comparison data not affected by marginal knowledge. The control data yielded few FOK ratings above 7 and an average of 28% correct recognition responses (not significantly above chance, $p > .05$).

The relearning of marginal knowledge

Table 7.2 shows the mean number of presentation trials required by a subject to reach the criterion of a correct test response as a function of

FOK ratings of the item. Separate data are presented for items passed on the recognition test, items failed on the recognition test, and items not subjected to recognition testing.

Clearly, relearning of marginal material is faster than initial learning of material of comparable difficulty. The extremes of this dimension are best illustrated by comparing the number of trials to criterion for PIC test portraits correctly recognized and rated 1 on the FOK scale and the number of trials required by the PIC control subjects to learn names arbitrarily assigned to portraits. Savings due to "marginality" are at least 55%. This estimate is conservative, because the validity of FOK ratings is imperfect; that is, even the group of items rated 1 includes some items that are not marginal, but were mistakenly judged to be familiar.

Comparing trials for items with and without prior recognition treatment reveals the savings attributable to the recognition test. The overall effect of the test is approximately 25%, but the magnitude of the effect depends as much on whether the response on the recognition test is correct or wrong as on the feedback provided on the recognition test per se. The rate of learning associations is approximately the same for items failed on the recognition test as for items never subjected to the recognition treatment. The latter group contains items for which the response would have been correct as well as items for which the response would have been wrong.

It is hardly surprising that relearning of marginal knowledge is more rapid than original learning of comparable material, but the available data make it possible to compare this effect for materials that are familiar to varying degrees. The data also confirm what Ebbinghaus (1885/1913) established long ago: Savings in relearning do not depend on conscious recognition that material is familiar. Even for material rated 5 to 7 on FOK, there are approximately 43% savings in comparison with the data for learning material de novo in the PIC control condition. Thus, of the total savings in relearning due to marginality (based on the comparison of the PIC control data with the material rated 1 on FOK), a large portion is obtained for material that appears unfamiliar to the individual. Nelson (1985) has shown that comparisons of the magnitudes of savings may not be meaningful, and this constraint limits further interpretation of these data.

Recall after an interval of 1 month

Table 7.3 gives the mean probabilities of recall as a function of treatment and FOK rating for the three knowledge areas. The data for each knowledge area were subjected to a 3×4 analysis of variance. In each case the results show highly significant ($p < .001$) main effects for type of treat-

Table 7.3. *Recall probability as a function of FOK rating and rehearsal treatment*

		Type of treatment				
	FOK	Recog.	Relearn.	Recog. + Relearn.	None	X
VOC	1	.77	.74	.61	.38	.63
	2–4	.37	.39	.51	.11	.36
	5–7	.16	.24	.30	.07	.19
	X	.43	.46	.47	.21	
GEN	1	.56	.63	.61	.29	.53
	2–4	.35	.36	.49	.17	.35
	5–7	.15	.17	.34	.07	.18
	X	.36	.39	.48	.18	
PIC	1	.66	.56	.64	.42	.57
	2–4	.44	.51	.59	.23	.45
	5–7	.29	.21	.51	.08	.28
	X	.47	.43	.58	.24	

ment and FOK rating, with no significant interaction. The significant treatment effects reflect mainly the inclusion of the control, or untreated, condition, which yields lower recall than the three treatment conditions. The differences among the three treatment effects are not large. The combined recognition and relearning treatment results in somewhat higher recall than either of the individual treatments, and the relearning treatment is somewhat superior to the recognition treatment, but these differences are relatively small and are found mostly for material rated low on FOK.

The most striking finding is the very high probability of recall for questions rated 1 on the FOK scale. For these questions, recall probability ranges from .29 to .42 for the no-treatment control condition. This finding shows that the accessibility of marginal material fluctuates considerably, so that a large portion can be recalled 30 days after a recall failure, even though it is highly improbable that the material was encountered during the interval. Incremental recall following a retention interval was reported long ago (Ballard, 1913) and has been discussed as *reminiscence* and more recently as *hypermnesia* (Payne, 1986). The present findings establish a strong relation between the reminiscence effect and metacognition, as reflected by the FOK ratings. This relation must be taken into account in interpreting fluctuations of recall for marginal knowledge.

Apparently, *a brief reexposure* is sufficient to boost accessibility very significantly for at least 1 month. Even the high recall probabilities of .56 to .77 associated with a single recognition test of material rated 1 on FOK

Table 7.4. *Thirty-day recall probability for the PIC control group*

Recog.	Relearn.	Recog. + Relearn.	None
.00	.03	.07	.00

Table 7.5. *Recall probability as a function of speed of relearning*

	Number of relearning trials		
Knowledge type	1	2	3+
VOC	.64	.34	.21
GEN	.66	.36	.10
PIC	.74	.42	.27
PIC control		.17	.03

underestimate the full effect, because this FOK category includes a portion of material (11–22%) that is not marginal, that is, questions failed on the recognition test (Table 7.1).

If we consider material rated lower on FOK (which includes a larger portion of nonmarginal material), the picture changes. For material rated 5 to 7 on the FOK scale, recall probabilities for the control condition are only .07 to .08, and the treatments have more differentiated effects. The double treatment of a recognition test followed by relearning is more beneficial than either treatment by itself, but differences between the two individual treatments remain small.

To obtain a complete perspective on the effect of the dimension of marginality, it is necessary to contrast the data in Table 7.3 with the PIC control data shown in Table 7.4. The PIC control data do not list separate recall levels for various FOK ratings. All of the material was new to the participants, and only a few of the FOK ratings were above 7. One month after treatment, recall probability was only .11 for the combined recognition and relearning treatment, .03 for the relearning treatment, and .00 for the recognition treatment.

Speed of relearning and probability of recall

Table 7.5 shows recall probability as a function of speed of relearning. This relationship is very strong in all three areas of knowledge; answers that were correct after a single presentation were far more likely to be recalled 1 month later than answers that required several presentations. The PIC control data also show this trend, although the number of answers correct after a single presentation was so small that no reliable recall probability could be established. The PIC control data also show much lower recall for nonmarginal material learned in the same number of trials as the marginal material of the other conditions. These data show clearly that the effect of marginality on long-term retention is independent of the effect on speed of acquisition.

It is not surprising that familiar but nonrecalled material is relearned more readily than unfamiliar material of comparable difficulty. Nor is it surprising that the access gained through relearning of marginal material will be more durable than the access achieved for equally difficult, but previously unfamiliar, material. Certainly these findings are consistent with those reported long ago by Jost (1897) and Ebbinghaus (1885/1913). Beyond this general consistency, however, this investigation permits estimates of the magnitudes of these effects and yields new and significant conclusions that are consistent for the three areas of knowledge examined. The principal conclusions are as follows:

1. Recall of marginal knowledge fluctuates greatly; 1 month after a free-recall failure, the probability of spontaneous recovery on a new recall test ranges from .29 to .42.
2. Feedback on a brief recognition test administered 1 day after the recall failure approximately doubles the high spontaneous recall probability at the end of a 1-month interval.
3. Ceiling effects make it difficult to determine the value of additional treatments.

These findings regarding the maintenance of marginal knowledge differ categorically from the findings for comparable newly acquired knowledge. One month after acquisition, recall of the newly acquired knowledge is negligible. Clearly, we must discover more about the manner in which the memory system maintains information over long periods of time. This knowledge will improve understanding of the system and will permit us to develop efficient strategies of rehearsals for knowledge we wish to maintain.

NOTE

This investigation was supported by the National Science Foundation under grant BNS-8417788. The authors are indebted to Jilliann Daly, Irene Jenkins, and Cara Wellman for help in the collections and analysis of data and to Lynda Hall for her contributions to the editing of the manuscript.

REFERENCES

Bahrick, H.P. (1979). Maintenance of knowledge: Questions about memory we forgot to ask. *Journal of Experimental Psychology: General, 108*, 296–308.

(1983). The cognitive map of a city: 50 years of learning and memory. In G. Bower (Ed.), *The psychology of learning and motivation: Advances in research and theory* (Vol. 17, pp. 125–163). New York: Academic Press.

(1984). Semantic memory content in permastore: 50 years of memory for Spanish learned in school. *Journal of Experimental Psychology: General, 113*, 1–29.

(1987). Functional and cognitive memory theory: An overview of some key issues. In D. Gorfein & R. Hoffman (Eds.), *One hundered years of memory research*. Hillsdale, NJ: Erlbaum.

(in press). The laboratory and the ecology: Supplementary sources of data for memory research. In L. Poon (Ed.), *Cognition in everyday life: Research approaches, aging effects, and enhancement methods*. Hillsdale, NJ: Erlbaum.

Bahrick, H. P., Bahrick, P. O., & Wittlinger, R. P. (1975). Fifty years of memory for names and faces: A cross-sectional approach. *Journal of Experimental Psychology: General, 104*, 54–75.

Ballard, P. B. (1913). Oblivescence and reminiscence. *British Journal of Psychology Monograph Supplement, 1*, No. 2.

Boring, E. G. (1954). *A history of experimental psychology* (2nd ed.). New York: Appleton-Century-Crofts.

Ebbinghaus, H. E. (1913). *Memory: A contribution to experimental psychology* (H. A. Ruger & C. E. Bussenius, Trans.) New York: New York Teachers College, Columbia University. (Original work published 1885.)

Gruneberg, M. M., & Monks, J. (1974). "Feeling of knowing" and cued recall. *Acta Psychologica, 38*, 257–265.

Harris, J. E., & Morris, P. E. (Eds.). (1984). *Everyday memory, actions and absent-mindedness*. London: Academic Press.

Hart, J. T. (1965). Memory and the feeling of knowing experience. *Journal of Educational Psychology, 56*, 208–216.

Jost, A. (1897). Die Assoziationsfestigkeit in ihrer Abhänigkeit von der Verteilung der Wiederholungen. *Zeitschrift für Psychologie, 14*, 436–472.

Julliand, A., & Rodrigues, E. (1964): *Frequency dictionary of Spanish words*. The Hague: Mouren.

Neisser, U. (1982). Memory: What are the important questions? In U. Neisser (Ed.), *Memory observed: Remembering in natural contexts* (pp. 3–19). San Francisco: Freeman.

Nelson, T. O. (1984). A comparison of current measures of the accuracy of feeling-of-knowing. *Psychological Bulletin, 95*, 109–133.

(1985). Ebbinghaus's contribution to the measurement of retention: Savings during relearning. *Journal of Experimental Psychology: Learning, Memory, and Cognition, 11*, 472–480.

Nelson, T. O., Gerler, D., & Narens, L. (1984). Accuracy of feeling-of-knowing judgments for predicting perceptual identification and relearning. *Journal of Experimental Psychology: General, 113*, 282–300.

Nelson, T. O., & Narens, L. (1980). Norms of 300 general-information questions: Accuracy of recall, latency of recall, and feeling-of-knowing ratings. *Journal of Verbal Learning and Verbal Behavior, 19*, 338–368.

Payne, D. G. (1986). Hypermnesia for pictures and words: Testing the recall level hypothesis. *Journal of Experimental Psychology: Learning, Memory, and Cognition, 12*, 16–29.

Poon, L. (Ed.). (in press). *Cognition in everyday life: Research approaches, aging effects and enhancement methods.* Hillsdale, NJ: Erlbaum.

8

The content and organization of autobiographical memories

LAWRENCE W. BARSALOU

As evidenced by many of the chapters in this volume, as well as in Rubin (1987), cognitive psychologists have become increasingly interested in the study of autobiographical memories.[1] But because this development is relatively recent, it understandably exhibits certain gaps and weaknesses. Although numerous experiments have addressed the retention of autobiographical memories, relatively few have addressed the content of autobiographical memories, how they are organized, or how they are related to world knowledge. Although a fair amount of empirical work has addressed autobiographical memories, no major theories have been proposed to account for them or to integrate them with other phenomena such as comprehension, learning, and problem solving.

A benefit of the cognitive science atmosphere that has grown with the development of cognitive psychology is that diverse methodological and theoretical frameworks contribute to one another's development. Insights from one approach fill gaps, stimulate new research, and occasionally restructure another approach. This chapter reflects such cross-fertilization. My initial interest in autobiographical memories was stimulated by Janet Kolodner's computational theory of autobiographical memories (Kolodner, 1978, 1980, 1983a,b, 1984; Schank & Kolodner, 1979), and our discussions of this work led to some very preliminary attempts to integrate psychological and computational perspectives (Kolodner & Barsalou, 1982, 1983).

In contrast to cognitive psychology, computational work on autobiographical memories has primarily been theoretical and has focused on the content and organization of autobiographical memories, along with their relation to world knowledge. It has also attempted to integrate autobiographical memories with the processes of comprehension, learning, and problem solving. My students and I found Kolodner's proposals sufficiently provocative that we initiated a research program to explore them. More complete reports of our work can be found in Barsalou, Lancaster, Spindler, George, and Farrar (1988) and Lancaster (1985).

Overview

The first of the remaining sections briefly summarizes Kolodner's (1983a,b, 1984) computational theory of autobiographical memories, as well as assumptions from a similar theory proposed by Schank (1982). Because these theories motivated the primary hypotheses in our work, and because they dictated the structure of our experiments, they provide essential background for what follows. The next two sections review the findings from our empirical explorations. The first addresses the kinds of information that comprise people's autobiographical memories and tests a hypothesis suggested by computational theories that people have extensive idiosyncratic, generic knowledge about events. The second section addresses how people organize this information and tests a hypothesis suggested by computational theories that activities and generalized actions form the primary organization of autobiographical memories. The final section presents a theory of autobiographical memories that has evolved from our work and that is serving as a framework for our current research. This theory assumes that (1) extended-event time lines form the primary organization of autobiographical memories, (2) idiosyncratic summarizations of events become nested within these time lines, (3) a specific event is represented as a collection of exemplars from different ontological domains, and (4) an event summarization is constructed from the experience of a single specific event. Each section also reviews recent findings from other laboratories that bear on particular issues of interest.

Computational work on the organization of autobiographical memories

Computational theories of autobiographical memories had their origin in computational theories of language comprehension. Early comprehension systems attempted to understand language with word-based semantics (e.g., Schank, 1975). Such systems retrieved meanings for the words in a sentence and combined them by various rules to determine its meaning. Because this approach could understand only the simplest forms of language, it was far from satisfactory.

A central problem with word-based semantics is its inability to generate the inferences necessary for understanding the bulk of human language. As a result, a second generation of language-understanding systems incorporated world knowledge to support extensive inferencing. Such knowledge has generally taken the form of scripts (Schank & Abelson, 1977) and frames (Minsky, 1975). Including such knowledge in language-understanding systems has led to substantial progress in machine comprehension.

The most recent generation of systems has gone a step further. The recent theories of Kolodner and Schank have proposed that successful language-understanding systems must also have knowledge of specific events (Kolodner, 1978, 1980, 1983a,b, 1984; Schank, 1982; Schank & Kolodner, 1979). These theories propose that specific events are important to language understanding for two reasons: First, memories of earlier events often provide a means of understanding later events by analogy. Second, memories of previous events are necessary for the continual abstraction of new generic knowledge that expedites the subsequent processing of similar events. Kolodner and Simpson (1984) and Kolodner, Simpson, and Sycara-Cyranski (1985) have extended this theoretical framework to learning and problem solving.

The comprehension hypothesis of event organization

In the process of implementing event-based comprehension systems, Kolodner and Schank encountered an interesting problem: How should information about specific events be organized in the memory of a language-comprehension system? I refer to Kolodner and Schank's solution to the organization problem as the "comprehension hypothesis of event organization."[2] This hypothesis first assumes that when one attempts to understand an event, or to understand text about an event, one retrieves generic knowledge relevant to comprehending it. This knowledge generates explanations about what has occurred so far, expectations about what may occur in the future, appropriate behaviors, and so forth.

Second, this hypothesis proposes that memories of events similar to the current event may become available and thereby generate more precise inferences. If one is reading about a visit to a Morrocan restaurant, for example, one may first retrieve generic knowledge about restaurants in general to help understand the event. However memories of specific trips to Morrocan restaurants may also be retrieved to provide more precise explanations and expectations.

Third, and most important, this hypothesis assumes that the memory for an event becomes integrated with the generic knowledge and specific episodes used to comprehend it. For example, the memory for the trip to a Morrocan restaurant would become integrated with knowledge about restaurants in general and with memories of Morrocan restaurants in particular. The comprehension process determines how memories for events become organized in memory.

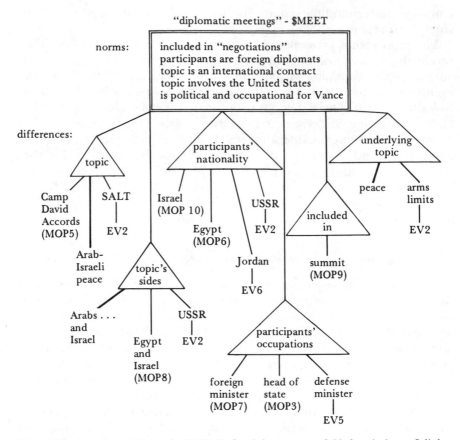

Figure 8.1. Event organization in CYRUS after it has processed 60 descriptions of diplomatic meetings (Kolodner, 1983a, p. 270). The E-MOPs in this figure are referred to as "MOPs," and events are indicated by "EV." Not all events instantiating subordinate E-MOPs are shown.

CYRUS

Kolodner (1983a,b, 1984) implemented an explicit account of an event-based comprehension system called CYRUS, which simulates Cyrus Vance's memory of his experiences as secretary of state. The basic unit used in CYRUS to represent classes of events is the *event-memory organization packet* or *E-MOP*. An example is shown in Figure 8.1 for the event type *diplomatic meetings*. As can be seen, an E-MOP contains two kinds of information: (1) prototypical information about its class of events (i.e., "norms") and (2) secondary organizational structures that organize instances of that kind of event by their differences.

Although Kolodner generally assumes that the memory for an event becomes organized with all the relevant knowledge structures used to comprehend it, she has primarily addressed the role of event types in organization (e.g., meetings, trips, restaurant visits). What constitutes an event type is not entirely clear. However the activity in an event, as specified by its goals and actions, seems most important in determining its event type.

This emphasis on event types manifests itself in a number of important ways in CYRUS and suggests that event types provide the primary organization of event memories. For example, CYRUS's highest level of memory organization is comprised of basic event types. As Kolodner (1983a, p. 249) states, "In general, we can expect an event memory to have E-MOPs for each major type of event it knows about," such as for "getting up in the morning, eating in a restaurant, going to the movies, and driving to the office." Other attributes organize more specific E-MOPs and event memories within these highest-level E-MOPs. In Figure 8.1, for example, subordinate E-MOPs and event memories are organized by topic, participant's nationality, and so forth within the E-MOP for *diplomatic meetings*.[3] In general, attributes such as these establish secondary organizations within the event types that comprise the highest level of memory organization.

CYRUS's emphasis on event types also manifests itself at retrieval. When searching for a particular event, CYRUS's first step is to determine the kind of event sought (see Figure 8 in Kolodner, 1983b). In fact, identifying an event type is a necessary step in retrieving an event. If a retrieval cue does not specify an event type (e.g., remember an event that occurred in *San Francisco*), then an event type must be inferred before search can begin (e.g., *eating in a restaurant*). It is impossible to retrieve an event directly from cues that do not specify an event type (e.g., from *San Francisco*). Furthermore, if CYRUS cannot find a sought-after memory in the context of the event type initially established, it employs various strategies to identify alternative event types whose memories are then searched (Kolodner, 1983b, pp. 299–305). Finally, as each event type is identified, secondary attributes provided by the retrieval cue direct search through attribute organizations within the selected E-MOP. For example, a retrieval cue might specify that a sought-after diplomatic meeting involved the *SALT treaty* and a *defense minister*. As subordinate E-MOPs are accessed via these secondary attributes, their norms provide further expectations in the form of inferred attribute values that also guide retrieval. As can be seen from Figure 8.1, a given event can generally be accessed by numerous unique paths of attribute values within its E-MOP (e.g., EV2). Barsalou and Bower (1984) discuss various issues associated with this form of organization.[4]

In general, CYRUS's organizational scheme clearly supports event comprehension. When an event is experienced, CYRUS's organization directs search toward E-MOPs and event memories that facilitate comprehension. The information retrieved about an event type establishes a rich context in which to explain an event and generate useful expectations about what has not yet been perceived. Conversely the process of comprehension alters memory organization. As an event is comprehended, it becomes part of memory, thereby changing it. In addition, integrating an event into memory usually causes new generic knowledge to be created along the path of comprehension (Kolodner, 1983a, pp. 264–266). All of these changes to memory organization make it better prepared to support comprehension of future events.

The activity dominance hypothesis

Reiser and his colleagues have performed a wide range of interesting studies closely related to Kolodner's theory in particular and to the comprehension hypothesis of event organization in general (Reiser, 1983, 1986; Reiser, Black, & Abelson, 1985; Reiser, Black, & Kalamarides, 1987). Similar to Kolodner and Schank, they have assumed that event memories are organized by the knowledge used to comprehend them. Similar to Kolodner, they have focusd on the role of event types in comprehension and retrieval (Reiser et al., 1985, pp. 91–93). Similar to Kolodner, this focus has led them to assume that event types provide the primary organization of event memories, stating that "activities . . . constitute the principal contexts used to store experiences," where "activity" is equivalent to "event type" as I have been using it (Reiser et al., 1985, p. 89). Following Kolodner, these theorists generally assume that organizational attributes such as participant and location are subordinate to event types (never vice versa) and that identifying an event type is necessary to retrieving an event memory.

This stress on event types reflects a focal interest on the roles of goals and causal reasoning in the comprehension and retrieval of events. Kolodner (personal communication, March 1985) and Reiser (personal communication, March 1986) both emphasize this, but also state that they accept the comprehension hypothesis of event organization in its full form, namely, that an event memory is stored with all the knowledge used to comprehend it, not just event types. However the assumption that event types provide the primary organization of event memories is strongly implied by their theories, in their conceptions of both event storage and event retrieval. This assumption seemed sufficiently important and provocative to us that we deemed it a hypothesis worth explicitly formulating and testing. Moreover, because goals and causal reasoning are so central to events, it seemed plausible that event types could provide the dominant organization of event memories. In fact, the research tradition that has evolved from Schank and Abelson (1977) can be viewed as resting heavily on this assumption.

So far I have been referring to the primary organization assumed by Kolodner and Reiser as organization by "event types." Actually Kolodner generally refers to event types as "contexts," and Reiser often refers to them as both "contexts" and "activities." For the remainder of this chapter, I follow Reiser in referring to this kind of organization as organization by "activities," primarily to contrast it with organization by participants, locations, and times, which will be addressed later. In addition, I refer to the hypothesis that event types form the dominant organization of event memories as the "activity dominance hypothesis."

Findings that address the content of autobiographical memories

The initial goal of our work was to test the activity dominance hypothesis. In the process of exploring organization, however, it became apparent that we needed to consider another issue first, namely, what kinds of information comprise the content of autobiographical memories. This next section presents findings from our experiments that bear on this issue. Of particular interest was the extent to which autobiographical memories contained event summarizations, as might be expected from the extensive formation of E-MOPs in the theories of Schank, Kolodner, and Reiser.

Free recall

At the beginning of a fall semester, an experimenter stopped people on the Emory campus and asked if they would participate in a survey. If they agreed, the experimenter continued:

What I would like you to do for the next five minutes is tell me about events you were involved in this past summer. In telling me what you did this summer, simply describe events you were involved in. *Most importantly, describe the events exactly in the order in which they come to mind.* When an event comes to mind, describe it immediately, and when the next event comes to mind, describe it. Simply describe events that occurred during your summer in the order in which they come to mind. Continue to remember events in this manner for the full five minutes.

The remainder of the instructions continued to stress that subjects remember "events" from their summer vacation and that they report them "in whatever order they come to mind." The experimenter tape-recorder the subject's protocol, which was later transcribed. In analyzing

Table 8.1. *Percentages of statement types and examples of statement types from the free-recall study*

Statement type[a] and examples	Percentage
Summarized events we also went to movies while we were there I watched a lot of TV everyday we would leave our house	32
Comments about aspects of events I did that for about four weeks the family is friends of ours . . . we had a lovely apartment	31
Specific events we saw a play we had a little picnic filled out an application at home	21
Extended events I worked there for two weeks I took a trip to Italy I went on a diet	9
Alternative events I had not taken a shower I'll probably go back to work at Christmas . . . they could have given me a job for a week . . .	3
Miscellaneous statements	4

[a]Statement types are defined in the text.

these protocols, and others discussed later, we developed various coding schemes. Across all coding analyses, interjudge reliability was .85 or higher.

To identify the kinds of information comprising subjects' protocols, we developed a coding scheme that divided each protocol into a sequence of statements, where each statement was coded as containing a particular kind of information. Some of the results from this analysis, along with examples, are shown in Table 8.1.

As can be seen, the most common kind of statement in subjects' protocols was what we refer to as a *summarized event*. A summarized event is a statement that refers to two or more events of a particular kind, such as many occasions of going to the movies, playing tennis, and so forth. These comprised nearly a third of all the statements in subjects' protocols. Another frequent kind of statement was a *comment* about some aspect of an event. Subjects often commented about themselves, how long an event lasted, the people involved, the location, the outcome, why the event occurred, and so forth.

The next most common kind of statement was a description of a *specific event*. These were single events that lasted less than a day, such as seeing a play, going on a picnic, and so forth. Although the instructions explicitly asked subjects to recall "events" from their summer vacation, only 21% of the statements in their protocols described specific events.

The next most common kind of statement was what we refer to as an *extended event*, which is a single event lasting longer than a day. Typically these events are not continuous, being frequently and systematically interspersed with other kinds of activities. Having a job, for example, is an extended event that is frequently interrupted because most people do not work 24 hours a day. Extended events and specific events differ in that extended events typically (but not necessarily) are long, interrupted, and significant, whereas specific events typically are short, uninterrupted, and insignificant.

An infrequent but nevertheless interesting kind of statement was what we refer to as an *alternative event*. These were events that (a) had not occurred during the summer, (b) were alternatives to what actually occurred, or (c) might occur in the future. Not only did subjects describe what occurred during their summer, they also described what had not occurred.

We were rather surprised by these results. We originally believed that the primary content of autobiographical memory was supposed to be memories of specific events. Yet subjects, when asked to describe "events" from their summer vacation, spent only 21% of their time recalling specific events.

We were sufficiently troubled by this outcome that we ran another version of the study in which we pointedly tried to elicit only specific events from subjects. In the instructions, subjects were told about the difference between specific and summarized events and were repeatedly asked only to recall specific events. In addition, if a subject did anything but retrieve specific events during this recall, the experimenter stopped the interview and reminded the subject to describe only specific events. We found that even under these conditions subjects had difficulty recalling only specific events. Subjects often retrieved other kinds of information and frequently had to be stopped. This new procedure appeared to disturb subjects' normal mode of recalling the past. The retrieval of summarized and extended events, along with other kinds of information, appears to play an important role in accessing information about periods of one's life.

Cued recall

In our next study, which also occurred at the beginning of a fall semester, each subject participated in three sessions. During the first session, subjects were told they would shortly perform a categorization experiment. But before starting this experiment, the experimenter asked the subjects to answer a short question that was part of an unrelated experiment. Subjects received one of four questions and verbally provided answers for 60 sec. Twenty-four of the subjects were asked to produce "the names of as many *people* as you can think of whom you did things with this summer." Another 24 subjects were asked to produce "the names of as many *places* as you can think of where you did things this summer." Another 24 subjects were asked to produce "as many different kinds of *activities* as you can think of that you did this summer." A final 24 subjects were asked to produce "as many *times* as you can think of when things occurred during the summer." The answers that subjects generated to these questions will be referred to as "cues," for reasons that will become apparent shortly.

Between 1 and 2 weeks later, subjects returned, believing they would continue with the categorization experiment. Instead they received the cues they had generated during the first session in a random order. As they received each cue, they were asked to "tell me as many events as you can remember" that involved the particular cue. Subjects then attempted to remember events for 60 sec before receiving the next cue.

Between 1 and 2 weeks later, subjects returned for a third session and provided various judgments about the cues and events they had generated during the first two sessions. One of the questions we asked subjects was whether the events they had generated during the second session were specific or summarized events. After receiving definitions and examples of specific and summarized events, subjects were asked to "indicate whether each event that you generated was a specific event, that is, something that occurred on one specific occasion, or a general kind of event, that is, something that occurred on more than one occasion" (these instructions used "general events" in referring to what I have been calling "summarized events"). Subjects were also allowed to indicate when they were not sure whether an event was specific or summarized. Examples of events judged as specific were "I went to the beach the day after graduation," "I visited her in the hospital," and "showed me everything he made with wood." Examples of events judged as summarized were "went to movies," "late night parties," and "long discussions."

As can be seen from Table 8.2, only around 40% of the events that subjects generated were specific events, by their own judgment. In con-

Table 8.2. *Average percentages of specific and summarized events as a function of cue type for the cued-recall study*

Measure	Cue type			
	People	Activity	Location	Time
Specific events	38.07	38.99	41.85	47.82
Summarized events	61.93	60.95	57.90	52.05
Unsure	0.00	0.06	0.25	0.13

trast, approximately 60% were summarized events. None of the differences between cuing conditions was significant.

The importance of summarized events

On the basis of these two studies, it is obvious that autobiographical memories are not exclusively memories of specific events. In fact, the most common kind of information retrieved by subjects in both studies concerned summarized events. Whereas summarized events comprised around 60% of the cued-recall protocols, specific events comprised only around 40%. Whereas summarized events comprised 32% of the free-recall protocols, specific events comprised only 21%. In addition, the free-recall protocols contained several other kinds of information, including extended events, alternative events, and comments about aspects of events.

Summarized events in CYRUS

The prevalence of summarized events in our data is what would be expected from Kolodner's (1983a,b, 1984) theory of autobiographical memory. Subordinate E-MOPs in CYRUS correspond to what we refer to as summarized events. Whenever CYRUS detects that two events of a given type share values on one or more attributes, it constructs a subordinate E-MOP for that new "kind" of event. For example, if two events are encoded about going to a movie with one's grandmother in the afternoon, then an E-MOP is constructed for *movies with one's grandmother in the afternoon* that is subordinate to the E-MOP for *movies*. The norm for this new E-MOP contains prototypical information about this kind of event, and subordinate attribute structures organize instances of it. Because events of a particular type often share attributes, CYRUS predicts continual evolution of new generic knowledge about specific events.

Our finding that summarized events dominate autobiographical protocols is consistent with CYRUS's proclivity for summarization. However it remains to be seen if the conditions under which CYRUS generalizes are the same as those under which people generalize. For example, if CY-RUS encountered two instances of going to a movie with one's grand-mother in the afternoon, it would construct summarizations for *movies with one's grandmother, movies in the afternoon,* and *movies with one's grand-mother in the afternoon* (but only if *grandmother* and *afternoon* were found to be predictive indices; Kolodner, 1983a, pp. 251–261). In contrast, people might form only the last of these summarizations.

Nelson and her colleagues have similarly argued for some time that children form event summarizations as soon as they experience two events of the same kind (Nelson, Fivush, Hudson, & Lucariello, 1983; Nelson & Gruendel, 1981). Hudson and Nelson (1986) and Watkins and Kerkar (1985) have addressed this issue directly and have found a robust tendency for people to summarize events. Brewer (1987) discusses additional findings that demonstrate the prevalence of summarization in autobiographical protocols.

Implications for the distinction between episodic and generic knowledge

Rather than viewing episodic and generic memories as sharply differenti-ated (e.g., Tulving, 1972, 1983), these findings suggest that it may make more sense to view episodic and generic memories as a continuum.[5] At one end are specific episodes (e.g., going to an Indian restaurant on one's 30th birthday). Next are those summarized events that were ab-stracted from a few highly specific and similar events (e.g., going to Indian restaurants on one's birthdays). Next are summarized events that were abstracted from events that have occurred often (e.g., going to Indian restaurants). Finally at the far end is relatively stable and abstract knowledge that may be culturally shared to a large extent (e.g., going to restaurants). Whereas intermediate generic knowledge often may be idio-syncratic to individuals because of its episodic basis, the generic knowl-edge that is least episodic may be so because of its origin in cultural and linguistic tradition.

Findings that address the organization of autobiographical memories

This next section addresses the organization of autobiographical memo-ries. In particular, it summarizes results from studies that bear on what I have termed the activity dominance hypothesis. As discussed earlier, this hypothesis stems from a basic assumption in the work of Kolodner and Reiser that activities provide the primary organization of autobiographi-cal memories.

Evidence for the activity dominance hypothesis

Reiser et al. (1985) suggested that if activities form the primary organization of autobiographical memories, then receiving an activity as a cue should result in faster retrieval of a specific event than receiving other kinds of information. To test this, they assessed whether activities (e.g., *went out drinking*) or generalized actions (e.g., *paid at the cash register*) provided faster access to event memories. On each trial of their Experiment 1, subjects received two descriptions, one of an activity and one of a generalized action, separated by 5 sec. Subjects' task was to remember a specific event that involved both pieces of information, the dependent measure being how long it took to remember the event. The critical manipulation was the order in which the two cues were presented. If activities provide better access to event memories, then receiving them before generalized actions should result in faster access than receiving them in the reverse order.

As predicted, Reiser et al. (1985) found that subjects were much faster in retrieving a specific event when activities came first than when they came second. In Experiment 2, they further found that activities, when presented as single cues, provided much faster access to event memories than did generalized actions. On the basis of these findings, they concluded that activities constitute the primary organization of autobiographical memories. Reiser (1983, 1986) and Reiser et al. (1987) reported further evidence for this position. It should be noted that Reiser's results frequently are inconsistent with Schank's (1982) proposal that generalized actions are more important organizers of event memories than are activities.

Alternative organizations of autobiographical memories

Reiser and his colleagues have clearly shown that activities are central to the organization of autobiographical memories. As Reiser et al. (1985, p. 132) point out, however, they have primarily focused on activities and have not examined other potentially important forms of organization. In addition, the competing organizations they have considered, such as generalized actions and emotions, are arguably not the strongest contenders available. Consequently one of the central goals of our research program has been to explore what we perceive as stronger contenders.

The alternative organizations we have addressed are organization by *participants*, organization by *locations*, and organization by *times*. For example, it often seems that people remember two or more events involving the same person, even though these events do not share a common activity (e.g., going to a baseball game, building a fence, and going camp-

Table 8.3. *Average time in seconds to retrieve an event as a function of cue order in an extension of Reiser et al. (1985)*

	Cue order	
Cue 1/Cue 2	Cue 1/Cue 2	Cue 2/Cue 1
Activity/Person	3.17	2.98
Activity/Location	2.58	2.88
Activity/Time	2.92	2.63
Person/Location	3.52	2.89
Person/Time	3.26	3.95
Location/Time	2.58	3.16

ing, all with one's father). Similarly people may organize events around locations (e.g., things I've done in Paris) and around times (e.g., things I've done on New Year's Eve), even though events within a cluster do not share an activity.

Kolodner and Reiser generally assume that event memories are not stored in these other ways. As can be seen in Figure 8.1, for example, Kolodner assumes that events can be clustered by participants' nationalities, but only if they share the same activity (also see Reiser et al., 1985, Figure 3). These theories also make a similar assumption about retrieval, namely, that an activity must either be given in a retrieval cue or be inferred from it before search can begin. Principle 5 in Kolodner (1983b, p. 302) states this explicitly, as does the section on "Finding a Context" in Reiser et al. (1987). In contrast, it seemed plausible to us that participants, locations, and times could provide unmediated access to event memories. As a result, we decided to examine their roles in organizing event memories and compare their relative importance to activity organization.

Extension of Reiser, Black, and Abelson (1985)

We performed an experiment similar to the one performed by Reiser et al. (1985) in which we compared organization by participant, location, time, and activity. Similar to Reiser et al.'s Experiment 1, subjects received two cues on each trial, their task being to remember a specific event that involved both pieces of information. Again the dependent measure was how long subjects took to retrieve an event.

We used four different kinds of cues: activities (e.g., *watch television*), participants (e.g., *your mother*), locations (e.g., *in the cafeteria*), and times (e.g., *noon*). Forming all possible pairs of cues resulted in six kinds of cue pairs (as shown in the left column of Table 8.3). Several instances were constructed for each of the six possible pairs in each of two stimulus lists.

As in the work of Reiser et al., the central manipulation was the order in which subjects received the two pieces of information from a given pair. For each pair, half of the subjects received the two pieces of information in one order, and the other half received them in the reverse order. For example, half the subjects received *watched TV/with your mother*, and half received *with your mother/watched TV*, this being an instance of an activity/ participant pair. Each subject received instances of each kind of pair in each order; however a subject received a given piece of information as a cue only once in the study (i.e., specific pairs were counterbalanced between subjects). An effort was made to construct each pair such that its two pieces of information were not highly predictive of one another.

On each trial, the first cue was presented for 2 sec before the second cue and remained on the screen during presentation of the second cue. Subjects pressed a response key as soon as they had remembered a specific event or decided they could not remember an event. When subjects remembered an event, they wrote a brief description of it. In the results that follow, only reaction times for trials on which subjects remembered an event are reported.

If activities are the primary organizers of autobiographical memories, with the other cues being subordinate indices, then receiving activity information first should result in faster access than receiving activity information second. As can be seen from Table 8.3, however, none of the differences between the two orderings for a given pair was significant. Order did not have an overall effect and did not affect any particular pair. Most important, order did not affect any of the pairs containing activity information (in the upper half of Table 8.3). In fact, receiving activity information first resulted in slightly slower retrieval than receiving it second for two of these pairs.

These results probably did not result from task insensitivity to differences in cue order. Reiser et al. found an effect of over 2 sec for the cues they studied, indicating that this task can clearly detect order effects. Instead these data suggest that none of these four types of information – activities, participants, locations, or times – is more important than another in organizing events. Consequently, other kinds of knowledge appear just as important in organizing event memories as activities. It does not appear that activities are the primary organizers of events, with participants, locations, and times providing subordinate indexing schemes within specific activities.[6]

Wagenaar's (1986) study of his own memory similarly compared the effectiveness of *who, what, where,* and *when* cues in retrieving events. Analogous to our result just described, he found that the order in which he received pairs of these cues did not affect the probability he would remember an event. Because his classification of cues appears fairly different from ours, however, care should be taken in comparing results. Wage-

Table 8.4. *Average frequency of recall as a function of cue type in the cued-recall study*

	Cue type			
Measure	Participant	Activity	Location	Time
Number of cues	19.54	11.79	11.50	5.13
Number of events	87.75	65.58	71.50	27.13
Number of events per cue	4.61	5.48	6.18	5.08
Number of events in first 5 sec	1.30	.62	1.05	.78

naar's only example of his classification scheme is of an event in which he saw da Vinci's *Last Supper* in a church in Milan on Saturday, September 10, 1983, with Elizabeth and Geoffrey Loftus. In this example, *who* is *Leonardo da Vinci, what* is *I went to see his Last Supper, where* is *a church in Milan,* and *when* is *Saturday, September 10, 1983.* Our scheme would have made different classifications. For example, we would have counted *Elizabeth and Geoffrey Loftus* as *participants* rather than *Leonardo da Vinci,* who is not a live participant. In addition, his *what* cues generally seem different from our *activity* cues and often seem to be a combination of several things, including actions and objects. Finally, our time cues were not specific dates and times but were more general, such as *springtime, weekend,* and *evening.*

Cued recall

These next data are from the cued-recall study described earlier. During the initial session, subjects generated cues for 60 sec and, a week or so later, generated events involving each cue for 60 sec. One group of subjects generated and used activity cues, and three other groups generated and used participant, location, and time cues, respectively. Of interest was whether or not activity cues would provide superior access to events. If events are primarily organized by activity, then activity cues should provide the fastest and most productive access.

Some of the relevant data from this study are shown in Table 8.4. The first row shows the average number of cues generated by subjects in each condition. Statistical analyses found that subjects generated more participants than any other kind of cue, generated equal numbers of activities and locations, and generated times less frequently than all other kinds of cues.

The second row shows the average number of total events generated by a subject, summed across all of the subject's cues. Statistical analyses found that participant cues generated more total events than activity cues, that location cues generated the same number of total events as participant and activity cues, and that time cues generated fewer total events than each other kind of cue. One could argue that these results are trivial because, after all, the total number of retrieved events reflects the total number of available cues. However it is perhaps interesting to note that if one wants to maximize the number of events retrieved with a single kind of cue, then the availability of a certain kind may make it more productive overall than other kinds.

The third row shows the average number of events generated per cue. Statistical analyses found that location cues generated more events on the average than participant and time cues. Although the difference between location and activity cues was not significant, location cues generated .70 more events per cue on the average than did activity cues.

The fourth row shows the average number of events generated in the first 5 sec of the 60-sec protocol period by a subject. This measure indexes how quickly subjects accessed events using a particular type of cue. Statistical analyses found that participant cues resulted in faster access than any other kind of cue, that locations resulted in the next fastest access, that times resulted in the next fastest access, and that activities resulted in the slowest access (each of these differences was significant). If in fact it were necessary to access an activity organization before accessing an event, then activity cues should have provided the fastest access, not the slowest access. To retrieve an event with a participant cue, according to the activity dominance hypothesis, it would first be necessary to infer a possible activity associated with that participant before an event could be found. Because other kinds of cues provide faster access than activities, retrieving an event does not appear to require the use of activity organization.

None of the measures in Table 8.4 shows an advantage for activity cues over nonactivity cues. Activity cues were not the most frequent kind of cue. They did not retrieve the largest number of total events, they did not retrieve the most events per cue, and they resulted in the slowest access of events. Similar to our reaction-time study, we failed to find an advantage of activity organization over organization by participant, location, and time. It should be noted that subjects were just as likely to access memories of specific events from nonactivity cues as from activity cues (Table 8.2). Nonactivity cues were at least as fast and productive as activity cues in accessing autobiographical information and provided equal access to memories of specific events.

Wagenaar (1986) compared the effectiveness of various kinds of cues and found, contrary to us, that effectiveness dropped sharply from *what* to *where* to *who* to *when* cues. As discussed earlier, however, his classifica-

Table 8.5. *Percentages of cluster types and examples of cluster types from the free-recall study*

Cluster type[a] and examples	Percentage
Parts of an extended event	29
and after this time I took a trip to Europe	
started out in Holland, Amsterdam, with my parents	
from which we went to Heidelberg, Germany,. . .	
then to Italy, Venice, Florence, up to . . . and over to England	
this trip lasted approximately 4 weeks	
at which time, I traveled around England for a week by myself by train	
and then I flew home around August 14th	
Instances of a kind of activity	17
went swimming at Red Oaks with a friend of mine	
went swimming at the University of Hartford because my brother went	
to summer school there	
went to the reservoir	
Parts of a summarized event	13
everyday we used to go and sit in this little restaurant before dinner	
and have coffee or something	
and watch the people walk by	
and got to know the waiters	
that was real interesting	
everyday we'd see different people walk by	
on my days off, I slept 'till about 10:00	
I layed around in the backyard by the pool	
I usually ate lunch with my dad	
on days I did work, I woke about 6:00 in the morning	
I went running	
after I went running about 2 or 3 miles, I got dressed for work	
Events organized chronologically or by a particular time	11
after school got out, I stayed home from graduation	
and flew home to Connecticut	
and rested a couple of days	
and I went to work in a retail store . . .	
Parts of a specific event	9
and we went to Circus World one day	
my brother . . . brought his girlfriend . . . I brought my boyfriend . . .	
my mom and dad went	
it was really good	
we rode all sorts of rides	
we saw a circus	
we spent most of the day there	

Table 8.5. *(cont.)*

Cluster type[a] and examples	Percentage
Events involving the same person or group of people	6
I also saw many of my friends from school before I left Italy	
and we went around Rome	
and we walked	
and we went shopping	
and we saw a lot of Rome	
Adding on to a previous grouping[b]	5
Events in the same location	4
we would take a lot of Metro rides, subway rides	
one time I had my sunglasses stolen in the Metro . . .	
another time we saw these bands of robber kids being caught . . .	
and they had musicians who stand in the middle and play	
then they'd ask for money	
Miscellaneous groupings	6

[a]Cluster types are defined in the text.
[b]These were cases in which a cluster of statements was a continuation of a cluster that had been generated earlier but that had been interrupted by at least one other different kind of cluster.

tion of cues was different from ours, and his *what* cues appeared to be a combination of several factors, including activities and objects. Most important, cues were sampled very differently in the two studies. Whereas he selected cues for each event as he experienced it, subjects in our experiment produced cues of one particular kind long after experiencing the events and produced cues in response to a very general type of retrieval request (e.g., produce "the names of as many *people* as you can think of [with] whom you did things . . . this summer"). Wagenaar's study shows that the cues he generated at encoding varied in potency, whereas our study shows that cues generated while thinking about the past do not.

Free recall

These next data are from the free-recall study described earlier. Subjects in this experiment were asked to describe events from their summer vacation in whatever order they came to mind for 5 min. In one analysis, we attempted to identify clusters of statements in a subject's protocol that reflected particular organizing principles. Table 8.5 shows the kinds of clusters we identified and how often they occurred.

The most frequent kind of cluster was a series of statements that comprised an extended event, where an extended event, as discussed earlier, is a specific event that lasts longer than a day and is typically significant and interrupted (e.g., a job, a course in school, a diet). The example in Table 8.5 contains three extended events, two of which are nested in a higher-order extended event (i.e., *a trip to the Continent* and *a trip to England* are nested in *taking a trip to Europe*).

The second most common kind of cluster was a series of statements that were all instances of the same kind of activity (e.g., instances of going swimming). Similar to the previous two studies, however, these data again indicate that activity organization does not dominate all other organizations. Although activity organization accounted for 17% of the clusters, organization by extended events accounted for a much larger proportion (29%).

The third most common kind of clustering was a series of statements that described a summarized event, where a summarized event, as discussed earlier, is a kind of event that occurs repeatedly. In a sense, the summarized events in these protocols are similar to scripts, which have received much attention recently (Abbott, Black, & Smith, 1985; Barsalou & Sewell, 1985; Bower, Black & Turner, 1979; Fivush, 1984; Galambos & Rips, 1982; Mandler & Murphy, 1983; Nelson et al., 1983; Nelson & Gruendel, 1981; Nottenburg & Shoben, 1980; Schank & Abelson, 1977).

However the summarized events in this study differ in two important ways from scripts as they are often discussed. First, whereas scripts often are assumed to represent culturally shared knowledge (e.g., going to a restaurant), these summarized events were highly idiosyncratic. Instead of being knowledge shared by a culture, they were generally unique to a person or to a very small group of people. Subjects often mentioned their daily routines and sometimes mentioned repeated events shared with family or friends.

These summarized events differ from traditional scripts in a second way as well. Whereas much work on scripts generally has focused on their action sequences, our subjects often failed to include an action sequence when recalling a summarized event. Instead subjects often described participants, locations, temporal properties, and other aspects of a summarized event at least as much as they described its actions. Consequently it appears that other kinds of ontological knowledge besides actions play an important role in summarized-event representations.

The remaining entries in Table 8.5 show examples of other kinds of groupings we observed and how often they occurred. Subjects clearly used a number of different organizational schemes when describing this period of their lives.

Higher-order organization of protocols

Although the frequency with which various clusters occurred provides an important source of information about organization, there is another important dimension of these data to consider. Clusters in all of these protocols were to some extent hierarchically organized, even though many protocols contained violations of strict hierarchical organization. Consequently it is also important to consider the kinds of organization that characterized the highest levels of organization. This is especially true because being a high-level organization could preclude being a frequent organization.

Generally speaking, the highest level of organization in subjects' protocols was *chronological order.* This kind of organization occurred infrequently – 9% of all the organizational clusters we identified – because it primarily operated at the high levels of protocols, organizing more numerous kinds of smaller organizational clusters. Subjects generally began by describing what occurred at the beginning of their summer and then progressed chronologically through the rest of their summer.

It is important to note again that the instructions for this experiment repeatedly asked subjects to remember events in whatever order they came to mind. If in fact autobiographical memories are primarily organized by activities, then these instructions should have resulted in the highest level of organization being different activities. Once subjects began recalling events of a certain type, they should have continued recalling events of that type, if they are in fact stored together. When a subject could no longer retrieve events of a particular type, the subject should then have switched to another type of event and begun recalling events of that type. Because activities rarely comprised the highest level of organization, they again do not appear to be the dominant organizers of autobiographical memories. In contrast, chronological order appeared important because it was often found at the highest level of organization.

What subjects chronologically organized were not specific events. Instead the highest level of organization in many protocols was a chronological sequence of extended events. Subjects often spent the first part of their recall describing an extended event that filled the first part of the summer and then progressed chronologically through subsequent extended events that filled the middle and later parts of the summer. For example, one subject first described the job that began his summer, then described summer school that followed in Europe, and then described staying at home until school started. Another subject first described a trip to Italy that began and extended through much of her summer and then described staying at home for the month before school started.

Although the highest level of organization in subjects' protocols was not always a chronological series of extended events, such organization occurred at least to some extent for 12 of the 13 subjects.

Another aspect of the highest level of organization was that subjects sometimes pursued *parallel tracks of events*. After subjects completed describing information about a particular extended event, they occasionally returned to the beginning of that time period and described another extended event, or activities of a different kind, that had occurred during the same time period. As a result, the highest level of organization in some subjects' protocols contained parallel tracks of chronologically ordered information. For example, one subject, in the middle of her protocol, described a project at school. When finished describing this project, she went back and described things she did with her family during the same period (organization by participant). Another subject began her protocol with a description of the job that began her summer. When finished describing the job, she went back and described social activities that had occurred during the same time period (organization by activity).

A final point about levels of protocols is that all of the other kinds of organization in Table 8.5 were generally subordinate to these global sequences of chronologically ordered extended events. Subjects often organized their protocols at lower levels by activities, summarized events, participants, locations, and so forth. Organization by extended events occurred at lower levels of organization as well.

In summary, the data from this study again indicate that activities do not form either the most frequent or the highest level of organization. Although people often organized events by activity, they typically did so at a relatively low level of organization. Instead chronological sequences of extended events appeared to dominate the organization of subjects' protocols. Linton (1987) reports similar kinds of organization in free-recall protocols, although she notes that there may be important organizational changes as the period being recalled becomes more distant in time.[7]

Clustering in the recall of artificial events

As is well known in the laboratory literature on memory organization, if subjects are presented with exemplars from taxonomic categories in a random order, they nevertheless cluster these exemplars by categories at recall (see Crowder, 1976, chap. 10, for a review; see Puff, 1979, for a relevant collection of papers). These results have generally been interpreted as showing that people use well-established knowledge about categories in long-term memory to organize incoming information. As each exemplar is encoded, it becomes integrated with information about its category. Because exemplars from the same category become integrated with the same category information, they become organized together in memory such that they are later clustered at recall.

Lancaster (1985) extended this theoretical framework to the organization of events. She argued that if activities are the dominant organizers of autobiographical memories, then when subjects receive randomly ordered descriptions of artificial events, they should cluster them by activity. Lancaster performed a series of experiments in which subjects received descriptions of artificial events that could be organized in multiple ways and observed how subjects organized them. Across experiments she generally found that subjects used a number of different organizational strategies. Although subjects often organized events by activity, they often organized them in other ways as well. In addition, there were large individual differences between subjects. Whereas some subjects primarily organized events by activities, other subjects primarily organized events in another manner (e.g., by participants). There was no overwhelming dominance of activities over other forms of organization. This fourth set of data from our laboratory again indicates that activities do not dominate other organizers of autobiographical memories.

Pivoting

Subjects in Lancaster's experiments sometimes switched between organizations in an interesting way, what she referred to as "pivoting." This occurred when the last event in one cluster of events initiated the retrieval of a different cluster of events. For example, a subject might first recall a cluster of events that all involve *Leonard Bernstein*, but that share nothing else in common. Having exhausted the cluster of events involving *Leonard Bernstein*, the subject switches attention from the participant dimension to another dimension, such as activity. If the value from this dimension for the last event retrieved was *went sailing*, the subject would then retrieve a new cluster of events that all involve *sailing*. Because the event involving *Leonard Bernstein going sailing* ends the *Leonard Bernstein* cluster and begins the *going sailing* cluster, it serves as an organizational pivot.

The observation of pivoting in these laboratory studies caused us to return to the free-recall study discussed earlier, where we found many interesting cases. One subject, for example, recalled a cluster of events involving *local travel* (organization by activity), the last of which took place in the subway. She then pivoted from events involving *local travel* to nontravel events involving the *subway* (organization by location). Another subject recalled a cluster of events that involved *friends* (organization by participant) and then pivoted to events that involved *swimming* (organization by activity).

As discussed by Lancaster, pivoting has been observed before in young children, who pivot between taxonomic and thematic clusters of words in free recall (Ayres, 1982; Ceci & Howe, 1978; Melkman & Deutsch, 1977; Salatas & Flavell, 1976). On the basis of casual observation, pivoting appears to be a ubiquitous and important characteristic of human thought. Consider conversations. As conversants progress through a topic, incidental features of a statement often trigger a new topic. For example, a statement in a conversation about movies might mention a comical plane flight, which thereby initiates a new conversational focus on comical plane flights, both in movies and in other contexts. Pivoting may also occur in other cognitive processes, such as in planning and decision making.

Pivoting may be a ubiquitous cognitive phenomenon whose purpose is to provide continuity of thought. Just as pivoting may serve as an important means of perpetuating conversations, it may also serve as an important means of perpetuating other processes, such as retrieval from long-term memory. Because this meandering and nonfocused quality seems so ubiquitous in human thought, it should be captured by the basic architecture of cognitive theories.

Distinguishing organization in memory from organization at retrieval

Before ending this discussion of organization, it is necessary to consider explanations of organization in recall. When subjects cluster information at recall, it could be for either of two reasons: First, subjects could be clustering information because it happens to be stored together. Once a piece of information is retrieved, information stored with it is also retrieved because of relations between them. Second, subjects could be clustering information because they are using a retrieval strategy that happens to select a certain type of information from memory. By focusing on a particular property, a strategy can direct search through many different suborganizations of memory and retrieve all information possessing that property.

It is often difficult to determine which of these two sources of organization underlies clustering. As discussed by Barsalou and Sewell (1985, pp. 650–652), however, certain data can increase one's confidence that clustering is mediated by underlying memory organization. The next two sections discuss data that can be diagnostic in this way.

Frequency of clustering. It is reasonable to assume that subjects frequently use the means of retrieving information that is easiest for them. Because following the underlying organization of memory is an easy way to retrieve information, it can be assumed that subjects frequently retrieve information in this manner. Imagine that autobiographical memories are actually stored by activity. If so, then it should be much easier to retrieve memories involving a particular activity than it would be to retrieve memories involving a particular participant. Whereas all the memories for the activity are stored in a single activity organization, all the memories for the participant are distributed throughout numerous activity organizations. Consequently much more search effort would be required to retrieve events by participant than by activity. When subjects are free to retrieve information in any manner, why should they use a retrieval strategy that does not maximize the ease with which they can retrieve information? To the extent that subjects can be assumed to be using the easiest strategy available, it follows that the clustering most frequently observed in recall reflects the clustering of information in memory.

As described in previous sections, when we have observed frequency of clustering in our studies, activities generally have not constituted the most frequent type. To the extent that one is willing to grant that subjects generally prefer to use underlying memory organization in our tasks, it follows that activities are not dominant organizers of autobiographical memories.

Retrieval time. Measures of the time to retrieve information provide stronger evidence of information being stored together. To the extent that subjects are faster at retrieving a certain kind of information, it is likely that the information is stored together in memory. Information that is not stored together, but is distributed throughout different suborganizations, should generally take longer to retrieve than information stored in a single suborganization. It is hard to imagine how searching many different suborganizations could be as fast as or faster than retrieving all of the information from a single suborganization.

As described in previous sections, when we have observed time to retrieve events in our studies, activity cues have not provided faster access than other cues. In fact, in the cued-recall study, activities provided the slowest access. Activities do not appear to be the primary organizers of autobiographical memories. If they were, they should have provided faster access than other cues.

Narrative styles. It is important to bear in mind, however, that people may employ various narrative styles when describing events from their lives. These narrative styles may in some cases be retrieval strategies that do not reflect underlying memory organization but instead reflect various cultural and linguistic conventions. For example, we found in our free-recall study that the highest level of organization often was a chronological sequence of extended events. This could represent a narrative style in which people begin at the beginning of a temporal interval and work toward the end, moving along in units of extended events—what in some sense might be considered personal story-telling. Most important, this organization may not reflect underlying memory organization. Information may instead be organized in a different way or be relatively unorganized.

Although further research is necessary to resolve whether chronologically organized sequences of extended events simply reflect narrative style or whether they actually reflect underlying memory organization, I assume for the remainder of this chapter that they reflect underlying memory organization. As discussed later, the many functions that chronologically organized sequences of extended events appear to serve suggest that they play a prominent role in the organization of autobiographical memories.

A theory of autobiographical memories

Findings reviewed in the previous sections led us to develop a theory of autobiographical memories. It should be borne in mind not only that this theory is post hoc but also that it is based on relatively few exploratory studies. Although this theory should be viewed as highly tentative at this point, it may nevertheless provide some value as a framework for thinking about autobiographical memories and for generating future research.

This theory was primarily motivated by the following three findings: (1) the centrality of chronologically organized extended events in structuring subjects' free-recall protocols, (2) the roughly equivalent use of other organizations across our studies (e.g., organization by activities, participants, locations), and (3) the prevalence of summarized events in subjects' protocols. It should again be noted that these results were obtained from a few exploratory studies and that further research is necessary to assess their generality.

Extended-event time lines: Structural characteristics

According to this theory, extended-event time lines are the primary organizers of autobiographical memories. Kolodner (1978), Schank and Kolodner (1979), and Reiser et al. (1987) have briefly considered a similar kind of knowledge that they refer to as "eras." Brown, Shevell, and Rips (1987), Linton (1987), and Neisser (1987b) have also considered this kind of knowledge. The following sections describe some of its possible characteristics.

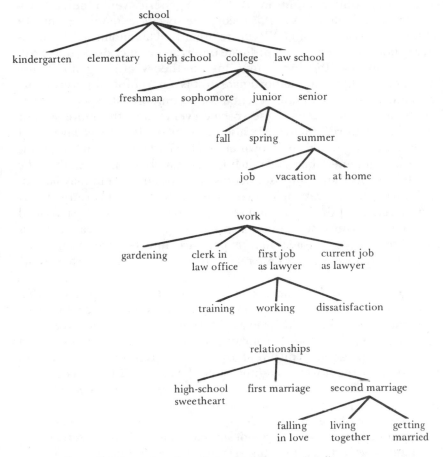

Figure 8.2. Examples of parallel, extended-event time lines.

Hierarchically and chronologically organized partonomies. An extended-event time line is a partonomy of extended events that are organized hierarchically and chronologically. As shown in Figure 8.2, for the extended-event time line for *school*, extended events such as *college, junior,* and *summer* are nested within one another hierarchically, and extended events that are parts of the same extended event are ordered chronologically (e.g., *job, vacation,* and *at home*). In general, extended-event time lines appear to be a type of highly idiosyncratic generic knowledge that is constructed in the process of reviewing, assessing, and organizing the events in one's life.

Extended-event time lines are fundamentally different from the primary organization in Kolodner's (1983a,b, 1984) CYRUS. Whereas the primary organizational units in CYRUS are generic event types, the primary organizational units in this theory are specific extended events. In addition, the basic units in CYRUS are organized taxonomically by inclusion relations, where each subordinate unit is an instance of its superordinate. In contrast, the basic units in this theory are organized into partonomies, where each subordinate unit is a part of its superordinate.

At some point, an extended event must decompose into specific events that last less than a day. These specific events (and the more specific events that comprise them) may also be parts of their respective event time lines, as suggested by Brown et al. (1987). However these specific events may generally become much less accessible in memory than the extended events they comprise. Because an extended event may be activated during the processing of many specific events, and because it may often be retrieved during reminiscence, it may become well established in memory. In contrast, because a specific event may receive much less processing, and because it may experience interference from many events of its type, it may become relatively inaccessible after a short time.

Parallel extended-event time lines. This theory further proposes that people have *parallel* extended-event time lines for each of the basic kinds of activities that comprise their lives. There may be extended-event time lines for family, school, work, romantic relationships, friendships, and so forth, each representing different aspects of a given temporal interval. Assuming that the horizontal dimension of Figure 8.2 represents time, extended-event time lines for school, work, and relationships parallel one another to a large extent. In support of this, subjects in our free-recall study, after describing one extended event that spanned a particular interval, occasionally went back through the same interval and described another kind of activity. Linton (1987) reported a similar finding.

Interrelation by the logic of goal attainment. The extended events in extended-event time lines may be interrelated by the logic of goal attainment, which may play the following two roles. First, it may specify how a particular extended event becomes divided into parts. For example, the extended events for *trip* and *travel* might be partitioned as shown at the top of Figure 8.3, because these parts reflect phases that are essential to goal attainment. Second, the logic of goal attainment may provide conceptual relations between extended events. As shown at the bottom of Figure 8.3, a gardening job may have served to earn money for dating a high school sweetheart.

Neisser's conjecture. As has often been noted, the structure of space often is metaphorically extended into other conceptual domains

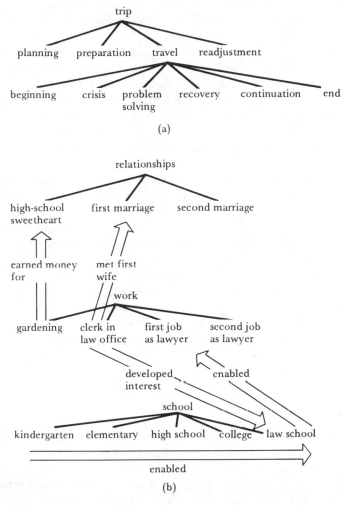

Figure 8.3. Examples of how the logic of goal attainment structures extended-event time lines: (a) specifies the composition of extended events; (b) interrelates extended events.

(e.g., Clark, 1973; Lakoff & Johnson, 1980a,b). Spatial terms enter into people's understanding of time (e.g., times that are close versus far), social relationships (e.g., people who are close versus distant), psychological states (e.g., feeling high versus low), and so forth.

Neisser (see chapter 14) makes some provocative points about this metaphorical extension of spatial structure. First, he suggests that spatial structure may be an important root metaphor because it has an innate neurological basis in the hippocampus. Because this inheritance enables all people to perceive the organization of space in relatively the same way, and because it may mature early in development, it provides a source of many socially shared metaphors.

Neisser further suggests that the organization of space may be extended to the organization of autobiographical memories. As he notes, people often use spatial terms to describe events from their lives (e.g., "I'm glad to have all of those events behind me," "that event occurred between two I would rather not remember"). Because events occur in time, and because time is often viewed spatially, events may be perceived spatially and thereby become organized temporally in memory.

Neisser's conjecture is highly compatible with the construct of extended-event time lines. Both schemes propose that the primary organization of events is chronological. In Neisser's scheme, the spatial organization imposed on events reflects their chronological order. In extended-event time lines, extended events are organized chronologically within a given hierarchical level. Both schemes also propose that events are organized hierarchically into partonomies. In Neisser's scheme, the understanding of how spatial locations are hierarchically nested within one another (e.g., cities within states within countries) is extended to events. Analogously, extended events in an extended-event time line are assumed to be hierarchically nested within one another. These parallels suggest that the metaphorical extension of space to time may provide the cognitive basis of extended-event time lines.

Extended-event time lines: Functions

Efficient summarization of life history.   Extended-event time lines provide an efficient means of summarizing a person's life. Because the concept for an extended event distills a large number of experiences into a single representation, extended-event time lines provide an efficient means of summarizing the tremendous amount of information that comprises a person's life history. Extended-event time lines also provide an efficient means of summarizing a particular period within a person's life. When people are asked to retrieve information from a particular period, they can retrieve the part of an extended-event time line that covers this period and thereby provide a global account of what occurred. For example, when our subjects were asked to describe their recent summer vacation, some began their protocols by briefly describing the sequence of extended events that spanned their summer. After completing this brief summary, they then returned to each extended event and expanded on what had occurred in its context. Initially accessing extended-event time lines in this manner may also have caused other subjects to globally organize their entire protocols around chronologically ordered extended events.

Primary organizers of autobiographical memories. Extended-event time lines may provide the primary organizers of autobiographical memories. As discussed earlier for the free-recall study, extended-event time lines generally provided the highest level of organization in these protocols. Casual observation further suggests their importance in retrieving events. For example, when one person asks another to remember an event from their life, the person requesting the event often provides extended events in which the sought-after event was nested. For example, a high school classmate might ask: "Remember that time in *the advanced Latin course* during our *junior year* of *high school* when the teacher kicked you out of class?" People may provide such cues when posing retrieval questions because it is culturally understood – as part of shared knowledge about metamemory – that autobiographical memories are organized around extended events. In support of this, Reiser et al. (1987) observed people using extended events in this manner, although Reiser et al. view organization by extended events as being subordinate to activity organization.

Elaborating cues with extended events is similar to the cue-elaboration strategies discussed by Kolodner (1983a,b, 1984), who proposes that subjects often elaborate retrieval cues extensively in the process of retrieving an event. However CYRUS assumes that the most important elaborations further specify event types, whereas this theory assumes that the most important elaborations further specify extended events. Cue elaboration has also been discussed by Norman and Bobrow (1979), Reiser (1983, 1987), Williams (1978), and Williams and Hollan (1981).

Certainly much more work will be necessary to determine whether or not extended-event time lines form the dominant organization of autobiographical memories. Studies similar to the ones in which we pitted various organizations against one another could be expanded to include extended-event time lines as a possible organization. To the extent that they are the primary organizers of autobiographical memories, they should emerge as a dominant form of organization where none has emerged so far. Brown et al. (1987) also suggest that this kind of knowledge may be central to the organization of event memories.

Temporal reference structures. Extended-event time lines may provide people with a means of "telling time in autobiographical memory." The extended events that comprise extended-event time lines provide salient temporal reference points for making temporal judgments. For example, when deciding when a political event occurred (e.g., when President Kennedy was shot), people may first attempt to determine what extended event was occurring at the time. Similarly when deciding which of two events came first, people may attempt to find an extended event that intervened between the two target events to determine their order.

Recent work by Brown et al. (1987) demonstrates the central role of extended events in making temporal judgments. Subjects in their second experiment went from high school to college at the same time that Reagan succeeded Carter as president. When judging events from their own lives, subjects were faster at knowing whether the event occurred during high school or college than whether it occurred during the Carter or Reagan presidency. In contrast, subjects were faster at knowing whether a national event occurred during the Carter or Reagan presidency than whether it occurred during high school or college. These results suggest that specific events are encoded into relevant extended-event time lines, which are later used to estimate when they occurred. Findings from Loftus and Marbuger (1983) and Robinson (1987) can be interpreted in a similar manner.

Self-concepts. Extended-event time lines can be viewed as personal histories. Because they organize memories chronologically, they enable people to construct explanations of how their lives have evolved. In a sense, extended-event time lines provide people with a sense of self, assuming that a significant aspect of people's self-concepts are what they have done with their lives (cf. Bem, 1972). To the extent that this conjecture is true, amnesics should have impoverished self-concepts (unless extended-event time lines are in fact a form of generic knowledge that is not affected by episodic amnesias). In general, changes in what a person remembers from the past may be accompanied by changes in self-concept. Barclay and DeCooke (see chapter 4), Brewer (1987), Fivush (see chapter 10), and Neisser (in press) also discuss the role of autobiographical memories in self-concepts.

Summarized events nested in extended-event time lines

The second structural component of this theory is the *summarized event*. As discussed earlier, a summarized event represents a kind of event that occurs repeatedly. Summarized events often are highly idiosyncratic in the sense that they summarize events unique to an individual or to a small set of individuals.

Because an extended event typically involves kinds of events that occur repeatedly, summarizations of these event types becomes nested within the extended event. For example, a job might typically involve making deliveries to ritzy neighborhoods, going out with co-workers to lunch at

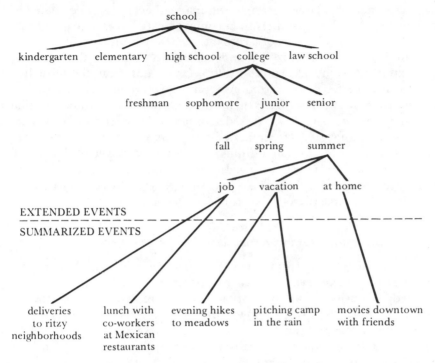

Figure 8.4. Examples of summarized events nested in extended events.

Mexican restaurants, and so forth. Similarly a vacation typically might involve evening hikes to open meadows and setting up camp in the rain. As a result, summarizations of these events become nested within their respective extended events, as shown in Figure 8.4. The summarized events that become nested within an extended event provide a representative account of the specific events that comprised it.

As discussed earlier, parallel extended events occur contemporaneously during the same time period (e.g., a job, a relationship, school). Consequently the problem arises as to how a summarized event becomes related to the relevant extended event. For example, if making deliveries frequently occurs for a job, then how does it become related to the extended event for the job and not to the ones for the relationship and school? The answer may simply be that a summarized event becomes related to an extended event only if the two are related by the logic of goal attainment. If making deliveries is not related to the goals for the relationship and school, it is never processed with these extended events in working memory and thereby does not become related to them in long-term memory. However some summarized events may be related to multiple extended events, thereby becoming related to each (e.g., if making deliveries were also part of a romantic relationship).

Assuming that summarized events become integrated only with relevant extended events explains why subjects do not recall the most frequently instantiated summarizations from a given time period. Why is it that subjects, when describing their summer vacation, do not describe brushing their teeth, getting dressed, eating breakfast, and so forth? One explanation is that subjects simply edit out these summarizations at retrieval because they are so mundane. Another account is that these summarizations are never retrieved. Because they are unrelated to the more interesting extended events that subjects initially access when describing a given time period, they remain inactive.

Hierarchically organized ontological knowledge

In order to discuss the formation of summarized events and the representation of specific events, it is first necessary to discuss ontological knowledge and its hierarchical organization. This aspect of the theory borrows from Keil's (1979, 1981) work on ontological categories (without advocating the controversial M constraint; see Gerard & Mandler, 1983). Keil has noted that children acquire knowledge about different kinds of ontological entities at different ages (e.g., objects, people, places, times, actions, thoughts, etc.). Significant developmental changes in children appear to underlie their ability to comprehend increasingly complex kinds of ontological entities and to construct knowledge for them. Because knowledge appears to be acquired in ontological stages, there may be a separate organization for each kind of ontological knowledge in memory. For example, people may have knowledge of objects organized together, knowledge of places organized together, knowledge of people organized together, and so forth.

Furthermore the generic knowledge for each of these ontological domains may be organized hierarchically to some extent. For example, objects may be organized into a hierarchical taxonomy, with abstract superordinate categories at the top and with more concrete categories at lower levels. Similarly locations may be organized into a hierarchical partonomy, with continents and oceans at the top, and with more specific locations at lower levels.[8]

Recent work on the basic level further supports the existence of hierarchically organized knowledge in different ontological domains. As discussed originally by Berlin, Breedlove, and Raven (1973), the basic level is the level of a hierarchy that people prefer to use when processing the entities it organizes. It has now been shown that there is a basic level in each of four different ontological domains. Rosch, Mervis, Gray, Johnson, and Boyes-Braem (1976), along with many others since, have shown that there is a basic level for objects. Cantor and Mischel (1979) have shown that there is a basic level for concepts of people. Tversky and Hemenway (1983) have shown that there is a basic level for locations. Rifkin (1985) has shown that there is a basic level for activities.

Most important, it is difficult to see how a domain of knowledge could have a basic level and not be hierarchically organized. The presence of a basic level in an ontological domain strongly suggests hierarchical organization. Consequently I assume that people have different kinds of ontological knowledge, each of which is hierarchically organized.[9]

An event as a collection of exemplars from multiple ontological domains

A physical event typically involves entities from many ontological domains. An event often includes objects, people, actions, a location, a time, thoughts, and so forth. Of course not all events involve an entity from every ontological domain, and events vary in the ontological domains that are relevant. However most events probably involve entities from at least several ontological domains.

When an event is experienced, according to this theory, information about each ontological entity in the event becomes integrated as an *exemplar* into the relevant body of hierarchically organized ontological knowledge. Consider the following event: A man drinks a bottle of wine after work in a Paris cafe and discusses art with his best friend. This event contains entities from many ontological domains, including actions (drinking), an object (bottle of wine), a time (after work), a location (Paris cafe), thoughts (about art), and a participant (best friend). As shown in Figure 8.5, each of these entities becomes represented in memory as an exemplar (e). Furthermore each exemplar becomes related to the most relevant and specific generic concept in the hierarchically organized, generic knowledge that comprises its ontological domain. For example, the exemplar for the bottle of wine becomes related to the generic concept for *bottle of wine;* the exemplar for the cafe becomes related to the generic concept for *Paris cafe;* the exemplar for the best friend becomes related to the generic concept for that friend; and so forth.[10]

Perceptual information in exemplars. As noted by Brewer (1987), remembering an event often is accompanied by imagery in several modalities (including the experience of motor movements). Because this perceptual information is a by-product of personally experiencing the original event, it provides memories of the event with a sense of self, that is, of an ego experiencing events in the physical world (Nigro & Neisser,

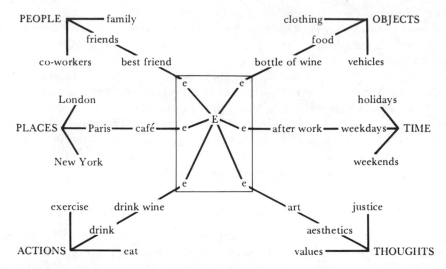

Figure 8.5. Example of an event stored as a collection of exemplars in the hierarchically organized knowledge for ontological domains. "E" represents the event, and "e" represents an exemplar.

1983). Such information is not present in memories based on hearsay (although perceptual information may have been encoded through mental imagery).

Because the exemplars comprising events may be represented perceptually to a large extent, they may underlie the imagery that often accompanies remembering events. Such perceptual information may also be responsible for exemplar effects, many of which appear to be controlled by perceptual information (Jacoby & Brooks, 1984; Kolers & Roediger, 1984). In addition, if perceptual information is repeated across exemplars, it may become abstracted into the generic knowledge they instantiate. This would provide a source for the perceptual generic knowledge that people have of events (Brewer, 1987).

Conceptual relations between exemplars. As shown in Figure 8.5, the representation of an event is an intersection of knowledge in different ontological domains. In a sense, events are the means by which different ontological domains become interrelated. However, Figure 8.5 depicts this intersection only as exemplars being related to a common superordinate (E) for the entire event. Although this is a convenient way to represent an event theoretically, it is probably incorrect. Instead of simply being related to a common superordinate, the exemplars that comprise an event probably are interrelated to each other in a much more complex manner by conceptual relations. For example, the location (e.g., cafe) could be related to the activity (e.g., drink wine) by relations of *allow* and *support* (i.e., cafes allow and support drinking wine). Similarly the participant (e.g., best friend) could be related to what was thought about (e.g., art) by the relation of *likes*. Some exemplars may be more interrelated in this manner than others. In addition, knowledge about goals may integrate these relations into hierarchical causal structures. Barsalou, Usher, and Sewell (1985) provide further discussion of conceptual relations. As suggested by DeJong (1983), these relations may be byproducts of the comprehension process.

Theoretical consequences of representing events as collections of exemplars

Exemplar-based knowledge evolution. Because Brooks (1978), Medin and Schaffer (1978), and Jacoby (see chapter 6) have shown that a wide range of cognitive tasks use exemplar knowledge, theories should provide a natural means of encoding exemplars into memory and relating them to relevant generic knowledge. Viewing events as collections of exemplars provides a natural means of explaining how knowledge in different ontological domains evolves with experience. Every time an event is experienced, it contributes new exemplars to many domains of knowledge. In addition, assuming that generic concepts are continually revised on the basis of new exemplars, this theory also provides a natural means of accounting for the continual evolution of generic concepts.

Sources of comments about events. As discussed earlier for the free-recall study, subjects often commented about the people, locations, and so forth, that comprised events. Generic knowledge related to each exemplar may provide the source of many of these comments. When retrieving an event, its exemplars may activate related generic knowledge, which subjects then include in their protocols.

Multiple access of events. Another consequence of this formulation is that an event can be retrieved directly with a wide variety of cues. Because an event deposits exemplars in many different ontological domains, it becomes possible to retrieve the event by searching any of them. More specifically, the hierarchically organized knowledge within any domain provides a ready supply of retrieval cues, one of which may be capable of eliciting an exemplar from a sought-after event. Once an exemplar is accessed from a generic cue, it may cue other exemplars in its event by the conceptual relations established between exemplars when the event was experienced. To the extent that many or all of the exemplars comprising the original event are retrieved, the event is remembered.

This view is consistent with our findings that no one kind of event information dominates all others as a retrieval cue (e.g., activity, participant, location) and that it is not necessary to first identify an activity to retrieve an event. Instead many different kinds of cues provide direct, parallel access to a given event.

Pivoting. As discussed earlier, the last event of an event cluster may sometimes initiate a new cluster based on a different organizational principle (e.g., when an event involving Leonard Bernstein going sailing pivots between a *Leonard Bernstein* cluster and a *sailing* cluster). Pivoting naturally follows from this theory. If search is focused on events involving a particular generic concept (e.g., *Leonard Bernstein*), then exemplars of that concept may be retrieved, each of which may access an event via conceptual relations to exemplars in other domains. Once no more exemplars of Leonard Bernstein can be retrieved, search may be redirected to a new generic concept in the most recently retrieved event (e.g., *sailing*). Exemplars of this concept may then be retrieved, each of which may provide access to an event, thereby resulting in an organizational pivot.

Reminding. Many theorists have recently proposed that reminding is central to learning (e.g., Kolodner, 1983a,b, 1984; Ross, 1984; Schank, 1982). An experienced event often will remind a person of a similar event, which then directs processing of the current event. As noted by Schank (1982), there are numerous bases of reminding. In fact, it appears that almost any characteristic of an event can serve to remind a person of another event having that characteristic. The theory proposed here provides a natural means of accounting for this wide variety of remindings: Any exemplar from a current event may retrieve a similar exemplar from a past event and thereby retrieve the past event. Because events can contain many kinds of exemplars, many kinds of reminding are possible.

Event fragmentation. Representing events in this manner also provides a natural way of viewing event fragmentation. It is well known that subjects often cannot remember the people involved in an event or the person who produced a message (i.e., source amnesia). This has recently been extended to showing that subjects often cannot remember where or when an event occurred (Jacoby & Brooks, 1984). One way to think about such loss of event information is that an exemplar in a particular ontological domain becomes inaccessible, perhaps because of interference, whereas all the other exemplars comprising the event remain accessible. Consequently when one tries to remember the event, one retrieves some of the exemplars, thereby partially remembering the event, but not all the exemplars, thereby producing a fragmented event.

Forgetting exemplars may result from interference. When exemplars from many different events become related to the same generic concept in an ontological domain, they may interfere with one another's retrieval, both proactively and retroactively, as well as through output interference. Although such exemplar loss may occur in all ontological domains to some extent, it may occur more often in particular domains. These may be domains in which more exemplars become related to particular generic concepts, thereby resulting in increased interference. Or these may be domains for which little mediating elaboration to other domains – via conceptual relations – is established when events are experienced. Because fewer mediating elaborations link the exemplars of these domains to exemplars of other domains, these exemplars are not as resistant to forgetting.

This interference view appears analogous to Wagenaar's (1986) file-system account of why some cues are more effective than others and why two cues do not function independently: A memory filed under an index with many memories is harder to find than a memory filed under an index with fewer memories, presumably because of more interference; and indexes with many memories function better as cues when a preceding index focuses search, presumably because it reduces interference.

Event confusion. This view of event representation also provides a natural way of accounting for the intrusion of one event into the recall of another. Because exemplars from many different events are related to a given generic concept, the wrong exemplar may be retrieved when accessing an event. For example, if someone is trying to remember an event involving drinking wine with a friend in Paris, the wrong cafe may be retrieved because the correct cafe is less accessible than the cafe in another event memory.

Actually this kind of error requires that memory contain a summarized event for drinking wine with friends in Paris cafes. When trying to remember an event involving drinking wine with a friend in Paris, generic knowledge must be used to generate the inference that the event took place in a cafe. Once this inference is made, search for an exemplar then produces the wrong cafe.

Exemplar accessibility may underlie some of the reconstructive biases observed in eyewitness testimony. For example, an incorrect presupposition embedded in a lawyer's question to an eyewitness may cause the eyewitness to integrate erroneous exemplar information into memory for an event (Loftus, Miller, & Burns, 1978). Because the incorrect exemplar was encoded more recently than the correct exemplar, it may be more accessible during later retrievals.

The construction of summarized events from specific events

Summarization after two or more events. Accounts of event summarization typically assume that summarization does not occur until after two or more events of the same kind have been experienced (e.g., Kolodner, 1983a,b, 1984; Nelson et al., 1983; Nelson & Gruendel, 1981; Schank, 1982). Such accounts typically propose that when a second event of the same kind occurs, the first event is retrieved to assist in processing the second. Similar aspects of the two events are then noted and become encoded into memory as a summarization of the two events.

Summarizations as temporary constructs in working memory. A second account of summarization is that an experienced event causes memories of similar events to be retrieved from long-term memory and be summarized in working memory. This summarization then guides processing of the event (e.g., Kahneman & Miller, 1986). An extreme form of this view – what could be construed as a hard-line exemplar view – holds that summarizations never become established in long-term memory. Instead long-term memory contains only exemplars, and summarizations exist only temporarily in working memory. As argued by Barsalou (1987), however, it would be surprising if summarizations were not transferred into long-term memory as a result of the extensive processing they often receive in working memory. This follows from a long tradition of memory research on the transfer of information from working memory to long-term memory (e.g., Craik & Watkins, 1973; Glenberg, Smith, & Green, 1977; Rundus, 1971). If exemplars become transferred to long-term memory through such processing, why not summarizations?

Summarization after one event. A third account of summarization, and the one proposed here, is that summarizations are constructed after experiencing a single event – summarization does not require that two or more events of the same kind be experienced. Consider the representation of an event memory shown in Figure 8.5. The memory is comprised of exemplars, each of which is an instance of a generic concept. The argument for summarization after one event rests on the following assumption: An exemplar cannot be related to a generic concept without that concept becoming active in working memory. Because a generic concept must become active to comprehend each exemplar, and because the generic concepts for all exemplars are therefore active simultaneously in working memory, they become interrelated and form a sum-

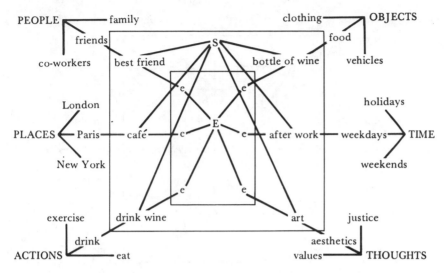

Figure 8.6. Example of summarization after one event. "S" represents the summarized event, "E" represents the event, and "e" represents an exemplar.

marized event that becomes transferred to long-term memory. An example is shown in Figure 8.6.

Consequently a single event creates two intersections of hierarchically organized ontological knowledge: one for the exemplars comprising the event (E), and one for the generic concepts used to encode it (S). Similar to how conceptual relations may integrate the exemplars comprising an event (as discussed earlier), conceptual relations may also integrate the generic concepts comprising its summarization. These relations, along with their higher-order goals, provide a *conceptual model* about that kind of event (Gentner & Stevens, 1983; Johnson-Laird, 1983; Lakoff, 1987; Murphy & Medin, 1985; Neisser, 1987a). Conceptual models serve important functions in processing events. During comprehension, they support causal inferencing (DeJong, 1983; Schank & Abelson, 1977). During retrieval, they guide cue elaboration and generate reconstructive distortions (Kolodner, 1983a,b, 1984; Reiser, 1983, in press; Reiser et al., 1987). During planning, they guide instantiation (Barsalou et al., 1985) (see chapter 9).

The construction of a new summarized event should occur only if an event activates a new combination of generic concepts. If an event activates a combination of generic concepts that has been activated by a previous event, then memory should already contain a summarization for that kind of event. Consider the example shown in Figure 8.7. Exemplars for the second and third events should activate the same

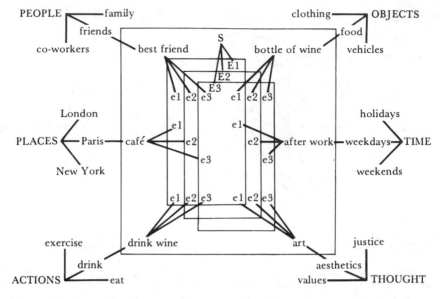

Figure 8.7. Example of three specific-event memories that instantiate the same summarized event. The specific events (E1, E2, and E3) are represented by the three inner rectangles containing their respective exemplars. The summarized event (S) is represented by the outer rectangle. Relations between exemplars in the same event, and relations between generic concepts in the summarized event, are not shown.

generic concepts as the first event and should therefore activate the summarization constructed from the first event. In addition, the second and third events may cause a "reminding" of the first event. This could occur (1) if a generic concept activates an exemplar from the first event or (2) if the summarized event activates the entire event as an instance (via a relation from S).

Because generic concepts generally may be better established in memory than exemplars, a summarization constructed after one event may become increasingly more accessible than the event memory as time passes. Consequently, even if a second event does not cue exemplars from the first event, it may cue the more accessible summarization, which then guides processing of the second event. In addition, a summarization should become increasingly established in memory as increasing numbers of its instances are encoded. In contrast, the exemplars comprising these instances should become increasingly difficult to access because of interference. As a result, this account reasonably predicts that increasing the number of instances should increase the gap between the accessibility of a summarization and the accessibility of its instances (Watkins & Kerkar, 1985).

DeJong (1983) has also proposed that summarizations are formed after encoding a single event, although for different reasons. He argues that comprehending a particular event may cause generic knowledge to be constructed, which explains that kind of event in general. For example, in trying to explain how a particular kidnapping occurred, someone might construct a causal account for that kind of kidnapping in general. As a result, this knowledge is available to help explain later events of this type. Kahneman and Miller (1986) also discuss summarization from a single event.[11]

The development of autobiographical memories

Children. This theory assumes that well-established, hierarchically organized knowledge for ontological domains exists in adults prior to the construction of a summarized event. However, this relationship is probably reversed for young children. As Nelson et al. (1983) and Nelson and Gruendel (1981) have noted, children construct summarized-event representations long before they construct taxonomic knowledge for ontological domains (Lucariello & Nelson, 1985). As Nelson has argued, taxonomic knowledge may in fact evolve from early event summarizations. The generic concepts that comprise these summarizations may provide the material from which bodies of ontological knowledge later develop.

An analogous reversal appears true of extended-event time lines. The theory proposed here assumes that adults integrate memories of specific events into preexisting extended-event time lines. However very young children may not possess such personal histories (see chapter 10), even though they do remember past events (Fivush, Gray, & Fromhoff, 1987).

One reason for the relatively late development of autobiographical memories in the form of personal histories may be children's limited opportunity to perceive extended events. The construction of this knowledge may become possible only when children understand that extended events exist and that life can be viewed as a succession of such events. Children's ability to extend the metaphor of space may ultimately determine when they begin to view events in this manner (see chapter 14). With this understanding, children may begin to construct extended-event time lines and to nest relevant summarized events within them. In addition, this newly acquired view of life may cooccur with an increased awareness of the cultural importance of developing a personal history (see chapter 10).

Because summarized events enable young children to cope with the repeated events that comprise their daily experience, summarized events are the primary products of children's initial memory development.

However these summarized events later provide the material from which ontological knowledge and extended-event time lines develop. Once this knowledge has evolved, the encoding of specific events may take place against it, and the organization and evolution of autobiographical memories may begin to look more like the theory proposed in this chapter for adults.

The elderly. Not only may extended-event time lines change substantially during childhood, they also may change substantially as people grow older. Rubin, Wetzler, and Nebes (1987) present evidence for a reminiscence effect. When people older than 30 years receive various cues and are asked to retrieve past experiences, they tend to retrieve more events from the ages of 10 to 30 than from after 30. Moreover, as these people grow older, the number of events from 10 to 30 increases relative to the number of events from years after 30. Rubin et al. suggest that this finding reflects increased reminiscing about the years from 10 to 30 as people become elderly.

Increased reminiscence about one's life may result in increasingly well-articulated and well-established extended-event time lines for the past. As a result, the elderly may provide much more information about a given period of life (e.g., 10 to 30) than people who are younger. They also may be able to generate this information much more quickly to the extent that they have reviewed the past more often and more recently.

This further suggests the possibility of extended-event time lines for the future. Younger people's extended-event time lines about the past may not be maximally developed because they are focusing more attention on what they foresee in their lives. The status of people with respect to their education, career, family, and so forth should determine the extent to which they project extended-event time lines into the future. People who have accomplished most of what they planned for their lives should have less-developed projections than people who have "their lives before them." In general, people's extended-event time lines for the past and future should reflect their current state of development.

The instability of knowledge

Barsalou (1987, 1988) argues that there are no invariant knowledge structures in memory. Instead, people continually construct unique representations from loosely organized generic and episodic knowledge to meet the constraints of particular contexts. Because no two contexts cause the same information to be incorporated from long-term memory into a representation, no two representations for a particular kind of thing are ever the same (e.g., *chair* is never represented identically across occasions).

This position may appear contradictory with proposals made here about knowledge for extended-event time lines and summarized events. However there is no reason why this knowledge should not also exhibit instability. For example, there may be substantial differences in how a person represents a particular extended-event time line in working memory across occasions. Although there would probably be similarities, there should also be context-dependent differences. Such instability should also occur for summarized and specific events, with no two representations of the same summarized or specific event ever being the same in working memory. Instability has been neglected in this chapter largely because of an interest in providing an initial and global account of autobiographical memories, and a more developed account would certainly require careful consideration of the mechanisms underlying it.

Conclusion

This theory is highly tentative. It was developed post hoc from a small number of exploratory studies, and all of its theoretical structures have been specified in the vaguest of terms. Clearly much more empirical investigation is needed to develop a sound and a complete empirical base that describes how people encode, organize, and retrieve autobiographical memories. Clearly a much better articulated version of this theory will be necessary for making unambiguous empirical predictions and for knowing how well it accounts for empirical findings. Nevertheless this theory in its current form may at least serve the purposes of suggesting research and stimulating discussion on what appear to be important issues.

NOTES

My collaborators on this project have been Juliana Lancaster, Jayna Spindler, Barbara George, and Jeffrey Farrar. Others who assisted with this work included Daniel Sewell, Robert Soloway, and Elaine Gendel. All of this research, along with work on this chapter, was supported by grant IST-8308984 from the National Science Foundation to the author. This chapter has benefited from the comments of Jeffrey Farrar, Robyn Fivush, Janet Kolodner, Christopher Riesbeck, Brian Reiser, and Jayna Spindler, who do not necessarily agree with everything it says. Correspondence and requests for reprints should be sent to Lawrence W. Barsalou, School of Psychology, Georgia Institute of Technology, Atlanta, GA 30332.

1 I am using "autobiographical memories" rather than "autobiographical memory" to avoid implying the presence of a separate autobiographical memory system or module.

2 It should be noted that neither Kolodner nor Schank uses the expression "comprehension hypothesis of event organization" in their writings. This hypothesis, as I state it here, is a summarization of several central assumptions that underlie their theories.

3 I follow the convention of using italics when referring to concepts.

4 It is important to note that CYRUS cross-indexes events to some degree by other organizational schemes besides events types. For example, locations within E-MOPs are organized across E-MOPs by geographical maps, and participants within E-MOPs are organized across E-MOPs by nationalities. However these alternative organizations generally appear secondary to organization by event types, providing subordinate indices of event types, never vice versa. In addition, the first, and arguably most important, step in retrieving an event memory is identifying its event type—identifying other attributes appears secondary and less important.

5 This episodic–generic distinction is roughly the same as Tulving's episodic–semantic distinction. Because "semantic" technically refers to the meaning of linguistic forms, I use "generic" to refer to a much wider range of knowledge.

6 One factor that may enter into why Reiser et al. found an order effect concerns part/whole relations between cues. Reiser et al. may have found an order effect for action and activity cues because actions are parts of activities. The effect does not occur for activity, participant, location, and action cues because they are not parts of each other but instead can be relatively independent. A general prediction that follows is that order effects should occur when one cue is a part of another. Consequently, order effects could occur for other kinds of cues besides activities. For participants, *Boston Celtics/center* should retrieve an event more quickly than *center/Boston Celtics,* because a center is part of a basketball team. Similarly for locations, *New York/stadium* might be faster than *stadium/New York;* for times, *summer/Saturday* might be faster than *Saturday/summer.*

7 The reader may wonder why we believe that a kind of time cue—chronologically ordered extended events—is so effective when time cues in our cued-recall study and in Wagenaar (1986) were so ineffective. However the time cues in these other studies were primarily dates and times, which are very different from extended events. Whereas dates and times are "conceptually bare" and do not have much potential for elaborating on specific events, extended events have much more elaborative potential and therefore make better cues.

8 It is likely that strict hierarchical organization is violated in these hierarchies (e.g., Conrad, 1972; Smith, Shoben, & Rips, 1974) and that several kinds of organization may exist in an ontological domain simultaneously (e.g., places may be organized both partonomically and taxonomically).

9 It is highly possible that knowledge is not divided neatly into different ontological domains. Although different ontological knowledge may be individually organized to a large extent, the distinctions between domains may not be as clear as Keil (1979, 1981) suggests. Some knowledge may be represented within more than one domain, and some knowledge may not fit neatly into any domain. The extent to which this is true has relatively little, if any, impact on the argument that follows. It is required only that people have bodies of

knowledge that are somewhat differentiated and that are hierarchically organized to some extent. Whether or not knowledge falls neatly into ontological domains and whether or not these domains are completely isolated from one another are not crucial. I further assume that each body of knowledge is integrated by intuitive theories about its respective domain (Murphy & Medin, 1985; Lakoff, 1987; Neisser, 1987a).

10 The use of "exemplar" in this theory is somewhat different from the senses proposed by Medin and Schaffer (1978), Brooks (1978), and Jacoby (see chapter 6). Whereas these theorists might assume that an entire event is stored as a single exemplar in memory, this theory assumes that an event is stored as a collection of exemplars from different ontological domains. Schank's (1982) theory of dynamic memory also proposes that an event is broken up into different parts, each of which is integrated into a different organizational structure. However the "parts" in Schank's theory are the various generalized actions that comprise an event, whereas the "parts" in this theory are the different ontological entities comprising an event. In general, an important and difficult problem is to determine how an event is broken up into exemplars, assuming it is broken up at all. A related problem is whether a single exemplar is stored for a given part of an event or whether multiple exemplars are stored. For example, is one exemplar stored for a participant in an event, or are multiple exemplars stored? If so, what determines the number of exemplars? Both of these problems also exist for current exemplar theories.

11 Trying to account for script action sequences substantially complicates the view of summarized events as intersections of generic knowledge from different ontological domains. How should we represent the hierarchically organized action sequences that comprise the "scriptiness" of many summarized events? Furthermore how should we represent the numerous tracks that such sequences can take (Schank & Abelson, 1977)? Accounting for the action sequences associated with a summarized event is likely to result in a proliferation of structure within the ontological domain for actions, which must then be related to relevant information in other ontological domains.

It may be useful to also view extended-event time lines as intersections of generic concepts from different ontological domains.

REFERENCES

Abbott, V., Black, J. B., & Smith, E. E. (1985). The representation of scripts in memory. *Journal of Memory and Language, 24*, 179–199.

Ayres, J. S. (1982) *Retrieval patterns in children's memory.* Unpublished masters' thesis, Emory University.

Barsalou, L. W. (1987). The instability of graded structure: Implications for the nature of concepts. In U. Neisser (Ed.), *Concepts and conceptual development: The ecological and intellectual bases of categories* (pp. 101–140). Cambridge University Press.

  (1988). Intra-concept similarity and its implications for inter-concept similarity. In S. Vosniadou & A. Ortony (Eds.), *Similarity and analogical reasoning.* Cambridge University Press.

Barsalou, L. W., & Bower, G. H. (1984). Discrimination nets as psychological models. *Cognitive Science, 8*, 1–26.

Barsalou, L. W., Lancaster, J. S., Spindler, J. L., George, B. L., & Farrar, M. J. (1988). The organization of autobiographical memories.

Barsalou, L. W., & Sewell, D. R. (1985). Contrasting the representation of scripts and categories. *Journal of Memory and Language, 24*, 646–665.

Barsalou, L. W., Usher, J. A., & Sewell, D. R. (1985). *Schema-based planning of events.* Paper presented at a meeting of the Psychonomic Society, Boston.

Bem, D. J. (1972). Self perception theory. In L. Berkowitz (Ed.), *Advances in experimental social psychology* (Vol. 6). New York: Academic Press.

Berlin, B., Breedlove, D. E., & Raven, P. H. (1973). General principles of classification and nomenclature in folk biology. *American Anthropologist, 75*, 214–242.

Bower, G. H., Black, J. B., & Turner, T. J. (1979). Scripts in memory for text. *Cognitive Psychology, 11*, 177–220.

Brewer, W. F. (1987). What is autobiographical memory? In D.C. Rubin (Ed.), *Autobiographical memory* (pp. 25–49). Cambridge University Press.

Brooks, L. R. (1978). Non-analytic concept formation and memory for instances. In E. Rosch & B. B. Lloyd (Eds.), *Cognition and categorization* (pp. 169–211). Hillsdale, NJ: Erlbaum.

Brown, N. R., Shevell, S. K., & Rips, L. J. (1987). Public memories and their personal context. In D. C. Rubin (Ed.), *Autobiographical memory* (pp. 137–158). Cambridge University Press.

Cantor, N., & Mischel, W. (1979). Prototypes in person perception. In L. Berkowitz (Ed.), *Advances in experimental social psychology* (Vol. 12, pp. 3–52). New York: Academic Press.

Ceci, S. J., & Howe, M. J. A. (1978). Age related differences in free recall as a function of retrieval flexibility. *Journal of Experimental Child Psychology, 26*, 432–442.

Clark, H. H. (1973). Space, time, semantics, and the child. In T. E. Moore (Ed.), *Cognitive development and the acquisition of language* (pp. 27–63). New York: Academic Press.

Conrad, C. (1972). Cognitive economy in semantic memory. *Journal of Experimental Psychology, 92*, 149–154.

Craik, F. I. M., & Watkins, M. J. (1973). The role of rehearsal in short-term memory. *Journal of Verbal Learning and Verbal Behavior, 12*, 599–607.

Crowder, R. G. (1976). *Principles of learning and memory.* Hillsdale, NJ: Erlbaum.

DeJong, G. (1983). An approach to learning from observation. In *Proceedings of the 1983 International Workshop on Machine Learning*, Allerton, IL. (Working Paper 45, Coordinated Science Laboratory, University of Illinois, Urbana.)

Fivush, R. (1984). Learning about school: The development of kindergarten school scripts. *Child Development, 55*, 1697–1709.

Fivush, R., Gray, J. T., & Fromhoff, F. A. (1987). Two years olds talk about the past. *Cognitive Development, 2*, 393–409.

Galambos, J. A., & Rips, L. J. (1982). Memory for routines. *Journal of Verbal Learning and Verbal Behavior, 21*, 260–281.

Gentner, D., & Stevens, A. L. (Eds.). (1983). *Mental models.* Hillsdale, NJ: Erlbaum.

Gerard, A. B., & Mandler, J. M. (1983). Ontological knowledge and sentence anomaly. *Journal of Verbal Learning and Verbal Behavior, 22*, 105–120.

Glenberg, A., Smith, S. M., & Green, E. (1977). Type I rehearsal: Maintenance and more. *Journal of Verbal Learning and Verbal Behavior, 16*, 339–352.

Hudson, J., & Nelson, K. (1986). Repeated encounters of a similar kind: Effects of familiarity on children's autobiographical memory. *Cognitive Development, 1*, 253–271.

Jacoby, L. L., & Brooks, L. R. (1984). Nonanalytic cognition: Memory, perception, and concept learning. In G. H. Bower (Ed.), *The psychology of learning and motivation: Advances in research and theory* (Vol. 18, pp. 1–47). New York: Academic Press.

Johnson-Laird, P. N. (1983). *Mental models.* Cambridge, MA: Harvard University Press.

Kahneman, D., & Miller, D. T. (1986). Norm theory: Comparing reality to its alternatives. *Psychological Review, 93,* 136–153.

Keil, F. C. (1979). *Semantic and conceptual development: An ontological perspective.* Cambridge, MA: Harvard University Press.

(1981). Constraints on knowledge and cognitive development. *Psychological Review, 88,* 197–227.

Kolers, P. A., & Roediger, H. L., III (1984). Procedures of mind. *Journal of Verbal Learning and Verbal Behavior, 23,* 425–449.

Kolodner, J. L. (1978). *Memory organization for natural language database inquiry.* Research Report 142, Department of Computer Science, Yale University, New Haven, CT.

(1980). Retrieval and organization strategies in conceptual memory: A computer model. Research Report 187, Department of Computer Science, Yale University, New Haven, CT.

(1983a). Maintaining organization in dynamic long-term memory. *Cognitive Science, 7,* 243–280.

(1983b). Reconstructive memory: A computer model. *Cognitive Science, 7,* 281–328.

(1984). *Retrieval and organizational strategies in conceptual memory.* Hillsdale, NJ: Erlbaum.

Kolodner, J. L., & Barsalou, L. W. (1982). Psychological issues raised by an AI model of reconstructive memory. In *Proceedings of the Conference of the Cognitive Science Society* (pp. 118–120). University of Michigan, August 1982.

(1983). A joint AI and psychology approach to the study of event memory. *Artificial Intelligence and Simulation Behavior Quarterly, 46,* 20–24.

Kolodner, J. L., & Simpson, R. L. (1984). Experience and problem solving: A framework. In *Proceedings of the Conference of the Cognitive Science Society* (pp. 239–243). Boulder, CO.

Kolodner, J. L., Simpson, R. L., & Sycara-Cyranski, K. (1985). A process model of case-based reasoning. In *Proccedings of the International Joint Conference on Artificial Intelligence* (pp. 284–290). Los Angeles, CA.

Lakoff, G. (1987). *Women, fire, and dangerous things: What categories tell us about the nature of thought.* University of Chicago Press.

Lakoff, G., & Johnson, M. (1980a). The metaphorical structure of the human conceptual system. *Cognitive Science, 4,* 195–298.

(1980b). *Metaphors we live by.* University of Chicago Press.

Lancaster, J. S. (1985). *Experimental investigations of the organization of memory for events.* Unpublished doctoral dissertation, Emory University.

Linton, M. (1987). Ways of searching and the content of memory. In D. C. Rubin (Ed.), *Autobiographical memory* (pp. 50–70). Cambridge University Press.

Loftus, E. F., & Marbuger, W. (1983). Since the eruption of Mt. St. Helens, has anyone beaten you up? Improving the accuracy of retrospective reports with landmark events. *Memory & Cognition, 11,* 114–120.

Loftus, E. F., Miller, D. G., & Burns, H. J. (1978). Semantic integration of verbal information into visual memory. *Journal of Experimental Psychology: Human Learning and Memory, 4,* 19–31.

Lucariello, J., & Nelson, K. (1985). Slot-filler categories as memory organizers for young chidren. *Developmental Psychology, 21,* 272–282.

Mandler, J. M., & Murphy, C. M. (1983). Subjective estimates of script structure. *Journal of Experimental Psychology: Learning, Memory, and Cognition, 9,* 534–543.

Medin, D. L., & Schaffer, M. M. (1978). A context theory of classification learning. *Psychological Review, 85,* 207–238.

Melkman, R., & Deutsch, C. (1977). Memory functioning as related to developmental changes in bases of organization. *Journal of Experimental Child Psychology, 23,* 84–97.

Minsky, M. (1975). A framework for representing knowledge. In P. H. Winston (Ed.), *The psychology of computer vision* (pp. 211–277). New York: McGraw-Hill.

Murphy, G. L., & Medin, D. L. (1985). The role of theories in conceptual coherence. *Psychological Review, 92,* 289–316.

Neisser, U. (Ed.). (1982). *Memory observed: Remembering in natural contexts.* San Francisco: Freeman.

(Ed.). (1987a). *Concepts and conceptual development: The ecological and intellectual bases of categories.* Cambridge University Press.

(1987b). Nested structure in autobiographical memory, In D. C. Rubin (Ed.), *Autobiographical memory* (pp. 71–81). Cambridge University Press.

(in press). The development of consciousness and the acquisition of skill. In P. M. Cole, D. L. Johnson, & F. S. Kessel (Eds.), *Self and consciousness.* New York: Praeger.

Nelson, K., Fivush, R., Hudson, J., & Lucariello, J. (1983). Scripts and the development of memory, In M. T. H. Chi (Ed.), *Contributions to human development: Trends in memory development research* (Vol. 9, pp. 52–70). New York: Karger.

Nelson, K., & Gruendel, J. (1981). Generalized event representations: Basic building blocks of cognitive development. In A. Brown & M. Lamb (Eds.), *Advances in developmental psychology* (Vol. 1, pp. 131–158). Hillsdale, NJ: Erlbaum.

Nigro, G., & Neisser, U. (1983). Point of view in personal memories. *Cognitive Psychology, 15,* 467–482.

Norman, D. A., & Bobrow, D. G. (1979). Descriptions: An intermediate stage in memory retrieval. *Cognitive Psychology, 11,* 107–123.

Nottenburg, G., & Schoben, E. J. (1980). Scripts as linear orders. *Journal of Experimental Social Psychology, 16,* 329–347.

Puff, C. R. (Ed.). (1979). *Memory organization and structure.* New York: Academic Press.

Reiser, B. J. (1983). *Contexts and indices in autobiographical memory.* Doctoral dissertation, Yale University. Cognitive Science Technical Report 24, Yale University.

(1986). The encoding and retrieval of memories of real-world experiences. In J. A. Galambos, R. R. Abelson, & J. B. Black (Eds.), *Knowledge structures* (pp. 71–99). Hillsdale, NJ: Erlbaum.

Reiser, B. J., Black, J. B., & Abelson, R. P. (1985). Knowledge structures in the organization and retrieval of autobiographical memories. *Cognitive Psychology, 17,* 89–137.

Reiser, B. J., Black, J. B., & Kalamarides, P. (1987). Strategic memory search processes. In D. C. Rubin (Ed.), *Autobiographical memory* (pp. 100–121). Cambridge University Press.

Rifkin, A. (1985). Evidence for a basic level in event taxonomies. *Memory & Cognition, 13,* 538–556.

Robinson, J. A. (1987). Autobiographical memory: A historical perspective. In D. C. Rubin (Ed.), *Autobiographical memory* (pp. 159–190). Cambridge University Press.

Rosch, E., Mervis, C. B., Gray, W. D., Johnson, D. M., & Boyes-Braem, P. (1976). Basic objects in natural categories. *Cognitive Psychology, 8,* 382–439.

Ross, B. H. (1984). Remindings and their effects in learning a cognitive skill. *Cognitive Psychology, 16,* 371–416.

Rubin, D. C. (1987). *Autobiographical memory.* Cambridge University Press.

Rubin, D. C., Wetzler, S. E., & Nebes, R. D. (1987). Autobiographical memory across the lifespan. In D. C. Rubin (Ed.), *Autobiographical memory* (pp. 202–224). Cambridge University Press.

Rundus, D. (1971). Analysis of rehearsal processes in free recall. *Journal of Experimental Psychology, 89,* 63–77.

Salatas, H., & Flavell, J. H. (1976). Retrieval of recently learned information: Development of strategies and control skills. *Child Development, 47,* 941–948.

Schank, R. (1975). *Conceptual information processing.* New York: American Elsevier.
  (1982). *Dynamic memory: A theory of reminding and learning in computers and people.* Cambridge University Press.

Schank, R., & Abelson, R. P. (1977). *Scripts, plans, goals, and understanding.* Hillsdale, NJ: Erlbaum.

Schank, R., & Kolodner, J. L. (1979). Retrieving information from an episodic memory. Research Report 159, Department of Computer Science, Yale University, New Haven, CT.

Smith, E. E., Shoben E. J., & Rips, L. J. (1974). Structure and process in semantic memory: A featural model for semantic decisions. *Psychological Review, 81,* 214–241.

Tulving, E. (1972). Episodic and semantic memory. In E. Tulving & W. Donaldson (Eds.), *Organization of memory* (pp. 381–403). New York: Academic Press.
  (1983). *Elements of episodic memory.* New York: Oxford University Press.

Tversky, B., & Hemenway, K. (1983). Categories of environmental scenes. *Cognitive Psychology, 15,* 121–149.

Wagenaar, W. A. (1986). My memory: A study of autobiographical memory over six years. *Cognitive Psychology, 18,* 225–252.

Watkins, M. J., & Kerkar, S. P. (1985). Recall of a twice-presented item without recall of either presentation: Generic memory for events. *Journal of Memory and Language, 24,* 666–678.

Williams, M. D. (1978). The process of retrieval from very long-term memory. Center for Human Information Processing Technical Report 75, University of California, La Jolla.

Williams, M. D., & Hollan, J. D. (1981). The process of retrieval from very long term memory. *Cognitive Science, 5,* 87–119.

9

The ontogeny of memory for real events

KATHERINE NELSON

The focus of this chapter is on how memory for real-life events – both specific episodes and general schemas – develops in the early years of childhood. To begin the discussion, it is useful to consider an example of such memory in a very young child. This example is taken from a very rich corpus of material that was obtained by periodically recording the presleep monologues of a child, Emily, between the ages of 21 months and 3 years. The first example in the Appendix is taken from the very earliest recordings to give a flavor of this material. At a later point I shall consider how the monologues changed and developed over time.

In this first example, Emily talks about a real event that, according to her mother's report, had occurred 2 months earlier when one of their cars was being repaired and they had to use the other one, an unusual event in Emily's experience. Her mother was sure that no similar event had taken place in the interim period. Evident in this example are some of the characteristics of presleep monologues of 2-year-olds that have been noted by other researchers, for example, repetition of utterances with substitution and rephrasing. Of some interest here are occasional apparent intrusions into the main topic (e.g., the reference to her friend Carl). However, more impressive is the sustained topic over roughly 30 separate (although not different) propositions. Although the statements do not cohere as a narrative, the nature of the event recalled becomes quite clear.

This and other examples from the same period raise a number of questions about the development of memory for real events. How can we describe the essential quality of such memories? Do the taxonomies of adult memory, for example, episodic and semantic, fit these data? Are these memories qualitatively different from the autobiographical memories of adults? If so, in what way? Do the differences reflect different encoding, storage, or retrieval mechanisms? If Emily's memory is not different from adults' memories, this provides a challenge to explanations of the infantile amnesia phenomenon, that is, the inability of adults to recall events that occurred earlier than 3 years of age, and often even later.

244

I am convinced that understanding the phenomenon of infantile amnesia is critical to our understanding of real-event memory and its development in humans. This phenomenon has attracted many theories, but relatively little empirical study (Meudell, 1983; Spear, 1979). Most of the research on this problem in humans has relied on the recall of childhood memories by adults. Although the relevant literature is for the most part quite old (see Dudycha & Dudycha, 1941, for a review), it does reveal a number of consistent findings. For example, adults almost always have an absolute block for memory of events prior to the age of 3 or 4 years, and the number of memories for a given year increases slowly from the age of the first memory over the next 3 or 4 years. The age of the first memory varies widely among individuals, and it has been reported in various studies that females, persons of higher social class and intelligence, and those with greater verbal ability have more and earlier childhood memories than do adults with the opposite characteristics. The age of a memory is unrelated to its recall; 40-year-old individuals have no difficulty recalling events that happened 20 years previously, although 20-year-olds cannot do so. Thus, length of time since the event was experienced cannot explain the childhood amnesia phenomenon.

Existing theories of infantile amnesia posit changes in encoding, storage, or retrieval mechanisms during childhood (Meudell, 1983). Encoding changes include the possibility that the rate of encoding is slower, leading to loss of information; that the cues or dimensions encoded are different in infancy than in later years; that young children do not employ effective elaborative encoding mnemonics. Proposals regarding retrieval failures suggest that young children are unable to use cues effectively in retrieval or that they rely on different cues. Freud's (1905/ 1963) theory proposed that memories from early childhood were unacceptable and painful and thus were repressed and/or replaced by screen memories, a type of retrieval failure. Theories offered as alternatives to Freud have proposed changes in storage or knowledge organization through a reorganization of cognitive schemas (Neisser, 1962; Schactel, 1947; White & Pillemer, 1979). Along a similar line, Piaget (1971) proposed that children's memories were all jumbled up because they were unable to sequence events.

These theoretical explanations of infantile amnesia have been based on findings from research with adults or with animals (e.g., Spear, 1979). What these accounts are missing are the findings from direct studies of memory in children within the age range in which the memory block has been found to occur. Such research is not abundant and has been undertaken only very recently (see, for example, the collected papers in Perlmutter, 1980). Thus, a reconsideration of the phenomenon, taking such research into account, is in order. As an example, the tapes of

Emily's monologues indicate that a child not yet age 2 recalls episodes from her experience in an extensive and elaborate verbal form. We need to inquire whether or not that form is different in important ways from that of adults, but it seems clear at the outset that the block for early memory in adults cannot be attributed to a total lack of such memories in early childhood. Moreover, because the material in these memories is unthreatening and even banal, Freud's mechanism of repression appears unnecessary. This leaves open the proposals regarding retrieval cues and possible reorganization as explanations. But I would propose in addition that we need to consider whether or not changes in the function of memories may explain the infantile amnesia phenomenon. Thus, among the questions to be addressed here are the nature of the content of early memories, their organization, and their function.

The ultimate goal of this endeavor is to develop a functional theory of memory development that incorporates an explanation for infantile amnesia as well as other findings emerging from studies of the memories of preschool children. Ideally, the explanation that I am seeking for early memory development is a functional one in the evolutionary sense (Bruce, 1985; Oakley, 1983). The fact that autobiographical memory is a late development in the cognitive functioning of humans suggests that it is a development unique to humans as well. Assuming that it is unique to humans, what is its function? This inquiry demands consideration of the general function of memory, and toward this end I have relied on the distinctions made by Oakley in his discussion of the evolution of memory and learning mechanisms.

Oakley (1983) has distinguished four levels of information gain and storage that place different types of memory in evolutionary perspective. He sees each level as a way of dealing with the stresses of environmental change. The first level involves the genetic adaptation of an organism to an unchanging environment, for example, a deep ocean trench or a polar ice cap. The obvious disadvantage of this strategy for the species is the vulnerability to possible radical changes in the environment and the lack of possibility for opportunism. If change cannot be avoided, other strategies may be invoked. If change is completely predictable, as in the daily light–dark cycle, a genetic program may be developed to take advantage of it.

A second level of information storage provides for variable epigenesis, that is, the possibility of the organism developing according to a different program depending on the environmental conditions that obtain. Oakley (1983, p. 23) presents imprinting as an example of this level, "where developmental programmes are 'open' for a specified period in order to gain a particular class of information which is needed for their completion" and subsequently become "closed."

Of central interest to the discussion here are Levels 3 and 4 in this system. Level 3 is necessary to handle environmental changes that are reversible, and possibly also short-lasting in the lifetime of an individual, and are exemplified in the systems of learning and memory in the individual. Oakley describes a number different types of memory within this model, with which I shall not be particularly concerned here. It may be noted in passing that within what he calls "Reference Memory" systems, he distinguishes between representational memory, including episodic or biographical memory, and abstract memory, including semantic memory and concept formation. This distinction is, of course, similar to the now common and pervasive distinction formulated by Tulving (1972) as episodic and semantic memory, and Oakley notes that information that is contained in representational memory may be reorganized into abstract memory in a different form. These notions are consistent with those developed in this chapter, and they also seem consistent with a functional view of Emily's memory processes, as will become clearer when more of that information is presented.

Oakley notes that "a major limitation of information gain and storage at the second and third levels is that the information so gained is restricted to a particular individual" (1983, p. 24). The development of means for sharing information between individuals and passing it on to future generations defines a fourth level of culturally disseminated information. Although limited means for cultural sharing exist among lower mammals, this level is primarily exploited by humans, in particular through the use of language. Level 4 makes possible cultural storage centers such as schools, libraries, academic conferences, and so on. Level 3, in turn, exploits the information available through Level 4, incorporating culturally represented and shared information within the individual memory system.

It is the thesis of this chapter that autobiographical memory is a Level 3 system, dependent for its development on Level 4 processes, and that it is for this reason that autobiographical memory is a late development in the human species and that early memories for specific episodes are not retained.

To examine this proposal, I first consider some evidence from previous studies of memory for real events in young children carried out by my research group at the City University of New York (CUNY) and the hypotheses about memory development that they suggested. As with the study of Emily's memories, the focus in these studies is on the evidence for spontaneous remembering of personally experienced episodes and the way in which these memories are organized. I then examine Emily's memories in some detail and finally draw some conclusions from this evidence that bear on the thesis set forth earlier and thus present a reasonably coherent picture of the early development of memory for personal experience.

The relation between general schema and specific memory

For the past 10 years, my students and I have been studying how children organize their knowledge of everyday routine events, that is, their event schemas or scripts. Early research on this topic (Nelson, 1978; Nelson & Gruendel, 1981) established that 3- and 4-year-old children could readily verbalize their script knowledge for such recurrent events as having lunch at the preschool or eating at McDonald's. However, pilot studies of children's memories for a specific episode of the preschool day indicated that in many cases young children could recall nothing of an episode from the previous day, for example, an outing to the park. This suggested the first hypothesis about the development of memory for real events, namely:

> *Hypothesis 1:* Episodic memories emerge only after the establishment of a general script for the event. That is, ontogenetically, general script formation precedes episodic memory.

The logical justification for this hypothesis was that the basic script needed to be established through a large number of experiences of the event, each of which contained minor variations. Only when the range of minor variations was sufficiently well established would a deviation from the expected script be noteworthy and memorable. Prior to that point, all variations would be entered as possible values in the general script format. The implication here is that episodes that follow an expected routine will not be retained in autobiographical memory. The further implication of this hypothesis is that unique events will not be retained in episodic memory because there is no script to support them. Indeed, our reading of the literature on autobiographical memory supported these implications. Most early childhood memories reflect unexpected variations on an expected routine, rather than truly novel events or invariant daily routines.

Scripts and memory 1

A systematic comparison of general script and specific memory for the same events was carried out in a study by Hudson and Nelson (1986), and it appeared to support Hypothesis 1. In this study, 3- and 5-year-olds were interviewed about their knowledge of two events, having snack at summer day camp and having dinner at home. Half the children were asked to report "What happens . . .?" for both events in one interview and "What happened yesterday . . .?" in an interview 1 week later. The remaining children were asked the same questions in the reverse order.

Responses were analyzed in terms of length, content, level of generality, and the use of past or timeless present tense. The contents and generality of the narratives were similar in the general and specific conditions. That is, contrary to what might be expected, children's specific reports did not provide more specific information than was included in their general scripts for the same events. As expected, however, children differentiated the two types of reports primarily in terms of tense used, with general accounts framed in the timeless present tense and specific reports utilizing the past tense. It is difficult to distinguish between the two types of reports except in the use of tense. In addition, however, the general scripts were almost one-third longer than the reports of episodic memories (a difference of means of 8.4 and 6.5 propositions). This difference seemed to indicate that children had more trouble formulating accounts of specific episodes of routine activities than they did for the general case, and indeed in some cases children were unable to answer the specific question at all.

This finding appeared to support Hypothesis 1, which states that general schemas are formed prior to specific memories and that the latter depend on the establishment of the former. There were no age differences in this study, however, except that 5-year-olds gave longer reports in both conditions. The lack of age differences between younger and older preschool children with respect to the relation between general and specific memory is troubling for Hypothesis 1, in that according to that formulation, as schemas become better established, memories for specific episodes should emerge more easily.

There was another finding from this study that also cast some doubt on the implications of Hypothesis 1. After the main interview data were obtained, most children were asked to recall episodes of less familiar events, a field trip or birthday party at camp (e.g., "What happened at Hilary's birthday party?"), as well as an episode of their own choice ("What happened one time when you did something really special?"). Analysis of these reports showed that they were longer and more elaborate than either the script reports or the specific episode reports in the main part of the study. These data suggested that the expectation that novel events (those that did not fit a script) would not be held in memory was unfounded. However, the data did not allow for a determination of how novel a reported episode was, and thus did not provide a good test of the proposition.

A diary study of early memory

Data from a study of children even younger than those who took part in the Hudson and Nelson experiment provided similar support for the suspicion that Hypothesis 1 was at best incomplete. In this study, mothers of toddlers 21 to 27 months of age kept diaries of their children's memories over a 3-month period (Nelson & Ross, 1980). Mothers recorded each occasion on which a child gave evidence of remembering a specific experience from the past, including information on the type of cue available, the length of time since the experience, and how often the event had been experienced. Ninety-eight memories presenting evidence of recall (rather than simple recognition) were collected in this way.

Analysis of the diary entries revealed that most memories recalled some aspect of an event, such as the fact that a friend broke a birthday gift at a birthday party, triggered by a photograph taken at the party. Another frequent category, especially at the youngest ages, was the recall of the location of an important person or object. All of the memories recorded were dependent on some kind of external cue, such as seeing the location of an object, or seeing an object or person associated with a remembered object or event. The fact that all of the memories were externally cued, however, might reflect only the fact that mothers could recognize a memory as such only when an external cue existed. That is, if a barely verbal child attempted to share an uncued memory, the mother might not be able to comprehend the reference. Very few memories at this age were cued by verbalizations, although the evidence for a memory was almost always verbal.

In this study, memories for both one-time and recurrent events were reported with about equal frequency. Some of the one-time memories were very striking and difficult to reconcile with a novelty-loss hypothesis. For example, one boy recalled the plot of a movie about a chemical that made animals grow bigger and then shrink. Seeing a glimpse of the movie on TV later, he announced, "Dog get bigger, monkey get bigger, dog get smaller." Most of the remembered events had occurred within the previous 3 months, although a few memories from 6 months or earlier were also reported. Many of the children had not been using language 6 months previously, and there were a few reports of memories in which children were able to verbalize about events or objects they had experienced before they were able to talk about them. For example, one child who had moved away from his old neighborhood before being able to say the name of a friend who had lived nearby yelled the friend's name when he passed the house 4.5 months later. Thus, the evidence from this study indicates that young children just beginning to use language can remember specific events over many months.

If 2-year-olds present evidence for memory of specific episodes retained over many months, this seems to go against the hypothesis that a general schema relevant to the episode must be established first. However, it might be that these apparent memories are being treated different than later "true" episodic memories would be. It might be that all remembered episodes were entered into a "general store," where those that were repeated would fuse into a general schema, whereas those that were not repeated would be lost, discarded, as it were, after a certain period of time. This led to the next hypothesis, namely:

> *Hypothesis 2:* In early development, memory for an experience is held for a limited period of time and during this time may be reported. If similar experiences occur, they are fused into a general schema in which details of the event may be confused with one another and eventually drop out. With development, discrepancies from the schema may be noted and entered into a separate autobiographical memory system.

It was also proposed in the Nelson and Ross study that the child would move from a state of dependence on external cues to one in which internal cues could provide the context for a memory. These proposals provided the framework for the next study undertaken by Hudson and Nelson (1986).

Scripts and memory 2

The second Hudson and Nelson study compared scripts and episodic memories of 3-, 5-, and 7-year-olds for events that varied systematically in terms of familiarity. Children were asked to report either "what happens" or "what happened one time" for three events: one that had been experienced more than five times, one that had been experienced two to five times, and a one-time experience, as designated by parental reports. The events included a variety of enjoyable experiences, such as birthday parties and trips to the circus, zoo, beach, and amusement parks. The analysis of the reports in the two conditions, script ("what happens") and episodes ("what happened"), showed that children differentiated between the two types of accounts in terms of tense use, content, and level of generality. But in contrast to the first study, there were no differences in the lengths of children's scripts and their episodic reports.

Familiarity of the experience had a strong effect on both types of reports, however. With increased experience with an event, children's reports concentrated on the skeletal framework, with fewer episodic details and less use of the past tense, and reports in the script condition included more optional qualifiers. Thus, increased experience led to more general and less episodic memory reports regardless of whether the child was asked about a specific episode or a general event.

Older children gave longer accounts in response to both questions, as expected, but there were no age differences on the other measures. Still, 3-year-olds were the only children who gave simple script reports rather than specific memories when asked to recall an episode of a very familiar event. Older children included both general and episodic information in these reports, for example, "You play games . . . We played pin the tail on the donkey." This difference suggests that older children may have used their scripts to generate episodic information, whereas younger children simply "read off" their scripts instead of formulating episodic accounts. This suggestion is in accord with other findings from our script studies that indicate that preschool children are more "script-bound" than older children.

The episodes of familiar events that children recalled seemed to stand out because they were very recent or because they involved personally salient people and places. A few memories included violations of the standard-event script, such as a thunderstorm at the beach, supporting the proposal that specific episodes are tagged in memory in terms of distinctive slot-fillers and deviations from the routine (cf. Reiser, Black, & Abelson, 1985). There was also evidence of confusion among slot-fillers in some reports, for example, a child who confessed confusion between two different visits to a zoo. Unfortunately, there was no systematic way to trace the effect of recency on memories in this study. However, recency was evaluated in a subsequent study.

Long-term memory for a unique experience

In this study (Fivush, Hudson, & Nelson, 1984) kindergartners' recall for a class trip to a unique museum of archaeology was studied immediately, after 6 weeks, and after 1 year. After 6 weeks, children's memories for the episode were as accurate and detailed as their immediate recall. After 1 year—although only 7% of the children were able to recall the trip given the original question "Can you tell me what happened when you went to the Jewish Museum?"—an additional 53% responded when they were asked "Do you remember you learned about archaeology?" The accuracy of recall did not decline over the year.

A comparison of children's "museum scripts" before and after the trip showed no change, suggesting that this atypical museum experience was not included in the general script. The fact that a year later memory for the trip was not accessible with the original cues, but could be accessed with additional cues, suggests that it may have been in the process of becoming inaccessible to recall. This would be in accord with the hypothesis that for young children, unique events, even when rehearsed (as this one was both immediately after the event and 6 weeks later), are lost to memory when not repeated.

Single and multiple experiences

Hudson's (1984) dissertation examined preschool children's recall of specific episodes when familiarity, time delay, and rehearsal were all controlled. Preschool and kindergarten children participated in either a single creative-movement workshop or a series of workshops once a week for 4 weeks. Four weeks after the first and last workshops in the series, children in the multiple condition were asked to recall those episodes. Children who experienced only a workshop identical with the first or the last of the series were also asked to recall the workshop 4 weeks later. In addition, half the children in each group were asked to recall (i.e., rehearse) the workshop on the same day.

The results from this study showed that increased experience with an event resulted in more extensive, but less accurate, recall. There were no effects of experience on children's immediate recall, but after 4 weeks, children in the multiple condition recalled more activities than did children in the episodic condition. However, they also produced more intrusions in recall, as they had difficulty in distinguishing between particular workshops. Even when they had rehearsed recall of particular workshops on the same day, these children confused individual episodes in recall at 4 weeks. This appears to be an example of what Neisser (1981) described as "repisodic" memory. Further, the younger children relied more heavily on specific cues in recall than did the older children, who overall recalled more activities. Thus, this study verified the main findings of the earlier studies in showing that repeated experiences are better remembered, but lead to confusion of episodes, and that provision of salient cues is essential to the younger child's recall, whereas older children appear to be able to access a memory from a variety of cues. A consistent finding is that the older the child the more extensive the memory of an episode and the more elaborate the script for an event.

Although these findings were generally consistent with Hypothesis 2, that hypothesis was modified and elaborated to take into account these more recent findings (Nelson & Hudson, in press):

> *Hypothesis 3:* Experience of an episode is entered into an event schema if one is available, and becomes fused with that schema, its unique details being retained as slot-fillers. In this process the schema shapes what will be remembered and also leads to confusions and inaccuracies in recall of a specific episode. If an episode does not fit an available event schema, it is retained for a limited period of time, but if not repeated it

becomes inaccessible to recall. The time of retention presumably varies with the perceived importance of the episode and may also vary with the child's age.

This hypothesis suggests further that in early childhood, repeated experiences are fused into a schema and cannot be reconstructed. With development, children become able to use the tags in their event schemas to reconstruct, often inaccurately, an account of a particular episode. Six months appears to be a likely limit on the time of retention of unique memories for the 2-year-old; this limit seems to be extended to 1 year or more during the preschool period; rehearsal apparently increases the likelihood of retention, although it does not increase accuracy. As unique memories age, their accessibility to a variety of cues decreases; this effect is apparently greater for younger children, who are more dependent on specific salient cues for recall.

The model that emerges from these studies suggests why early memories should be blocked and thus provides an explanation for the infantile amnesia phenomenon that does not rely on repression or reorganization. The claim is that the memory system of the young child is similar to that of the older child and adult in content and organization. It is different primarily in its relative inability to reconstruct episodes and in its dependence on specific cues. The inaccessibility of unique memories after a limited time and the changing dependence on and importance of particular cues then explain why early memories are lost.

However, this model does not provide the necessary other half of the theory, that is, an explanation for the later retention of memories in an autobiographical system. As a background to the consideration of that development, I present some evidence from Emily's monologues that is relevant to these issues.

Evidence from crib talk

The transcripts of Emily's presleep monologues are unique in that they reveal so much about her private thought processes. Other collections of this kind (Kuczaj, 1983; Weir, 1962) have been analyzed primarily for evidence of language practice and play, but examination of their content does not show anything like the richness we find in Emily's musings. We can trace the development of her thought over the 16-month period covered by this study because she was such a facile and accomplished verbalizer. Her command of language was extremely good and at 2 years was comparable in many ways to that of children a year or more older. Thus, she cannot be considered generally representative of development at 2 years, but her monologues may still provide an insight into the processes we are concerned with here, especially as they form a picture that is consistent with other evidence.

Over the 16 months of this study, Emily's monologues, and usually the pre-bed talk with parents that preceded them, were recorded on 122 occasions, but they were recorded much more frequently in the early months than later, with 43 recordings during the first 4 months and only 20 during the last 4 months. This variability in part reflected the parents' interest and other events that intruded, such as vacations, but also reflected changes in Emily's disposition to engage in presleep talk. For the purposes of analysis of the content of the talk, each measure is reported proportional to the number of recording sessions in a given period of time. The transcripts lend themselves to a variety of different analyses and approaches to the data, and these will be brought out in a forthcoming report (Nelson, in press). For the present purposes, I am considering only the possible different functions of Emily's memory in both dialogue and monologue.

It is necessary first to comment further on the nature of the material and the problems we face in coming to grips with it. Emily's parents determined when to record and for how long, and her mother went over each recording to clarify a reference and to provide documentation of a remembered episode. For example, in an early monologue, Emily says "Mormor come . . . so . . . Mommy Daddy to cocktail party." Her mother noted that they had gone to a cocktail party the week before when Mormor (her maternal grandmother) had come to baby-sit, and also that they had told her that Mormor was coming that afternoon. This example is indicative of some of the problems. Was Emily remembering the former occasion? Was she anticipating and inferring the next occasion on the basis of the former experience? Was this a random association of ideas? Beyond ascribing some type of memory to this excerpt, further inference is unwarranted on the basis of the data available from this period. But we can note in passing how dependent this memory (like many others) is on verbal material proffered by parents. Emily had not experienced a cocktail party, and although she had experienced Mormor coming, she could know only indirectly (if in fact we attribute the knowledge to her) through parent talk that Mormor would come that afternoon.

The analysis of memory episodes in the transcripts consisted in identifying each episode of a remembered event in both dialogue and monologue. An episode consisted of a sequence of uninterrupted talk in which the memory was one of the topics. It might be that a sequence contained more than one memory. In that case, two memories would be coded for the same sequence. If the talk was interrupted by a pause of more than a few seconds or by the intrusion of a different topic, and the first topic was then resumed, it was counted as another memory episode. In order to be coded as memory, the context or mother's notes had to provide evidence that a specific episode might have provided the basis for the recall, even if it was a recurrent event. Thus, memories were either specific or novel, where "novel" refers to a one-time episode. These guidelines applied to both dialogue and monologue.

In the present coding system, if Emily remembered and talked about a coming event that her parents had told her about, as she not infrequently did, this was counted not as a memory but as an anticipation, although it obviously reflected memory for verbal information.

A rough estimate of how extensive her memory episodes were was obtained by counting the number of conversational turns in the dialogues and number of idea units (Chafe, 1980) in the monologues. An idea unit is identified primarily in terms of pauses in the discourse. These measures are not comparable, but they provide patterns that can be compared over time. The count of idea units is preferable to the use of clauses or propositions because of the frequently fragmented nature of the monologues (see Chafe's discussion of this point). Thus, the most that can be claimed for the length measure is that it is a rough estimate, useful for providing a general picture of development over time.

As noted with respect to talk about coming events, specific reference to remembered episodes was not the only material that reflected memory. Other important types of talk reveal the function of memory episodes themselves. Two that occur to a significant extent in both the dialogues and the monologues are anticipatory talk – that is, what will happen in the future, this afternoon, tomorrow morning, this weekend, or next year – and talk about routines, how things are in general. These can be compared with memory episodes both quantitatively and qualitatively. As she grew older, Emily began not only to anticipate but also to speculate about different possible alternatives for action on the basis of her previous experience. I have included these here under anticipations, but they provide additional important evidence regarding the function of memory. In some cases she transformed a memory, either from direct experience or from a parental report, into fantasy. These fantasies are not direct reference to memory, nor are they inaccurate memories, but rather represent an additional use of memory. I do not consider fantasies here specifically, although they also rely on memory. Distinguishing among these different types of talk is not an either/or issue. In the actual coding, I have not tried to construct mutually exclusive categories, because a given stream of talk might include both specific memory references and anticipations, routines, or fantasies. In particular, a differentiation between routines and anticipations frequently is nonexistent, as will become clear in the subsequent discussion.

With these caveats in mind, let us consider some quantitative relations

Table 9.1. *Relative frequencies of anticipations, routines, and specific memories in monologue and dialogue (no. of episodes/recording session)*

Age (months)	Anticipation		Routine		Memory	
	D	M	D	M	D	M
21–22	0.48	[1.07]	0.33	[0.87]	0.27	[0.67]
23–24	[0.54]	0.48	0.29	[0.54]	0.29	[1.03]
25–26	[0.50]	0.18	0.09	0.45	0.09	[0.59]
27–28	[1.30]	0.30	0	0.20	[.60]	[1.20]
29–30	[.50]	0.36	0.14	0.14	0.07	0.14
31–32	0.30	[0.50]	0.20	[0.50]	0	[0.90]
33–34	0	0	0	0	0.21	[0.79]
35–36	[0.50]	0	0.33	0	0.33	[1.17]

Note: D = dialogue; M = monologue.

in the data. Of some interest to the hypothesis put forth earlier is the relation between general memory – here coded as routines – and specific memory. Table 9.1 shows the relations between the categories of episodes per session collapsed over 2-month periods to smooth out the data. (The figures for amount of talk per session in each category reveal the same patterns, with one exception. The rise in anticipatory talk at the 6th point [31–32 months] is much more pronounced.) Frequencies greater than 0.5 (indicating one episode in every two sessions or more) are bracketed in the table for ease of interpretation.

Looking at the right-hand column under each type, it can be seen that in the earliest period, anticipations and routines are more frequent than specific memories in Emily's talk, but the latter are more frequent after that point. (During the 29–30-month period, Emily primarily spent her nap time looking at books and reciting stories and songs, and there is a low occurrence of all types.) Routine and anticipation talk showed a general decline over the first year, but rose again at 31–32 months, and then fell off to zero in the last 4 months. Specific memories show a general rise through the peak at 27–28 months and then rise again from the low point to another high point at 35–36 months. Note that, in contrast to the monologues, the most frequent type of parent–child dialogue is anticipatory, with very little memory or routine discussion.

In order to make sense of these changing relations over time, it is necessary to consider the content of each type of talk and how it changes over time, as well as to take into account relations between such talk and Emily's life experience as well as parental pre-bed talk. A central interest in the analysis of the memories was whether they were novel or everyday incidents of repeated events. A number of events that were novel to Emily occurred during the months of these recordings – trips to visit relatives, holidays, the birth of a sibling, her own second birthday, the beginning of nursery school, for example, as well as seemingly less momentous but possibly memorable episodes such as being sick and going to the doctor. Identifying which of these events show up in her presleep talk and how they are remembered should provide us with some clue as to what she found important to remember, and how accurate and long-lived that memory was.

Some novel events were recalled, but they did not include those that seemed special to the adult observer. The broken car, as in Example (1) in the Appendix, was referred to four times over the first 5 months. The fact that Emily's bedroom had been changed 2 months before the baby's arrival formed the basis for a memory three times, beginning the week her mother arrived home with the new baby. Other novel memories occurred in the transcripts once only: a trip to the library on the bus (her only bus trip); the time she watched a tow truck tow away a car; a dream about an alligator; an episode concerned with getting her own TV; a clown at a birthday party. Sickness, medicine, and doctor visits were referred to very frequently – a total of eight times – over the first 5 months, but not thereafter. In contrast, although baby Stephen appeared as an actor in some memories, his birth or homecoming was not a memory topic. Holidays, excursions, her visits to relatives – with the possible exceptions of brief mentions of planes and trains – did not show up as memories. The only reference to an episode from her trips to Minnesota and California was to taking a bath with a cousin, and, according to her mother's report, this was confused with another episode of taking a bath with a friend at home, who had cried (the cousin had not). On the other hand, she used her plane experience to formulate a general rule, as will be discussed later.

What she remembered tended to be specific variations on daily routines, and the content of these changed over time. In the early months, in addition to sickness, sleep activities, beds, and bedding were the most frequent topics – for example, that her blankets were changed, or that one time she slept in Mommy and Daddy's bed. She also mentioned visits to stores, and food episodes, in particular an occasion when Daddy made cornbread, which she liked. In the latter half of the study, these topics were infrequent or absent. Instead, she referred to incidents involving friends, incidents that happened at nursery school, stories retold from books, incidents from the premonologue interaction, and her father's activities, particularly his running in races. A topic that came up not infrequently during this period involved incidents of fighting, biting, poking, and pushing by other children. Thus, over the period of the study, as life arrangements changed, memory topics changed. We may assume that the earlier topics of sleep, food, and doctor visits became well integrated into her general personal knowledge system by 2.5 years and therefore were no longer particularly memorable. Instead, incidents involving other people – children at nursery school, friends at her baby-sitter's house, Daddy – became prominent. It should be noted that her life experience widened considerably as she entered nursery school at 2.5 years. Even though she had been in group care at a neighborhood baby-sitter's house from her earliest months, the experience at nursery school was clearly very different for her and something that needed to be reflected on.

In addition to focusing on different topics, her memories became more coherent and better organized over time, as might be expected with increasing linguistic ability. In contrast to the rather loosely organized strings of related propositions found in the early months, and exemplified in the first excerpt in the Appendix, her later memories of events often were formulated quite succinctly. For example, a true incident when she was 33 months of age is remembered in the brief and nonredundant Example (2).

We might expect that Emily's memories would be reflective to some extent of the things emphasized by her parents as important to remember. Thus, comparing the content of the dialogues with the monologues is of interest. It is not possible to be wholly systematic in this respect, because the recordings did not always catch significant portions of the dialogue. Nonetheless, there were sufficient samples of lengthy pre-bed dialogue to provide evidence on this issue. However, in contrast to anticipations and routines, relatively little specific-memory talk occurred in the pre-bed dialogues. Of all memory episodes, only 22% occurred in dialogues. Of these, a large portion concerned the location of objects, in which Emily asked for a toy or a book, and then told her parents where it could be found. There was, however, a brief period when Emily was 27 to 28 months old when her father recounted the day's events to her as a pre-bed routine, and Emily began to contribute to these accounts. An example of this routine is found in Example (3) in the Appendix. It can be seen there that although Emily picks up a bit from the lengthy dialogue recounting in her subsequent monologue, it is a very brief segment, adding a new element (John's daddy) to the narrative. On the basis of this and similar examples from this period we can speculate that the memory talk in the dialogue provides a sufficient replay of the day's incidents to satisfy whatever need she might have for reflecting on them. That is, as long as these memories are shared, they do not seem to need to be repeated in the monologue. Indeed, this was the only example in which any material from the day's recount in the dialogue was repeated in the monologue.

Example (3) also illustrates the father's use of anticipatory talk as a pre-bed routine. Unlike memories, the majority (56%) of all anticipation episodes occurred in the dialogues. In the early months, however, most anticipations were found in the monologues and seemed to be used by Emily as a kind of self-reassurance. For example, she would repeat phrases such as "Daddy coming get me . . . after my nap." Her parents sometimes referred to what would happen after nap or the next day during this early period, but anticipatory talk did not play a large part in the pre-bed routine. Interestingly, after baby Stephen was born (when she was 23 months), her father hit on the technique of using "what's going to happen after you wake up" as a comforting routine. At first, this occurred primarily when Emily was anxious, upset, or fussing, as a way of calming her down, but 6 months later, as in Example (3), anticipatory talk was used together with "what we did today" as a regular pre-bed routine. It is interesting that in contrast to the memory episodes, Emily frequently did attempt to replay these anticipations to herself in her monologues. An early example of this when Emily was 23.5 months is found in Example (4) in the Appendix.

In this example, Emily tries very hard to repeat what Daddy has told her, but has difficulty with the intercom, a topic totally novel to her. She then slides into talk about other things to buy at Childworld, including a new infant seat because the one at Tanta's house (her baby-sitter) is broken, thus demonstrating her general knowledge of what needs to be bought where. Here we see memory (for things that are broken), routines (for store-buying), and anticipation of tomorrow's activities all coming together. This is the first example in the transcripts where Emily picks up on what her father tells her specifically about tomorrow or after nap, rather than repeating what can generally be expected, such as "Daddy coming," "Carl [her best friend] coming," and so on.

At about 2 years, Emily began to use her memory for past events to speculate about the future. An example from one of the dialogues at this time is provided in Example (5) in the Appendix. In this example, Emily proposes that an incident remembered from the day's experiences might happen again. Her confusion of tenses and temporal markers (i.e., "what we do today" and "what we did now") makes it difficult for her father to interpret her intentions, and incidentally shows the difficulty of interpreting her understanding of past, present, and future at this time.

Example (6), from about the same time, also illustrates speculation about the future on the basis of past experience. It follows a dialogue that has included mention of a visit to the doctor the next day. It is impossible to say why in this example Emily is concerned about her pajamas; her mother reported that they had never taken her to the doctor in her pajamas, although she had visited the doctor several times that winter, enough times to understand the relations among doctors, sickness, medicine, and presumably taking clothes off. Emily apparently was struggling with how to integrate all of this information together with her current state of dress.

One more example, Example (7), from the later period – when Emily was 28 months – illustrates the further development of this propensity to speculate on the future. It should be noted with respect to this monologue that Emily had never been to the ocean, nor had she ever previously eaten a hot dog. Her speculation about the cars is based on the fact that the car seats had been moved that day from one car to the other. Her parents had said nothing about which car would be used for the beach expedition. Thus, it can be seen that by the age of 28 months Emily was using her general knowledge, her specific memory, what her parents told her, and her powers of inference in combination to construct an account of what might happen in the future.

One might expect that the actual experience of the projected events of this packed weekend would lead to a reconstruction that would show up in her memory talk afterward. But it is noteworthy that in the monologue recorded on the Sunday night after this series of novel episodes, no reference to any of the events was made. Indeed, it was generally the case that novel material was much more likely to occur in an anticipation than in a memory.

Parental use of "what will happen tomorrow" as a pre-bed routine tended to condense and drop out after midyear, although Emily sometimes demanded and got it. Anticipations in the monologues, however, rose to a high point at 31 to 32 months, as shown in Table 9.1. At the same time, talk about routines rose from a low point at 29 to 30 months after a long decline. To understand these facts, we need to consider the content and organization of routine talk.

As shown in Table 9.1, routines follow a course very similar to that for anticipations. Indeed, often they are indistinguishable from one another. In the early months there are fragmentary references to sleeping and waking, as illustrated in Example (8) at 21 months. Although the fragments of talk in this example are difficult to interpret, they seem clearly to represent Emily's trying to come to grips with sleeping and waking routines and with the rules that govern them. Later, Emily began to encode variations on the day's routine into her monologues, which nonetheless remained unorganized and somewhat incoherent. Example (9) is from the 23-month tapes and refers both to the fact that she sometimes stays with her grandmother (Mormor) and to the fact that Stephen sleeps in her old room and she now sleeps in a different room.

A month later, she formulated a somewhat incorrect but quite coherent rule about how things go, as shown in Example (10). It must be noted that

Emily's routine at this time was very complicated, with both parents work-ing, her weekdays spent with her baby-sitter Tanta or her grandmother Mormor, and her evenings and weekends spent with her parents.

By 28 months her parents had begun introducing the distinction be-tween different days of the week. Sunday was distinguished as waffle day (that is, the day waffles are served for breakfast), the weekends in gen-eral as Mommy and Daddy days. At this time, the excerpt found in Example (11) appeared in the monologue. This somewhat confused ef-fort at distinguishing between different types of buses is based on a distinction discussed earlier with her mother between city buses (blue) and school buses (yellow) that come only on weekdays. This account is illustrative of what seems to be important to Emily–to discover how things are and should be, that is, to set up a normative account of events in the real world as she has experienced it.

It is noteworthy that Emily formulated norms based on novel experi-ences, as well as routine ones, as illustrated in Example (12), which appeared in a monologue during the summer, after her plane trips to Minnesota and California. This example demonstrates that although she apparently did not retain specific memories of the trips, she used them to formulate general rules.

At 2.5 years, Emily's routine became even more complicated, as nursery school alternated with her baby-sitter 2 days a week. At this time she began practicing the daily and weekly routines both in the dialogue and in the monologue. Example (13) shows how she had formulated her routine about a month after she began going to nursery school, when she was 32 months. This remarkably detailed (but general) account produced on a Thursday evening was verified by her mother as being a correct represen-tation of how things generally went on Fridays at that time.

Conclusions

We can summarize the most relevant findings from the Emily data in the following terms. Routine everyday experiences and arrangements appar-ently were very important to her and formed the content of much of her monologues. They showed up as anticipations, based on prior experi-ence and particularly on the pre-bed discussions with her parents. They appeared also as formulations of how things go in general, eventually in the well-organized account of what will happen tomorrow presented in the last example, which consists of over 50 propositions correctly se-quenced.[1] Specific memories in the monologues were primarily of varia-tions on daily routines, very rarely of novel events. On the other hand, novel episodes were anticipated and discussed by parents, and these frequently showed up also as anticipations in the monologues.

Overall, parents talked about how things are or should be and about what would happen in the future, rather than about what had happened during the day or in the more distant past. This well might not be characteristic of the parental talk in general; they quite probably talked about past events at other points during the day. When they did talk about the past in the pre-bed dialogue, it was almost always about what had happened that day. In contrast, Emily's monologic references to the past often were to events that had happened days, weeks, and even months earlier. Moreover, when a memory was discussed in the dialogue, it generally did not reappear in the monologue.

Monologue topics seemed to be ones that Emily was struggling to make sense of, either because she needed to organize her knowledge of a routine, including the incorporation of unusual variations, or because her parents had presented new information that she tried to come to grips with, as in Example (7). In making sense of direct and indirect experience, she called on all aspects of her knowledge system, including general knowledge, specific memory, and speculations based on logical (but often incorrect) inference.

From this perspective, distinguishing between memory episodes and other types of material in these transcripts may be misleading inasmuch as all of the topics reflect memory in some way, and they vary primarily in terms of how memory is used. Other types and other uses of memory, not discussed here, can also be identified in the data. I have noted that in the later transcripts (at 2.5 to 3 years), memories often were transformed into fantasies. In addition, episodes of songs, stories, book "reading," playing out caretaking routines with dolls and stuffed animals, practice of numbers, letters, and colors, all reflecting memory for types of material not based directly on daily experience, also occurred with some frequency. Further, there was evidence of the formation of what we have called "slot-filler categories," that is, categories of items that fill slots in scripts, such as the listing of different foods that she liked. Thus, the varieties of memory and memory functions are more extensive than the specific episodic recounts that I have focused on here. The point that I want to emphasize, however, is that what gets talked about in these presleep monologues are those aspects of her experience that Emily apparently feels the need to incorporate into her organized knowledge system; episodic memory is one source of systematized knowledge.

In order to integrate these observations with the findings from prior studies and to see their implications for the development of early memory, infantile amnesia, and the establishment of an autobiographical memory system, we need to consider further the organization of personal knowledge. To begin with, as she progresses through her third

year, Emily is increasingly able to organize the material in her monologues more coherently, although unlike her interactive speech at this
time, her monologues remain somewhat loose, often with what seem to
be random associations between topics.[2]

We cannot ignore the possibility that the apparent developmental
increase in organization reflects only a general increased ability to organize verbal material, that is, to construct narratives. Nonetheless, it
seems probable that this increase in organization reflects a real increase
in the ability to impose organization on the personal knowledge base.
Moreover, there is evidence in the data that supports this conclusion.
Note in Table 9.1 the initial decline and subsequent rise in routines and
anticipations. The decline is associated with a decline in the topics of
sleeping, eating, going to Tanta's, and Mormor coming, all topics concerned with the organization of Emily's daily routine at that time. Presumably, talking about these topics in the monologues enables her to
get them under control, in the sense that she understands the content
and structure of these daily events and is able to predict their occurrence and sequence. When this level of understanding is achieved,
these topics are abandoned, and the monologues then focus on different types of material – stories, songs, and so on.

But routines and anticipations rise again in frequency as Emily's life
changes, after she enters nursery school at the age of 2.5 years. As we
have seen in Example (13), this material in turn comes under control and
becomes well organized within a month of this new experience. Unlike
the lengthy period devoted to organizing knowledge of her earlier routine (6 months or more, depending on when we assume her organizing
efforts to have begun), the organizing process takes place very quickly,
presumably because she is now more practiced at such organization than
she was 6 months earlier. Note that after this point, anticipations and
routines again disappear completely from the monologues, presumably
an indication that she has gotten this new material under control and no
longer needs to focus on it.

Are these data supportive of Hypothesis 3 set forth earlier? I believe
they are in that they reflect the organization of general knowledge and
the incorporation of specific episodic variations on routines into general
event schemas. Memory for novel episodes is rare in Emily's monologues, and such episodes are not remembered for more than a few
months. It is interesting in this regard that nothing appears in the transcripts between 2.5 and 3 years from episodes that could be dated to the
previous year.

Our original expectation that early memories would depend on external cuing was clearly wrong, however, in that in these presleep monologues no external cues to the memories are present. Rather, the need to

organize experience apparently provides all the necessary cues for remembering an experience.

With regard to the explanation for infantile amnesia, the evidence from the preschool studies reviewed earlier and from the detailed examination of Emily's monologues does not support any of the earlier proposed theories. There does not appear to be an encoding problem, nor a general retrieval problem for young children (although the particular cues that are successful for a young child may be different than those for older children). Moreover, organization of knowledge for very young children appears similar to that for older children and adults. Although this organization may become more focused with development, there is nothing to suggest the need for or the existence of a general reorganization of memory. Contrary to Piaget's suggestion, all of our research shows that children as young as 2 years have a fairly good ability to impose or abstract a temporal sequence on events (O'Connell & Gerard, 1985).

However, taking a functional and evolutionary view of memory, as suggested by Bruce (1985), and using the distinctions outlined by Oakley (1983), suggests a more adequate explanation of the infantile amnesia phenomenon that complements Hypothesis 3. As outlined earlier, Oakley distinguished between information gain and storage at the individual level (Level 3) and at the culturally shared level (Level 4) and noted that Level 3 may exploit the information available at Level 4. How does this taxonomy bear on the questions raised here? In this perspective, memory is one aspect of the total adaptive system of information gain and storage. As an adaptive system, the general function of memory is to predict and prepare for future encounters, actions, and experiences. That is, memory as such has no value in and of itself, but takes on value only as it contributes to the individual's ability to behave adaptively.

This view provides a way of accounting for the various facts that we have encountered here, but it also raises further questions about the autobiographical memory system. Under this view, the formation of general schemas of routine events is of highest adaptive priority. Noting the variations in routines is important to the organization of schemas that will provide reliable expectations about future encounters. Highly novel events—ones that do not fit prior schemas—may be retained, available for schematizing when another such episode is experienced. However, if another episode similar to the first does not appear, memories for these events will have no apparent adaptive value. We have seen that in fact novel episodes play little role in Emily's memory talk. I have also suggested that she talks primarily about events that need organization and resolution. When a single novel episode occurs, there is no way to organize and resolve its similarities and differences with other events. Presumably, novel episodes are not available indefinitely and thus are lost to the memory system. If the single novel event is of great adaptive significance (e.g., is life-threatening), information about it may be retained for an indefinite period (although not necessarily in an episodic form). Such events are rare in the lives of children, and they do not occur in the Emily data. Under this view, all that we have observed in Emily's monologues are efforts at organizing information that will be available as a support for understanding and acting in the future. What we have not observed is precisely the establishment of an autobiographical memory system per se as it exists in older children and adults.

The proposal here is that whereas general event memory is a product of the individual memory system and is derived from the organization of information from the personal experience of episodes, the autobiographical memory system is a product of social and cultural construction. In the terms that Oakley (1983) set forth, its source is Level 4 (cultural) memory rather than Level 3 (individual) memory. As such, it is a uniquely human system, dependent on language and the sharing of experiences between individuals. This view is in accord with Tulving's claim: "Remembering past events is a universally familiar experience. It is also a uniquely human one. . . . Other members of the animal kingdom . . . cannot travel back into the past in their own minds" (1983, p. 1). I would add to this that establishing a past that can be traveled through probably depends on socially shared remembering experiences. Although it is clear that Emily remembered events that had happened in the past, there is little or no evidence that she had developed an organized set of specific memorable experiences from the past. Indeed, the fact that the topics of her memory changed substantially over the year, with earlier topics dropping out, indicates that she did not travel back through the same past at different points in development. For example, she did not go back to the broken-car episode or to the trip-to-the-library-on-the-bus episode a year later and replay them to herself. Indeed, why should she? These incidents, like others she remembered, had no value simply as memories, but rather as information-laden experiences to be organized along with other such experiences in order to form a functional "world model" that could be used to interpret and predict events in the future.

The distinctive thing about the autobiographical memory system is that the memories it contains do appear to be valued for themselves. Of course, many such memories serve the adaptive function of increasing predictability, but many seem to be held solely for their social or personal enjoyment (or, in some cases, embarrassment). Sharing memories with others is in fact a prime social activity. The suggestion here is that this activity is learned in early childhood, and the result of this learning is the establishment of a store of memories that are shareable and ultimately reviewable by the individual, forming a personal history that has its own value independent of the general memory function of prediction and preparation for future events.

We have noted that Emily's parents did relatively little pre-bed talking about past events, and when they did they talked about events of the day, not about the distant past. They did not say "Remember when we went to the ocean?" Of course, being a very verbal family, they may have engaged—and probably did engage—in this kind of talk on other occasions. But during the period in question, in the data we have available, they emphasized to a marked degree what would happen in the future and how things were and should be in general. These topics can be seen to fit the adaptive hypothesis very neatly; that is, they prepared Emily— as did her own experience—for what to expect and how to behave.

Sharing memories is a type of activity altogether different from instruction about how things are and should be, however pleasantly such information is presented. A few studies have begun to look specifically at how adults talk about the past with their young children (de Loache, 1984; Eisenberg, 1985; Engel, 1986; Sachs, 1983), and we can draw some lessons from this work. First, it appears from all of these studies that young children are quite explicitly taught how to talk about the past. As Eisenberg notes, children seem to have to learn the point of talking about the past. Mothers in our culture frequently begin drawing their children into such talk during the second year, but it is not until the third year or later that most children take an active part in this type of talk. Sachs (1983) did not find evidence of memory sharing in her study of a single child until 3 years of age. De Loache (1984) found that mothers tended to focus on general information, rather than specific episodes, in their memory talk with 2- and 3-year-olds, a finding that accords well with the adaptive hypothesis. Engel (1986) found that some of the mothers she studied engaged in memory talk of a reminiscing type during the second year, whereas others focused on practical memory, such as locating lost objects. Interestingly, the children of reminiscing mothers had begun to take an active role in contributing to such talk by the age of 2 years, whereas the children of practical rememberers took little part in memory talk, although the two types of children did not differ on other variables such as language competence.

Studies of adults' childhood memories are consistent with the suggestion that autobiographical memory is learned from others in the finding that early memory is correlated with verbal ability, high social class, and female gender. All of these factors can be expected to be associated with more and earlier memory sharing between parents and their children. We might also expect to find that children with more siblings have more early memories, because the older children might readily talk to the younger about these topics.

Because this proposal is based on evolutionary considerations, it is worth emphasizing that the autobiographical memory system as it is conceived here is unique to humans, as Tulving suggested. To say that it depends for its establishment on the socially valued sharing of memories is not quite the same as claiming that it depends on language, although the two claims are obviously related. But the implication is clear that the infantile amnesia problem in humans is quite different from that of infrahuman animals such as rats (Spear, 1979), and the two cannot be accounted for in the same terms.

At first consideration, Emily might seem to be an exception to the claims set forth here, in that she engaged in extensive memory talk in the apparent absence of a model for this type of talk. But the claim here is that her solitary memory talk was different from shared reminiscing as a social activity; she engaged in such talk in the service of organizing knowledge, not in the service of social bonding. As such, the memories talked about would be expected to disappear as specific episodes as they became integrated into her personal knowledge system. In contrast, socially shared memories are expected to be retained in specific narrativized form.

In brief, the claim here is not that early autobiographical memory is lost in infantile amnesia, but rather that it never existed as such. That is, the Level 4 autobiographical system that is set up is different in function and kind from the Level 3 system that exists in the early years. That Level 3 system presumably continues serving its function, with the same relationships between specific episodic memory and general schemas obtaining. Our Hypothesis 3 seems to explain the data on early memory quite well. In considering that hypothesis, I pointed out that whereas it could explain why early memories are lost, it did not explain why later ones are retained. The proposal here is that what changes in the system is that instead of being lost, novel memories may be shared and thus retained in a newly established autobiographical system, perhaps throughout life. Of course, once established, the autobiographical system need no longer be dependent on sharing; that is, after early childhood, an experience does not need to be socially shared to be retained in the system, although it frequently will be, and may be held longer if it is. This, like many other implications of this proposal, is a problem for further research.[3]

APPENDIX

Note: Square brackets indicate uncertain transcriptions. Question marks indicate verbalizations that cannot be interpreted. Phrasing is roughly indicated by line separation and punctuation.

(1)
Car broke,
The – Emmy can't go in the car.
Go in green car.
No. Emmy go in the car
Broken. Broken. Their car broken,
so Mommy Daddy go in their their car,
Emmy Daddy go in the car,
Emmy Daddy Mommy go in the car, broke,
Da . . . da car . . .
their, their, car broken.
So go in the green car.
Fix the car broken,
So go in the green car . . .
Car fix their car broke,
So their car broke . . .
So my Daddy went in the meeting in, in the, in the car.
So Emmy put the [circles] in the, [w-] in the way.
Daddy stop it, in the [circles] over there,
Emmy put over there,
So car broke,
Car [name],
Car broken,
So have to go in the green car,
The – then, green car broken,
So my go to nap.

(2)
We bought a baby . . . cause . . . the, well, because, . . . when she, well, we *thought* it was for Christmas, but when we went to the s-s-store we didn't have our jacket on, but I saw some dolly and I *yelled* at my mother and said "I want one of those dolly." So *after* we were finished with the store, we went over to the dolly and she *bought* me one. . . . So I have one. And I need a [broke].

(3)
F: We sure have had a busy day today! You want me to explain what we did? And I'll tell you about tomorrow? Today was Sunday, and we got up, and we changed the sheets, and we had French toast, and then, after we read the newspaper, mommy went down to the basement, I think, and played with you.
E: I came down to get the laundry!
F: And you went down to get the laundry. And Daddy went and ran, in a race. And then we came back, and we went to *Child* World, and we we

bought a, we were going to buy a swimming pool, but it was too big to carry back in the car, so we're going to have to have Mormor take her car and get it, and, but we did buy an easel, and we came back and *pain*ted. After your nap we came back and painted, and Caitlin came over,

E: (laughs)

F: And you had a *lot* of fun with Caitlin and [Caitlin's parents].

E: Tell it to me again.

F: I can – Well, we had a, we had a good dinner of a cheeseburger, and juice and ice cream,

E: And everybody went home, everybody's home.

F: And they went home so Caitlin's going to go to sleep. Well, Caitlin and Emmy both have to go to sleep now, cause it's nighttime. Let me tell you what we're going to do tomorrow. Tomorrow is a Tanta [Emily's baby-sitter] day, so we're going to see Carl again, and Julie, and Chris, and Jeannie and Annie, and Tanta, and then Mommy's going to pick you up, and if it's not raining, we'll play outside.

E: I goin' to the park!

F: Maybe we'll go to the park, we'll see how muddy it is. . . . I don't know how muddy it will be, but we might be able to. We hope it's a nice day, we hope it's not raining. If it's raining you can probably play in the basement. We're going to spend most of June in the basement some-how, if it keeps raining, but we're hoping for nice weather. So you have a good night's sleep, hon, and I'll see you in the morning.

E: [unclear request for more talk]

F: Well, I'm only going to do it one more time, sweetie-pie, and then I'm going to say good-night, okay? What we did today, we got up, and we had French toast, and you played in the basement, and Daddy went for a race, and we went to Childworld, bought an easel,

E: And then you were a *ti*ger racing!

F: I was a *ti*ger, I raced like a, ran like a tiger, huh? I did!

E: Yeah!

F: And *then,* we came back and after our nap we painted, and Caitlin came over. Tomorrow we're going to Tanta's and see all the kids at Tanta's and then we're going to pick you up, and maybe go to the park, or at least play outside if it's a nice day. So you have a good night's sleep, honey.

[The monologue that follows after father leaves consists only of the following]

E: And he *ran* in a race. A race, a regular race. And, and John's daddy went with him, but when he came back, then John's daddy was going back, and he did. Hou . . . ses, houses, houses are houses [etc. to end]

(4)

F: You know what we're going to do, you know what we're going to do this weekend? . . . We're going to go . . . to Childworld . . . and we're going to buy some diapers for Stephen and some diapers for Emily, and we're going to buy an intercom system, so that we can hear Stephen in differ-ent parts of the house. I think you're going to like it because we'll be able to hear Stephen downstairs, when Stephen's uptairs. It's going to be a neat gadget. . . .

E: [going get it?]

F: When we, go to Childworld and buy diapers for Stephen and diapers for Emily and what is called an intercom system that we plug in, Stephen, into Stephen's room, and then we go downstairs and we plug it in, and we get to hear Stephen! Making a, when Stephen wakes up we'll hear him cry, through the intercom system. It's a neat gadget.

E: ???

F: Yeah.

E: ???

F: One more time and now go to bed. . . . On Saturday we're going to go to Childworld and get diapers for Emily, and diapers for Stephen, and an intercom system so we can hear Stephen, in different parts of the house. . . . Okay, hon, I love you.

[After more talk about not crying, father leaves and Emily's monologue begins]

E: I 'member the . . . ? I [went to sleep] and daddy said buy diapers for Stephen and Emmy and buy some-thing for Stephen, plug in, and say ah-h-h (simulates baby cry) and put the in. . . . On Saturday go Childworld buy diaper for Emmy, and diaper for the baby, and then buy something for the, and . . . seee . . . for . . . that . . . baby, plug in and get diapers for anybody. . . . And buy more that that day at Childworld, and buy [croutes] [and maybe??] Childworld, cause the one that broken at *Tanta*'s. The one that's broken. The one that's broken here, the . . . the infant seat . . . dada actually at home.

[The monologue continues on the crying topic]

(5)

E. What we do today!

F: What did we do today. Well, we went to Tanta's today, and you saw a tow truck. Then we came back here, and we painted, and we read "Hansel and Gretel," and we had, and you helped daddy make pasta [gucoe?], and tortellini, and daddy played the tortellini man, the pasta man, and Emmy played the pasta girl. We had a good time.

E: What we. . . .

F: And daddy had a little nap, just now, huh?

E: What we did t-, *now!*

M: Well, now we're going to bed. Honeybunch we have a lot of things to do tomorrow, stay at Tanta's again, and tomorrow afternoon Mormor's going to get you to play outside.

E: May, maybe the tow truck come back, and my can get it go for, towing the blue, towing the blue, the *blue* car.

M: Well, maybe that tow truck would come back. That would be fun to see it towing the blue car like that. Maybe it would tow a different color car, I don't know.

(6)

E: Maybe the doctor, took my jamas (I don't know [very soft]). Maybe, *maybe* we take my *jamas* off. But leave my diaper, take my *jamas* off, and *leave* them off, at the doctor, my have get my check up, so *we* take my *jamas* off. My don't know this looking all better. Doctor, doc, the boys take back home. The, and we maybe take my jamas off. I don't know what we do with my, maybe the doctor take my jamas, my jamas off cause my maybe get check up, have to go take my jamas.

[After an interval of several minutes on other topics, monologue continues as follows]

Could be my go see *doc*tor. My doctor Mor-. Maybe we take my jamas off. We do take jamas off near the doctor. We put them off back on have here. We take off at the *doc*tor cause *doc*tor there. But the doctor puts . . . the stetheskethis, but this is medicine. Emmy feel . . . better.

[Monologue continues on the sick theme]

(7)
F: Well, we're going to get up tomorrow morning, and it's a nobody day! . . . And we're going to get up, and it's Saturday, and we're going to have breakfast.
E: Whose this one? [This refers to a game they've established of Daddy being nobody and Emily being somebody.]
F: Whose that? Anyone. And we're going to have breakfast, and then play outside in the yard. . . .
E: I am nobody!
F: Are you nobody, too? Well, you know, tomorrow. . . .
E: (??) be, I am, what I am?
F: You're anyone . . . you're anyone, and I am nobody, and nobody is going to . . . mow the *lawn* tomorrow morning . . . and anyone can help . . . and after that we are going to go on an excursion to see some antique stores, and we're going to come back and have lunch. . . .
E: And I can have a hot dogs!
F: Well after, then we're going to come back and have lunch, and then you're going to have a nap, and then after your nap we're going to have a hot dog at the ocean, with the Schultzs, and Mr. and Mrs. Schultz, and, and their kids, and a bunch of other kids are going to have hot dogs at the ocean. And then we're going to come back. . . .
E: We can sit in the ocean!
F: Yeah, we can sit in the ocean, yeah, if it's a warm day, in the sand, you can sit in it, we'll be, take your bathing suit . . . it's like your pool, only it's much bigger. And there's sand.
E: And I can splash!
F: And you can splash, you bet!
E: And I can . . . kicking.
F: Yes you can. Well, we're going to have a lot of fun, but you know, you've got to be rested, so, in order for us to have all that fun. . . .
E: I want everybody and Caitlin.
F: Tell you, tell you about what?
E: Caitlin.
F: Caitlin? Well, that's on Sunday. Well, Sunday we're going to get up and I think nobody's going to make, uh, French toast. And . . . then, we're going to, probably go on another excursion, I-don't-quite-know-what we'll-do-Sunday-morning, but then after your nap on Sunday, Caitlin is going to come over with [her mommy and daddy], and we're going to have barbe*cued ham*burgers! With cheese. Called cheeseburgers! . . . Okay, well, it's night-night right now.

E: Tell me again!
F: Well I'm only going to tell you quickly, one more time, and then we're going to go to sleep.
E: ??
F: Okay, (quickly) but tomorrow is a nobody day, and we're going to get up and have breakfast and mow the lawn, go to an antique store, have a nap and go to the ocean and have some hot dogs. And so that's. . . .
E: Caitlin's coming there.
F: And on Sunday Caitlin's going to come over and we're going to have cheeseburgers . . . so you have a good night's sleep, Pookie, I love you.

[Emily had probably heard this account more than twice by the evidence of her contributions. In the monologue that follows, she says]

E: We are gonna . . . at the ocean. Ocean is a little far away. Baw, baw-buh-buh (×2) . . . far away . . . I think it's . . . couple b*locks* . . . away. Maybe it's down, downtown, and across the ocean, and down the river, and maybe it's in, the hot dogs wd be in a fridge, and the fridge wd be in the water over by a shore, and then we could go in, and get a hot dog and bring it out to the river, and then [sharks? Schultz?] go *in* the river, and [bite] me, in the ocean, we go in to the ocean, and ocean be over by, I think a couple of blocks away. But we could be, and we could find any hot dogs, um, the hot dogs gonna be for the beach. Then the bridge is gonna, we'll *have* to go in the green car, cause that's where the car seats are. Um, I can be in the red car, but, see, I be in the *green* car. But you know who's going to be in the green car—both children. . . . I'm going to be in the green car in my car seat, he's gonna be . . . , and nobody's gonna be, just . . . you know, th-e-se people, we don't know, and too far way from the beach, and two things.

(8)
Mormor says no,
So why my kids go sleep, my,
Mormor say night, have go sleep,
So why, uh, so why my k-, have to go sleep.
I can't go sleep. . . .

(9)
One morning . . . when Emmy go morm in the daytime. . . . That's what Emmy do so*meti*me. Sometimes Emmy go sleep and have read . . . Daddy no an back to missing woman. Mormor said this truck. Did di Daddy . . . keep this, run away. Go away . . . big one. Time will [barrel] make big, now you can, I need the barrel.

[Approximately 5 min later the monologue picks up again]

Daddy didn't bring in the baby room, cause the baby and (?) and diaper the baby room, but Daddy moved Emmy in this room cause the baby sleeping in own . . . room, ca- . . . Daddy brought this in the [ma-goo]. Emmy sleeping in this [magoo-goo] cause the bassinet in the baby in there. . . . There Emmy's that other room, that's where the baby. This is Emmy room. This where Emmy sleeps. Naptimes Emmy go bed and napped. Sometimes Emmy take napping. Sometimes Emmy take bedroom. Time go bed. Emmy sometimes take nap. . . . Nap sometimes my bed . . . do-o-o.

(10)

I can't go down the basement with jamas on. I *sleep* with jamas. Okay *sleep* with jamas. In the night time my only put big girl pants on. But in the morning we put *jamas* on.. . . . But, and the morning gets up . . . of the room. But, *afternoon* my *wake* up and play . . . play with mommy, daddy.

(11)

yellow buses . . . 1 2 3 4 days, we have yellow buses, but not 5 4 5 4 5 have blue buses. I like. . . . These days we're going to have the yellow buses, and the, right *now*, it's Thursday, and Friday, and S-s . . . and Sunday, so it's, umm . . . a yellow bus day. And on Friday and Sunday it's blue day, so I going on y*ellow* and a blue. One day going on a yellow bus and one day going on a blue bus. When Mormor comes, one day we'll maybe yellow bus that day, and just, n-now. . . . O*n*ce I am going on, one, again, I know, I'm going on a yellow bus, this day, but on a weekends, when we have the waffle day, and we, it's not what the . . . it's a blue, y*ellow* bus day. And we're gonna walk downstairs as . . . I've finished. On blue bus days we just get blue. I can see yellow and I can see black.

(12)

If ever we go to the airport we have to get some luggage. If have to go to the airport, hafta take something for the airport, to the airport or you can't go. Need your own special bus [carry me]. And they z-o-o-m. Zoom! Zoom! Zoom! Zoom!

(13)

Tomorrow, when we wake up from bed, first me and Daddy and Mommy, you, eat breakfast . . . eat breakfast, like we u*su*ally do, and then we're going to p-l-a-y, and then soon as daddy comes, Carl's going to come over, and then we're going to play a little while, and then Carl and Emily are both going down the car with somebody, and we're going to ride to nursery school, and then we when we get there, we're all going to get out of the car, go in to nursery school, and Daddy's going to give us kisses, then go, and then say, and then we will say good bye, then he's going to work, and we're going to play at nursery school. Won't that be funny? Because sometimes I go to nursery school cause it's a nursery school day. Sometimes I stay with Tanta all week, and sometimes we play mom and dad. But usually, sometimes I um, oh go to nursery school. But today I'm going to nursery school in the morning. In the morning, Daddy in the, when, and u*s*ual, we're going to eat breakfast like we usually do, and then we're going to . . . and *then* we're going to . . . *play* and then we're, then the doorbell's going to ring, and here comes Carl in here, then Carl, and then we are all going to play, and then wha-, and then go in the car with somebody, and drive to nursery. When we get to nursery school, we're to, *all* going to get out of the car . . . and then we're going to ummm . . . I think then we're going to . . . they're going to give us kisses, . . . and t-h-e-n, she's [this reference is to Mommy] going to *go* to work, with somebody with her, and meet her new students, and then she's going to pick us up, and work, and Daddy's going to bring us, and Mommy's going to pick us up, a-n-d then she's going home, and we're going to go to nap, and t-h-e-n when you awake, then we are going to-o-o . . . school . . . uh, uh (monologue tapers off)

(*M notes:* This is in fact a description of her Friday routine.)

NOTES

1 Compare this with the average of four to eight propositions from the 3-year-olds in our script studies! Although Emily was an unusual and precocious child, the difference between her narratives and those produced by children in the studies described earlier may reflect factors other than individual differences, possibly including the child's uncertainty about the experimenters' intent and the availability of a more practiced automatic and thus concise event schema.
2 It is probable, however, that the latter characteristics would be found in adult covert presleep monologues as well.
3 Robyn Fivush, in her discussion of this chapter, made the very important point that autobiographical memory represents the establishment of an autonomous self-concept. I concur with this point, but cannot take credit for it and therefore have not attempted to integrate it into the argument set forth here. Both of us agree that it is a complementary rather than competing claim about the function of the autobiographical memory system.

REFERENCES

Bruce, D. (1985). The how and why of ecological memory. *Journal of Experimental Psychology: General, 114,* 78–90.
Chafe, W. (Ed.). (1980). *Advances in discourse processes. Vol. 3: The pear stories.* Norwood, NJ: Ablex.
de Loache, J. S. (1984, October). What's this? Maternal questions in joint picture book reading with toddlers. *Quarterly Newsletter of the Laboratory of Comparative Human Cognition, 6* (4), 87–95.
Dudycha, G. J., & Dudycha, M. M. (1941). Childhood memories: A review of the literature. *Psychological Bulletin, 38,* 668–682.
Eisenberg, A. R. (1985). Learning to describe past experiences in conversation. *Discourse Processes, 8,* 177–204.
Engel, S. (1986). *Learning to reminisce: A developmental study of how young children talk about the past.* Unpublished dissertation, City University of New York.
Fivush, R., Hudson, J., & Nelson, K. (1984). Children's long-term memory for a novel event: An exploratory study. *Merrill-Palmer Quarterly, 30,* 303–316.
Freud, S. (1963). Three essays on the theory of sexuality. In J. Strachey (Ed.), *The standard edition of the complete works of Freud* (Vol. 7). London: Hogarth Press. (Original work published 1905).
Hudson, J. A. (1984). Constructive processes in children's memory for a real-world event. Unpublished doctoral dissertation, City University of New York.

Hudson, J., & Nelson, K. (1986). Repeated encounters of a similar kind: Effects of familiarity on children's autobiographical memory. *Cognitive Development, 1*, 253–271.

Kuczaj, S. A., II (1983). *Crib speech and language play.* New York: Springer-Verlag.

Meudell, P. (1983). The development and dissolution of memory. In A. Mayes (Ed.), *Memory in animals and humans* (pp. 83–133). Workingham, UK: Van Nostrand Reinhold.

Neisser, U. (1962). Cultural and cognitive discontinuity. In T. E. Gladwin & W. Sturtevant (Eds.), *Anthropology and human behavior.* Washington, DC: Anthropological Society of Washington DC.

(1981). John Dean's memory: A case study. *Cognition, 9*, 1–22.

Nelson, K. (1978). How young children represent knowledge of their world in and out of language. In R .S. Siegler (Ed.), *Children's thinking: What develops?* (pp. 225–273). Hillsdale, NJ: Erlbaum.

(Ed.). (in press). *Narratives from the crib.*

Nelson, K., & Gruendel, J. (1981). Generalized event representations: Basic building blocks of cognitive development. In A. Brown & M. Lamb (Eds.), *Advances in developmental psychology* (Vol. 1). Hillsdale, NJ: Erlbaum.

Nelson, K., & Hudson, J. (in press). Scripts and memory: Interrelations in development. In F. Weinert & M. Perlmutter (Eds.), *Memory development.* Hillsdale, NJ: Erlbaum.

Nelson, K., & Ross, G. (1980). The generalities and specifics of long-term memory in infants and young children. In M. Perlmutter (Ed.), *Children's memory: New directions for child development* (Vol. 10, pp. 87–101). San Francisco: Jossey-Bass.

Oakley, D. A. (1983). The varieties of memory: A phylogenetic approach. In A. Mayes (Ed.), *Memory in animals and humans* (pp. 20–82). Workingham, UK: Van Nostrand Reinhold.

O'Connell, B., & Gerard, A. B. (1985). Scripts and scraps: The development of sequential understanding. *Child Development, 56*, 671–681.

Perlmutter, M. (Ed.). (1980). *Children's memory.* San Francisco: Jossey-Bass.

Piaget, J. (1971). *The child's conception of time.* New York: Ballantine Books.

Reiser, B. J., Black, J. B., & Abelson, R. P. (1985). Knowledge structures in the organization and retrieval of autobiographical memories. *Cognitive Psychology, 17*, 89–137.

Sachs, J. (1983). Talking about the there and then: The emergence of displaced reference in parent-child discourse. In K. E. Nelson (Ed.), *Children's language* (Vol. 4, pp. 1–28). New York: Gardner Press.

Schactel, E. G. (1947). On memory and childhood amnesia. *Psychiatry, 10*, 1–26.

Spear, N. E. (1979). Experimental analysis of infantile amnesia. In J. F. Kihlstrom & F. S. Evans (Eds.), *Functional disorders of memory* (pp. 75–102). Hillsdale, NJ: Erlbaum.

Tulving, E. (1972). Episodic and semantic memory. In E. Tulving & W. Donaldson (Eds.), *Organization of memory* (pp. 382–403). New York: Academic Press.

(1983). *Elements of episodic memory.* New York: Oxford University Press.

Weir, R. H. (1962). *Language in the crib.* The Hague: Mouton & Co.

White, S. H., & Pillemer, D. B. (1979). Childhood amnesia and the development of a socially accessible memory system. In J. F. Kihlstrom & F. J. Evans (Eds.), *Functional disorders of memory* (pp. 29–47). Hillsdale, NJ: Erlbaum.

10

The functions of event memory: Some comments on Nelson and Barsalou

ROBYN FIVUSH

This book represents an emerging theme in the field of memory research: a shift in focus from examining what memory *is*, a structural approach, to what memory *is for*, a functional approach (Bruce, 1985; Oakley, 1983). As Nelson points out, one of the primary and developmentally early functions of event memory is to organize our knowledge about the world, and as Barsalou's data demonstrate, this remains an important function of event memory throughout development. But there is another function of event memory. Event memory not only organizes our knowledge about the world, but also helps organize our knowledge about ourselves. Our sense of self and event memories are interwoven systems. We learn about ourselves by interacting with the world. Who we are is largely defined by what we *do* – the kinds of activities and events that we engage in.

Moreover, it is the sense of self that is crucial for *autobiographical memory*. Autobiographical memory is not simply memories of previously experienced events; it is memory of the self engaging in these activities. It is the sense of self that makes the memories cohere as a life history that expresses the essence of who we are. Whereas event memory serves the function of organizing our knowledge of the world, a predictive function, autobiographical memory serves the function of organizing our knowledge about ourselves, a self-defining function. I am not arguing for two separate memory systems, only for multiple functions. The same memories can simultaneously allow us to anticipate and predict the world around us and help define how we think about ourselves. But when we examine the data presented by Nelson and Barsalou using the distinction between event memory and autobiographical memory, it appears that these two functions may follow different developmental courses.

Even a cursory perusal of Emily's presleep monologues indicates that she is actively engaged in the process of remembering and understanding real-world events even at the very earliest period studied. This is why we see such a heavy emphasis on routine events and especially on devia-

277

tions from those routines. Emily is in the process of understanding and representing how things happen in the world so that she can better understand and predict future events. This process has obvious adaptive value. Organisms existing in an environment need to be able to predict routine occurrences in that environment and to understand the dimensions along which events can and cannot vary. So it is not surprising that we see such a heavy emphasis on routine events in the event memories of a very young child.

What is surprising is that we see the same type of content when adults recall their past experiences, as Barsalou's data demonstrate. When asked to recall their summer vacation, adults do not report highlights or special events, but focus instead on everyday routines and activities. Even when explicitly asked to recall specific events, adults slip into reporting summarized events. The high percentage of extended events and summarized events demonstrates that adults provide information about what usually happens. Thus, the content of event memory remains relatively constant across a wide developmental age span. Two-year-olds and 20-year-olds focus on routine events when recalling the past, suggesting that the predictive function of event memory remains relatively stable throughout development.

However, there are substantial changes in the organization of event memory, especially in the relatively short period during which Emily was studied. In addition to the changes Nelson highlights, there is another aspect of organizational change that I would like to comment on. It seems that Emily's earliest monologues are about events that span a relatively short time duration – sleeping routines, store routines, and so on. With development, Emily's monologues became more coherently organized, as Nelson mentions, and they also become more temporally integrated. Emily starts talking about events that span a greater and greater time duration.

We can see this process in several of the excerpts Nelson provides, including the excerpt on the different buses that come on the different days of the week, and especially in the excerpt of Emily's rendition of the weekly routine. In this excerpt, Emily gives a very complex extended-event sequence that integrates aspects of her weekly routine and her differing daily routines. Within the daily routines, Emily embeds subroutines about eating breakfast and getting dropped off and picked up at nursery or at the baby-sitter and includes information about what she herself is going to do and what several other people are going to do. This organization is somewhat different from what Barsalou has called an extended-event sequence, but it shares some basic characteristics with that type of organization. Most important, it is hierarchically organized. Emily embeds several different routines in a larger temporal framework.

Some of the embedded routines are temporally organized routines that span a shorter duration than the framing event, and some of the embedded routines are more like what Barsalou has called summarized events.

As Barsalou points out, these hierarchies organize not only our knowledge about events in the world but also knowledge about people, objects, places, and so on. We see the beginnings of these knowledge structures in Emily's monologues. Emily includes information about the various roles that people can play and about different objects that may or may not occur in a given event sequence in her retelling of events. Very early on, event structures provide the framework for the kinds of taxonomic knowledge structures that we see in the adult data. Comparison of the findings of Nelson and Barsalou, then, indicates that for both 2-year-olds and 20-year-olds, a primary function of event memory is to organize our knowledge about the world.

But I believe that the organizational changes we see in Emily's event memories also reflect changes in how Emily is perceiving her *self*. It makes sense that as Emily develops extended-event structures, that is, begins to represent events that span an extended period of time, she is also developing the idea of a self that continues to exist through time, and this is the crux of autobiographical memory. Barsalou discusses this issue briefly; he argues that extended-event time lines provide the "story line" for the individual's life history, which helps define the self-concept. I would argue that we are seeing the beginnings of this story line in Emily's later excerpts. The fact that Emily is organizing events in longer time frames indicates that she is developing a stable concept of herself continuing to exist through time. I am not arguing that Emily is not aware that it was she who engaged in the activities she recalls in the early excerpts. Rather, at this early stage, there is only a loose collection of memories that are not coherently organized in time. Because event memories are not integrated into extended time lines, there is no sense of a self extended into the past and future, but only an immediate awareness of one's surroundings.

This idea has also been discussed by Neisser (in press); he calls this early self-concept the "ecological self" and defines it as being objectively aware of where one is in the environment and what one is doing. It is very much a here-and-now kind of self-concept. The ability to recall past events and imagine or anticipate future events depends on an ability to extend the self in time, and so Neisser calls this self the "extended self." Obviously, the fact that Emily recounts past events at all in the early excerpts indicates some burgeoning awareness that she has been in other places at other times, but this awareness has not yet developed into an extended self-concept. There is not yet a sense of an enduring self that is *continuous* in time.

Two other changes in how Emily talks about past and future events implicate changes in how she is perceiving herself. The first is the growing tendency to discuss social relations and roles. This is particularly evident in the last excerpt, in which Emily discusses her weekly routines. Emily not only talks about what she does but also talks about what other people do, including what her parents do when she is not with them. This suggests that Emily is becoming increasingly aware that other people continue to be independent and active agents even when they are not interacting with her. This is related to, but somewhat different from, a person-permanence argument. Emily is aware not only that people continue to exist when out of her sight but also that they have independent lives. As Emily becomes more and more aware that she herself has a stable existence and life history through time, she is also becoming aware that other people have their own independent life histories.

Second, Emily begins to reference internal states over time. In the early excerpts, Emily focuses on what happened in the external world, but over time she begins to reference what she thought about the event or how she felt about it. Again, in the last excerpt, Emily uses the phrase, "I think," and she remarks that playing at nursery school will be "fun." In the excerpt about buying the doll at the toy store, Emily remarks that "we *thought* it was for Christmas" and also comments on what she said and how, by yelling, she manipulated her mother into buying her the doll she wanted. These examples demonstrate that Emily is increasingly commenting on the internal workings of her mind. Remembering what she said and thought suggests that Emily is developing an internally defined self-concept (see Bretherton, McNew, & Beeghly-Smith, 1981, for related arguments about the child's developing theory of mind). Her memories are no longer confined to what happened in the external world; they are being interpreted from the perspective of the internal self.

The argument, then, is that very young children (and probably infants) remember events that have occurred in the past, but these memories are not organized into a coherent time line. Although very young children are aware that it was they who engaged in these experiences, because events are not yet organized as extended time lines, there is not yet an enduring sense of self that continues to exist through time. As children begin to represent events that extend over longer time periods, from daily routines, to weekly routines, and so on, they also begin to develop a sense of self that continues to exist through time. The self-concept and memories of past experiences develop dialectically and begin to form a life history. The life history, in turn, helps organize both memories of past experiences and the self-concept. The life history is essentially what Barsalou calls the extended time lines, or the person's "story line." It is only with the construction of the life history that we have true autobiographical memory.

If we accept this position for a moment, what implications does it have for the phenomenon of infantile amnesia? Nelson proposes that the early memory system is geared only toward generic-event knowledge and that children in the first few years of life are not able to retain memories of specific events over extended periods of time. An autobiographical memory system is the product of social-cultural interaction and is not established until later childhood.

However, very young children do recall specific, novel events over a very long period of time. In some recent research (Fivush, Gray, & Fromhoff, 1987), we asked 2.5-year-olds to recall special one-time events that they had experienced at various points in the past. Not only were children easily able to participate in these interviews, but all the children recalled events that had happened more than 6 months earlier. So infantile amnesia cannot be explained in quite the way that Nelson is proposing. There are specific memories of one-time events available and accessible in the memory system over a long period of time, even very early on.

However, I do agree that social interaction is essential in the development of autobiographical memory. There is growing evidence that young children learn how to structure a coherent verbal report of an event through social interaction with adults (Eisenberg, 1985; Engel, 1986; Hudson, 1986). That is, children learn how to tell a coherently organized narrative about a past experience through conversations with others. Although the verbal report is not isomorphic to the underlying event memory, it seems likely that as children learn to structure their verbal reports more coherently, it has some effect on the underlying memory representation. We can speculate that children's growing ability to organize extended events more coherently develops through social interaction. Because the organization of event memory is constructed through social interaction, it follows that the organization of the self-concept is constructed through social interaction as well. That is, the sense of an enduring self that continues to exist through time is the product of a social-cultural process. Until there is an enduring sense of self, there can be no life history, no autobiographical memory. I would argue that although there are memories of past events even in very early childhood, we cannot remember these experiences easily because they have not been integrated into our life history, which was constructed after these experiments occurred.

These arguments must remain speculative for now. Nelson and Barsalou have presented important and intriguing research on event memory. Perhaps most surprising are the similarities in event memory over the large age range represented in these data. Although there were a great many changes in Emily's memories over a short period of time, there is remarkable consistency between Emily's last excerpts and Barsalou's adult subjects. However, I would argue that in order to really understand autobiographical memory, we must begin to examine the relationships between event memory and the self-concept.

REFERENCES

Bretherton, I., McNew, S., & Beeghly-Smith, M. (1981). Early person knowledge as expressed in gestural and verbal communication: When do infants acquire a theory of mind? In M. Lamb & L. Sherrod (Eds.), *Infant social cognition* (pp. 333–373). Hillsdale, NJ: Erlbaum.

Bruce, D. (1985). The how and why of ecological memory. *Journal of Experimental Psychology, 114,* 78–90.

Eisenberg, A. R. (1985). Learning to describe past experiences in conversation. *Discourse Processes, 8,* 177–204.

Engel, S. (1986, April). The role of mother–child interaction in autobiographical recall. In J. A. Hudson (Chair.), *Learning to talk about the past.* Symposium conducted at the Southeastern Conference on Human Development, Nashville, TN.

Fivush, R., Gray, J. T., & Fromhoff, F. A. (1987, April). Two year olds talk about the past. *Cognitive Development, 2,* 393–409.

Hudson, J. A. (1986, April). Effects of repeated recall on autobiographic memory. In J. A. Hudson (Chair.), *Learning to talk about the past.* Symposium conducted at the Southeastern Conference on Human Development, Nashville, TN.

Neisser, U. (in press). The development of consciousness and the acquisition of skill. In P. M. Cole, D. L. Johnson, & F. S. Kessel (Eds.), *Self and consciousness.* New York: Praeger.

Oakley, D. A. (1983). The varieties of memory: A phylogenetic approach. In A. Mayes (Ed.), *Memory in animals and humans* (pp. 20–82). New York: Von Nostrand Reinhold.

11

"The Wreck of the Old 97": A real event remembered in song

WANDA T. WALLACE AND DAVID C. RUBIN

"The Wreck of the Old 97"[1]

They gave him his orders at Monroe, Virginia
Saying Steve you're away behind time
This is not thirty-eight but it's old ninety-seven
You must put her in Spencer on time

Steve Brooklyn said to his black greasy fireman
Just shovel in a little more coal
And when we cross that White Oak Mountain
You can watch old ninety-seven roll

It's a mighty rough road from Lynchburg to Danville
And a line on a three mile grade
It was on this grade that he lost his air-brakes
And you see what a jump he made

He was going down grade making ninety miles an hour
When his whistle began to scream
He was found in the wreck with his hand on the throttle
And was scalded to death by the steam

Come all you young ladies you must take warning
From this time now and on
Never speak harsh words to a loving husband
For he may leave you and never return

Number 97 was a fast mail train, owned by the Southern Railway, which ran between Washington and Atlanta from 1902 to 1907. The real event described in the ballad occurred on December 27, 1903. Number 97 reached Monroe, Virginia, about an hour behind schedule. Joseph A. Broady, the engineer taking charge at Monroe, was new to the Southern Railway and was unfamiliar with treacherous points in Number 97's route (Cohen, 1981; *Newsleader*, 1903). Broady was nicknamed "Steve" after Steve Brody, who leaped from the Brooklyn Bridge on a bet and survived (Cohen, 1981; Hubbard, 1945).

From Monroe to Lynchburg, Virginia, Number 97's route passed the White Oak Mountain grade. Just north of Danville, Virginia, the tracks crossed the Stillhouse Trestle. The trestle, 75 to 100 feet above the creek, was preceded by a curve and another descending grade. It was at this trestle that the wreck occurred. Apparently, Broady approached too fast (Hubbard, 1945; *News and Observer*, 1903; *Newsleader*, 1903). The engine and the five cars behind it left the track 50 feet before the trestle and landed in the creek ravine. Nine people died, including the engineer, fireman, conductor, and flagman. According to reports of nearby residents, Broady was not killed instantly in the crash, but was badly scalded (Cohen, 1981; Yarbough, 1978).

More than the usual information is known about the development of the ballad "The Wreck of the Old 97" as a result of a copyright suit in which a folklorist served as consultant. Current opinion holds that the ballad began with a variation of "The Ship That Never Returned" (Cohen, 1981). Several such songs, some involving trains, are known to have existed in the ballad tradition at the time of the wreck of Number 97. In addition, "The Wreck of the Old 97" has roots in "Parted Lovers," which is a traditional American ballad of unknown origin. The last verses of both contain similar warnings to young maidens to be kind to a faithful lover or else he will never return. One supposed author claims to have used "Parted Lovers" as the basis for his version of "The Wreck of the Old 97" (Cohen, 1981).

More than one person claimed authorship of "The Wreck of the Old 97." Copyrights were granted to two different people, and early recordings were made by four different artists. A lawsuit between David Graves George and Victor Talking Machine Company over royalties was brought to court in 1931. The court found in favor of George; however, subsequent appeals reversed that decision (Cohen, 1981). At the trial, the judge acknowledged that two other people, Noell and Lewey, and possibly others could have authored other versions of the ballad, but that these versions were not those involved in the records made by Victor (Cohen, 1981; *Victor Talking Machine Company* v. *George*, 1934).

At the court trial, almost 30 years after the wreck, five people gave five different versions of the ballad. The versions from these five people, which vary from 5 to 14 verses, are listed in the first half of Appendix Table 11.A. The versions from Lewey and Noell are taken from R. W. Gordon's collection (Gordon, 1925) as recorded in 1925. The other versions are taken from the *Federal Reporter* (*Victor Talking Machine Company* v. *George*, 1934). Across all five versions there are five common verses that are roughly the same as those given in the version cited at the beginning of this chapter. The main differences between versions concern the opening verses, the inclusion of various details spoken by the engineer or observers, and the use of the verse beginning "Did she ever pull in."

That so many people would claim to have composed one song is not surprising given the nature of the ballad tradition. Ballads are part of a living tradition in which variants are passed orally among the singers and over generations and into which new ballads can enter. In fact, most of the singers we tested were able to generate a ballad quickly from a newspaper clipping of a train wreck.

There is no "right" version of any ballad, according to the singers we have interviewed. Each singer has an individual version, usually learned from a particular person, that is equally as valid as any other version. Singers admit that on occasion a line or verse is intentionally changed to improve the ballad. Additionally, it is not uncommon to find verses from one ballad incorporated into a different ballad. At the time "The Wreck of the Old 97" was popular, many songs in the tradition had similar lines telling the story of a train or ship wreck and the loss of lives (White, 1952). Given a memorable and much-talked-about event such as this wreck, it is likely that more than one person would have attempted to compose a song about the event. Furthermore, these singers would have had the same traditional background from which to compose the song. It is also likely that several singers could have composed similar songs, given the norms in the tradition. Furthermore, once such songs circulated in the tradition, singers would likely borrow from each other. Because ballads typically have no known author, it would not be important for singers to remember from where verses were borrowed.

Our studies of counting-out rhymes, epic poetry, and ballads have led us to the view that multiple constraints play large roles in keeping oral traditions stable over time. In ballads, the multiple constraints are based on music, poetics, narrative structure, and imagery. These constraints limit the possible choices for any one word or phrase and thereby reduce the memory load. That is, the constraints, plus a minimum of detailed information, can be transmitted instead of the exact words. This view of multiple constraints is much the same as Bartlett (1932) suggested for the single constraint of meaning. Here, however, we assume that singers display not only effort after meaning but also effort after all the forms of organization present in the ballad tradition. The combination of these forms of organization, or constraints, in oral traditions leads to a much more stable transmission than Bartlett observed in material that lacked forms of organization other than meaning.

All that is needed in addition to these general constraints to keep a particular ballad, such as "The Wreck of the Old 97," stable is the memory for the details of which particular memory, poetics, story line, characters, places, and so forth, are to be used. These numerous rules severely constrain the ballad that can be sung and thereby increase its stability. Changes can occur in some of the details selected on each telling, but the multiple constraints will tend to limit systematic drift over tellings of the same ballad. It is as if the rules, or constraints, rather than the particular telling, are being transmitted.

Although ballads and oral traditions in general are stable over retellings, these traditions are not transmitted verbatim (Goody, 1978; Havelock, 1978; Hunter, 1985; Lord, 1960; Ong, 1982). Changes, which are considerable in some traditions, occur in retellings. Ballads are not an exception.

The noteworthy event of the wreck of Number 97 was captured in the ballad tradition. The ballads conformed to the existing norms in the tradition, which include, among other things, high imagery, a four-line verse with four beats per line, a rhyming scheme involving the last words in the second and fourth lines, and a simple rhythmical structure. As shown in Appendix Table 11.A, the ballad existed in the tradition, commercially and noncommercially, in the mid-1920s. White (1952) listed six versions, including the one at the beginning of this chapter, that were collected from traditional, noncommercial sources between 1912 and 1944.

"The Wreck of the Old 97" is still sung in North Carolina and, for the most part, is transmitted not by written text or recording but by memory.[2] The question we address in the remainder of this chapter is how memory influences the retelling of this ballad and how the characteristics of the tradition influence memory. We begin by asking how recall of this ballad varies between two performances by the same singer and how recall varies between singers.

Versions of "The Wreck of the Old 97" by current singers

As part of a larger project, traditional ballad singers were asked to sing all the train and shipwreck ballads they knew. A person is considered a traditional ballad singer if that person knows several ballads and reports learning most of that repertoire orally from another singer. Singers were never prompted or cued during the interview. Five of the 11 traditional singers interviewed gave a full rendition of "The Wreck of the Old 97." Each of the five singers sang the ballad on two different occasions separated by a mean of 6 months. All five singers have always lived in North Carolina. Each singer plays a guitar, fiddle, or another stringed musical instrument, but none reads music.

Each singer's version is unique. No singer gave exactly the same version on the two performances. The last half of Appendix Table 11.A gives the words to the song as recalled by each singer. The changes from the first to the second session are indicated in parentheses. Singers are identified by their initials. The characteristics discussed next are abstracted from the songs as sung by these singers. In actual renditions, these characteristics are not isolated, but interact and intertwine.

Table 11.1. *Changes in singing from first session to second session*

Singer	Word substitutions	Word additions (+) and deletions (−)
BM	straight–tall Border–Border's can't you–saying it's–on is–was message–news said–read ye–you learn–on the whistle–his whistle	said (+)
TS	well it's–this is it's a line–lined great white mountain–white oak mountain	well (+) said (+) when his (−) was (−)
WM	he was–they were	all (+)
DW	she–he the whistle–his whistle	then (+) and (+) yes (+)
WA	Blowee–victory Captain–Buddy thirty–ninety зауз–заying he was–and we'll–we're going to	well they (+) he (+) going down grade making (+)

Changes in recall within a singer

Changes in singing the same ballad on two different occasions, like errors in recall, can provide clues to how material is recalled. If our hypothesis about the role of constraints is correct, then we would expect changes on less constrained words as well as changes that tend to preserve the existing constraints.

The changes that singers made were characterized into four categories: (a) substitutions, (b) adding/deleting words, (c) adding/deleting verses, and (d) inverting order of phrases. As will be demonstrated, these changes are mostly variations within the poetic and semantic constraints of the ballad. All word substitutions, additions, and deletions found within singers are listed in Table 11.1.

There are very few changes between versions by the same singer. Of these 34 changes listed in Table 11.1, there are 10 instances involving words with poetic ties to another word in the line. The first versions from all singers have an average of 21% words involved in poetics. Thus, for 34 changes, 7 would be expected to involve poetics if word changes were random. From these numbers there is no reason to conclude that poetically constrained words are less likely to change than any other words. However, some of these changes preserve the poetic constraint even if the specific word changes. Three of the four rhyme changes preserve the rhyme sound. The other rhyme change involves the weak end rhyme "learn–return" and the frequently observed alternate "on–return." The remaining six poetic changes involve words that alliterate or assonate with an adjacent word in the line. Words alliterate when they begin with the same sound, usually a consonant, but end with different sounds. Assonance occurs when two words have the same vowel sound in the accented syllable, but not the same consonant sounds. None of these changes preserves the poetic sound. However, 50% of these changes involve a weak assonance: "his–whistle." Strong alliterations such as "rough–road" and assonances such as "grade–making" do not change between versions by the same singer. Although the changes observed here indicate that poetically constrained words change randomly, there is reason to suspect that poetic constraints, especially rhymes, are preserved and to expect that the stronger the poetic constraint, the less likely the word is to change.

There are two instances in these songs in which the order of phrases within a line is inverted:

> "It's a mighty rough road from Lynchburg to Danville" versus "From Lynchburg to Danville it's a mighty rough road"
> "I stood on the mountain one cold frosty morning" versus "One cold frosty morning I stood on the mountain"

Both phrase inversions occur for the same singer (BM) and on the first line of a verse. One might expect to find more such inversions. However, inversions can occur only on the first and third lines of a verse, or else the end-rhyme found in the second and fourth lines is lost. Second, most of the remaining lines in the ballad are sentences that are not easily inverted.

In two instances, a verse is dropped in one of the versions by a singer. In one case, singer WM did not recall the verse until he had finished the song in the second session. He noted that something was missing. Humming and singing through the first line of each verse, he recalled the omitted verse at the correct location and then sang that verse in full.

In the second instance, singer WA had difficulty recalling the last verses in both sessions. In the first session, the first two lines are found in other versions of "The Wreck of the Old 97"; however, the last line is not the standard last line of this verse. In the second session, the first three lines of the last verse, often found in a different train-wreck song, were imported. The last lines in both sessions have essentially the same gist.

In most ballads, each verse is a four-line structure with four beats on the first and third line and three or four beats on the second and fourth lines. Sometimes the second and fourth lines with three beats are counted as four-beat structure by considering the musical rest after the third beat as an unspoken stress (Bronson, 1969). "The Wreck of the Old 97," as presented at the beginning of this chapter, has four beats on lines 1 and 3 and three beats plus one unspoken beat at the ends of lines 2 and 4. This four-line structure with four beats per line is maintained across sessions, with one exception: singer WA. In the first session, two verses have more than four lines. In each of those two verses, the melody and rhythm are repeated for the extra lines. In the first verse of session 1, the first two lines are sung as if they were the last two lines of a previous verse; thus, the melody and rhythm are those used in all third and fourth lines. In the next to the last line of the first session, the third line repeats the melody and rhythm of the second line. Apparently, even though the singer violated the usual four-line structure, the constraint was known. The only way to compensate for the violation was to repeat part of the structure. Furthermore, in the second session, all verses have only four lines.

The preceding has considered only the changes in words between the first and second sessions. The melodies also vary between sessions for the same singer. Most of these changes occur in the rhythm, such as singing two eighth notes instead of a dotted eighth and a sixteenth note. Thus, the same total time is given to the two notes; what varies is the rhythm. Additionally, as a line requires more syllables, a quarter note will be sung as two eighth notes to accommodate the additional syllables, or vice versa if a line contains fewer syllables. This same type of change occurs for eighth notes sung as two sixteenths. Finally, on occasion, a note one step above or below the note will be sung instead of repeating the same note. Similar changes are observed between verses in the same session.

One singer, BM, made a melodic change between the two sessions. In session 1, he sang the second line with an entirely different melody than in the first session. Instead of descending on the scale, he sang ascending notes. The melody in the second session was closer to that of the other singers. This change varies the melodic scale from a hexatonic to heptatonic scale; that is, the melodic scale changes from one employing only six tones to one employing seven tones.

What does not change across sessions is the number of beats per line, the number of measures in the song, and the notes sung on the quarter beat in each measure. Singers may vary the rhythm and the specific notes around the quarter beats, but the notes sung on the quarter beats do not change. All first and third lines were sung with four beats per line, and all second and fourth lines were sung with three beats, with a held note or a rest at the fourth beat. All verses had eight measures with 4/4 time. Only one singer, DW, changed the key between the two sessions.

Changes across singers

There are five common verses in Appendix Table 11.A that are similar to the ones given at the beginning of this chapter. When these five verses are recalled, they are recalled in the same order, even though two singers (BM and DW) insert other verses between the common ones. When singers recall the same verse, they use the same end rhyme except in the last verse, as previously discussed. The singer with the longest version incorporates additional verses that round out the details of the song, give the setting, and justify the final "warning to the ladies" verse. The verse that WM omits in one singing "It's a mighty rough road . . .") is also omitted by WA in both singings. The story line flows equally as well without this verse.

Within these five common verses there are changes across singers. For example, consider the line about the "black greasy fireman." For all versions in the last half of Appendix Table 11.A, the gist of the line is the same, although none of the versions have identical wording.

    BM: He turned around to his black and greasy fireman
     TS: Well then he turned around to his black greasy fireman
    WM: Well Steve Broadway turned to his black greasy fireman
    DW: He turned all around to his white faced fireman
    WA: The engineer whispered to his black greasy fireman

Each version indicates that someone made a gesture to a fireman; however, the versions differ in the name of the person making the gesture, the word indicating the gesture, and the adjectives for the fireman. This line is not unique. Inspection of Appendix Table 11.A will show that most lines have similar differences.

Several aspects remain relatively constant across singers. When singers recall the same verse, the gist of each line in that verse is the same across singers, and the sequence of lines is the same except for the last verse by WA. The end rhyme is also identical except for the "on/learn–return" rhyme. The number of lines and the number of beats per line remain constant. There are few possible phrasings that preserve these constraints. Within the ballad tradition, it seems that most of these possible phrasings occur.

Across singers, the melodic variations are similar to those variations observed within a singer. The specific rhythm may vary. For example, one variation observed between singers is as follows:

Table 11.2. *Notes sung on the quarter beats of each measure*

Singer	Measure								
	1	2	3	4	5	6	7	8	
BM	5531	4468	5513	2225	8883	4468	5323	111	(session 1)
	5531	4465	5898	7778	8881	4468	5532	111	(session 2)
TS	5531	4468	5598	7778	8881	4468	5532	111	(session 1 = session 2)
WM	5531	4468	5898	7776	8881	4468	5532	111	(session 1 = session 2)
DW	5531	4468	5898	7776	8881	4468	5532	111	(session 1 = session 2)
WA	5531	4468	5588	7776	8881	4468	5533	111	(session 1 = session 2)

or-ders in   versus or-ders in

The difference lies in which syllable is stressed: "or" or "ders." A similar variation occurs in the first line at "Monroe" and in the third line at "old ninety." Another example of a rhythmical change between singers' melodies occurs in the first line:

Vir-gin-ia   versus Vir-gin-ia

Again, the difference lies in which syllable is stressed and thus in the time given to each syllable. A similar change occurs in the fourth line at "put her in."

Looking at just the notes sung on the quarter beats of each measure, we can easily identify the constants across singers. Singers vary the incidental notes sung around the quarter beats; however, the notes sung on the quarter beats change only slightly across singers. Bayard (1950) asserted that over time a melodic line becomes fixed at the basic intervals. Bronson (1969) used the notes sung on stressed beats to identify tune families in the Child ballads. In "The Wreck of the Old 97," the stressed beats occur at the first and third quarter beats.

Quarter notes in the time signature of this song are also the locations at which guitar strums should occur. Not all of the singers perform this song with accompaniment; however, all of these singers do play a musical instrument and would be aware of this additional physical constraint whether or not they have ever sung "The Wreck of the Old 97" accompanied by a musical instrument. Whether or not this additional motion on the guitar or other stringed instrument increased the stability of the quarter notes could be tested by examining the quarter notes for two singers—one of whom plays a musical instrument and one who does not.

Table 11.2 gives the scale step sung on each quarter beat by each singer. All singers perform this ballad in an Ionian, major, authentic scale. The tonic note in the scale is represented by 1: a C in the key of C, or a G in the key of G, and so on. The number 3 represents the third step: an E in the key of C, or a B in the key of G. An 8 represents the octave above the tonic. Across singers, the melody varies in the third, fourth, sixth, and seventh measures only. These changes correspond to the middle of the second line, the first and last beats of the third line, and the middle of the fourth line. There is no question that singers know the same general melody; however, as with the words, none of the melodies are identical.

Summary

There is no evidence of rote recall of this ballad. Each singer makes changes in the wording of the ballad between the two performances. However, these changes are limited by the constraints in the ballad and in the ballad tradition. End-rhyme sound, number of beats per line, and number of lines per verse remain relatively constant. Meaning or gist of verses, sequence of lines within a verse, and sequence of verses remain constant. Singers may add or delete verses that embellish the story. Melodic changes occur, but are also limited by the constraints of the particular type of scale used, the time signature, and the basic melodic line of the quarter beats. None of the singers performs the ballad exactly the same. Yet there are commonalities among singers that are defined by these constraints.

Words and music, although considered separately in the foregoing discussion, are intertwined. The words have a metrical pattern, which must correspond to the rhythmical pattern, the beat structure, and the time signature of the music. A metrical pattern is the series of stressed and unstressed syllables. In this ballad, the meter consists of two unstressed syllables followed by a stressed syllable. Usually the unstressed syllables are shorter in length than the stressed syllable. The meter is defined by the words and limits the number of syllables that can occur at any place. In two-syllable words, the stress falls on the accented syllable. The meter and rhythm are closely related in that the number of stressed syllables equals the number of beats in the music and in that the rhythmical outline is set by the meter. Thus, the music and words constrain each other.

Experiment 1: Learning and recalling "The Wreck of the Old 97"

From the analysis of variation and stability in traditional singers' versions of "The Wreck of the Old 97," we have argued that the constraints within the ballad and the ballad tradition limit possible variations singers can make in recalling a ballad and that these constraints contribute to stability in recall across singers and across performances by the same singer. Next, we asked undergraduates who were not familiar with the ballad tradition to learn and recall "The Wreck of the Old 97" in order to determine if these recalls were also governed by similar constraints. That is, we asked whether the effects of similar constraints can be observed in a broader population or whether the effects of the constraints are observed only when the learner is familiar with the general characteristics of the tradition.

Method

Subjects. Twenty-seven undergraduates participating in an introductory psychology class served as subjects in this experiment.

Materials. The first version of "The Wreck of the Old 97" from the Frank C. Brown collection (White, 1952) contains the five common verses and served as the stimulus (see Appendix Table 11.B). The last word of line 2 in verse 5 was changed from "on" to "learn" in order to maintain the same rhyme scheme for each verse in the ballad. This variation is found in Appendix Table 11.A (versions by BM, TS, and DW).

A female singer from North Carolina recorded this version of "The Wreck of the Old 97." The melody was learned by listening to five versions performed by traditional ballad singers. She was instructed to enunciate words carefully and to preserve the rhythm present in the melody. No slurred pronunciations were allowed, even if the traditional singers had slurred the words. For example, saying "ol' ninety-seven" rather than clearly pronouncing the "d" in "old" was not allowed. This step minimized the chances that subjects would not understand the words and simplified scoring.

Procedure. Subjects were instructed that they would hear a tape of a ballad and would be asked to recall the ballad. They were told that they would be asked to recall the words exactly as they heard them and in the same order. Over a period of 12 min, subjects heard the recorded song 10 times, with 3-sec pauses between repetitions. There was 1 min of silence at the end of the 10th repetition. Subjects then solved multiplication and division problems for 10 min, after which they were given 10 min to recall in writing the ballad they had heard earlier.

At the end of the recall, subjects were asked to answer several questions, including whether or not they had ever heard the ballad before.

All subjects reported that they had "definitely not" heard the ballad prior to the experiment.

Results

Recalls were scored for the percentage of correct words. A line had to be recalled in the correct sequence in order to be counted as correct. The first correct line in the sequence set the scale for what could follow that line; thus, a line could be omitted without affecting the scoring of subsequent lines. For instance, if line 2 was recalled after line 3, only line 3 was scored as correct. Less than 2% of the total lines (10 of 540) scored were marked as zero recall because they were recalled in the wrong sequence. The number of words correctly recalled in a line divided by the number of words in that line yielded the percentage recall score. Misspellings that preserved the sound of a word were counted as correct recalls. Contractions, where the original song did not have a contraction, and changes in number were counted as incorrect. Words recalled out of sequence within the line were scored as correct. Reliability (Cronbach's [1951] alpha) across subjects for recall of lines equals .95.[3]

Predicting recalls with ballad characteristics

The constraints and characteristics considered include the meaning value of each line, the imagery value of each line, the percentage of words in each line with a poetic tie to another word in the line or with an end rhyme, the percentage of agreement of each line with the metrical pattern, and the number of causal connections (Trabasso & Sperry, 1985) for each line.

Five observers rated the meaning and imagery values for each line. Meaning value was defined as the importance of that line to understanding the story and its meaning. Imagery value was defined as the importance of that line in obtaining an overall picture or image of the story. A scale from 0 to 9 was used to rate the imagery and meaning values, where 0 indicated *not important at all* and 9 indicated *most important*. Reliabilities (Cronbach's [1951] alpha) for imagery and meaning ratings were .82 and .86, respectively.

Poetic ties consisted of words that alliterated, assonated, or rhymed with other words in the line. Words alliterate when they begin with the same sound, usually a consonant, but end with different sounds. Assonance occurs when two words have the same vowel sound in the accented syllable, but not the same consonant sounds. For example, *lake* and *light* alliterate, whereas *lake* and *made* assonate. Alliterations and assonances were restricted to those words that occurred next to each other within the line. This restriction was imposed because we thought subjects could not hear instances of alliteration or assonance that were separated from each other. Such instances are extremely difficult to identify reliably even with a great deal of experience.

Words rhyme if they begin with different sounds but the last syllable of each ends in the same sound. Words that rhymed with other words in the same line were counted as having poetic ties. In addition, words were also counted as having a poetic constraint if they were part of an end rhyme. End rhyme occurs when the last words of two lines rhyme.

All such instances of alliteration, assonance, rhyme, and end rhyme were marked within each line. The percentage of words per line involved in one of these poetic constraints was calculated.

There are several common metrical patterns in ballads. In "The Wreck of the Old 97," the metrical pattern is anapestic (that is, two unstressed syllables followed by a stressed syllable). This metrical pattern is set up by the rhythmical beat of the music and the pattern of accented syllables in the line. In this ballad, the first and third lines contain four stressed beats, whereas the second and fourth lines contain three stressed beats (not counting the unspoken beat). The metrical pattern limits the possible word choices that can fit into a line in that the number of syllables and the stress pattern of those syllables are specified. Some exceptions can occur to the metrical pattern that are not very disruptive. For example, a single syllable can be stretched to cover two unstressed syllables, and an extra syllable can sometimes be incorporated into the two unstressed syllables. For each line, the number of exceptions to the metrical pattern was counted. The percentage of agreement between the metrical pattern and the line equals the number of possible metrical units (stressed plus unstressed units) minus the number of units that do not agree with the pattern divided by the number of metrical units for that line.

The number of causal connections for each line was determined according to the method outlined in Trabasso and Sperry's (1985) study. A causal connection occurs from line x to line y when the event described in line y could not have occurred if the event in line x had not occurred. Four judges were given this definition and asked to draw all possible causal connections between lines. Two lines were defined as causally connected when three of the four judges agreed. For each line, the number of causal connections to and from another line was counted.

Lines that are high in these characteristics were expected to have better verbatim recall. Table 11.3 gives the Pearson product-moment correlation between all characteristics and the mean percentage verbatim recall. The mean percentage recall for each line is significantly correlated with imagery ratings, metrical agreement, and number of causal

Table 11.3. *Pearson product-moment correlation between variables*

Variable		(1)	(2)	(3)	(4)	(5)	(6)
Mean recall (%)	(1)						
Imagery	(2)	.49[a]					
Meaning	(3)	.06	.43[a]				
Poetic ties (%)	(4)	.15	.03	.28			
Metrical agreement (%)	(5)	.44[a]	.17	.40[a]	.43[a]		
No. causal connections	(6)	.42[a]	.20	.17	.18	.37	

[a]Indicates correlations that are significant at $p < .05$.

Table 11.4. *Results for regression of characteristics on mean percentage recall*

Variable coefficient	Standardized
Imagery	.54[a]
Meaning	−.37
Metrical agreement	.40
Poetic ties (%)	.03
No. causal connections	.23

Note: Multiple $R = .72$; $R^2 = .52$; $F(5,14) = 3.02$[a]
[a]Indicates $p < .05$.

connections under the liberal assumption that each line is independent. Imagery and meaning are significantly correlated; however, causal connectedness is not correlated with meaning or imagery. Lines such as "It's a mighty rough road from Lynchburg to Danville" are high in imagery and high in meaning, but are not viewed as causally related to other lines in the ballad. Here, causal connectedness assesses a different characteristic than that assessed by meaning and imagery ratings. Furthermore, causal connectedness (not meaning) is significantly correlated with the mean percentage recall for each line.

The mean percentage recall for each line was regressed on each of the five characteristics. This regression equation is given in Table 11.4. The five independent variables account for 52% of the variance. Only imagery significantly contributes to predicting recalls.

Imagery is a constraint. The picture of the story identifies the primary event and limits what will be included in descriptions and scenes of that event, as well as implying some causes and sequences. Imagery integrates components into a whole scene and thus constrains the whole, but not the specific words. For undergraduates, the contribution a line makes to the image of a ballad better predicts recall than does the contribution a line makes to an understanding of the story. Whether or not this same observation holds for experienced singers remains to be tested; however, we expect experienced singers to make use of both imagery and meaning of lines.

Recalls of "The Wreck of the Old 97" by undergraduates are governed by some constraints observed in recalls by traditional singers. Undergraduates who are not familiar with the ballad tradition have better recalls of lines with higher imagery. Lines that have strong metrical agreement and greater causal connectedness also show higher recalls.

Experiment 2: Recalls of the ballad without poetic ties

Multiple constraints, we claim, limit the range of possible variation in recall and lead to increased stability in recall and subsequently in transmission. Removing even one constraint should increase the variability in recall. The results from Experiment 1 indicate that imagery, metrical agreement, and causal connectedness significantly correlate with recall. Poetics, however, was not correlated with recall; yet, poetics should have some effect even for a relatively few words. The purpose of this experiment is therefore to demonstrate that recall accuracy is reduced and variability is increased when poetic constraints within a line are reduced. This experiment will hold the other characteristics constant while varying only the percentage of words poetically linked to other words.

Method

Stimulus. Twenty-four words of "The Wreck of the Old 97" were changed in order to eliminate some of the obvious poetic constraints. All but three instances of assonance and alliteration in words that occurred next to each other were removed. In addition, all but two instances of alliteration, assonance, or rhyme in words that were separated by one other word were removed. The words altered from the original version examined in Experiment 1 are given in parentheses in Appendix Table 11.B.

The word changes were selected so that only poetic characteristics were altered. These changes preserved the number of syllables and the stress pattern in the original words. No instances of end rhyme were altered; thus, the most apparent aspects of poetics remained intact. Most of the word changes came from other versions of the ballad. Word changes were selected so that the meaning and tenor of all lines were preserved. Two observers were asked to compare the altered and original versions and determine if the meaning or implication of any lines was changed by the altered words. Both observers found no such changes. Because of the difficulty in meeting all the constraints mentioned, some of the substitutions may seem better than others to the careful reader. Nonetheless, the results hold even for the very best of the substitutions.

The song was recorded by the same singer with the same tune as in Experiment 1.

Subjects. Twenty-seven subjects from the same population as in Experiment 1 participated in this experiment.

Procedure. The procedure was identical with that in Experiment 1.

Results

The mean percentage of verbatim recall for the ballad equals 55% (SE = 4%), which is not statistically different from the mean percentage of recall from the original version (60%) examined in Experiment 1 – $F(1, 52) = 0.93$, not significant.

The differences in recalls for the two versions appear in comparisons of the poetic word pairs. If verbatim recall is scored for just those words that differ between the two versions, then words with poetic constraints are recalled more often than the nonpoetic substitutes – 51% versus 24%, $F(1, 52) = 24.81$.

There are five cases in which two words occurring next to each other assonate or alliterate and in which one of the pair is not a pronoun, article, or preposition (i.e., "they," "the," "his," "this," or "with"). These five word pairs represent the clearest instances of poetics that were changed between the two versions. These word pairs as they occurred in each recording are given in Table 11.5 along with all variations recalled by subjects and with the number of subjects recalling each variation.

There are fewer variations in the original version (left column) than in the altered version (right column). In the left column, most subjects recalled the word pair that was sung. However, in the right column, few or no subjects recalled the exact word pair. When poetic characteristics are removed, there is greater variability in the words subjects recall.

In addition, even normal college students sometimes recovered the original poetic phrases instead of recalling the altered, nonpoetic phrases. These instances are underlined. For example, with the altered

Table 11.5. *Recalls of poetic word pairs from the original and the altered versions*

Recalls from original version		Recalls from altered version	
"beh<u>i</u>nd t<u>i</u>me"		"beyond time"	
behind time	17	beyond time	4
behind Tom	1	<u>behind</u> <u>time</u>	7
running late	1	behind the line	1
running behind	1	ahead of your time	1
(not recalled)	7	righty on time	1
		mighty long time	1
		before your time	1
		get May on time	1
		past his time	1
		(not recalled)	9
"<u>S</u>aying <u>S</u>teve"		"telling Steve"	
saying Steve	9	telling Steve	0
said Steve	6	<u>saying</u> <u>Steve</u>	2
Steve	4	said Steve	1
said you're	1	they said Steve	1
said he	1	Steve	3
told him	1	(no name or verb)	1
Dan Brooklyn	1	calling Steve	1
Saying John	1	well Steve	1
(not recalled)	3	Johnny	1
		to tell Steve	1
		tell us Steve	1
		and how Steve	1
		(not recalled)	13
"mighty <u>r</u>ough <u>r</u>oad"		"mighty tough road"	
mighty rough road	13	mighty tough road	0
long rough road	3	<u>mighty</u> <u>rough</u> <u>road</u>	1
road is rough	1	long tough road	2
road is . . . mighty rough	1	road is tough	1
long long line	1	long way	3
hard long road	1	long hard track	1
mighty long track	1	mighty long trip	1
long hard road	1	long hard road	1
long haul	1	treacherous run	1
(not recalled)	4	long tough hall	1
		long long way	1
		hard road	2
		long road	2
		long hard way	1
		mighty long line	1
		mighty hard road	1
		real rough road	1
		treacherous & steep trail	1
		(not recalled)	5

Table 11.5. *(cont.)*

Recalls from original version		Recalls from altered version	
"grade making"		"grade running"	
grade making	3	grade running	1
grade at	6	grade	2
at . . . grade	1	grade going	1
going . . . grade	1	grade doing	1
mountain making	1	doing . . . grade	1
grade	1	grade at	2
making	1	mountain at	3
that at	1	hill at	1
hill making	1	at	1
grade doing	3	going	1
going	2	doing	1
(not recalled)	6	went at	1
		grade 'round	1
		riding . . . grade	1
		(not recalled)	9
"you young"		"you fine"	
you young	14	you fine	14
young	6	you young	2
you	3	ye fine	3
ye	1	fine	3
you fine young	1	you	2
(not recalled)	2	young	1
		your fine	1
		fair	1
		(not recalled)	0

word pair "tough road," recalls contain alliterations with the "t" or with the "r," as in "real rough road" or "treacherous trail." Even if some of the constraints are temporarily lost, there is a chance of their being recovered. With ballad singers, who are more sensitive to the constraints of the tradition, the effect should be even greater. This effect, more than the absolute differences in recall, indicates the way in which poetics adds to the stability in recall and thus in transmission. It is as if the rules, not the instances constructed from those rules, are being transmitted. To the extent that the rules can be fulfilled with only one word pair, recall and thus transmission will not vary (Rubin & Wallace, 1986).

Even though subjects more often recalled the exact wording of the original version, there is no statistical difference between ratings of recall accuracy for the two versions. In both experiments, subjects rated their confidence in the accuracy of verbatim recall at the end of the experimental session using a rating scale from 1 to 7, where 7 indicates no lines recalled verbatim, and 1 indicates all lines recalled verbatim. The mean ratings for the original and the altered versions were 4.33 and 4.35, respectively – $F(1, 52) = .002$, not significant.

In summary, the overall percentage recalled for the altered version does not statistically differ from the percentage recalled for the original version. However, when only the altered word pairs are scored for recall, the percentage of verbatim recall is greater for the original poetic pairs than for the altered nonpoetic pairs. Furthermore, when poetic constraints are removed, recalls have greater variation in word choices. Poetic constraints limit possible word choices and thereby increase stability in recall.

Experiment 3: Effect of rhythmical information on recall

In the preceding experiments, the words to be learned were presented as a song. This experiment concentrates on an aspect of the song, the rhythm, another constraint that contributes to stability in recall.

When traditional ballad singers are asked what they do to recall a ballad, singers often reply that one must get the rhythm and/or melody in one's head before one can sing the song. Furthermore, singers report difficulty recalling a song with an irregular rhythm.

By "rhythmical pattern" is meant an idealized combination of the metrical pattern and the timing constraints of the ballad. The metrical pattern is the series of stressed and unstressed units that repeat throughout the ballad and is primarily determined by the words. In this ballad, the metrical pattern consists of two unstressed units followed by a stressed unit, where a unit is usually one syllable. In the musical score of this ballad, there are four beats per measure, with a stressed beat falling on the first and third beats of each measure. These stressed beats correspond to stressed units in the metrical pattern. In this ballad, two unstressed syllables are spoken or sung as fast as one stressed syllable. The pauses incorporated into this ballad occurred at the ends of lines 2 and 4. Here, the pause acts as an additional (unspoken) stressed beat or metrical unit. This definition of rhythmical pattern considers the basic, regular, constant case. In singing, the rhythmical pattern might be livelier and not so monotonous.

In the following experiment, the rhythmical pattern is either omitted or emphasized in the stimulus. If rhythmical information is a good learning or recall cue, then recall should be greater when the rhythmical information is given.

Method

Stimulus. The same ballad was again used in this experiment. Here, the ballad was spoken rather than sung. The ballad was read with either (a) normal voice intonation, as if a story were being read, (b) rhythmical intonation in which stressed syllables were clearly emphasized, or (c) the same rhythmical intonation as in (b) and with a beat tapped in the background corresponding to each stressed syllable. The last two conditions differed only in the addition of the tapped beat. This tap is much like what an audience would do when clapping along with a song. A male voice recorded all three stimulus variants.

Procedure. The procedure was identical with that in the previous experiments.

Subjects. Eighty-seven subjects from the same subject population participated in this session. Each group of 27 subjects heard one of the three stimulus tapes.

Results

The mean percentage recall in the three conditions (normal voice, rhythmical voice, rhythmical voice plus beat) averaged 57%, 56%, and 64% words correct, respectively. Using a repeated-measures analysis of variance, a significant main effect of line – $F(38, 1,482) = 18.02$ – and a significant interaction of condition and line – $F(38, 1,482) = 1.43$ – were found. The main effect of condition was not significant – $F(2, 78) = 1.24, p > .29$.

The interaction of line and condition indicates that some lines are better recalled in one condition than in another. Lines that fit the rhythmical or metrical pattern best should have more accurate recalls when rhythmical information is present. To assess this explanation of the interaction of condition and line, the mean percentage recall for each line was correlated with the metrical-agreement measure from Experiment 1. The recalls significantly correlate with metrical agreement in the rhythmical-voice condition and in the rhythmical-voice-plus-beat condition – $r = .52$ and $r = .57$, respectively. However, in the normal-voice condition, metrical agreement does not significantly correlate with percentage recall – $r = .38$.

Rhythmical information is yet another constraint present in ballads that contributes to stability in recall. The rhythmical pattern limits the number of syllables and the number of words in a line and thereby increases verbatim recall or decreases variation in recall. The rhythm and the beat emphasize certain words. The musical notes corresponding with beats are also the stable points in singers' recalls. The rhythmical pattern links the words and the music.

Summary

"The Wreck of the Old 97" describes a real event that occurred in 1903. That event entered the ballad tradition using a form that appears to have been adopted from other songs about ships. Ballads describing that event are still sung in North Carolina.

By examining the versions of this ballad from five singers, we observed that every singer made changes in the song between two performances. Singers were not performing by rote. Furthermore, although each singer was clearly singing the same ballad, none of the renditions were identical across singers. There was variation, but that variation occurred within bounds that inhibited systematic changes over time and limited the set of possible variations. Stability was maintained without maintaining a fixed text.

The changes that did occur followed constraints within the ballad. Rhyme pairs, verse content, story sequence, meter, number of beats per measure, and number of measures did not change across singers. The melody line was stable around the quarter beats in each measure. Verses that embellish the story by adding details but do not change the story line may be added or omitted by different singers. When the phrasing of a line is altered, all these characteristics are still preserved. The combination of these characteristics then limits the possible variations a ballad can have.

The memory for the ballad is not the exact song, nor is it a collection of words; rather, it is a collection of rules and constraints. This notion is the same one that Bartlett (1932) labeled "schema." Here, however, we have not only a schema for gist but also a schema for poetics, rhythm, imagery, and music. Together these schemata, and possibly others, constrain recall to the extent that it almost appears rote or verbatim.

Finally, by examining recalls of the ballad from undergraduates in a learning paradigm, we observed that undergraduates could make use of many characteristics. Lines with high imagery values or many poetic constraints were recalled more accurately. When the metrical agreement and the poetics were high, recall was more accurate. When poetic constraints were removed, recalls had greater variability across subjects. Finally, when rhythmical information was emphasized in the stimulus, recalls were more accurate.

All of these characteristics interact together to limit variations in recall and thus increase the stability in recall and in transmission of a ballad. Moreover, the variation that does exist is variation within constraints. As long as the constraints do not change over generations, neither will the ballad "The Wreck of the Old 97."

Appendix Table 11.A. *Versions of "The Wreck of the Old 97"*

Fred Jackson Lewey (recorded 10-14-25 by R. W. Gordon) (from Gordon, 1925, NC 4)	Charles Weston Noell (recorded 10-14-25 by R. W. Gordon) (from Gordon, 1925, NC 1)
Last evening I stood on a mountain Just watching the smoke from below It was springing from a long slender smokestack Way down on the Southern Road	
	Come all of you fellows and gather around me And a sad sad story to hear All about the wreck of old Ninety-seven And the death of the brave engineer
	At the Whiting Station on that wet Sabbath morning Twas just at the rising of the sun When he kissed his wife said "My children God bless you Your father must go out on his run"
	Steve Broady was the engineer And a brave brave man was he For a many poor man have lost his life For the railroad company
It was Ninety-seven the fastest train That the South has ever seen But she run too fast that fatal Sunday evening And the death list numbered fourteen	Ninety-seven was the fastest train That was ever on the Southern Line All the freight trains and passengers had to hold for 97 She's compelled to be at stations on time
	At Monroe, Virginia he received his orders Saying Steve you are way behind This is not Thirty-eight but it's Ninety-seven You must put her into Danville on time
	He climbed in his engine at Monroe, Virginia Saying fireman it's do or die I'll reverse the lever throw the throttle wide open We'll watch old Ninety-seven fly
Well the engineer was a brave fast driver On that fatal Sunday eve And his fireman leaned far out at Lynchburg Waiting for the signal to leave	Steve Broady he was that engineer On that fatal Sunday eve And his fireman was leaning far out at Lynchburg Just waiting for the signal to leave
When he got on board well he threw back his throttle And although his air was bad People all said as he passed Franklin Junction That you couldn't see the men in the cab	When they gave him the post he threw back his throttle Although his airbrakes was bad And the people all said when he passed Franklin Junction It seemed like the engineer was mad
	Steve Broady he said to his black and greasy fireman Just put in a little more coal And when we turn over White Oak Mountain You just watch my drivers roll
There's a mighty bad road from Lynchburg to Danville And although he knew this well He said he'd pull his train on time into Spencer Or he'd jerk it right square into hell	Now it's a awful bad road from Lynchburg to Danville And from Lima it's a three mile grade It was on this grade that his airbrakes failed him And look what a jump she made
When he hit the grade from Lima to Danville His whistle began to scream He was found when she wrecked with his hand on the throttle Where he'd scalded to death from steam	Falling down this grade at eighty miles an hour His whistle began to scream He was found in the wreck with his hand on the throttle Where he scalded to death from the steam
	When the news came slipping o'er the telegraph wires And this is the way it read That brave engineer that pulled Ninety-seven Is lying in North Danville dead
Did she ever pull in No she never pulled in [a] Though at one forty-five he was due For hours and hours has the switchman been watching For that fast mail that never came through	Did she ever pull in No she never pulled in You could hear it in silent breath His poor little wife fell back and fainted When the news came home of his death

[a]This verse was sung as a chorus after every second verse.

Appendix Table 11.A. *(cont.)*

Vernon Dalhart (recorded for Victor Talking Machine Company, 1924) (from Victor Talking Machine Company v George, 1934)	David Graves George (hand written copy - unknown date) (from Victor Talking Machine Company v George, 1934)
	On a cold frosty morning in the month of September When the clouds were hanging low Ninety-seven pulled out from the Washington station Like an arrow shot from a bow
They gave him his orders at Monroe, Virginia Saying Pete you're way behind time This is not Thirty-eight but it's old Ninety-seven You must put her in Center on time	They gave him his orders at Monroe, Virginia Saying "Pete you are way behind time It's not Thirty-eight but it's old Ninety-seven You must put her in Spencer on time"
He looked round then to his black greasy fireman Just shove on in a little more coal And when we cross that White Oak Mountain You can watch old Ninety-seven roll It's a mighty rough road from Lynchburg to Danville And a line on a three mile grade It was on that grade that he lost his average And you see what a jump he made He was going down grade making ninety miles an hour When his whistle broke into a scream He was found in the wreck with his hand on the throttle And a-scalded to death with the steam	He looked at his black greasy fireman And said shovel in a little more coal For when we cross that White Oak Mountain You can see old Ninety-seven roll It's a mighty rough road from Lynchburg to Danville And Lima it's a three mile grade It was on this grade that he lost his average And you see what a jump he made They was going down grade making ninety miles an hour Who when the whistle whistle whistle broke into a scream He was found in a wreck with his hand on the throttle And scalded to death with the s[team]
Now ladies you must take warning From this time now and on Never speak harsh words to your true love and husband He may leave you and never return	Now ladies you must take warning From this time on Never speak harsh words to your true loving husbands For they may leave you and never r[eturn] Did she ever pull in No she never pulled in For hours and hours . . . . as watching For the train that never pulled . . . . . .

Appendix Table 11.A. *(cont.)*

Henry Whitter from Victor Talking Machine Company v George, 1934)	Singer BM [b] (Recorded June 17, 1983 and November 16, 1983)
	I stood on the mountain one cold frosty morning (One cold winter morning I stood on the mountain) Watching the smoke from below It was strolling out of a long straight (tall) smokestack Way down on the southern railroad
	The old Ninety-seven was the fastest mailtrain That the South had ever seen She run so fast on that fatal Sunday morning And her detect was number 14
	Steve Border's (Border) kissed his loving wife Just at the rise of the sun And he said God bless you to my children Your pop is going out on his run
	The old Ninety-seven was the fastest mailtrain Ever run on the southern line And when she pulled into old Monroe, Virginia She was Thirty-seven minutes behind
They gave him up his order at Monroe, Virginia Saying Steve you're way behind time This is not Thirty-Eight but it's Old Ninety-Seven You must put her in Spencer on time	They give him his orders at Monroe Virginia Saying Steve you're away behind time This is not Thirty-eight but it's old Ninety-seven You must put her into Spencer on time
	Steve Border(s) mounted to his cabin Says pal she's due or die He reversed his engine threw open the throttle (Said) Now watch old Ninety-seven fly
	But when they crossed that White Oak Mountain [c] His air brakes was mighty bad And the people did say as they passed Franklin junction That you couldn't see the man in the cab
Steve Brooklyn said to his black greasy fireman Just shovel on a little more coal And when we cross the White Oak Mountain You can watch old Ninety-Seven roll	He turned around to his black and greasy fireman Can't you (Saying) shovel in a little more coal And when we cross that White Oak Mountain You can watch my drivers roll
It's a mighty rough road from Lynchburg to Danville And a line on a three mile grade It was on this grade when he lost his airbrakes And you see what a jump he made	It's a mighty rough road from Lynchburg to Danville (From Lynchburg to Danville it's a mighty rough road) And Lima it's (on) a three mile grade It were on this grade that he lost his air brakes And you see what a jump he made
He was going down grade making ninety mile an hour When his whistle began to scream He was found in the wreck with his hand on the throttle And was scalded to death by the steam	They were going down grade making ninety miles an hour When the (his) whistle begin to scream He was found in the wreck with his hand on the throttle And was scaulded to death by the steam
	The message (news) came in on the telegram wire And this is what it said (read) That the brave engineer who left Monroe this morning Is (Was) a lying over Danville dead
So come you ladies you must take warning From this time now and on Never speak harsh words to your true loving husband He may leave you and never return	Come all ye (you) ladies and take fair warning From this time now and learn (on) Never speak harsh words to your true loving husband He may leave you and never return

[b]For the last five versions, words in parentheses indicate variations as sung in the second session.

[c]This verse was actually sung after the ballad was completed in session 2.

Appendix Table 11.A. *(cont.)*

Singer TS (Recorded August 8, 1983 and January 6, 1984)	Singer WM (Recorded November 4, 1984 and June 16, 1985)
(Well) They gave him his orders in Monroe Virgina Saying Steve you're way behind time Well its (This is) not Thirty-eight but she's old 97 You must put her in Spencer on time	They gave him his orders in Monroe Virginia Saying Steve you're way behind time This is not Thirty-eight but it's old Ninety-seven You must put her into Spencer on time
Well then he turned around to his black greasy fireman (Said) Shovel in a little more coal And when we reach that great white (White Oak) mountain You will watch old Ninety-seven roll	Well Steve Broadway turned to his black greasy fireman Saying shovel on a little more coal And it's when we hit that White Oak Mountain You can watch Ninety-seven roll
It's a mighty rough road from Lynchburg to Danville It's a line (Lined) on a three mile grade It was on that grade that he lost his air brakes You should a seen what a jump he made	(It's a mighty rough road from Lynchburg to Danville) [a] (On the line there's a three mile grade) (It was on this grade that he lost his air brakes) (You should see what a jump he made)
He was going round a curve making ninety miles an hour When his whistle (Whistle) broke into a scream He was found in the wreck with his hand on the throttle Was scaulded (Scaulded) to death by the steam	He was (They were) going down the curve doing 90 miles an hour When his whistle broke into a scream He was found in the wreck with his hand on the throttle He was scaulded to death by steam
Now listen to me all you railroad women From this time now and learn Never speak harsh words to your true loving husband He may leave you and never return	Now (all) you ladies won't you please take warning From this time and now on Don't you speak harsh words to your true loving husband He may leave you and never return

[a] This verse was recalled after the ballad had been completed in session 2.

Appendix Table 11.A. *(cont.)*

Singer DW (Recorded September 26, 1984 and June 3, 1985)	Singer WA (Recorded March 22, 1982 and April 4, 1982)
	It's not Thirty-eight but it's old Ninety-seven [e] It'll make it to Blowee on time
Oh they gave him his orders at Monroe Virginia Said Steve you're away behind time This is not Thirty-eight it's old Ninety-seven You must pull her into Spencer on time	(Well they) Gave him his orders in Monroe Virginia Saying Captain (Buddy) you're way behind time It's not Thirty- (Ninety) -eight it's old Ninety-seven It'll take you to Blowee (victory) on time
(Then) He turned all around to his white faced fireman Said shovel in a little more coal (And) When we get on top of that White Oak Mountain You can watch Ninety-seven roll	The engineer (he) whispered to the black greasy fireman Says (saying) shovel in a little more coal And when we cross that great Smokey Mountain We'll (We're going to) watch old Ninety-seven roll
Now it's a mighty rough road from Lynchburg to Danville And it's on a three mile grade It was on this grade that he lost his airbrake You can see what a jump she made	
She (He) was going down grade making ninety mile per hour When the (his) whistle broke into a scream He was found in the wreck with his hand on the throttle And scaulded to death by the steam	They was going (down the grade making) ninety miles an hour When the whistle began to scream They found him in the wreck with his hand on the throttle He was (And) scalded to death by steam
Then a call came into Washington City And here is what it said The brave young engineer who pulled old Ninety-seven Is lying here in Danville dead	
	It's not thirty-eight but it's old Ninety-seven [e] So it took him to Blowee on time The engineering was all he had on his mind They buried him today with all high honors Resting from the wearies of his great troubled mind
Now young wives be kind to your true loving husband And from this a sad lesson learn (Yes) Always be kind to your true loving husband He may leave you to never return	Now ladies be true to a kind loving husband [e] They'll leave you to never return It's not Thirty-eight but old Ninety-seven And it's on his way with his last run
	(Well his breath slowly waned while his message he said) (To the maiden he thought would be his bride) (Oh ladies take warning to your fair lady) (They may be on his last ride)

[e]This verse was omitted in session 2.

Appendix Table 11.B. *Versions of "The Wreck of the Old 97" used in Experiments 1 and 3*

They gave (told) him his (the) orders at Monroe, Virginia
Saying (Telling) Steve you're away behind (beyond) time
This is (And it's) not thirty-eight but it's (the) old ninety-seven
You must put her in (it at) Spencer on time

Steve Brooklyn said (called) to his black (tired) greasy fireman
Just shovel in a little more coal
And when we cross that White (Red) Oak Mountain
You can watch old ninety-seven roll

It's a mighty rough (tough) road from Lynchburg to Danville
And a (the) line on a three mile grade
It was on this grade that (where) he lost his air brakes
And you see what a jump he made

He was going (heading) down grade making (running) ninety miles an hour
When (And) his whistle began to scream
He was found in the wreck with his (a) hand on the (a) throttle
And was scalded to death by the steam

Come all you young (fine) ladies you must take warning
From this time now and learn
Never speak harsh (mean) words to a loving husband
For he may leave you and never return

Note: Alterations used in Experiment 2 are given in parentheses after the words that were changed.

NOTES

Preparation of this chapter was supported in part by National Science Foundation grant BNS 84-10124.

We gratefully acknowledge the singers whose versions are presented here for their participation and willingness to share their tradition. We also gratefully acknowledge the assistance of Kevin Mallory and Mary Baker in preparing recordings of the ballad. We thank Archie Levy for the suggestion that guitar strums coincide with quarter notes. We thank Ian Hunter for helpful comments on the manuscript.

1 Version A of "The Wreck of the Old Ninety-Seven" as contributed by W. Amos Abrams of Boone, NC, from *The Frank C. Brown Collection of North Carolina Folklore: Vol. 2. Folk Ballads from North Carolina* (pp. 516–518), edited by N. I. White, 1952, Durham, NC: Duke University Press. Copyright 1952 by Duke University Press; renewed 1980 Duke University Press. Reprinted by permission.
2 The most popular of all recordings of "The Wreck of the Old 97" was Dalhart's version, which was last released in 1926. If the song were transmitted from Dalhart's recording, the character would be *Pete*, not *Steve*, going to

Center, not *Spencer,* and he would lose his *average,* not his *air brakes.* Among our singers, these words are not found.

3 All reported statistics occur at $p < .05$ unless otherwise indicated.

REFERENCES

Bartlett, F. C. (1932). *Remembering a study in experimental and social psychology.* Cambridge University Press.

Bayard, S. P. (1950). Prolegomena to a study of the principal melodic families of folk song. *Journal of American Folklore, 63,* 1–44.

Bronson, B. H. (1969). *The ballad as song.* Berkeley: University of California Press.

Cohen, N. (1981). *The long steel rail: The railroad in American folksong.* Urbana: University of Illinois Press.

Cronbach, L. J. (1951). Coefficient alpha and the internal structure of tests. *Psychometrika, 16,* 297–334.

Goody, J. (1978). Oral tradition and the reconstruction of the past in northern Ghana. In B. Bernadi, C. Poni, & A. Triuli (Eds.), *Fonti orali. Antropolgia e storia* (pp. 285–295). Milano: Franco Angeli.

Gordon, R. W., Collection (1925, October–December). *North Carolina collection.* Unpublished texts numbered NC 1–NC 298 of field recordings A1–A298. Archive of Folk Culture, Library of Congress.

Havelock, E. A. (1978). *The Greek concept of justice: From its shadow in Homer to its substance in Plato.* Cambridge, MA: Harvard University Press.

Hubbard, F. H. (1945). *Railroad avenue: Great stories and legends of American rail-roading.* New York: McGraw-Hill.

Hunter, I. M. L. (1985). Lengthy verbatim recall: The role of text. In A. Ellis (Ed.), *Progress in the psychology of language* (Vol. 1, pp. 207–235). Hillsdale, NJ: Erlbaum.

Lord, A. B. (1960). *The singer of tales.* Cambridge, MA: Harvard University Press.

News and Observer. (1903). Death's black blank swallowed up nine. *The News and Observer,* Raleigh, NC (September 29).

Newsleader (1903). Nine are killed by train's wild leap. *The Newsleader,* Richmond, VA (September 28).

Ong, W. S. (1982). *Orality and literacy: The technologizing of the world.* London: Methuen.

Rubin, D. C., & Wallace, W. T. (1986, November). *Rhyme and reason: Integral properties of words.* Paper presented at a meeting of the Psychonomic Society, New Orleans, LA.

Trabasso, T., & Sperry, L. L. (1985). Causal relatedness and the importance of story events. *Journal of Memory and Language, 24,* 595–611.

Victor Talking Machine Company v. *George, Federal Reporter,* 2nd Series (April–May, 1934), *69,* 871ff.

White, N. I. (Ed.). (1952). *The Frank C. Brown collection of North Carolina folklore* (Vol. 2). Durham, NC: Duke University Press.

Yarbough, J. (1978, July). [Interview with John C. Wiley, eyewitness to the wreck of Number 97]. (Cassette recording available from Danville Public Library, Danville, VA).

12

Passive remembering

DONALD P. SPENCE

I am particularly glad to join in a conference on ecological memory, and I am glad for at least two reasons. First of all, it lets me focus on the domain of passive remembering – the general experience of having things come to mind without their being requested. When we are under the spell of the past, captive to one or more past events; when we suffer from reminiscences, as did Freud's hysterical patients – in all these cases, we are engaged in passive remembering.

The second reason to be happy with an ecological approach is that it would seem the only way to study passive remembering. By definition, this type of recall can hardly be studied experimentally; the amount of data gathered per subject in the usual laboratory procedure is too small to be useful, and only by following a subject over a long period of time can we ever accumulate very much. Consider the findings from a typical setting for inducing unbidden thoughts, a sensory-deprivation experiment. Subjects tend to show enormous individual differences in the number of thoughts that come to mind under such conditions, and differ again in their willingness to report them. We are next faced with the difficulty of establishing the memorial validity of these thoughts – did the event really happen as remembered, and, if not, how was it changed? And finally, we have no way of comparing, within a given subject, the form and content of passive memories with the form and content of active memories, because an experiment designed to produce the former usually is all wrong for the latter. We have to turn to a more natural setting.

Consider the following statement from Barrett Mandel:

I am going about my business when something happens and I "get" a memory. Whenever a certain tune plays on the radio, it triggers a memory of the high-school prom. Or I may not notice that I am noticing a button on someone's coat because what I do notice I am noticing is that I am remembering my grand-mother pressing me, as a child, to her bosom, pinching my skin with her button. This always happens when I don't notice that I am noticing that kind of button. Or, my eye glances up at my index cards and my mind glides to a weekly card game played by the grownups in the early forties. Something happens *now* and a memory is triggered. What happens now is unpredictable, while the memory is hinged to the mysterious, fleeting present more than to the past. The picture never develops to a new stage, it does not elaborate itself, does not clarify through successive reappearances, ends abruptly as time goes on, leads nowhere. The truth is not in these pictures, but behind them. The pictures—part of a survival mechanism—are there to *prevent* self-discovery. (Mandel, 1980, p. 51)

I think this excerpt is instructive on several counts. Many of these unbidden memories are repetitive and familiar; we recognize that we have had them before—and yet they are curiously isolated from anything else. To dwell on them or associate to them often leads nowhere, and one possible reason is hinted at in the paragraph just quoted. The memory may exist to protect us from discovering something more; its isolated nature may be more than accidental. The following is an excerpt from Richard Wright's 1945 autobiography, *Black Boy*, that may further clarify this defensive function:

Many times in the years after [my father went off with a strange woman] the image of my father and the . . . woman, their faces lit by the dancing flame, would surge up in my imagination so vivid and strong that I felt I could reach out and touch it; I would stare at it, feeling that it possessed some vital meaning which always eluded me. (Wright, quoted in Mandel, 1980, p. 51)

The unbidden and recurring memory finally dissolved when Wright paid a visit to his aged father, some 25 years later.

An important aspect of these repeated memories bears on the problem of context. Many cases of inadvertent recall are triggered by a repetitive context—the example with the button is a good one—and the memory takes on significance only within that context. That may be why people often will feel dissatisfied when they attempt to verify such a memory—when they go back to their elementary school or their college fraternity—because looking at the real object does not substitute for remembering it, because the remembering, often inadvertent, is embedded in a specific situation with its special context and its own dynamics. A trip to the fraternity house is simply a trip, and it produces a sense of disappointment because it is deprived of the critical surround.

The first two memories quoted—the one triggered by the button and the one about the index cards—may have come into being for highly specific reasons. To obsessively notice the button on someone's coat may prevent him from looking at her face; the memory of the grandmother with her painful embrace may parallel his mixed feelings of wanting to stay and talk, and also wanting to get away. Thus, the unbidden memory may be a piece of insight, concretely represented. Much more study needs to be carried out on the relationship between unbidden memories and their enabling contexts.

The second memory, triggered by the index cards, would seem to have a more defensive meaning. It sounds as if he were settling down to some writing, perhaps working over a manuscript – and the memory of the card game may be a call to abandon the work and have some fun. But maybe not. He mentions grownups, as if he were a child looking on. Could this particular cast of characters say something about his concern with the reading public – especially the critics – and what they will say about his manuscript when it is published? Is he worried that they can "play the game" better than he can? Perhaps, after all, he is only a child and has nothing important to say.

Once we see the importance of the enabling context, we see, first, how passive remembering can be studied only in the natural environment. Second, we begin to realize – particularly in the example with the button – how difficult it may be to fully establish the context. "I may not notice," Mandel writes, "that I am noticing a button on someone's coat"; this particular kind of experience takes special ingenuity to recapture. It has the flavor of a peripheral scotoma, and to focus attention on it only drives it farther from the line of sight. Third, we realize that the repeated memory cannot be treated in isolation, but must be studied together with its enabling context. Each sheds light on the other, and in many cases the reason why the memory keeps recurring can be understood only if we know the conditions under which it appears. We know from experience how context controls meaning, how what Gadamer (1975) calls the horizon of understanding will determine the sense of a text; for just this reason, it is important that a repeated memory can be understood only within its triggering surround.

Where and when do unbidden memories tend to occur? We have lots of anecdotes, many from authors and playwrights, but little in the way of firm facts. Eugene O'Neill, in the last 10 years of his life, appeared to live almost continually in the past. During the time he was writing *A Long Day's Journey,* he would come in from his study with his eyes streaming with tears; his wife feared he might go mad. We can assume that much of this remembering was involuntary, and we might suspect that it happens quite frequently in writing both fiction and autobiography. Here is another example, from Nabokov's autobiography, *Speak, Memory* (1966). It concerns a French governess who lived with the family when Nabokov was a young boy. He describes her as enormous and morose, somewhat hard of hearing, and essentially helpless because she knew only one word of Russian, and that was usually the wrong one. He went to visit her in Switzerland, many years later, and after saying good-bye, he found himself walking by a lake.

Below, a wide ripple, almost a wave, and something vaguely white attracted my eye. As I came quite close to the lapping water, I saw what it was – an aged swan, a large, uncouth, dodo-like creature, making ridiculous efforts to hoist himself into a moored boat. He could not do it. The heavy, impotent flapping of his wings, their slippery sound against the rocking and splashing boat, the gluey glistening of the dark swell where it caught the light—all seemed for a moment laden with a strange significance. (1966, p. 116)

It comes as no surprise to hear that when he discovered, several years later, that his governess had died, the image of the swan came to mind. It takes no great imagination to see the links between the enabling context and the unbidden memory.

Autobiography is clearly a rich source of passive memories, and it would be interesting to make a collection of similar examples to see what they all have in common. Even allowing for the author's frequent temptation to smooth the facts here and there, we would still learn something of interest about what settings seem most likely to evoke this kind of experience. Nabokov draws attention to one condition that deserves particular attention—the moment of falling asleep, or altered state of consciousness. You may have noticed that very often, a transition occurs between the time that you are controlling your thoughts and the time when some other voice takes over, and this other voice is very close to the voice of unbidden memory. Nabokov describes it well:

Just before falling asleep, I often become aware of a kind of one-sided conversation going on in an adjacent section of my mind, quite independently from the actual trend of my thoughts. It is a neutral, detached, anonymous voice, which I catch saying words of no importance to me whatever—an English or a Russian sentence, not even addressed to me, and so trivial that I hardly dare give samples, lest the flatness I wish to convey be marred by a molehill of sense. (1966, p. 33)

This example brings out one of the difficulties in collecting good data. One of the significant characteristics of the passive memory, when it first appears, is that it may speak in a whisper, and we may not notice its presence. It is particularly hard to capture under conditions of falling asleep. At other times, we may recognize the memory, but be unaware of the enabling context, precisely because one of the functions of the former is to make us unaware of the latter. To gather data on *both* phenomena demands both special interest and special training.

We can begin to summarize what we have learned so far. A passive memory, first of all, may indicate that another mode of functioning has taken over, as in falling asleep. Second, it may be a way of summarizing— even symbolizing—a particular reaction, as in Nabokov's memory of the helpless swan occurring to him at the moment when he learned of the death of his French governess. Third, it may function to distract us from something going on in the present. It should be obvious why we have so few data of this kind, because the full force of the memory is intended to *prevent* us from noticing the surrounding circumstances, and recall of the circumstances would take place only when the memory failed to distract us. We are faced with a methodological puzzle.

Putting together the clues we have gathered so far, we might hypothesize that although an enabling context may be a necessary condition for an unbidden-memory condition to appear, it is clearly not sufficient. Also needed, as the evidence from studies of sleep states seems to suggest, is a shift of consciousness that allows the passive voice to speak. Evidence supporting this shift may be found in Mandel when he writes that "I may not notice that I am noticing . . ."–some change in level of awareness seems to be taking place, and it may be this change that allows the memory of the grandmother to appear.

We now begin to understand just how the unbidden memory can distract. It is not that something else pops into mind at that particular moment; rather, it is a combination of distracting memory along with an alteration of consciousness. The unbidden memory is somewhat distracting, to be sure, but the fact that it has appeared is a signal that a crucial shift in awareness has already taken place, and for that reason we are not attending to the enabling context quite as keenly as before. Thus, the unbidden memory often can be the *result* of the distraction as much as the cause.

From what I have said so far, it is clear that the mind is not a camera, snapping everything that comes along: An event that arouses anxiety may bring about a lapse of attention and, quite possibly, an unbidden memory. We now begin to see why autobiography tells its own kind of truth–narrative truth (Spence, 1982)–even though it may not match with archival accounts of what "really happened." If unbidden memories, for example, are substituted for real events with no awareness of the difference, then it is perfectly possible for authors to be quite sincere in recounting their lives while, at the same time, including any number of "events" that simply never happened. In such cases, one's personal past has been enlarged and now includes other pieces of one's life that belong to some other time and place. Perhaps this is what Gusdorf had in mind when he said that the "author of an autobiography gives himself the job of narrating his own history; what he sets out to do is to reassemble the scattered elements of his individual life and to regroup them in a comprehensive sketch" (1980, p. 35). Notice that certain kinds of errors, such as the transformation of memory into experience, are not entirely false, because they represent a truth about the narrator at another time and place; they tell us, quite accurately, that the narrator had such-and-such a string of impressions; what is in error is their relation to real time. Listen to Mandel:

The autobiographer who speaks the truth about him or herself may produce a book that would most assuredly strike a close relative or an enemy as distorted or even false. Yet, if he is courageously open to the synthesizing process of meaning-making, the autobiographer will have produced a valid, honest, and perfectly true revelation of his life, couched in and defined by his horizons. The truth of the author's *life* will doubtless undergo erosion or alteration if he lives on for many years, but the truth of the *book* cannot change if it has vividly and honestly illuminated the past as experienced in a moment of now. (1980, p. 70)

A moment of now. It can be both truth and false – true with respect to its inner content, a faithful report of a moment of time, and false with respect to a certain slice of the outside world. I think it is this distinction that repeatedly appears in John Dean's testimony: He was trying to be sincere, as Neisser (1982) makes clear, and give an account of the now of his mind, whereas the committee kept trying to turn him into a reporter and draw connections between this moment of now and the world of facts.

Change of voice

Once we admit that the truth of memories is not always the same as the truth of the world, we begin to see that special precautions must be taken in any investigation, naturalistic or experimental. If we hold too strongly to the correspondence theory of truth, then we are in danger of striking out any sign of noncorrespondence. Freud is a useful guide in this connection; even though he was something of a positivist who held strongly to the correspondence theory, he also had the wit to see that transformations might sometimes take place and that slips of the tongue and other parapraxes could often be meaningful and significant.

How can we identify these moments, these substitutions of unbidden memory for lived experience? The concept of negative ratification, suggested by Mandel in connection with our reaction to an autobiography, may be relevant here. In certain autobiographies, he writes, "the reader experiences dis-ease with the autobiography. It seems as if the author is lying . . . although readers cannot always easily put their fingers on the lie. Lionel Charlton creates just such an impression, as do Cellini and Maugham" (1980, p. 65). I would argue that these moments come to pass when an unbidden memory is unwittingly substituted for an experienced event; rather than being a lie, it is simply a failure to mark a change in the mode of experience, a failure to become aware that remembering has displaced recollection.

Most of the examples presented here are drawn from autobiography, and of course there are many more where these came from. In fact, this particular genre, so much maligned as a strange blend of fact and fiction,

may be our best source of data and deserves much more careful attention than it has received up to now. The first order of business would
seem to be a list of rules by which we could detect when narrators are
changing voice and shifting their attention from the outside world to
their inner experiences.

One warning flag, of course, is age; whenever we hear reports of
incidents that are supposed to happen before age 4 years, I would suspect that we may be in the presence of some kind of substitution. A
second has to do with a subtle shift of tone, the quality that Mandel has
described as negative ratification and that often results in a strange kind
of discomfort in the reader. Third, we might be suspicious of obvious
changes in time and place and of discontinuities in tense; a close look at
the verb forms might provide evidence of some kind of substitution
(assuming that some eager proofreader has not got there first).

Of particular interest are those substitutions that have entered into the
family myth. Freud was rightfully suspicious of stories that others have
told us and how easily they are confused with real happenings. These
stories, of course, do not come out of the blue, and in certain cases they
might take advantage of an unbidden memory. Something of this sort
seems to have given rise to Robert Graves's earliest memory. He recalls
"being loyally held up at a window to watch a procession of decorated
carriages and wagons for Queen Victoria's Diamond Jubilee in 1897"
(1929, p. 1). When we learn that he was only 2 years old at the time, we
are naturally suspicious; when we notice the word "loyally," we are even
more suspicious, because certainly this word belongs to the parent more
than to the child. Does this not sound like something the parents might
tell other relatives and friends about baby Graves, who, after hearing it
so often, begins to believe he must have experienced it himself?

And yet it would be a mistake to let skepticism take over. There are
some accounts (notably Salaman, 1982) of passive memories that gradually and progressively unfold, on each new remembering, until they fill
in the dark corners and connect a series of still-life pictures. When this
kind of discovery takes place, we are once again impressed by the staying
power of what really happened, by the suspicion that historical truth
(Spence, 1982) can also be preserved and recovered.

I have a memory of being bitten by a dog when I was three. I have always
remembered this: I am standing outside the closed front door when I suddenly
see a big dog bounding towards me, his broken rope trailing on his left; there is
no snow or mud, the season is late spring. There is a lull in the traffic—no cabs
going to and from the station, no peasants yet going home from the market—it is
a middle-of-the-day hour. Another moment which I have always remembered
holds the noise of people rushing towards me and lifting me from the ground—a
vague moment. But the moment which came back after fifty years was this: the

dog has knocked me over, and I am actually turning my head away and burying my face in the earth while the dog is searching between my petticoats and the long black stockings on my left leg for bare flesh to dig his teeth into. . . . The new moment was a panel which fitted between the other two which had always been in my conscious mind. (Salaman, 1982, p. 56)

The accumulation of new details adds to the sense of veridical recovery and parallels my own experience, which appears later in this chapter. It is unfortunate that we have no clearer picture of the enabling context—the surrounding time and place that allowed the "middle panel" to emerge in Salaman's memory.

Defensive memories

I now want to turn from the experience of an occasional repetitious memory to what Wollheim (1984) has called "the tyranny of the past." Consider this example from the beginning of his chapter by the same title:

> For years after the event, during his exile in Siberia and after his return to Russia, Dostoevsky's mind was haunted by the moment when he stood below the scaffold, waiting his call for execution, and his reprieve was suddenly announced. At the end of the second book of the *Confessions*, Rousseau tells the story of how he falsely accused an innocent young servant girl of stealing a piece of blue and silver ribbon, an object of no value, which he had taken himself and had not even troubled to conceal. Not a day passed, he writes, without the memory of what he chose to call the "sole offence" he had ever committed returning to plague him, and at various points he claimed that his writing the *Confessions* was chiefly motivated by the desire to rid himself of his burden on his conscience, which he had been unable to disclose even to his most intimate friends. (1984, p. 131)

These are more than memories; the interminable repetition hides something pathological. It was the repetition that first attracted Freud and that prompted him to arrive at his famous formulation: "Hysterics suffer mainly from reminiscences." But the more he studied these so-called memories, the more he became impressed by their defensive significance. In other words, the remembering did not just happen; rather, it was motivated and paradoxical. The patient remembers A, over and over, so as not to remember B or become aware of C.

There are many ways in which this can happen; let me offer a few hypothetical examples. When Richard Wright keeps seeing in his mind's eye the image of his father going off with the other woman and is impressed by their "faces lit by the dancing flames," we would suspect that the fascination with their faces keeps him from noticing (or remembering) something else about the scene that is even more troubling. Let us assume that it had something to do with his own anger or helplessness or jealousy.

Repeating the memory in its iconic form serves as a way of warding off these more difficult feelings; going a step further, we might argue that the memory emerges whenever these other feelings tend to surface. A similar argument could be applied to Nabokov's image of the helpless swan. We have no idea how often this image occurred to him throughout his life – I have not attempted to search his autobiography for clues – but I would guess more than once. If it substitutes for feelings about his governess, we might guess that this memory might surface whenever he thought of the governess and perhaps prevent him from looking too closely at his last visit and at his feelings on seeing her for the last time.

Repetitive remembering of this kind is clearly defensive, because it protects one from views of the past or present that one would prefer not to experience. The repeated memory can be either real or make-believe or some combination of the two, but the essential point is that its repetition is lawful and open to study. And because it is lawful, it prompts us to look with particular curiosity at the triggering context.

Here is where the standard autobiography is most apt to fail us. When repeated memories are described, usually they are presented in a rather pedestrian fashion that is essentially uncurious about the triggering context; their repetition is more important than their surround. We have seen one of the reasons for this oversight: The memory, when it appears, is much more striking than the evoking circumstances, and any memory of the latter tends to be swept away by a reminiscent recognition of the former. But there is no reason that further research could not be carried out on the heels of a standard autobiography, no reason that the author could not be queried as to the time and place at which particular memories occurred, in an effort to track down the triggering circumstances.

For a more systematic approach, consider the raw material of Marigold Linton (1982). We are told that she collected a file of some 5,500 memories over a 6-year period by writing down a brief description of at least two events that happened to her every day. Suppose we assume that some of these initial events also occurred to her as repeated memories at some later time. Whenever a repeated memory occurred, she could check (a) its historical truth, (b) additional features of its narrative truth, and (c) the triggering conditions that prompted the recall. My guess would be that the slippage between historical and narrative truth – the transformations that turned the original event into the remembered event – would have something to do with the triggering condition, the circumstances of recall. Preliminary hypotheses, gathered from the early trials, could be tested against a later series of passive memories, and a fairly rigorous experiment could be carried out that would identify, for Linton at least, the extent to which repeated remembering was under the influence of the enabling context. We could also study how slightly transformed memories might have protected her from veridical recall and the specific kinds of transformations that allowed this to happen. A number of experiments of this kind would begin to identify a family of transformations that would seem to operate in such cases, and we would be on the way to developing a grammar of these transformations, a grammar that might parallel the grammar of the primary process that was started in Freud's famous seventh chapter of *The Interpretation of Dreams*, but that has never been completed.

If memories serve a defensive function, then the repetition may be more apparent than real. Wollheim makes the distinction between "the tyranny of the past and the tyranny of something that began in the past and has persisted" (1984, p. 226), and I think we may experience much more of the second than of the first. It may happen that each time we use a given memory in a defensive manner, we make some permanent alteration in its structure; as a result, we keep encountering a Bartlett-like chain of reminiscences that belong to the same family but that diverge more and more from the original event. Some of these, provided the transformations are sufficiently small, might be experienced as repeated memories; others, with larger transformations, would be experienced as different memories. One can see how the link to the original event could change so radically in the course of remembering that we would be left with something that would seem to have no connection with the original. It would follow that the experience of serial remembering may be much more common than we may have assumed simply because the subjective sense of repetition often is not there; a radical transformation makes it seem as if the specimen is completely new. I am making two points: (1) Seemingly repeated memories may actually be quite dissimilar. (2) Many seemingly disconnected memories may really belong to the same family. Phenotype is never the same as genotype. Subtle transformations in the "repeated" memory may allow for the emergence of new material, as in Salaman's memory of the dog.

How can this problem be investigated? If my argument is correct, all memories evoked by the same triggering context should have something in common, and a close examination of memories that share a given experiential surround should reveal a grammar of transformations. If we are lucky, this grammar will have something in common with that discovered by Bartlett in his studies of serial remembering: Small details are lost in favor of larger outlines; unlikely or unfamiliar details give way to more commonplace events; sharpening gives way to leveling. Perhaps Freud's seventh chapter can be filled out by the *Studies in Remembering* — an unexpected, but very satisfying, convergence.

Wollheim's first kind of tyranny — the simple tyranny of the past in which the triggering event is preserved in aspic and is always coming back to haunt us—is, as I have argued, relatively rare. It also parallels computer memory and, for that reason, should further increase our suspicion. As is becoming quite clear, one of the central differences between computers and the rest of us is that memory in the former is unchanging, veridical, and uninfluenced by use. That clearly is not the way human memory is organized; a gradually changing content—as reflected in Wollheim's second tyranny—is much closer to the laws of all living things. We may feel that we are haunted by particular moments that occur to us over and over, but careful study of these "repetitions" will show, I think, that there are gradual changes over time and that these changes are rule-governed.

To sum up: When passive memories occur to us—when we find ourselves thinking about a particular piece of "pastness" that is imbued with the feeling that it is part of our lived experience—when this feeling dawns on us, we are very likely in a special mode of awareness. An altered state of consciousness probably is a necessary, but not sufficient, condition for this experience to appear. Second, the content of the memory can be triangulated against two other referents—the historical truth of the original event and the circumstances surrounding the experience of passive remembering—that I have called the enabling context. By triangulation, I mean that each of these two factors intersects with, and brings an influence to bear on, the passive memory. The influence may be defensive, in which case the enabling memory emerges to distract us from what is going on in the enabling context or from what that context arouses in the way of feelings or ideas. The influence may be metaphoric, as when Nabokov found himself thinking of the helpless swan at a time when he learned of the death of his childhood teacher. Or the influence may represent some combination of the two.

Passive memories are sometimes repetitive, but I do not think very often. Even though repeated memories are experienced as repetitious, in actual fact the series may be continuously changing—Wollheim's tyranny of "something that began in the past and has persisted." We can imagine how the series of transformations has something in common with Bartlett's chain of rememberings, and if the sequence is long enough, we may lose sight of the fact that it originated in the past. Specific and unchanging memories may also exist—we have the example from Dostoevsky—and in this case the influence of the past is very clear and specific. But, as I mentioned, I think such examples are the exception.

One memory, two recollections

To investigate these matters further, I carried out an experiment on myself. My aim was to study changes in the recall of a specific traumatic incident—an unexpected belly landing in Colorado some 15 years ago. I have frequently found myself remembering this incident, in varying degrees of detail, and I wanted to document two separate transcriptions of this memory and their relation to the enabling context. I was first reminded of the event when some friends went off to Colorado to go skiing. That recollection yielded the first version. I next recalled the event shortly after the *Challenger* disaster of January 28, 1986, and that recollection yielded the second version.

First version

Friends have left for Aspen to go skiing and I'm thinking of that famous flight. I had saved myself a weekend on the way home from the West, flew into Denver late Friday night and planned to catch the early plane to Aspen in the morning. Some confusion about finding the plane—I don't remember the details—and then we were airborne, heading north along the Front Range.

I remember very clearly seeing a firm line of clouds running the whole length of the Range—clear on the East and socked in on the West. As soon as we left the high plains, we were in the clouds—or rather, above them because the front wasn't very high. We turned West and droned along. About 15,000 feet, I would guess, never seeing the ground—flying along. Time moved ahead—9:20, 9:30, 9:40—well past our expected arrival.

Now we seemed to be circling—not too much, just a little—looking for the field, looking for the high peaks, looking for the way in. The hostess handed out hot cider. The boy behind me started to cry and his father shut him up. During all this, no word from the cabin, no news from the stewardess who only looked worried.

Then we seemed to be starting down, and in one spot we could see the ground. Amazing—it was the field. We came in low over the highway and I have a clear image of cars underneath, as if stopped, everyone staring up at the plane. What were they looking at? We might have been Lindbergh coming into Paris.

Then we touched down and taxied past the tower and the main building, but we weren't taxiing at all—we were going 60, maybe 70 miles per hour, and the plane was fishtailing along, weaving back and forth, gradually slowing down until one wing hit a snowbank and we stopped.

"Everyone out! Now!" cried the stewardess, and we raced for the door. One man dove out through the window. I looked back. We had made a belly landing! I remember thinking, "I better find my rubbers because I'm standing in deep snow."

Second version

The *Challenger* disaster started me thinking about the dangers of air travel and my close call on Aspen Airways. I had planned my trip to the Coast so that I could come back to Denver Friday night and catch an early plane on Saturday morning. Coming up from L.A., I started talking to another skier who was making plans to join friends in a cabin near Aspen; we made plans to talk Friday night, but he never called.

Saturday morning was cold and foggy, and the bus to the airport was late. The hotel doorman persuaded me to take a taxi, and once we got to the airport, I had some trouble finding the right gate. Ground fog delayed our take-off a few minutes; once airborne, we came out into clear sunshine and we could see the

Front Range in all of its snowy wonder. We headed North, which surprised me because I knew that Aspen was somewhat southwest from Denver – perhaps we needed to gain altitude before crossing the Rockies. (Reminded me of flying out of Innsbruck on a propeller plane in the 60's. A hair-raising flight. To gain the altitude necessary to cross the Alps, we had to fly up and down the Inn valley three or four times. The first time we looped back, I thought something had gone wrong and we were returning to the field.)

Was I thinking about this, then, while flying to Aspen, or is this a new association? I have absolutely no way of knowing. I also realize that, at the time of the Aspen flight, I was not really sure where we were going and I could not have said that our true course was southwest; this information came to me years later when we drove to Aspen one summer.

Now we are over the Front Range, heading West, and the weather has thickened. Can no longer see the ground, the seat belt sign has come on again, and the flight is getting bumpy. Very little talking in the cabin, and the longer we fly, the quieter it gets. (As I write this, I become aware of a slight change in certainty. Where I clearly remembered the ground fog and the stark view of the Front Range, I am somewhat less certain about the silence in the cabin. Am I preparing the reader for what happened later? Or more exactly, am I letting what happened later cast a shadow over what led up to it?)

We are still flying and well past our expected arrival time. No sign of the airport and I overhear some talk about alternate landing fields. A bad sign. Eagle is mentioned. How far is Eagle from Aspen? How big a field? I picture the weekend getting smaller and smaller, and I look for something to read. All I have with me is a brief-case full of grant applications. I turn back to the window and wonder where we are. Still bumpy, and the boy behind me starts to cry. This time I seem to hear the father trying to comfort him. The stewardess comes down the aisle with hot cider, and I think, What will she give us when things get really serious? Do they have anything stronger on board? I see her going into the pilot's cabin and I wonder what they're saying. More talk about other fields. More time has passed.

Suddenly we're coming down – this must be Aspen. I look out to see more clouds; the ride gets even more bumpy; then we see the ground. No time to think – we're over a highway, we're coming down, we're down, but we're going much too fast – the tower shoots by in a blur, we're weaving our way down the runway, finally – thank goodness – we're slowing down, now we've stopped. We made it – enormous relief.

Some interesting differences appear when the two versions are compared. The second account is about 50% longer than the first, contains much more feeling, and is structurally much more complex because it contains associations to other time periods (the plane ride at Innsbruck, for example) and reflections on the nature of the evidence. Does the greater amount of affect somehow reflect the impact of the *Challenger* disaster?

I had expected, in planning the experiment, to find that repeated remembering would lead to stereotyping, à la Bartlett, and that the second version would be a tired and more condensed version of the first. It seems clear that just the opposite had happened: The second version is richer, more affect-laden, and structually much more complex, and it surprised me with new information. My experience parallels that of Salaman (whose piece I read only after the experiment was over). Subsequent rememberings would very likely add further detail to the skeleton account.

In writing both versions, I was acutely aware that I was engaged in a kind of unpacking. The memory "inside my head" was much more condensed than either written version, and in going from memory to written text, I was aware of a complicated kind of translation that sometimes preserved the original sense and sometimes added its own meaning. The initial memory, what is more, had no clear boundaries, and it is worth noting that the second version began earlier in time than the first; I also had trouble in deciding where it should stop. The second version contains several details of which I was less certain – the silence in the cabin, for example – and at first I was not sure I should include them. While writing the second version, I became aware of setting a kind of "acceptance threshold"; events that failed to rise to this level of clarity or intensity or certainty were not included. But I was also aware that the threshold was quite arbitrary, depending mainly on my state of mind at the moment of recovering the memory. Perhaps the enabling context serves mainly to set the acceptance threshold.

We have seen how the tone of the first version is more factual and repressed than that of the second. The image of the father sitting behind me changes accordingly – in the first version, he is scolding, in the second, permissive. Was the freer expression of emotion in the second version projected onto him, or did this freer expression allow a more faithful memory to emerge? In either event, we see how the enabling context (partly inspired by the *Challenger* disaster) has influenced the form and content of the memory.

If repeated attempts to recall a particular incident could be checked against an on-the-spot account, written immediately after the event, we would have a clearer picture of how memories are formed, how they change over time, and the extent to which some details can disappear only to be recovered again under the influence of a more benign enabling context. If we combined a Linton type of real-time report with the Salaman procedure of successive remembering, we would have a way of studying how events are transformed over time and some sense of how a "repetitive" memory may actually be changing each time it is recovered.

In closing, I would like to make a special plea for studying this process from another vantage point. I have mentioned autobiographies as one possible source of data; I would now like to call attention to another data base that is starting to become available – the complete text of a terminated analysis. Think of how a series of passive rememberings of a given incident could be traced over time and studied for Bartlett-like transformations of form and content. Consider how the enabling context (the transference) is always available for comparison (implicitly or explicitly). Finally, consider how the defensive function of remembering will naturally come into focus. If the enabling context were particularly repressive, we would expect that important details of the skeletal memory would be forgotten; as the enabling context becomes more positive, these details may reappear. Although the use of this material would not provide us with an archival record of the original event, it would allow for more careful study of the enabling context. It seems clear that the moment of remembering may be just as important as the moment remembered, and until we understand the first, we probably can never understand the second.

REFERENCES

Brown, R., & Kulik, J. (1982). Flashbulb memories. In U. Neisser (Ed.), *Memory observed* (pp. 23–40). San Francisco: Freeman.
Gadamer, H.-G. (1975). *Truth and method*. London: Sheed & Ward.
Graves, R. (1929). *Good-bye to all that*. New York: Doubleday.
Gusdorf, G. (1980). Conditions and limits of autobiography. In J. Olney (Ed.), *Autobiography: Essays theoretical and critical* (pp. 28–48). Princeton, NJ: Princeton University Press.
Linton, M. (1982). Transformations of memory in everyday life. In U. Neisser (Ed.), *Memory observed* (pp. 77–91). San Francisco: Freeman.
Mandel, B. J. (1980). Full of life now. In J. Olney (Ed.), *Autobiography: Essays theoretical and critical* (pp. 49–72). Princeton, NJ: Princeton University Press.
Nabokov, V. (1966). *Speak, memory*. New York: G. P. Putnam's Sons.
Neisser, U. (Ed.). (1982). *Memory observed*. San Francisco: Freeman.
Olney, J. (Ed.). (1980). *Autobiography: Essays theoretical and critical*. Princeton, NJ: Princeton University Press.
Salaman, E. (1982). A collection of moments: A study of involuntary memories. In U. Neisser (Ed.), *Memory observed* (pp. 49–63). San Francisco: Freeman.
Spence, D. P. (1982). *Narrative truth and historical truth*. New York: Norton.
Wollheim, R. (1984). *The thread of life*. Cambridge, MA: Harvard University Press.

13

Remembering without experiencing: Memory for reported events

STEEN F. LARSEN

There is a class of real events that we know about and remember, though we have not experienced them. Learning about such events does not require clairvoyance or divine revelations, but only listening to a friend, reading a newspaper, or watching television. The fact is that we may know about real events in the world in two different ways, either by personal experience (directly, firsthand) or by the report of someone else (indirectly, secondhand). I shall call events that are known in these two ways *experienced events* and *reported events*, respectively. This chapter attempts, first, to demonstrate the pertinence of this distinction to research on real-event memory; second, to advance a theoretical analysis of memory of the two classes of events in terms of the information available to specify them; and, third, to examine some empirical results relevant to this analysis.

A little personal background is in order to set the topic and the approach in perspective. My interest in these issues stems from several years of research into memory for texts and particularly news reports (Larsen, 1983). News reports are different from the texts of most memory experiments because they are about real events and because they are important in everyday life. Therefore, news memory seemed to deserve a place in the emerging field of ecological memory research (Neisser, 1982a). But in this research the emphasis was heavily on autobiographical memory. Thus, the question arose if news memory was to be seen as just another variety of ecological memory, or if its relationship to autobiographical memory could be more precisely defined and theoretically motivated.

However, the distinction between experienced and reported events has an older and deeper background that I had completely forgotten until it was pointed out by T. Nielsen (personal communication) during the revision of this chapter. This background derives from the "Copenhagen school of phenomenological psychology," a branch of Gestalt psychology founded by E. Rubin around 1920 (Woodworth, 1945, pp. 114–118). When I received my training at the Copenhagen school in the

1960s, the head of the school was E. Tranekjaer Rasmussen, its last influential figure. Rasmussen (1956) distinguished phenomena themselves (i.e., "anything of which one can be conscious," whether physical or mental) from the conscious appearance of these phenomena. He proposed a dimension from immediate to mediate modes of appearance as fundamental for describing our consciousness of phenomena. The immediate mode of appearance is characterized by the experience that we deal directly with a phenomenon, without awareness of any intermediaries that represent, refer to, or imply it. The paradigmatic example is everyday sensory experience. In the mediate mode of appearance, on the other hand, our experience of a phenomenon includes elements that specify it—represent, refer to, or imply it. Rasmussen (1956, pp. 54–56) ascribed particular importance to appearances mediated through "a human form of expression," usually language, as, for example, becoming conscious of phenomena through reading or listening. This so-called *anthropic* mode of appearance was primarily meant to include scientific theories and descriptions as fully valid means of experience, in contrast to the tendency of phenomenological epistemologies to focus exclusively on sensory experience. But it may also serve to remind ecological approaches to psychology that everyday objects and events are often known through anthropic mediation, namely, through reports.

The Copenhagen school is relevant to the current ideas in other respects, too. Unlike those in other phenomenological schools (in psychology as well as in philosophy), Rasmussen (1956, p. 23) held that description of experience turns into a psychological method only if two requirements are fulfilled:

1. It must be coupled with a description of the *stimulation* from the environment that gives rise to the experience.
2. It must be assumed that the experience is a result of "psychophysical" *processing* and is codetermined by the structure of such processes.

Despite this program, the Copenhagen school limited itself to pure description of experiences, except for a few studies like Rubin's (1915) founding work on figure and ground. However, the first requirement is close to asking for an ecological description of stimulation similar to that of Gibson (1979). The second requirement is reminiscent of the view of much of current cognitive psychology. The influence of both will be evident in this chapter.

Reported events in everyday life

People have two different avenues to knowledge of real events: their personal experience and reports they receive from others. Any individual experiences personally only a tiny proportion of the events that occur in the world at large. Some of the events that are not experienced become known anyway through the reports of other people, including reports in the communications media. Information about both kinds of events may be remembered, of course, but not necessarily in the same way and equally well. Different types and amounts of information may be available, and it may be organized and processed differently. However, these issues have only occasionally been touched on by memory researchers, and never in a systematic fashion. Does the distinction merit discussion at all?

Most people probably regard autobiographical memory as the typical kind of memory. But memories of events described in reports are also very common in everyday life—news, gossip, friends' stories, minutes of meetings, and so on. Without such reports, we would be confined to know only that narrow and shallow slice of the world that we are able to observe by our senses. For example, those who attended this conference would be the only ones who would ever know and remember anything that happened here; to anyone else, it could just as well not have taken place, as Bishop Berkeley might indeed have claimed. Again, without memory of reported events, none of us would know about Ronald Reagan, that there have been men on the moon, and that there are wars going on in Afghanistan, the Persian Gulf, and Nicaragua. Similar to the view that memories of experienced events are "some of the things of which selves are made" (see chapter 4), memories of reported events may therefore be regarded as "some of the things of which history is made." This is true in two senses. First, reported events provide each of us with a knowledge of current history. Second, reports about events are important materials for writing "real" history.

In many situations, it is considered very important whether a remembered event is experienced or reported. One reason has to do with the veridicality of information, because we are much more easily fooled by reports about events than when we experience them directly. This is most clearly demonstrated by the importance attached to eyewitness testimony in the judicial process. But we also attach importance to the distinction more generally. If someone consistently confuses reported events with experiences, that person will appear quite strange, like the paranoid who mistakes hallucinations and fantasies for reality, or habitual liars who believe in their own stories.

The veridicality problem with reported events is probably the reason for the phrasing of the common question "Did you see it with your own eyes, or did you only hear about it?" The small word "only" discloses the evaluation of reported events as being inferior to personal experience. This inferiority view apparently extends to memory, too. Common sense suggests that experienced events are remembered better than reported events—"better" meaning longer, more vividly, more accessibly, more accurately. We do not worry about forgetting news or other people's stories, but if we generally forget our personal experiences, it is considered a "memory problem."

That there is a difference of memorability between experienced and reported events may appear self-evident, which is perhaps the reason that few attempts have been made to investigate it empirically or to explore its theoretical implications. The strategy of this discussion is to throw light on the way reported events are remembered by contrasting them with experienced events – comparing the little known phenomenon to the (relatively) well known. Most of the time, rather extreme cases of experienced and reported events will be in focus, namely, autobiographical events and mass-communicated news events (sometimes called personal and public events, respectively). I shall disregard the facts that some autobiographical events are not experienced personally (e.g., an assessment of a proposal of mine by a grants committee) and that some reported events are not public news (e.g., experiences told by family members). Another complication, the relation between reported events and the experienced events of receiving the reports, is treated in a later section.

When we consider early periods of human history, the distinction between experienced and reported events is clear-cut. Either one was present to observe and possibly participate in events or one was told about them afterward. With present-day technologies of observation and communication, the distinction may appear blurred. By means of telescopes and remotely controlled TV cameras, events may be observed at a distance that prevents participation. Are they still to be counted as personal experiences? By means of movies, video recordings, holograms, and so on, events may be communicated in a form that approaches actual experience, while satellite transmission provides for worldwide simultaneity. Are such cases still to be counted as reported, secondhand events? I think the answer to both questions should be yes, because the basic feature of possibilities for action is not changed. In experienced events, but not in reported events, one has at least some freedom to act, to influence what is happening (including at least some freedom to explore and pick up information directly). For present purposes, however, our focus on the clear cases of personal experience and news reports should render it immaterial whether experienced and reported events constitute a dichotomy or a dimension.

The neglect of reported events in memory research

Philosophical background

It is of some theoretical interest to examine the reasons that reported events have escaped the attention of memory researchers, despite 100 years of studying the learning and memory of almost exclusively verbal materials. With the use of verbal materials, it would seem unavoidable to take into account that linguistic utterances typically refer to phenomena in the surrounding world. But psychologists working in the Ebbinghaus tradition have largely ignored this fact. Part of the background may be philosophical. Brewer and Pani (1983) pointed out that philosophers have generally distinguished personal, autobiographical memory and "habit memory" (practical memory, skill). Whereas the philosophers themselves tended to find autobiographical memory the more interesting, psychologists followed Ebbinghaus by emphasizing a particular kind of habit, namely, rote learning, probably for reasons of methodological control. More recently, generic or semantic memory has appeared as an object of study, and psychologists have begun to redress the balance by starting empirical research on autobiographical memory. But the basic view prevails that only personally experienced events count as real, in psychology as well as in philosophy.

An explanation for the stubbornness of this view is suggested in another paper by Brewer that provides a more penetrating discussion of the philosophical assumptions underlying psychological theories of knowledge and memory. Brewer and Nakamura (1984) show that the development from stimulus–response theory to modern, cognitive schema theory in Britain and America represents a movement from the assumptions of British empiricism toward those of Continental philosophy (in particular, Kant). One assumption they do not discuss, however, is the basic assumption of empiricism that all knowledge is acquired by immediate sensation (and the corollary that language is a mechanical transmission channel). The alternative to empiricism in classical Continental philosophy was nativism, which few psychologists would want to endorse. Only in more recent Continental philosophy (Marxism and French philosophy, e.g., Halbwachs, 1925) was another alternative developed – namely, that knowledge may have a social origin, that it may be acquired from other people and social institutions. Mainstream cognitive psychology still seems peculiarly unaware of this possibility, in respect to exploring its theoretical implications as well as in choosing objects of research.

Episodic and semantic memory

Consider a few examples of how events in general and reported events in particular have slipped through the theoretical nets cast by psychologists. Taken at surface value, Tulving's (1972) distinction between episodic and semantic memory set experienced events apart from all the rest that human beings remember. According to Tulving, episodic memory concerns "information about temporally dated episodes or events . . . always stored in terms of its autobiographical reference" (p. 385) – that is, personally experienced events. However, Tulving's use of the concept is not consistent with the definition (as noted by Brewer & Pani, 1983, and others). Thus, he viewed episodic memory as the field of traditional verbal learning research. For example, when subjects in a verbal learning experiment are told to remember a list of words, they do not have to remember the words as such, because they already know them; what they have to remember is that the words occurred at a particular time and place, namely, in the experimental situation where they were presented. Therefore, Tulving argued, later memory tests will concern the subject's memory of this autobiographical event. But such memory tests really presuppose memory of the event rather than investigating it. They concern isolated details of the experimental event (namely, the words on the list), whereas memory of the event itself is taken for granted. This problem was actually admitted by Tulving (1983), who suggested that it is "reasonable to separate the remembering of a personal episode from the knowledge of its 'semantic' contents" (p. 31) and that most laboratory experiments tell us only about the latter. But that is once again beside the point. The words used in an event cannot be regarded as its "semantic contents" in any accepted sense. The words may carry semantic contents if they can be taken to refer to things in some world – for instance, an event they describe – but otherwise they are just factual details. Tulving failed to realize this, however.

As for reported events, Tulving's definitions left them in no-man's-land, outside the taxonomy that came to guide memory research for a decade. Semantic memory, the other side of his dichotomy, concerns general knowledge of all sorts (facts, rules, concepts, etc.) and does not include specific-event information. Therefore, memory for reported events is neither episodic nor semantic. The Tulvingian scheme does not recognize that information about events can be acquired except by immediate perception, that is, that the social world provides symbolic systems and technologies for transmittting information about specific occurrences to people who are absent from events. Some researchers who have studied reported-event memory anyway seem to have recognized that classification is problematic. For example, Thompson (1985b) notes that autobiographical memory is only a "portion of episodic memory," but still classifies reported events as belonging to semantic memory.

Stories and scripts

The numerous studies of stories, texts, and "connected discourse" published during the past decade are much closer to dealing with real events that the Tulvingian tradition. But investigators have been concentrating

on the *structure* of the materials (story grammars, narrative patterns, etc.)
(Mandler & Johnson, 1977; Rumelhart, 1975) rather than the contents,
or, more precisely, the extralinguistic phenomena specified by the linguistic materials. This *structural bias* probably can be traced all the way
back to the pioneering studies of Bartlett (1932), who was not very clear
about what it was in a story like the famous "The War of the Ghosts" that
made it so difficult to remember – its unusual structure or the unusual
events it described or both. The structural bias is evident, for instance, in
the theory of text memory proposed by Kintsch and van Dijk (1978), and
it can be seen from the fact that experimental materials almost invariably
deal with purely fictional events – folk stories, fairy tales, short stories –
thus limiting the subjects' opportunities for applying general knowledge
of the real world to the task of remembering.

One group of recent studies of text memory might appear to concern
memory for reported events directly. These studies build on the *script*
concept introduced by Schank and Abelson (1977). Scripts are assumed
to reflect the properties of routine events known by personal, firsthand
experience. Memory experiments attempting to demonstrate the effects
of scripts have employed texts describing events that conform to specific
scripts or deviate from them in certain respects (e.g., Bower, Black, &
Turner, 1979). However, two assumptions of this research cast serious
doubt on its relevance. First, the equivalence of experiencing an event
personally and reading a text describing it is assumed without question
(e.g., Brewer & Pani, 1983; Schank, Birnbaum, & Mey, 1982). With one
or two exceptions, to be discussed later, the possibility that reports about
events are different from experiences has therefore not been investigated, and it is unclear to what extent results from studies of "scripted"
texts are applicable to memory of personal experience. Second, there is
again a structural bias: The content of the text does not matter as long as
it conforms to the structure of the script. This structure is assumed to be
the same whether the events are experienced or read about. It is not
considered that scripts might also develop from knowledge of reported
events (e.g., from news) and then be applied to experienced events – vice
versa – with inappropriate understanding as a possible consequence.

Internal and external origins of information

Consider, as a final example of neglect of reported events, Johnson and
Raye's (1981) ingenious research on remembering the "source" of information, whether it originated internally (from thinking) or externally
(from observation). Memories of external events are hypothesized to be
richer in contextual, sensory, and semantic detail, whereas internal
events provide richer information about the cognitive operations per-

Table 13.1. *Categories of events jointly distinguished by origin of information and mode of reception*

Origin of information	Mode of reception	
	Experienced events (observation)	Reported events (communication)
External	Autobiographical events	Public events History
Internal	One's own thoughts, imagery, fantasies, lies	Others' thoughts, lies, etc. Fiction

formed to generate the internal events. However, Johnson and Raye do not acknowledge that there are external sources of memories besides observation, namely, social sources, and that these sources may give information about real events that has quite different characteristics. It is even possible through reports to learn about events that originated internally in somebody else's thinking, for instance, lies and purely imaginary events which are most prominently reported in fictional literature. The experienced events versus reported events distinction seems to cut across Johnson's distinction of internal versus external origin of information, thus defining four classes of event memories (Table 13.1).

Ecological investigations of event memory

Until quite recently, only occasional studies of real-event memory were carried out. They were usually outside the mainstream verbal learning tradition and had an applied focus, like the validity of eyewitness testimony or the question of childhood amnesia (see the historical review by Robinson, 1986a). Though most of this research concerned autobiographical events, reported events were sometimes studied to get some control of the acquisition conditions (e.g., in the case of amnesia, questionnaires about very long-term memory; Squire & Slater, 1975; Warrington & Sanders, 1971) or to elucidate practical problems (e.g., studies of factors affecting the memorability of news broadcasts; Findahl & Höijer, 1975, 1982; Gunter, Berry, & Clifford, 1981). However, the important point is that research on memory of events, whether experienced or reported, had no clear theoretical rationale and therefore led a life in limbo.

It is the so-called ecological approach to cognitive psychology that must be credited with calling attention to everyday memory of real events as an object of study in its own right (Neisser, 1976, 1978, 1982a).

Until quite recently, the ecological approach to memory was just a methodological rule of thumb rather than a theoretical program. Memory research should start by examining tasks that occur in everyday, "naturalistic" situations in order not to miss interesting and important phenomena. This recommendation has already generated a number of innovative studies, simply by legitimizing researchers' interest in what goes on outside the laboratory. In a review of research on ecological memory, Bahrick and Karis (1982) introduced a distinction between "individual" and "shared" episodic memory. As viewed by Bahrick and Karis, shared episodes are similar to the present concept of reported events, but in addition include "meaningless" experimental materials as well as fictional events (contents of books, etc.). Nevertheless, Bahrick and Karis's concept may be seen as a move to put reported events on the agenda of psychological memory research. The review showed, however, that by far the largest amount of effort had been spent on individual (autobiographical) episodes. Work in the category of shared episodes consisted primarily of Warrington's and Squire's studies of amnesia questionnaires about news events, as mentioned earlier.

Since the Bahrick and Karis (1982) study, a few more experiments have appeared. This work is briefly reviewed in the next section, followed by a discussion of what kinds of theoretical principles are needed to account for the results and at the same time be compatible with the ecological approach to memory.

Memory for reported events and theory of ecological memory

Empirical investigations comparing reported and experienced events

As mentioned earlier in this chapter, common sense and everyday experience would suggest that reported events are remembered less well than experienced events – a "report-inferiority" views. Herrmann and Neisser (1978) found that people believed that forgetting of TV news was among the most common forgetting experiences. However, the questionnaire study by Warrington and Sanders (1971) of "striking and significant" public events showed that such memories can be surprisingly stable even after several decades. A couple of experiments comparing memory of a live, staged classroom incident with a verbal description have also found little or no report inferiority. Thus, Brown, Heymann, Preskill, Rubin, and Wuletich (1977) found that memories based on experience and those based on description were equally susceptible to misleading questions 1 week after the incident. (Note, though, that the tape-recorded description lasted 50% longer than the original event, possibly allowing better processing of reported-event information to take place during the extra exposure time.) Toglia, Shlechter, and Herrmann (1984) reported slightly larger declines in recall and recognition of the described event as compared with the experienced event after 2 weeks, but floor and ceiling effects make these results equivocal.

In contrast to these findings, several studies of natural events appear to offer support for the report-inferiority view. Lieury, Richer, and Weeger (1978) found that only 18% of the "12 most remarkable events" that subjects remembered from the last 8 years were reported events. Similarly, Rubin and Kozin (1984) reported that less than 3% of the 174 "most vivid events" recalled by their subjects were public events. Comparable results are available from experiments that have examined the events people use as reference points when they try to date public events. The great majority of such reference points turn out to be experienced events (Brown, Shevell, & Rips, 1986; Friedman & Wilkins, 1985; Lieury, Aiello, Lepreux, & Mellet, 1980). More direct evidence about the characteristics of the two types of remembered events comes from a study by Reisberg, Heuer, O'Shaughnessy, and McLean (1984), who obtained ratings of personal and public memories that subjects had recalled themselves. Experienced events yielded higher ratings of vividness, affect, and consequentiality ("whether the event changed your life").

These results show that the representation of reported events in memory is in some respects "inferior," but do not imply that they are particularly likely to be forgotten. Experienced events may simply be more remarkable and vivid from the beginning, and perhaps more numerous. Such an interpretation is suggested by the finding of Larsen and Plunkett (1987) that cued recall of reported events was slower than for experienced events, while, at the same time, faster forgetting of reported events seemed unlikely, because the estimated ages of the two classes of recalled events were equal. On the other hand, a strong indication of higher forgetting of reported events comes from an investigation by Thompson (1985b), who let subjects rate the memorability of events for which they had written short descriptions several weeks before. Thompson found that ratings of memorability were higher for personally experienced events than for events that were originally reported to the subjects by roommates. Furthermore, Thompson (1985b) demonstrated that it did not matter whether the subject participated in or only observed an experienced event; the important difference in terms of memorability was whether the event was experienced by or reported to the subject. This finding strongly supports the validity of the present distinction between experienced and reported events. (To alleviate concern that subjects' memorability ratings might not correspond to their ability to recall events, it can be mentioned that Reisberg et al., 1984, demonstrated the validity of memory ratings for predicting amount recalled.)

This empirical work indicates that reported events generally are less prominent in memory than experienced ones—less vivid, less remarkable, less consequential, less affectively loaded, more difficult to access. It is not entirely clear whether or not reported events are also more easily forgotten. There is an obvious need for more research in this area. But the problems remain of accounting for such differences as may exist and giving theoretical direction to the empirical efforts. The next sections explore some possible theoretical accounts.

Refutation of some obvious intuitions

A sufficient theoretical account should tell us, first, what the psychologically important differences are between reported and experienced events that allow us to distinguish them at all and, second, how these differences affect memory, resulting in a generally (but not necessarily universal) inferior remembering of reported events.

Event contents. Intuitively, the primary difference appears to be in the "contents" of the events. Mass-communicated reports, like newspaper or television news, describe events that very few people would mistake for their own experiences—shaking hands with the U.S. president, disarmament talks in a Vienna park, a Greenpeace ship being sunk in New Zealand. As Brown et al. (1986) noted, if one had experienced an unusual event like this, one would assume that the fact of this personal experience would be remembered. Therefore, from lack of such a memory, it can be inferred that the event was reported, not experienced. But this argument just shifts the problem to one of explaining why the personal experiences of such events would be particularly well remembered. More generally, inferior remembering of reported events is hard to explain in this way. If reported events are unusual and spectacular—and of course the news media attempt to select them to be just that—one would expect them to be inherently more memorable than run-of-the-mill personal experiences. Most reported events are certainly different from experienced events in content, but that cannot account for their inferior memorability.

Tag theories. A simple assumption, familiar from multicomponent, associative theories of memory (e.g., Bower, 1967), would be that a special *tag* is assigned to the memory trace indicating that it is personally experienced and helping it to resist forgetting. This conforms to the usual constructivist view of memory: The mind of the subject must add information to enrich the impoverished impressions from the environment. Such a view was suggested by Kihlstrom (1981), who talked about "the attribute of self-reference" to explain superior memory of personally relevant information. When applied to the distinction between experienced versus reported events, this *self-tag theory* predicts that, over time, experienced events should increasingly be mistaken for reported events because the tag is weakened by forgetting. We should begin to think of our own past as if it were a story told by somebody else. In normal people, that seems totally absurd, though I would not exclude the possibility in cases of pathologic changes.

Another version of tag theory would hold the reverse, namely, that reported events are tagged (a *report tag*), whereas no tag would be necessary for experienced events, because they may be considered the primary, unmarked type of event in terms of frequency, order of development, and so forth. This report-tag theory also implies that confusions of experienced and reported events should be quite common, because the tag is subject to degradation or loss of strength by forgetting. In this case, however, as reported events recede into the past, they should increasingly often be mistaken for personally experienced events. That seems to happen only if the reports concern events that might (or actually did) take place as personal experiences. For instance, some early childhood memories may actually be stories that we have heard from parents and relatives. But such mistakes seem to occur when the events have been talked about repeatedly, illustrated with photographs, and so forth – in short, when the information has been refreshed and enriched, not when it has become degraded, as the report-tag theory would have it. Anyway, the theory does not give any indication why the addition of the tag should engender inferior forgetting of reported events.

Tag theories are insufficient because they postulate a single differentiating feature (the tag), existing solely in the person's cognitive system, instead of analyzing the information available in the world when the two types of events occur. For instance, if you remember taking part in a demonstration in front of the South African Embassy, your presence will be indicated by much more than a single piece of information: by your memory of the trip to get there, the weather, bumping into Jane Fonda, the terrible spongy hamburger you had for lunch, the good feeling of singing antiapartheid songs together, and so on. Similarly, but perhaps less strongly, that you saw the demonstration on television may be indicated by several things (besides the absence of "personal" information): by your memory of how the story was introduced, the constant focus on well-known people, the commentators' discussion afterward, and so on. It is therefore reasonable to assume that our distinction of experienced and reported events is not based on a single feature, but rather on multiple pieces of information, so that the two classes can be identified even when memory of an event is vague and incomplete. The character and interrelations of such features should, at the same time, provide the explanation for differential memorability of the events.

Theoretical aspects of the ecological approach

The ecological orientation has drawn the attention of memory researchers toward more naturalistic instances of remembering, as mentioned earlier. Is this approach more than advice on methodology, and what can it offer toward the understanding of memory for events? In the field of perception, the work of Gibson (1979) has certainly proved that the ecological approach reaches into both research strategy and theory. Current studies by Neisser (1984, 1985, 1986) are attempting to extend Gibson's observations to memory. Let me outline two implications of the ecological approach to memory that have given shape to the theoretical proposal described in the remainder of this chapter. These implications precisely concern research strategy and theoretical principles.

Neisser (1985) has advocated what he terms the "genuinely ecological approach," which follows the example of Gibson's ecological optics by trying to "get a better understanding of the sorts of things that are remembered" (p. 274). Neisser contrasts this approach with the two kinds of theories that Bruce (1985) describes: The traditional, "general principles memory research" (asking about *causes*: the "how" of memory) and the "Darwinian" approach proposed by Bruce himself (asking about *functions*: the "why" of memory). We may say that Neisser's proposal is to begin with the "what" of memory, to ask for systematic *descriptions* of the phenomena that are remembered – the memorabilia – as a prerequisite for posing any other questions. The descriptive work is not intended to replace causal and functional analyses. The idea is rather that such descriptions of the information that is available to specify past events for remembering should serve as a basis for causal and functional studies by highlighting potentially important variables and suggesting what relationships are worth investigating. Note that ecological descriptions are not phenomenological in the ordinary psychological sense; they do not concern experiences, mental images, or the like, but properties of the human-in-environment system that provide information that in the future may specify events in the past to these human beings.

It is important to realize that Gibson's ecological optics cannot be extended to memory without fundamental modifications. An analogous "ecological mnemonics" cannot be limited to describing properties of the present human-environment system. It would have to take into account that most of the information that in the past specified states and events in the world is not available in the environment at the time of remembering. Even when some consequences of past events can currently be observed (a scar on a face, a newly mended roof), they usually will not specify their past origins unambiguously. The relevant information must have persisted as a trace or representation of the original information. Moreover, in addition to traces of information specifying the original event, the rememberer will possess traces of information that specify both succeeding and preceding events. Such organized representations of interconnected events will reduce ambiguities in specification of the original event. In short, without allowing for a concept of memory traces or cognitive representations specifying past events (plus principles of organization of such traces), an ecological theory of memory does not seem possible. However, whereas conventional theories of mental representations are constructivist – they assume that representations arise from mental processes that add information to a basically fragmented and ambiguous stimulation from the environment – an ecological theory of representations should be realistic. It must assume that sufficient information is normally available from the organism-environment system to constitute an adequate representation that, in ensuing events, becomes part of the functional environment from which information may be picked up.

The following analysis of the information available to specify experienced and reported events attempts to put these rather abstract principles of an ecological approach to memory into practice.

Information specifying reported and experienced events

The basic characteristic of reported events is that the information that specifies them has already been processed and is presented to the perceiver by another human being in an act of communication. This "preprocessing" gives rise to a number of peculiar features that contrast with those of experienced events in which the perceiver is present in the midst of the event and therefore can influence what happens as well as what information to pick up about it. I suggest that, as a consequence, the information available to specify reported and experienced events is characterized by the differentiating properties that are shown in Table 13.2, loosely ordered on a dimension from superficial and narrow to deep and comprehensive. In the following sections, each pair of properties is more closely argued, and some interesting implications for remembering the two classes of events are described.

Perceptual versus symbolic information

Whereas experienced events are primarily specified by *perceptual information* impinging on the person's senses, reported events are first and fore-

Table 13.2. *Properties of experienced and reported events*

Properties	Characteristics of available information	
	Experienced events	Reported events
Type of information	Perceptual	Symbolic
Origin of selection	Self	Social
Structure of information	Event structure	Event + narrative structure
Context of information	Original event	Reception event
Causal-temporal organization	Nesting	Fragmentation

most known from information in *symbolic* form, most often linguistic, but also gestural, graphic, and so forth. In general, the availability of information depends both on the properties of the symbolic medium and on the skill of the reporter. But symbolic coding is never exhaustive, and we may therefore assume that the information available about reported events has less perceptual detail (including the bodily sensations that are prominent in emotional experience) and is less vivid than that for experienced events (on top of the selection factor). In line with trace-strength theories (Wickelgren, 1970), this might be expected to put memory for reported events at a disadvantage.

As mentioned earlier, there is evidence that memories of experienced events are indeed perceptually more vivid than those for reported events (Reisberg et al., 1984, among others). Visual information may be particularly strong. Brewer and Pani (1983) even go so far as to include in the definition of "personal memories" that they are "experienced in terms of visual imagery." White's (1982) study of experienced events recording during 1 year indicates that vividness of experience also facilitates remembering, as does the amount of perceptual detail, provided it is visual. Similar studies of reported events have not been published.

The role of affect has received more attention, but with mixed results. Again, Reisberg et al. (1984) showed a much higher level of affect in experienced events than in reported events. Robinson (1980) and Thompson (1985a) found that the intensity of affect in experienced events was related to short retrieval time and high memory ratings, respectively, whereas the type of affect (pleasant or unpleasant) played no role. This agrees completely with the vividness data. However, White (1982) found no relation at all between affective intensity and memory ratings, and Wagenaar (1986) reported that only pleasant events (not unpleasant ones) were more accurately recalled at higher intensity; Wagenaar attributed this finding to a suppression of strongly unpleasant memories that seems to vanish in a couple of years when the contents of the events are largely forgotten. The only data on affective information in reported events come from Larsen and Plunkett's (1987) study of retrieval cued by object and emotion words. Results concerning retrieval time and dating showed exactly the same effect of emotion-word cues on reported events as on experienced events, but with longer latencies for reports. That is, no effect of a lower level of emotionality in reported events was observed (decreased accessibility, increased forgetting).

To summarize, the memorability of reported events may be expected to suffer because of lack of perceptual vividness, including emotional information, but this prediction still needs to be adequately tested. On the other hand, it should be recognized that skillful and creative report-ers are able to elicit quite intense imagery and emotional involvement in the public. For writers of fiction, this is often considered a criterion of excellence, and it is increasingly being pursued by TV and newspaper journalists (as in so-called human-interest journalism). Along with many other aspects of reported events, the effects of such factors are not known.

Self-selection versus social selection of information

The selection of what information to pick up from an experienced event is made by the person involved (*self-selection*), whereas information about a reported event is previously selected by other people or organizations (*social selection*) before it reaches the receiver. Perception inevitably in-volves selection of information from the continuous flux available in the environment and in the person. In personal experience, this selection is largely automatic and in part governed by the person's knowledge, pur-poses, and interests. When events are reported, however, selections are made by the people who report them. In mass-communication research, this is called *gatekeeping* on the flow of information (after Kurt Lewin; see McQuail, 1969). Gatekeepers necessarily and sometimes intentionally bias the available information, partly by what they exclude, partly by presenting it from a specific perspective, and even by inferring or invent-ing things. In sum, information about reported events probably is less extensive and subject to different biases than that about experienced events.

The problems of overcoming omissions and biases in one's own percep-tion and in reports about events are beyond the scope of this chapter. Here we mention only a few implications for memory of this difference of selection. First, as a general rule it is to be expected that the less extensive and detailed information about reported events will result in lower chances of retrieving these events. Second, one kind of bias in reports may be that important and unimportant details are more sharply differentiated than in personal experience, thus counteracting retrieval difficulty for details that are singled out as significant. Third, memories for reported events may appear inferior because people are reluctant to reconstruct them. Neisser (see chapter 14) has pointed out that informa-' tion about an experienced event exists at several nested levels, from the very detailed, such as the particular words used, to the very general, such as the ultimate purpose of uttering them. When we attempt to remember an experienced event, we are so confident that information at every level once existed that we almost inevitably reconstruct it if we do not remember it. This may be true for experienced events, but with reported events people will hardly believe that they once had complete information. It is therefore reasonable to expect less reconstruction of information in recall of reported events than for experienced events. People may reason, "The report didn't mention that," rather than attempt to reconstruct an answer that they feel they must have known.

Event structure and narrative structure

The internal structure of information about experienced events may differ from that for reported events because of what could be called the double structure of reports. Two types of internal structure may be identified: event structure and narrative structure. *Event structure* refers to the temporal, causal, and hierarchical relationships among parts of the event. Causes precede consequences, provocations precede retaliations, intentions precede actions, goals serve superordinate purposes and are realized by subordinate goals, and so forth (Lichtenstein & Brewer, 1980). Information specifying event structure is available in the spatiotemporal flow of stimulation that can be picked up by anyone personally present. All real events, reported as well as experienced events, exhibit this structuring. When information is reported, another kind of structure is imposed in addition. This structure comes from the "storytellers" through whom we receive the information and who respond to the constraints and conventions of communication (Robinson & Hawpe, 1986). The generic term *narrative structure* is used to refer to this second structure. Note that autobiographical events may become narrativized, of course, like the "repisodes" in John Dean's memory (Neisser, 1981). The point is that narrativization of experienced events does not necessarily take place, only to the extent that the events are told to others. Therefore, each reported event might be represented in a more tightly organized and schematic format than experienced events, which could counteract forgetting of the rather scarce information available to specify reported events in the first place.

The distinction between event structure and narrative structure is common in literary theory, but has only recently been recognized by psychologists (Brewer, 1980; Brewer & Lichtenstein, 1981). The most prominent account of event structure is Schank and Abelson's (1977) *script theory.* Scripts represent generic knowledge of routine events, acquired from everyday experience, and they are assumed to direct actual behavior as well as perception and memory of such events. The role of scripts in recognition and recall of everyday routines has been confirmed in numerous studies (Bower et al., 1979).

Most people do not, from personal experience, know the structure of news events like summit meetings, trade negotiations, national economy crises, or terrorist activities. They may therefore not be able to take advantage of the inherent structure of these events – they lack appropriate scripts. However, some studies suggest that people tend to understand reported events in terms of experienced events, for instance, by applying scripts known from interpersonal conflicts to reports of international conflicts (Collins & Wellman, 1982; Roloff, 1981). This may aid comprehension and memory, and it frequently seems to be encouraged by treatment in the news media, even though international conflicts seldom follow the same pattern as family quarrels – they have different causes and must be resolved in different ways. But people may not always misapprehend the structure of news events in this way. The assumption that scripts have to be learned from personal experience could be wrong. In a recent unpublished study, Kim Plunkett and I found results suggesting that scripts can develop from reports of events. Subjects read stories of typical news events: a strike among construction workers and negotiations concerning a United Nations resolution. In a later recognition test, they made exactly the same kinds and numbers of errors of inference with these events as they did with purely personal events like "getting up in the morning" and "shopping" (Bower et al., 1979). For routine reported events, people may thus possess event schemas that are equally familiar as those of experienced events. To the extent that this is the case, comprehension and memory will be equally facilitated without necessarily being distorted by inappropriate script application.

Consider next the *narrative structure* that is imposed on events by reporting. The type of narrative structure most thoroughly investigated is that of traditional folk stories (Mandler & Johnson, 1977; Rumelhart, 1975). Mandler and Johnson, in particular, emphasize that the very tight organization of such stories probably reflects the fact that they are meant for oral presentation – the structure has evolved as a means to make events in the story easy to comprehend and remember. Therefore, even quite different events are cast in the same format: A setting is outlined; one person is depicted as the protagonist, the hero; a problem besetting the hero is stated; the whole course of events is described as the hero's attempts to solve the problem. Large numbers of studies have shown that the story structure is familiar, even to quite young children, and that it may direct attention during reading or listening, facilitate comprehension, generate inferences, and aid recall (Brewer & Nakamura, 1984; Kintsch & van Dijk, 1978; Mandler, 1984).

The purposes and constraints of modern news communication have produced a different type of narrative structure (Findahl & Höijer, 1975; Larsen, 1983; Thorndyke, 1979). In news, the narrative characteristically starts with a short summary of the main event, followed by a more extensive description that includes details about the where, when, and who of the event, then (optionally) some elaboration of the causes and background of the event, plus some evaluation of possible consequences. The news story structure serves the purposes of catching attention initially, identifying the geopolitical location and eventual political actors in the event, and perhaps relating it to previous occurrences and indicating its future significance. Elements of the structure are ordered on the basis of decreasing "journalistic importance," because if space limitations arise, it is most convenient for the editor to cut the end. A story that cannot be cut at the end risks being omitted altogether. (Note that Brown et al., 1986, use the term "public narrative" to denote more extended structures, "interconnected historical episodes." Such interstory relations are treated in a later section. The present discussion concerns intrastory organization.)

Little empirical evidence exists regarding the role of the news structure in memory. Thorndyke (1979) found the newspaper versions of stories to give slightly *inferior* recall compared with a chronological description (which would be the format of a pure event structure; real events are, of course, chronologically ordered). Unpublished data from our laboratory showed equivalent recognition when artificial news events were presented in the news story format and a chronological format. With authentic news reports, I have previously found that both news structure and chronological structure contribute to determining what information is produced in free recall (Larsen, 1983).

To summarize, it appears that both event structure and narrative structure may contribute to remembering news reports, but event structure is probably the more potent factor (unlike the case with folk stories and perhaps other fiction). Thus, the particular narrative structure of news and similar reported events may not assist remembering significantly as compared with personal, nonnarrated experience.

Original event and reception event

Information about an experienced event is picked up by the perceiver as an integral part of the unfolding of the event. The information that specifies a reported event, on the other hand, is received by the subject as part of an entirely separate, personally experienced event. Every reported event is embedded or nested in what may be termed a *reception event:* the particular time and place in one's life at which one is told a story, watches television, reads a newspaper, and so on. Memories of reported events are born with a shadow, so to speak; there is a duality of the original event and its personal context (Brown et al., 1986); note that this feature may be seen as a more precise and detailed formulation of the report-tag theory. It is interesting that recent studies of the phenomenon of "source amnesia" (Schacter, Harbluk, & McLachlan, 1984) indicate the importance of this distinction and even suggest that retention of the "source" of information (by which is actually meant the entire reception event) has a neuropsychological location in the frontal lobes.

In the present discussion, the question is whether or not the "shadow" – information about the reception event – can facilitate later remembering of the original event described in the received message. Reception events appear to add pieces of information to that of the messages themselves. If some of this information and its links to the particular reported event are retained, then it might assist memory of the reported event. As Brown et al. (1986) pointed out, this would be similar to the common phenomenon that information about the situational context may later facilitate recognition and recall of events (see the review by Davies, 1986). However, two characteristics of reception events render such a facilitation less likely. First, the relation between what is told in a report and the situation in which it is told is almost completely arbitrary. A particular piece of news might equally well be picked up from television, radio, newspaper, or even a discussion. The reception context of a report cannot substitute for the natural context of the original event (or an experienced event), which is stripped in the communication process. This difference is reminiscent of Baddeley's (1982) distinction between independent and interactive contexts that seems to be important for context effects in laboratory studies. Second, reception events tend to be similar to each other, one instance of newspaper reading or television watching being much like any other. Such receptive events are, of course, difficult to distinguish; usually, only the most recent one remains distinct in memory (Linton, 1982).

Rather than reception events contributing to make reported events memorable, it is probably the other way around: In some cases the distinctiveness and impact of a reported event may cause the reception event to be exceptionally well remembered. This is seen most dramatically in so-called flashbulb memories (Brown & Kulik, 1977; Pillemer, 1984; Winograd & Killinger, 1983), where subjects claim to have very vivid memories of the circumstances in which they had news about a public event, often remembering more about the circumstances than about the event reported. The prototypical example of a flashbulb is people's memories of receiving the news of the assassination of President Kennedy in 1963. Flashbulb memories of this classic type are apparently rare, much more rare than equally vivid memories of experienced events (Rubin & Kozin, 1984).

Because flashbulbs are examples of vividly remembered reported events, it is of interest to examine what factors are responsible for such memories. Brown and Kulik (1977) originally suggested intensity of affect created by surprise. Surprise was later disconfirmed in studies by Reisberg et al. (1984) and Rubin and Kozin (1984), who nevertheless found intensity of affect to be effective per se, as did Pillemer (1984). However, Neisser (1982b) suggested that the basic cause of flashbulbs might be that the reported event is seen as a "benchmark" in the course of historical events that becomes linked to our personal history by repeated use as a distinctive reference point in thinking and talking about other events. Neisser's view is supported by the data of Reisberg et al. (1984), which showed high vividness of memories for events judged to "change one's life" and be "used as a reference point"; but intensity of affect was also a prominent correlate of vividness in this study. Affectivity and benchmark quality may well be independently responsible for flashbulb memories, though probably correlated. The point is, however, that it takes something special to make reception events memorable in their own right—unusually intense affect or being the occasion of an unusually important and therefore frequently referenced message. (Note that flashbulbs do not require a constructivist theory of memory— something like "firing a mental flashbulb." The experience is vivid from the beginning; we only need to explain why it stays that way. Later references to the event, in thought or speech, are not constructions; they are real.)

I have argued that reception events most likely are unable to aid in remembering reported events. This is not to say that reception-event information is useless, however. Brown et al. (1986) proposed that such information, retrieved together with the reported event, might help to place it in relation to other events. For instance, fragments of information about the reception event—the personal context—might be used to narrow the period of time during which the original event could have occurred. This is precisely the idea of the reference-point function of flashbulbs mentioned earlier. Brown et al. (1986) found supporting evidence in verbal protocols from subjects who attempted to date reported events. Three-quarters of the datings included references to other events that were used to home in on the answer, and most of these auxiliary events were experienced events. Similar results were reported by Lieury et al. (1980, Exp. 2) and Friedman and Wilkins (1985). In this way, reception-event information may be important to maintain the temporal organization of sequences of reported events, that is, knowledge of the course of current history. This function goes beyond the one proposed by Neisser (1982b) that the personal aspect of flashbulbs serves to "line up our own lives with the course of history itself." Rather, the course of current history would appear to be organized in terms of the structure of one's personal life. This aid to organizing historical events is needed because, as discussed in the next section, information about such events is generally poorly organized.

To sum up, the reception context of reported events is relatively arbitrary and indiscriminable compared with the original context of experienced events. In most cases, memories of reported events are thus at a disadvantage because they cannot be facilitated by contextual information. Flashbulb memories constitute a rare exception to this rule; however, they also highlight what may be a more general (though less conspicuous) phenomenon, that current historical events are organized in terms of personal experiences. This is the theme of the next section.

Autobiographical nesting versus causal-temporal fragmentation

Finally, we consider the relations among individual events: interevent organization. Every experienced event is nested within broader, more comprehensive structures of information (see chapter 14), and ultimately within a single, well-integrated structure, namely, the person's autobiography. Autobiographical knowledge is no doubt organized into temporal segments corresponding to major life periods, delimited and further subdivided by "landmark events" of various sorts (Robinson, 1986b). However, there will also be overarching features knitting events together within and across segments: basic personal motives, values, interests, "life themes," and so forth. Therefore, one's autobiography may be considered a very rich and highly integrated knowledge structure. A reported event, on the other hand, may belong to one or more of a large number of separate knowledge structures (the public narratives of Brown et al., 1986), each of them more limited in scope, less complete, and less coherent. Of course, some events do belong to the same chain (e.g., " 'Contra' terrorism in Nicaragua"), and sometimes different chains intersect and interact (when the Nicaragua chain crosses the "U.S. presidential conduct" chain). But, in general, there are substantial numbers of separate reported-event chains about which we possess information. Reported events are thus by necessity relatively fragmented temporally and causally, and this is reinforced by the far too common piecemeal presentation in the news media (Findahl & Höijer, 1982).

Similar views on autobiographical knowledge have been proposed by many previous investigators, often using the term *self-schema* to convey the idea of integrated unity (Barclay & Wellman, 1986; Greenwald, 1981; Johnson, 1983; Thompson, 1985b). These theories assume that individual events are integrated into the self-schema by constructive cognitive processes carried out by the person—abstracting common features, establishing associative or semantic relations to the schematic "network," and so forth. In contrast, I assume that there is information available in the personally experienced event itself to specify this integration. As the person acts in accordance with personal goals, motives, and interests, adapted to the present circumstances, the new event is already related to and subsumed under higher-level self-knowledge; it is related to what happened before and what happens afterward, and it may remind the person of previous experiences in terms of which the new one is interpreted (Winograd & Soloway, 1985). After the event, some "construction" may, of course, take place (e.g., if it is discussed with others or reflected on in solitude), but that is not a necessary condition for integration in the autobiography. If special explanations are needed, it is rather to deal with experienced events that are nevertheless remembered as being totally unrelated to the rest of one's autobiography. Such insulation is actually so strange that it is considered a symptom of severe personality disorder (Talland, 1968).

A number of empirical studies have shown that information related to the self-schema is better remembered as compared with relating it to one's knowledge of somebody else or subjecting it to "semantic processing" (Bower & Gilligan, 1979; Rogers, Kuiper, & Kriker, 1977). These investigations dealt with experimentally constructed materials that required subjects to construct or imagine the self-schema relation rather than perceiving it. Moreover, the interpretation in terms of self-schema has been challenged (Klein & Kihlstrom, 1986). With real-life events, however, Barclay and Wellman's (1986) results point to an adverse effect of the self-schema, namely, that events tend to lose their uniqueness, blending with similar or closely related events so that reconstruction and misrecognition of events that "just might have happened" become frequent. More generally, Greenwald (1980) emphasized the bias imposed on new information to make it conform to the self-schema. Thus, autobiographical memory may not be very precise, but it might still be superior to reported-event memory because of the nesting of events in the solid autobiographical framework.

In psychology, the structure of public, historical knowledge is an almost untouched problem. Some evidence comes from studies of memory for news reports. Findahl and Höijer (1975, 1982) have repeatedly shown that the persons involved and the places of occurrence of news are remembered far better than the causes and consequences. This suggests that information specifying interevent organization tends not to be picked up by people, perhaps because they lack appropriate schemas. Rather, the organization of knowledge apparently is in terms of geography, famous persons, and perhaps event types. This account of historical knowledge is similar to the view of autobiographical memory put forward by Kolodner (1983). But Kolodner's theory is built on a simulation of the memory of Cyrus Vance's public activities as U.S. secretary of state. It would therefore not be surprising if her theory were more pertinent to reported events than to autobiographical events (see chapter 8).

The most direct investigations of structuring of public knowledge were reported by Brown et al. (1986). As mentioned earlier, these authors found that the knowledge recruited by subjects to assist in dating public events was predominantly autobiographical, suggesting that public events are more closely related to experienced events than to each other in memory. Moreover, when public events were recruited, they most often belonged to the same public narrative – the same event chain – as the to-be-dated event. These authors further distinguished between "political" and "nonpolitical" events, the latter typically exemplified by incidents in the lives of persons known from the sports and entertainment world. Political events were assumed to be integrated in more extended event chains than nonpolitical events; in particular, it was hypothesized that to the subjects (who were U.S. citizens), political events often would be related to which U.S. president was in office when an event occurred, thus providing a comparatively firm link to calendar time. Their results confirmed these assumptions. They showed that more public-event and same-narrative knowledge was recruited to date political events than to date nonpolitical events. Furthermore, it was faster to locate political events in relation to presidential periods than in relation to periods of the subjects' own lives (periods of attending different schools), whereas nonpolitical events were located faster in autobiographical periods than in presidential periods.

The work of Brown et al. (1986) suggests that in some cases there is sufficient information available about the temporal interrelations of reported events to allow a coherent organization in memory. But more frequently, memories are fragmented, and subjects need to take recourse to the better integrated autobiographical domain to supply the organizational framework for temporal estimates. If that strategy does not succeed, people may employ the "accessibility principle" proposed by Brown, Rips, and Shevell (1985) as a dating heuristic, implicitly assuming that the more one knows about an event, the more recent it is. This heuristic seems uncommon with autobiographical memories, according to C. P. Thompson's data (personal communication), except among people who do poorly in dating their own, previously recorded, experiences.

The argument in this section has been that experienced events are naturally nested within a rich and coherent framework of autobiographical knowledge, whereas reported events are relatively fragmented. This may lead to errors of remembering if events fit into the autobiographical framework but did not actually take place. On the other hand, this framework seems important to maintain temporal order among reported events, not only in the rare case of flashbulb memories. It is personal experience that gives structure to our knowledge of current history, we might say. However, direct comparisons of the organization of experienced and reported events – for instance, by studying retrieval strategies – have apparently not been made.

Conclusions

We experience only a tiny proportion of the events that occur in the world at large. Some of the events that we do not experience become known to us through the reports of other people and, in particular, through the mass-communication media. This discussion of memory for such reported events has had three purposes: first, to argue that memory for reported events is ecologically important and to examine why both traditional and ecological memory research has neglected this topic; second, to analyze what information may be available to specify events reported in the past, that is, to remember them; third, to review empirical studies that bear on this analysis.

Part of the background for the traditional neglect of memory for reported events is philosophical, namely, the empiricist neglect of social origins of knowledge; phenomenological descriptions like that of Rasmussen (1956) remind us of the importance of anthropic mediation, that is, experience relayed by fellow human beings. Another factor is that psychology has in general ignored memory for real events, being satisfied with studying "minievents" in the laboratory. More recent research informed by the ecological approach to cognition seems to have inherited the presumption of Tulving's (1972) concept of episodic memory that all real events are personally experienced and thus autobiographical. But it cannot be taken for granted that autobiographical events and reported events are equivalent in respect to memory. Indeed, the everyday view apparently is that memory for reported events is inferior. The handful of empirical investigations that have directly compared experienced and reported events have not yielded entirely consistent findings. However, the studies that concerned natural, nonlaboratory events suggested that reported events are actually less well remembered.

To better understand memory of reported events as well as experienced events and to provide a frame for research into their differences, an ecological analysis of the information that may specify experienced and reported events is proposed. This analysis is primarily descriptive; it attempts to characterize experienced and reported events in terms of a number of contrasting features (or dimensions), each of which might be relevant to the ease and accuracy of remembering the events. The basic assumption is that memory of events should be understood in terms of the information available to the individual to specify these events, whether past or present, rather than assuming that information is constructed by the individual and added to the impoverished data obtained from the environment.

According to the present analysis, information available about reported events is symbolically coded, socially selected, narratively structured, acquired in the rather arbitrary and indistinctive context of an autobiographical message-reception event, and relatively isolated from other pieces of information possessed by the individual. Information about experienced events, in contrast, is perceptually rich, self-selected, not necessarily subjected to narrative structuring, perceived in the natural context of the original event, and nested within the individual's autobiographical knowledge. The evidence reviewed suggests that, generally speaking, reported events are more difficult to remember because experienced events are favored by more complete and unselected information, by richness of perceptual and affective features, by familiarity of event scripts, and by being integral elements of one's autobiography. In comparison, it is insignificant that reported events exhibit a double structure (event structure plus narrative structure) and are occasionally linked to vividly remembered experienced events (as in flashbulb memories).

Perhaps the most important empirical result is that autobiographical knowledge seems to form the backbone for organizing and ordering remembered events, whether experienced or reported. Theoretically speaking, the main message has been to put reported events on the research agenda and to suggest that the understanding of autobiographical memory, by now well advanced, can benefit from being viewed in the perspective of the world beyond immediate experience.

NOTE

The idea of writing this chapter was conceived during a stay at the Emory Cognition Project as a Fulbright Visiting Scholar. Valuable discussions with researchers and students at the project—in particular with the editors of this volume—are gratefully acknowledged and too numerous to detail. In addition, Mariane Hedegaard, Jesper Hermann, Steinar Kvale, Thomas Nielsen, Kim Plunkett, Henrik Poulsen, Daniel Reisberg, and Charles Thompson deserve credit for helpful comments during various revisions. In addition to support from the Fulbright Commission, this work was supported by the Danish Research Council for the Humanities and by the University of Aarhus Research Foundation. Correspondence should be addressed to Steen F. Larsen, Institute of Psychology, University of Aarhus, 4 Asylvej, DK-8240 Risskov, Denmark.

REFERENCES

Anderson, R. C., & Pichert, J. W. (1978). Recall of previously unrecallable information following a shift in perspective. *Journal of Verbal Learning and Verbal Behavior, 17,* 1–12.

Baddeley, A. D. (1982). Domains of recollection. *Psychological Review, 89,* 708–729.

Bahrick, H. P., & Karis, D. (1982). Long-term ecological memory. In C. R. Puff (Ed.), *Handbook of research methods in human memory and cognition* (pp. 427–465). New York: Academic Press.

Barclay, C. R., & Wellman, H. M. (1986). Accuracies and inaccuracies in autobiographical memories. *Journal of Memory and Language, 25,* 93–103.

Bartlett, F. C. (1932). *Remembering: An experimental and social study.* Cambridge University Press.

Bower, G. H. (1967). A multicomponent theory of the memory trace. In K. W. Spence & J. T. Spence (Eds.), *The psychology of learning and motivation* (Vol. 1, pp. 230–326). New York: Academic Press.

Bower, G. H., Black, J. B., & Turner, T. J. (1979). Scripts in memory for texts. *Cognitive Psychology, 11,* 177–220.

Bower, G. H., & Gilligan, S. G. (1979). Remembering information related to one's self. *Journal of Research in Personality, 13,* 420–432.

Brewer, W. F. (1980). Literary theory, rhetoric, stylistics: Implications for psychology. In R. J. Spiro, B. C. Bruce, & W. F. Brewer (Eds.), *Theoretical issues in reading comprehension: Perspectives from cognitive psychology, linguistics, artificial intelligence, and education* (pp. 221–239). Hillsdale, NJ: Erlbaum.

Brewer, W. F., & Lichtenstein, E. H. (1981). Event schemas, story schemas, and story grammars. In J. Long & A. Baddeley (Eds.), *Attention and performance* (Vol. 9, pp. 363–379). Hillsdale, NJ: Erlbaum.

Brewer, W. F., & Nakamura, G. V. (1984). The nature and function of schemas. In R. S. Wyer & T. K. Srull (Eds.), *Handbook of social cognition* (Vol. 1, pp. 119–160). Hillsdale, NJ: Erlbaum.

Brewer, W. F., & Pani, J. R. (1983). The structure of human memory. In G. H. Bower (Ed.), *The psychology of learning and motivation* (Vol. 17, pp. 1–38). New York: Academic Press.

Brown, L., Heymann, S., Preskill, B., Rubin, D., & Wuletich, T. (1977). Leading questions and the eyewitness report of a live and a described event. *Psychological Reports, 40,* 1041–1042.

Brown, N. R., Rips, L. J., & Shevell, S. K. (1985). The subjective dates of natural events in very-long-term memory. *Cognitive Psychology, 17,* 139–177.

Brown, N. R., Shevell, S. K., & Rips, L. J. (1986). Public memories and their personal context. In D. C. Rubin (Ed.), *Autobiographical memory* (pp. 137–158). Cambridge University Press.

Brown, R., & Kulik, J. (1977). Flashbulb memories. *Cognition, 5,* 73–99.

Bruce, D. (1985). The how and why of ecological memory. *Journal of Experimental Psychology: General, 114,* 78–90.

Collins, W. A., & Wellman, H. M. (1982). Social scripts and developmental patterns in comprehension of televised narratives. *Communication Research, 9,* 380–398.

Davies, G. (1986). Context effects in episodic memory: A review. *Cahiers de Psychologie Cognitive, 2,* 157–174.

Findahl, O., & Höijer, B. (1975). Effects of additional verbal information on retention of a radio news program. *Journalism Quarterly, 52,* 493–498.

(1982). The problem of comprehension and recall of broadcast news. In J. F. Le Ny & W. Kintsch (Eds.), *Language and comprehension* (pp. 261–272). Amsterdam: North Holland.

Friedman, W. J., & Wilkins, A. J. (1985). Scale effects in memory for the time of events. *Memory and Cognition, 13,* 168–175.

Gibson, J. J. (1979). *The ecological approach to visual perception.* Boston: Houghton Mifflin.

Greenwald, A. G. (1980). The totalitarian ego: Fabrication and revision of personal history. *American Psychologist, 35,* 603–618.

(1981). Self and memory. In G. H. Bower (Ed.), *The psychology of learning and motivation* (Vol. 15, pp. 202–236). New York: Academic Press.

Gunter, B., Berry, C., & Clifford, B. R. (1981). Proactive interference effects with television news items: Further evidence. *Journal of Experimental Psychology: Human Learning and Memory, 7,* 480–487.

Halbwachs, M. (1925). *Les cadres sociaux de la memoire.* Paris: Presses Universitaires de France.

Herrmann, D. J., & Neisser, U. (1978). An inventory of everyday memory experiences. In M. M. Gruneberg, P. E. Morris, & R. N. Sykes (Eds.), *Practical aspects of memory* (pp. 35–51). New York: Academic Press.

Johnson, M. K. (1983). A multiple-entry, modular memory system. In G. H. Bower (Ed.), *The psychology of learning and motivation* (Vol. 17, pp. 81–123). New York: Academic Press.

Johnson, M. K., & Raye, C. L. (1981). Reality monitoring. *Psychological Review, 88,* 67–85.

Kihlstrom, J. F. (1981). On personality and memory. In N. Cantor & J. F. Kihlstrom (Eds.), *Personality, cognition, and social interaction* (pp. 123–149). Hillsdale, NJ: Erlbaum.

Kintsch, W., & van Dijk, T. A. (1978). Toward a model of text comprehension and memory. *Psychological Review, 85,* 363–394.

Klein, S. B., & Kihlstrom, J. F. (1986). Elaboration, organization, and the self-reference effect in memory. *Journal of Experimental Psychology: General, 115,* 26–38.

Kolodner, J. L. (1983). Maintaining organization in a dynamic long-term memory. *Cognitive Science, 7,* 243–280.

Larsen, S. F. (1983). Text processing and knowledge updating in memory for radio news. *Discourse Processes, 6,* 21–38.

Larsen, S. F., & Plunkett, K. (1987). Remembering experienced and reported events. *Applied Cognitive Psychology, 1,* 15–26.

Lichtenstein, E. H., & Brewer, W. F. (1980). Memory for goal-directed events. *Cognitive Psychology, 12,* 412–445.

Lieury, A., Aiello, B., Lepreux, D., & Mellet, M. (1980). Le rôle des repères dans la récupération et la datation des souvenirs. *L'Annee Psychologique, 80,* 149–167.

Lieury, A., Richer, E., & Weeger, I. (1978). Les événements privés et publics dans les souvenirs. *Bulletin de Psychologie, 32,* 41–48.

Linton, M. (1978). Real world memory after six years: An in vivo study of very long term memory. In M. M. Gruneberg, P. E. Morris, & R. N. Sykes (Eds.), *Practical aspects of memory* (pp. 69–76). New York: Academic Press.

(1982). Transformations of memory in everyday life. In U. Neisser (Ed.), *Memory observed: Remembering in natural contexts* (pp. 77–91). San Francisco: Freeman.

McQuail, D. (1969). *Towards a sociology of mass communication.* London: Collier Macmillan.

Mandler, J. (1984). *Stories, scripts, and scenes: Aspects of schema theory.* Hillsdale, NJ: Erlbaum.

Mandler, J., & Johnson, N. S. (1977). Remembrance of things parsed: Story structure and recall. *Cognitive Psychology, 9,* 111–151.

Neisser, U. (1976). *Cognition and reality.* San Francisco: Freeman.

(1978). Memory: What are the important questions? In M. M. Gruneberg, P. E. Morris, & R. N. Sykes (Eds.), *Practical aspects of memory* (pp. 3–24). New York: Academic Press.

(1981). John Dean's memory: A case study. *Cognition, 9,* 1–22.

(Ed.). (1982a). *Memory observed: Remembering in natural contexts.* San Francisco: Freeman.

(1982b). Snapshots or benchmarks? In U. Neisser (Ed.), *Memory observed: Remembering in natural contexts* (pp. 43–48). San Francisco: Freeman.

(1984). *Toward an ecologically oriented cognitive science* (Emory Cognition Project, Report No. 1). Atlanta, GA: Emory University, Department of Psychology.

(1985). The role of theory in the ecological study of memory: Comment on Bruce. *Journal of Experimental Psychology: General, 114,* 272–276.

(1986). Nested structure in autobiographical memory. In D. Rubin (Ed.), *Autobiographical memory* (pp. 71–81). Cambridge University Press.

Pillemer, D. B. (1984). Flashbulb memories of the assassination attempt on President Reagan. *Cognition, 16,* 63–80.

Rasmussen, E. T. (1956). *Bevidsthedsliv og erkendelse* (Conscious life and cognition). Copenhagen: Munksgaard.

Reisberg, D., Heuer, F., O'Shaughnessy, M., & McLean, J. (1984, November). *Memory vividness.* Paper presented at Psychonomic Society Conference, San Antonio, TX.

Robinson, J. A. (1980). Affect and retrieval of personal memories. *Motivation and Emotion, 4,* 149–174.

(1986a). Autobiographical memory: An historical prologue. In D. C. Rubin (Ed.), *Autobiographical memory* (pp. 19–24). Cambridge University Press.

(1986b). Temporal reference systems and autobiographical memory. In D. C. Rubin (Ed.), *Autobiographical memory* (pp. 159–190). Cambridge University Press.

Robinson, J. A., & Hawpe, L. (1986). Narrative thinking as a heuristic process. In T. R. Sarbin (Ed.), *Narrative psychology: The storied nature of human conduct* (pp. 111–125). New York: Praeger.

Rogers, T. B., Kuiper, N. A., & Kriker, W. S. (1977). Self-reference and the encoding of personal information. *Journal of Personality and Social Psychology, 35,* 677–688.

Roloff, M. E. (1981). Interpersonal and mass communication scripts. In G. C. Wilhoit & H. de Bock (Eds.), *Mass communication review yearbook* (Vol. 2, pp. 428–444). Washington, DC: Sage.

Rubin, D. C., & Kozin, M. (1984). Vivid memories. *Cognition, 16,* 81–95.

Rubin, E. (1915). *Synsoplevede figurer* (Visually experienced figures). Copenhagen: Gylendal.

Rumelhart, D. E. (1975). Notes on a schema for stories. In D. G. Bobrow & A. Collins (Eds.), *Representation and understanding. Studies in cognitive science* (pp. 211–236). New York: Academic Press.

Schacter, D. L., Harbluk, J. L., & McLachlan, D. R. (1984). Retrieval without recollection: An experimental analysis of source amnesia. *Journal of Verbal Learning and Verbal Behavior, 23,* 593–611.

Schank, R. C., & Abelson, R. P. (1977). *Scripts, plans, goals, and understanding.* Hillsdale, NJ: Erlbaum.

Schank, R. C., Birnbaum, L., & Mey, J. (1982). *Integrating semantics and pragmatics.* Paper presented at 13th International Congress of Linguistics, Tokyo.

Squire, L., & Slater, P. C. (1975). Forgetting in very long-term memory as assessed by an improved questionnaire technique. *Journal of Experimental Psychology: Human Learning and Memory, 104,* 50–54.

Talland, G. A. (1968). *Disorders of memory and learning.* Harmondsworth, UK: Penguin.

Thompson, C. P. (1985a). Memory for unique personal events: Effects of pleasantness. *Motivation and Emotion, 9,* 277–289.

  (1985b). Memory for unique personal events: Some implications of the self-schema. *Human Learning, 4,* 267–280.

Thorndyke, P. W. (1979). Knowledge acquisition from newspaper stories. *Discourse Processes, 2,* 95–112.

Toglia, M. P., Shlechter, T. M., & Herrmann, D. J. (1984, November). *Event memory and modality of experience.* Paper presented at Psychonomic Society Conference, San Antonio, TX.

Tulving, E. (1972). Episodic and semantic memory. In E. Tulving & W. Donaldson (Eds.), *Organization and memory* (pp. 381–403). New York: Academic Press.

  (1983). *Elements of episodic memory.* New York: Oxford University Press.

Wagenaar, W. A. (1986). My memory: A study of autobiographical memory over six years. *Cognitive Psychology, 18,* 225–252.

Warrington, E. K., & Sanders, H. I. (1971). The fate of old memories. *Quarterly Journal of Experimental Psychology, 23,* 432–442.

White, R. T. (1982). Memory for personal events. *Human Learning, 1,* 171–183.

Wickelgren, W. A. (1970). Multitrace strength theory. In D. A. Norman (Ed.), *Models of human memory* (pp. 65–102). New York: Academic Press.

Winograd, E., & Killinger, W. A. (1983). Relating age at encoding in early childhood to adult recall: Development of flashbulb memories. *Journal of Experimental Psychology: General, 112,* 413–422.

Winograd, E., & Soloway, R. M. (1985). Reminding as a basis for temporal judgments. *Journal of Experimental Psychology: Learning, Memory, and Cognition, 11,* 262–271.

Woodworth, R. S. (1945). *Contemporary schools of psychology* (4th ed.). London: Methuen.

14

What is ordinary memory the memory of?[1]

ULRIC NEISSER

This chapter consists of three relatively independent sections. The first provides an overview of recent developments in various fields of memory, the second suggests an ecological way of thinking about memory for personally experienced results, and the third offers a conjecture about the relation between personal memory and spatial orientation. My own confidence in the several sections is mirrored by their order of presentation: I think of section I as almost incontrovertible, of section II as an essentially reasonable proposal, and of section III as frankly speculative.

I. The new memoria

In the past 10 or 15 years, the psychology of memory has undergone a fundamental change. This shift, which began well before the current interest in the possibilities of an ecological approach, has not been the work of any one individual or research group. What has happened is not merely the emergence of a new method or a new theory, but a change in our notions of what kinds of things people remember in the first place. In effect, we have a new definition of what memory is *of*.

   Twenty years ago, the principal function of memory was assumed to be the storage of individual experiences and actions. The strings of numbers, words, or pictures that subjects were asked to remember in the laboratory were surrogates for the sequences of specific stimuli (or percepts or responses or ideas or whatever) that they presumably experienced and remembered in the outside world. What has been developing in recent years is not merely a new skepticism about the representativeness of such experiments, but a new conception of what we should be trying to represent. The recent revival of interest in autobiographical memory is perhaps the *least* radical aspect of this shift; most theorists still think of personal memory as if it were just a set of remembered concrete experiences. (I present a different view of the matter in section II.) It is now generally agreed that we remember many other kinds of things as well: Even a cursory list would have to include general knowledge, skills, the grammar of stories, scripted behavior, and material learned in school. Borrowing a term from Reiff and Scheerer (1959), I shall call them all *memoria*–things that we remember.[2]

The "new memoria" of my title are not new to human memory, of course, just to psychology. Psychologists have occasionally tried to study them before–Bartlett and Freud are obvious examples–but their efforts only scratched the surface of the wide field that is now taking shape. The real cultivation of that field did not begin until the 1970s. Its first significant manifestation, I think, was Endel Tulving's (1972) contrast between episodic and semantic memory. "Episodic memory," for Tulving, was what we had been studying all along: memory for specific and personally experienced events, especially including stimulus presentations in standard experiments. "Semantic memory," however, was something relatively new. The term had originally been introduced by Quillian (1968) to refer to stored knowledge about word meanings, as that knowledge might be organized for a language-using computer. Tulving broadened it to include every kind of stable, nonpersonal fact that people can know–that the formula for salt is NaCl, for example, or that summers are hot in Katmandu.

Most cognitive psychologists, including Tulving (1985), think of semantic memory as an information-processing system (i.e., as something in the head). Many specific models of this system have been proposed, mostly based on hypothetical networks of labeled associations. But the vitality of Tulving's concept does not derive from any of these theories, not even from his own. In my view, his major contribution was to introduce an entirely new subject matter into the psychology of memory (i.e., to recognize the existence of a vast new class of memoria). People do not just remember momentary experiences, it seems; they also remember what I shall call–for lack of a more impressive technical word–*facts*.

It was also in the 1970s that Bartlett's old term "schema" began to enjoy a new popularity, which continues even today. The first modern schema theorists (Mandler & Johnson, 1977; Rumelhart, 1975) were concerned with memory for stories, just as Bartlett (1932) had been. Their research suggested that people have mental representations of the general characteristics of stories and that these representations develop with age and experience. Since then, various models of story schemata and their development have been proposed. Once again, I believe that the most significant contribution of this work is not the formulation of any particular schema model; rather, it is the recognition of a new class of memoria. Story structure, which exists objectively in every culture and transcends the details of any particular story or myth, is apparently something that people remember. What is more, remembering this rather abstract entity serves an important function: It helps one to recall specific and particular stories as they are encountered.

Stories were only the beginning: Analogous schema concepts were soon applied in many other domains. It has been suggested that there are schemata for scenes (Mandler & Parker, 1976), for the self (Markus, 1977), for goal-directed events (Lichtenstein & Brewer, 1980), for other people (Fiske & Linville, 1980), for rooms (Brewer & Treyens, 1981), and so forth. The fate of these theories is still in doubt; it is not obvious that postulating, say, "room schemata" adds much to the observation that one can remember rooms. What is *not* in doubt is that we do remember such things. Although rooms and people and such are not temporally specific stimuli – they exist over extended periods of time and have enduring properties – they must be included on any list of currently accepted memoria.

Scripts (Schank & Abelson, 1975) came along at about the same time as schemata. Everyone's cultural experience includes certain familiar sequences of events. In America, visiting a restaurant or going to the doctor are good examples. In the mid-1970s, psychologists began to explore (and students of artificial intelligence began to model) people's knowledge of these sequences, defining a class of mental representations they called "scripts." Their initial accounts of those scripts ("first you sit down at a table, then you consult the menu, then you give your order to the waiter or waitress . . .") had an almost ethnographic flavor: Each was a description of the sequence of actions that usually takes place in a certain situation. Because such structures eventually seemed too linear and rigid to explain the characteristic flexibility of human memory, Schank (1982) has recently proposed a revised theory that postulates more dynamic and hierarchical forms of mental representation: His concepts include generalized scenes, memory organization packets (MOPs), and thematic organization points (TOPs). Whatever the ultimate fate of these theories, no one doubts that routines, both personal and cultural, are among the things we remember.

In the case of scripts, there has been a further development. A series of important studies by Katherine Nelson and her associates has shown that young children are quite good at remembering such routines – as good as or better than they are at remembering the individual episodes of which each routine is apparently composed. (For reviews, see Nelson, 1986, and chapter 9 in this volume.) In most current discussions, this finding is described in terms of mental representations: The child is assumed to transform one type of representation into another (i.e., to convert stored memories of several episodes into a "script" that includes the properties they have in common). I would prefer to describe the same phenomenon in a more ecological way. What the research shows, I think, is that memories of young children are more closely attuned to one class of objectively existing memoria (repeated sequences) than to another (unique episodes).

This way of describing scripts, like my earlier account of story grammars as objectively existing memoria, may seem somewhat perverse. Although we are used to thinking of single episodes (or single story-tellings) as things that really happen in the world, we tend to assume that a *series* of related episodes can have only whatever unity is conferred on it by our mental representations. Although this assumption is very common, it has no basis in logic or necessity. From the ecological point of view, both the single concrete event and the sequence of such events are things that happen in the world, though on different time scales. Either of them can be selected as an object of memory or of thought.

An example from a different domain may help to clarify this notion. It seems likely that young children notice and learn reduplicated syllables ("ma-ma") more easily than they notice and learn the component syllables occurring alone. Although one might try to explain this difference by postulating two separate mental representations of "ma" together with some process that combines them, it seems more natural to assume that the repetitive stimulus structure is picked up in its own right. I am essentially suggesting that something similar occurs when the child notices a repeated routine.

In another important development, cognitive psychology has finally begun to consider a class of memoria that we should have been studying all along: the information that is acquired in school and college courses. Some years ago (Neisser, 1978) I complained vigorously about the absence of significant research on this problem. How can we be so indifferent about whether or not our students remember what we teach them? It turned out, however, that not everyone was as indifferent as I had supposed. Harry Bahrick's (1984) study of memory for Spanish (as learned in school and college courses) shed a good deal of light on this problem, and the new research he has conducted together with Elizabeth Phelps (see chapter 7) illuminates it further.

Bahrick's careful and statistically sophisticated study of Spanish produced a major discovery—one of the most important yet made in the ecological study of memory. Some of the material that people learn in classroom settings is essentially immune to forgetting. Retest scores do decline for the first few years after one stops studying Spanish, but after that they level off; nothing more is forgotten for two or three decades. In his published article, Bahrick described this finding in terms of *responses:* After enough practice, some responses get into a state he called "perma-store." I would put it differently (Neisser, 1984): Students of Spanish do not merely learn responses; they acquire knowledge. That knowledge is structured, and aspects of the structure that are sufficiently unique (for a given subject) will suffer little interference in subsequent years.

Where is that structure located? At the time of Bahrick's test, it was obviously in the heads of the subjects, who used it to generate their answers to the test questions. At that point it was presumably the residue of much richer representations that the subjects had first developed in their courses—representations that roughly mirrored the *objective* structure of Spanish and its relation to English. A major goal of their original study of Spanish had been the discovery of that structure, which, in my view, comprises the essential memoria in Bahrick's experiments.

Another example of the new memoria (and one that still has not been adequately studied) is the spatial layout of the personally known environment. Spatial knowledge is often described as if it depended on mental representations called "cognitive maps," but this usage may take too much for granted. For one thing, it tends to bypass the more difficult questions; any aspect of spatial memory can be explained by postulating a corresponding property of the map. It also suggests that a single, coherent representation underlies all forms of spatial orientation—something that is unlikely to be the case (Lorenz & Neisser, 1986). An ecological analysis would begin, instead, by asking what aspects of environmental structure can be remembered and how those aspects are specified to perceivers. Comparative and neurological studies also have something to contribute to the problem of spatial memory; I consider them further in section III.

Although my survey of the new memoria has turned up a considerable range of examples, those considered up to this point have two characteristics in common. First, all of them are based on repeated rather than unique experiences. People discover story grammars by hearing many different stories, acquire the restaurant script by going to many different restaurants (or one restaurant many times), learn Spanish by attending many classes and doing lots of homework, come to know their environment by traveling through it on many occasions. What is remembered in these cases is an underlying structure that has become manifest on several different specific occasions. Second, those occasions themselves may not be recalled at all. Generic memories can persist even when the individual episodes that gave rise to them have been entirely forgotten. (For a very similar effect obtainable under laboratory conditions, see Watkins & Kerkar, 1985.)

These two characteristics of generic memories are not unrelated. Most everyday forgetting surely results from interference among similar items—the greater the similarity, the more the interference. When a number of experiences are very much alike, their common structure tends to become salient even as their individual characteristics are forgotten. Marigold Linton has called this the "transformation from episodic to semantic memory" (1982, p. 79). The effect of the interference is often proactive: We may forget the most recent of a set of highly similar episodes, even when it is very recent indeed. One of my favorite examples occurs in the game of bridge, where the responsibility for dealing rotates clockwise each time a new hand of cards is dealt. Surprisingly, it often happens that none of the four players (not even the dealer!) can recall who dealt the cards of the present hand only a few moments ago. Each player knows the script for dealing extremely well, but the most recent instantiation of that script can vanish within minutes.

Such failures of episodic memory may be less complete than they seem. As Larry Jacoby has shown (see chapter 6), a recent experience may continue to affect us even when we have forgotten its autobiographical component. This is dramatically true of amnesics, who can acquire a completely new skill without any recollection of ever having practiced it. In Jacoby's ingenious experiments, it is also true of more ordinary people. They may fail to recognize that a given word was among those recently shown to them on a memory list, for example, and yet exhibit several different mnemonic consequences of that very exposure. I interpret these experiments to mean that the personal aspect of an experience – the fact that you yourself saw a given word on a given occasion – is separable from other memoria that were noted at the same time and can have an independent fate in memory. This, too, is an important discovery. But it would be a mistake to assume that personal memory is made up only of specific and particular experiences; I believe that it includes larger and more complex structures as well. What happens when the notion of memory for temporally extended structures is extended to the autobiographical case?

II. Autobiographical memory

Autobiographical memory is, by definition, the form of memory in which the events of one's own life comprise the significant memoria. But what are "the events of one's own life"? Although it is difficult to give a clear definition of "event," it is easy to give examples: The event closest at hand can serve as well as any other. Right now, everyone in this room[3] is experiencing the 1985 Emory Cognition Project Conference, and we all expect to remember it. Conferences certainly belong among the memoria that can be included in autobiographical memory.

A conference is an event, and it is not surprising that we remember events – that is what episodic memory is all about. But this one is an event of substantial duration, beginning as it did on Thursday evening and continuing through Saturday. A "memory" of an event lasting for 2.5

days may have significant theoretical implications. Indeed, the importance of temporally extended memoria is beginning to be widely recognized. Linton (1986) has already given them a special name: "extendures." It seems to me that memory for such long-lasting events cannot plausibly be reconciled with most of the standard accounts of memory. The classical theories (associationism, behaviorism, Gestalt psychology) dealt only with very much smaller units (sensations, ideas, responses, S–R bonds, percepts), and could have explained memory of an entire conference only as a concatenation of such elements. Bartlett's schema theory did allow for remembering a whole story at a time, but the stories he used were only about a page long; I do not know what he would have thought about a conference.

Of the more recently developed concepts mentioned in section I, only two seem to be applicable here. One is the original notion of *script:* Perhaps people remember a conference by assimilating it, piece by piece and slot by slot, to a mental representation that they already have. This seems unlikely to me. The conference as we experience it is surely richer than any general representation we could have had ready in advance. The other is the more elaborate set of knowledge packets, thematic points, scenes, and scripts postulated by Schank in *Dynamic Memory* (1982). I do not yet understand Schank's theory very well and shall not attempt to evaluate it here. Instead, I shall try to develop a different and more ecological approach to the same issues.

The term "episodic" suggests relatively brief and isolated events, but we recall enduring and recurrent experiences as well. Indeed, such experiences may be among the most salient things in our memories. The reports elicited in Barsalou's "What did you do last summer?" study (see chapter 8) strongly support this view. Only 21% of the subjects' responses described brief and specific events; they were much more likely to summarize recurrent patterns (32%) or to make general comments (31%). There was also a substantial number (9%) of reports of extended events like being on a diet or taking a trip. When the subjects in another instructional group were explicitly asked to confine their responses to brief concrete events, they experienced great difficulty in doing so. The request for specificity "appeared to disturb subjects' normal mode of recalling their past" (p. 201). Individual episodes have no privileged status in memory; it is at least as natural to remember extended situations or typical patterns. Why not? The latter are often far more important in the long run.

What is the relation between events at different levels of analysis? J. J. Gibson put it this way:

Environmental sequences commonly have cycles embedded in larger cycles, that is, *nested* events. Consider the events in speech or music or pantomime or ballet (or in the sexual courting behavior of animals, for that matter). There are some different events and some similar events in the sequence. There will be shorter events that make up longer events and these making up still longer events. All are units of a sort, in the way that syllables, words, phrases, sentences and discourses are units. Units are nested within other units. And the remarkable fact is that both the superordinate and the subordinate events can be perceived. (J. J. Gibson, in Reed & Jones, 1982, p. 208)

An equally remarkable fact, I think, is that both superordinate and subordinate events can be remembered.

This conference is a present event, taking place right here and now. But it is not the *only* present event; I am giving this talk here and now too. To use Gibson's term, the talk is nested in the conference. Nesting can occur at many levels. Right now, I am uttering a sentence that began with the words "right now" and, as it happens, will end with the very same pair of words; I am completing it right now. That sentence was nested in my talk as well as in the conference, and three separate occurrences of "right now" were themselves nested in the sentence.

The events I have been considering—words, sentences, talks, conferences—are (or were) all real. They are not figments of my imagination, or yours; they are not hypothetical constructs or intervening variables; they are not codes or mental representations or schemata or scripts. In describing them, I am referring to something that actually happened. Of course, my description is not the only one possible; different people may see the same situation quite differently. A visitor from some exotic culture who knew nothing of conferences—if there still are any such cultures—would describe what is happening here in ways that might surprise us. That possibility does not affect the reality status of the events as I have chosen to describe them.

As I have suggested elsewhere (Neisser, 1987a), we perceive and remember events at many levels of analysis. We remember conferences, talks, and sentences; lasting personal relationships, special evenings, and pregnant moments; graduate school years, particular seminars, memorable remarks. The organization of autobiographical memory evidently parallels the hierarchical organization of the remembered events themselves. Mental representations (they used to be called "memory traces") are nested in one another just as events are: There are representations of conferences as well as of talks and sentences, and the latter are nested inside the former. Representations of the more comprehensive events are sometimes assembled after the fact by linking elements together (Schank, 1982, offers one possible account of those links), but they may also result from perceiving higher-order events directly.

We are usually aware of the nested structure of events as they occur, although our awareness is rarely explicit. Listening to my argument at this moment, you are probably not thinking about the higher-order units in which it is nested – about my talk as a whole, the conference as a whole, or your visit to Atlanta as a whole. But you do know that the argument is part of *something* and that you could turn your attention to its setting if you wanted to. It seems to me that we experience the nesting of events somewhat in the way that we experience the analogous nesting of places. As you sit in this room, you are probably not explicitly aware of its location – that it is in this odd-shaped building[4] on the Emory campus in Atlanta – but you know that it is *somewhere,* in some nested set of places where you arrived only recently and which you confidently expect to leave again. In the same way, you know that what is happening right now is set in a whole nest of more inclusive events that began some time ago, and can be expected to end sooner or later. (I pursue the analogy between events and places further in section III.)

The structure of autobiographical memory, then, is basically hierarchical. It is not a strict hierarchy in the mathematical sense, but it is rich enough in overlapping and nested relations to make that term appropriate. We use our memories in ways that reflect this hierarchical organization. Directed recall usually moves either downward from context or upward from particulars. In the downward mode, you may begin by remembering "what happened at the memory conference" or "what Neisser said in his talk" and only then arrive at particular details of this argument. In the upward mode, you might start with a detail ("Where did I hear that odd argument about nesting in memory?") and (hopefully) get back to me and to the conference. There are also links between successive events, which may be said to go "horizontally" rather than upward or downward, but the ability to remember such a sequence often depends on recalling the larger context in which both events took place.

The links in the hierarchical structure of autobiographical memory do not last forever. All levels of memory are subject to forgetting; both events and the relations between them can be lost. Lower levels of the hierarchy seem to be more vulnerable than higher ones: You will forget most of the individual incidents that took place at this conference long before you have forgotten the conference itself. As the Gestalt psychologists might have said, the whole is more memorable than its parts. The speed with which we forget nested details probably stems from the similarities that inevitably appear when there are many structures at the same level of analysis; larger structures tend to be unique.

However it arises, loss of detail in memory often puts us in an odd situation. We may remember an overall event, perhaps well enough to infer some of its more specific characteristics, but we do not remember those characteristics themselves. That is why memory is so vulnerable to unintended distortion and why it often seems "true" even when it is false.

We can never do full justice to what Spence (1982) has called *historical truth,* because what really happened was too rich for anyone's memory to preserve. But it is relatively easy to remember events in a way that is accurate with respect to some overall characteristic of the situation; such a recollection always has some degree of validity even if it suggests nested details that are by no means accurate themselves. In the end, the episode-as-remembered may have only the kind of validity that Spence called "narrative truth": It will be truthful in some respects and yet very far from historically accurate. (In chapter 12, Spence himself offers a rather different interpretation of the sense in which an altered autobiographical memory may still be "true.")

A recent study by Freeman, Romney, and Freeman (1986) provides a useful illustration of these points. The subjects of the study were the people who attended an ongoing colloquium series at the University of California in Irvine. In the spring of 1985, Freeman et al. unobtrusively recorded the names of everyone who attended nine consecutive colloquia. The last of these meetings was designated as the "target session"; 5 days later, the 17 people who had been there on that day were asked to recall the names (or give descriptions) of everyone else who had been there too. There were many errors, both of omission and commission. Of 272 recall opportunities (each of the 17 subjects could have recalled the 16 others), 115 were missed. There were also 26 false reports: People who had not attended the target session were nevertheless "remembered." Most of the false reports (22 of them, or an average of 2.8 per subject) were generated by eight subjects who belonged to an independently defined "in-group" – they all had offices on the same floor of the same building. These false reports were by no means random; most of them were names of people who had attended more than half of the *other* colloquia in the series but happened to miss the last one. In short, the reports of the in-group subjects were a better fit to the overall structure of the colloquium series than to the particular meeting they had been asked to remember. The nine "out-group" subjects, in contrast, made only 4 false reports altogether (for a mean of 0.4); they were indeed remembering the target meeting. But they remembered *less* about that meeting than the (false-report-prone) in-groupers, forgetting an average of 8.1 people (i.e., about half of those who had been present), whereas the in-group averaged only 4.7 such omissions apiece.

For the in-group, each meeting was perceived as part of the colloquium series as a whole. That large-scale event, being relatively unique, was very well remembered. What the subjects remembered about the series, however, was its overall structure (e.g., who was usually present); they were less likely to recall details of the individual meetings of which the series was composed. Those details themselves had often been forgotten; nevertheless, they could be reconstructed in light of the general characteristics of the series as a whole. Such reconstructions are often accurate (hence these subjects made relatively few omissions), but they may also be wrong (hence they made occasional errors of commission). Because the out-group subjects were not so likely to have seen the final meeting as part of a more extended event, these processes played a much smaller role in their recollection of it.

Freeman et al. did not ask their subjects for confidence ratings, but it seems likely that some would have expressed considerable confidence in their own erroneous responses. Data on eyewitness testimony, as reviewed by Loftus (1979), suggest that people often are surprisingly (and inappropriately) confident about the accuracy of their answers to memory questions. This effect has also appeared in two of my own studies. An analysis of John Dean's Watergate testimony, for example (Neisser, 1981), showed that Dean had far too much confidence in his recollections of detailed conversations with President Nixon. A similar result has also begun to appear in a new study of memory for seminar discussions, presently being conducted by Ira Hyman and myself.

Actually, the surprising faith that such subjects have in their own memories is not entirely misplaced. There is even a sense in which they are quite correct, though it is not the sense that they themselves intend. They are wrong about what happened on some specific occasion, but they are not wrong about the larger event in which that occasion was nested, nor about the meaning of that larger event, as they originally understood it. Freeman et al.'s in-group subjects were quite right about who had attended the colloquium series as a whole; they were just wrong about the final meeting. John Dean was quite right about what was basically going on in the White House; he was just wrong about who said what to whom in particular conversations. These subjects believed themselves to be recalling particular episodes, but their recollections were more accurate with respect to other, more superordinate memoria. Because such recollections do not fit comfortably on either side of Tulving's (1972) distinction between episodic and semantic memory (they seem to be episodes, but really represent something else), I have occasionally described them as "repisodic" memories (Neisser, 1981).

One final aspect of memory for extended events is worth considering. By definition, the memory of an entire conference or a series of meetings preserves information about their overall characteristics, not about any specific visualizable moment. Surprisingly, however, such memories are often accompanied by visual images. A subject in Barsalou's what-did-you-do-last-summer study, for example (see chapter 8), may well have had a specific image of a particular *piazza* in mind as he answered "I took a trip to Italy." Similarly, subjects in the Freeman et al. study may have visualized some particular colleague's face (wearing some typical expression!) at the very moment when they were erroneously identifying that colleague as having attended the target meeting. Generic memories often are accompanied by specific images. Indeed, these imagery experiences may account for the widely held assumption that autobiographical memory is essentially a collection of specific moments from the past. If I am right, introspection has misled us on this point.

In my view, these accompanying mental images do not function primarily as carriers of information. Images can certainly serve informational purposes in other contexts – for example, in "mental rotation" experiments – but that is not their role when they accompany the recall of generic memories. Because such an image is produced internally as a result of the activation of the generic memory itself, it tends to "illustrate" that memory (i.e., to present some subjectively important aspect of the generic event in visual form). A mental image generated in this way need not be an accurate representation of any particular experienced moment; sometimes a never-experienced or even an impossible view of some event illustrates a general recollection particularly well. This may explain the prevalence of so-called observer memories, first discussed by Freud (1899/1950) and more recently studied by Georgia Nigro and myself (Nigro & Neisser, 1983). A memory image that "visibly" includes the experiencing subject (i.e., one in which the subject "sees" himself/herself much as an outside observer would) may illustrate the most salient aspect of the event in question, namely, that the subject was at the center of it! This hypothesis would explain why these so-called observer memories are very often accompanied by explanations that focus on the self (Rozett, 1986).

III. Events and places: A conjecture

Autobiographical memory is a remarkable achievement of the human species. Events in the real world can be described in infinitely many ways. How did we happen to hit on the nested hierarchies that serve us so well? I would like to suggest a hypothesis on this point – one that goes beyond the ecological description of memoria to implicate a specific cognitive mechanism. My conjecture starts with the observation that events are not the only nested entities in our experience. The concept of nesting applies even more naturally to the places in our environment.

A *place* is a location in the environment as contrasted with a point in space. . . . Whereas a point must be located with reference to a coordinate system, a place can be located by its inclusion in a larger place (for example, the fireplace in the cabin by the bend of the river in the Great Plains). (Gibson, 1979, p. 34)

Recent years have witnessed a surge of interest in how animals and people find their way around. The ability to get from one place to another, to take shortcuts as appropriate, and to recognize familiar places on arrival is usually called "spatial orientation" (Ellen & Thinus-Blanc, 1987). In many mammals, spatial orientation is mediated by mechanisms in the hippocampal system of the midbrain (O'Keefe & Nadel, 1978). There are neurons in the rat's hippocampus that fire whenever the rat reaches a certain place in a familiar maze, regardless of how it got there or of the specific visual cues available on a given occasion (Olton, 1987). Destruction of the hippocampus renders the animal incapable of normal orientation: It can still learn responses, but it can no longer find its way effectively. The hippocampus is apparently the neural substrate of a well-defined cognitive module – a system that works in a specialized way to deal with its own special domain.

The idea that there are "cognitive modules" – hard-wired systems with their own neural substrates, innately specific to particular domains – has recently become rather popular (Fodor, 1983; Gardner, 1983). Indeed, it is now difficult to think why it was resisted so long; the simple fact that the nervous system evolved through natural selection makes modular organization virtually inevitable (Simon, 1962). There is no incompatibility between the modular hypothesis and the ecological approach to cognitive psychology. To be sure, ecological theorists have not been much concerned with the organization of the nervous system. They believe that one must understand the information that is objectively available before one can hope to understand the mechanisms that pick it up. Nevertheless, there is no reason to doubt that specific neural mechanisms have developed during evolution to take advantage of specific informational domains.

Despite the increasing acceptance of the modularity hypothesis itself, there is still no general agreement on what specific modules actually exist. For reasons that I have elaborated elsewhere, however (Neisser, 1987b), the mammalian spatial-orientation system is an excellent candidate for modular status. The human version of that system, then, would be responsible for our general ability to know where we are and get where we want to go (i.e., for our so-called cognitive maps) (O'Keefe & Nadel, 1978; Tolman, 1948). As noted earlier, however, the term "cognitive map" too easily suggests that people find their way around by examining internal images; moreover, it too confidently assumes that a single unified representation underlies all aspects of spatial behavior. Because I doubt both of these propositions, I prefer to avoid "cognitive map" and just talk about spatial knowledge.

Spatial knowledge depends in part on memory. People and other animals *remember* places where they have been, as well as the spatial relationships among those places. This does not mean, however, that such information is stored in some general memory system from which it is retrieved as necessary. It seems more likely to me that the spatial module preserves the needed information itself, on its own terms and in its own format. In other words, it is a memory system. Chimpanzees can recall the locations of 16 or more pieces of food that they have just watched the experimenter hide (Menzel, 1987); the common marsh tit can remember a hundred different places where it has cached bits of food (Sherry, 1987); and we all know our way around in lots of different territories.

Spatial memory is so dependable that it can even be used as a deliberate mnemonic for the recall of nonspatial material. In the well-known *method of loci*, for example, one can remember an otherwise unconnected set of items by pretending that each of them has been put at a particular place in a familiar region of the environment. To recall the items, one need only imagine that one is traveling through that region again. The effectiveness of the method of loci is sometimes attributed to the use of visual imagery, but this is misleading; even congenitally blind persons can employ it successfully (Jonides, Kahn, & Rozin, 1975). The method of loci apparently is not based in the visual system, but in the spatial module.

The spatial cognitive system, then, has several intriguing characteristics. First, it operates on a domain that has a clearly nested structure. Everyone present at this conference got here by first coming to Atlanta, then getting to Emory, then finding this building, and finally locating this room. All of us understand this hierarchy in principle, even if we cannot successfully retrace the path on which we came. Second, the system stores information about the spatial domain in a way that captures that hierarchical structure very effectively. Common experience suggests (there have been very few relevant systematic studies) that one can remember spatial information in considerable detail and for long periods of time. Third, the system enables us to "mentally revisit" places that we have once encountered without actually returning to them. Indeed, it even allows us to rearrange the furniture of those places in our imaginations.

All these features of the spatial module are equally characteristic of autobiographical memory. Our memories of our own past are also organized in terms of nested units (at least if the argument of section II is valid); they also preserve information for very long periods and with great richness of detail. Autobiographical memory enables us to "revisit" previously experienced events just as the spatial module enables us to "revisit" previously visited places, and perhaps even to rearrange some of their details. My conjecture, then, is that the spatial module may be the principal vehicle of personal memory. A system that originally evolved to deal only with movement through space now helps us to keep track of "movement through time" as well. If this is true, it would be a good example of what Rozin (1976) has described as a fundamental process in the evolution of intelligence: the organism's increased ability to use old and specialized cognitive subsystems for new adaptive purposes.

The plausibility of this conjecture is somewhat enhanced, I think, by neuropsychological considerations. Damage to the hippocampus—as in the case of H.M., or in Korsakov amnesia—is known to impair personal memory as well as spatial orientation. There is also reason to believe that the human hippocampus does not fully mature until a year or two after birth (Nadel & Zola-Morgan, 1984). If this is true, it may be a factor in infantile amnesia (i.e., in our inability to remember our earliest early experiences later on). Although this is surely not the only cause of infantile amnesia—Nelson's arguments (see chapter 9) are persuasive on this point—it may well be a factor.

Even more persuasive, for me, are certain theoretical considerations. If autobiographical memory depends on a separate and specialized system, we can understand how it might become dissociated from other forms of memory—as it apparently is in Jacoby's experiments and in certain cases of amnesia. If it depends on a system that is naturally tuned to hierarchically organized structure in the stimulus information, we can understand why scripted sequences and extended events often take precedence over individual episodes in memory. Finally, if personal memory depends on a system that is already known to have a large capacity for hierarchically organized information, we can understand how it is possible to remember so much about our own lives for such long periods of time.

Much remains to be explained. The spatial module itself is complex, and it is difficult to know what aspects of its operation should be most directly reflected in autobiographical memory. We do not even know what aspects are most directly served by the mechanisms in the hippocampus: memory for landmarks? Memory for routes? Directional orientation? I mention these three "aspects" because they emerged as separate factors in our preliminary study of individual differences (Lorenz & Neisser, 1986). But the results of that study also produced some tentative evidence *against* the present conjecture: There were no correlations between our measure of personal memory and any of the spatial dimensions! Perhaps we did not use the right memory measure (subjects were asked specific questions about particular past occasions, e.g., "your first day of school"), or perhaps the conjecture is simply wrong. Further research probably will tell, perhaps all too soon.

It is no accident that this ecologically slanted review of the state of the art has ended with a testable hypothesis. The study of memory is moving fast – faster than I can ever remember. By enlarging the accepted scope of nonautobiographical memory – so that it now includes facts, story grammars, scripts, skills, places, and all sorts of other extended entities – we have also enlarged the range of the theoretical possibilities that we can see for autobiographical memory itself. Regardless of the fate of my particular suggestions here, that wider scope will make many new theories and hypotheses possible in years to come. Some of them are bound to be right.

NOTES

1 The original conference talk was entitled "Places and Events: Hierarchical Organization in the Real World and in Memory"; the present chapter title seems more appropriate, as well as less cumbersome. I am happy to acknowledge its debt to John Flavell's (1971) well-known paper.
2 My definition of "memoria" is different from that of Reiff and Scheerer (1959). Their usage was roughly equivalent to Tulving's (1972) later formulation of semantic memory; they contrasted memoria with "remembrances," or episodic memory. I am not using "memoria" to refer to any kind of memory at all, but rather to the real entities that memories (of every kind) represent. The word "memoranda" might have been more appropriate (by analogy with Tolman's terms "manipulanda" and "discriminanda"), but unfortunately it already has another well-established meaning in English.
3 This section of the chapter retains certain verb tenses and phrases verbatim from the original conference talk. Because there was no obvious way to transpose these phrases from the context of listening to that of reading, I must ask my readers to interpret them as if they were hearing the talk itself. For an analogous analysis of the act of writing a chapter, see Neisser (1987a).
4 The site of the 1985 conference was the same building used in Lorenz and Neisser's (1986) study.

REFERENCES

Bahrick, H. P. (1984). Semantic memory content in permastore: Fifty years of memory for Spanish learned in school. *Journal of Experimental Psychology: General, 113,* 1–29.

Bartlett, F. (1932). *Remembering.* Cambridge University Press.

Brewer, W. F., & Treyens, J. C. (1981). Role of schemata in memory for places. *Cognitive Psychology, 13,* 207–230.

Ellen, P., & Thinus-Blanc, C. (Eds.). (1987). *Cognitive processes and spatial orientation in animal and man.* Dordrecht: Martinus Nijhoff.

Fiske, S. T., & Linville, P. W. (1980). What does the schema concept buy us? *Personality and Social Psychology Bulletin, 6,* 543–557.

Flavell, J. H. (1971). First discussant's comments: What is memory development the development of? *Human Development, 14,* 272–278.

Fodor, J. (1983). *The modularity of mind.* Cambridge, MA: M.I.T. Press.

Freeman, L. C., Romney, A. K., & Freeman, S. C. (1986). *Cognitive structure and informant accuracy.* Unpublished manuscript, University of California, Irvine.

Freud, S. (1950). Screen memories. In *Collected Papers of Sigmund Freud* (Vol. 5). London: Hogarth Press. (Original work published 1899)

Gardner, H. (1983). *Frames of mind: The theory of multiple intelligences.* New York: Basic Books.

Gibson, J. J. (1979). *The senses considered as perceptual systems.* Boston: Houghton Mifflin.

  (1982). The problem of event perception. In E. Reed & R. Jones (Eds.), *Reasons for realism: Selected essays of James J. Gibson* (pp. 203–216). Hillsdale, NJ: Erlbaum.

Jonides, J., Kahn, R., & Rozin, P. (1975). Imagery instructions improve memory in blind subjects. *Bulletin of the Psychonomic Society, 5,* 424–426.

Lichtenstein, E. H., & Brewer, W. F. (1980). Memory for goal-directed events. *Cognitive Psychology, 12,* 412–445.

Linton, M. (1982). Transformations of memory in everyday life. In U. Neisser (Ed.), *Memory observed: Remembering in natural contexts* (pp. 77–91). New York: Freeman.

  (1986). Ways of searching and the contents of memory. In D. C. Rubin (Ed.), *Autobiographical memory* (pp. 50–67). Cambridge University Press.

Loftus, E. F. (1979). *Eyewitness testimony.* Cambridge, MA: Harvard University Press.

Lorenz, C. A., & Neisser, U. (1986). *Ecological and psychometric dimensions of spatial ability* (Emory Cognition Project Report 10). Atlanta: Emory University Psychology Department.

Mandler, J. M., & Johnson, N. S. (1977). Remembrance of things parsed: Story structure and recall. *Cognitive Psychology, 9,* 111–151.

Mandler, J. M., & Parker, R. E. (1976). Memory for descriptive and spatial information in complex pictures. *Journal of Experimental Psychology: Human Learning and Memory, 2,* 38–48.

Markus, H. (1977). Self-schemata and processing information about the self. *Journal of Personality and Social Psychology, 35,* 63.

Menzel, E. (1987). Behavior as a locationist views it. In P. Ellen & C. Thinus-Blanc (Eds.), *Cognitive processes and spatial orientation in animal and man.* Dordrecht: Martinus Nijhoff.

Nadel, L., & Zola-Morgan, S. (1984). Infantile amnesia: A neurobiological perspective. In M. Moscovitch (Ed.), *Infant memory.* New York: Plenum.

Neisser, U. (1978). Memory: What are the important questions? In M. M. Gruneberg, P. E. Morris, & R. N. Sykes (Eds.), *Practical aspects of memory* (pp. 3–24). New York: Academic Press.

  (1981). John Dean's memory: A case study. *Cognition, 9,* 1–22.

  (1984). Interpreting Harry Bahrick's discovery: What confers immunity against forgetting? *Journal of Experimental Psychology: General, 113,* 32–35.

  (1987a). Nested structure in autobiographical memory. In D. Rubin (Ed.), *Autobiographical memory* (pp. 71–81). Cambridge University Press.

  (1987b). A sense of where you are: Functions of the spatial module. In P. Ellen & C. Thinus-Blanc (Eds.), *Cognitive processes and spatial orientation in animal and man, Vol. 2, Neurophysiology and developmental aspects* (pp. 293–310). Dordrecht: Martinus Nijhoff.

Nelson, K. (1986). *Event knowledge: Structure and function in development.* Hillsdale, NJ: Erlbaum.

Nigro, G. N., & Neisser, U. (1983). Point of view in personal memories. *Cognitive Psychology, 15,* 467–482.

O'Keefe, J., & Nadel, L. (1978). *The hippocampus as a cognitive map.* Oxford University Press.

Olton, D. S. (1987). Temporally constant and temporally changing spatial memory: Single unit correlates in the hippocampus. In P. Ellen & C. Thinus-Blanc (Eds.), *Cognitive processes and spatial orientation in animal and man, Vol. 2, Neurophysiology and development aspects* (pp. 16–27). Dordrecht: Martinus Nijhoff.

Quillian, M. R. (1968). Semantic memory. In M. Minsky (Ed.), *Semantic information processing* (pp. 227–270). Cambridge, MA: M.I.T. Press.

Reed, E., & Jones, R. (1982). *Reasons for realism: Selected essays of James J. Gibson.* Hillsdale, NJ: Erlbaum.

Reiff, R., & Scheerer, M. (1959). *Memory and hypnotic age regression.* New York: International Universities Press.

Rozett, A. (1986). *Determinants of point of view in personal memory.* Unpublished B.A. thesis, Emory University.

Rozin, P. (1976). The evolution of intelligence and access to the cognitive unconscious. In *Progress in psychobiology and physiological psychology* (Vol. 6). New York: Academic Press.

Rumelhart, D. E. (1975). Notes on a schema for stories. In D. G. Bobrow & A. M. Collins (Eds.), *Representation and understanding: Studies in cognitive science.* New York: Academic Press.

Schank, R. C. (1982). *Dynamic memory: A theory of reminding and learning in computers and people.* Cambridge University Press.

Schank, R. C., & Abelson, R. (1975). *Scripts, plans, goals, and understanding.* Hillsdale, NJ: Erlbaum.

Sherry, D. F. (1987). The function and organization of memory in food-storing birds. In P. Ellen & C. Thinus-Blanc (Eds.), *Cognitive processes and spatial orientation in animal and man.* Dordrecht: Martinus Nijhoff.

Simon, H. A. (1962). The architecture of complexity. *Proceedings of the American Philosophical Society, 106,* 467–482.

Spence, D. P. (1982). *Narrative truth and historical truth.* New York: Norton.

Tolman, E. C. (1948). Cognitive maps in rats and men. *Psychological Review, 55,* 189–208.

Tulving, E. (1972). Episodic and semantic memory. In E. Tulving & W. Donaldson (Eds.), *Organization of memory* (pp. 381–403). New York: Academic Press.
    (1985). How many memory systems are there? *American Psychologist, 40,* 385–398.

Watkins, M. J., & Kerkar, S. P. (1985). Recall of a twice-presented item without recall of either presentation: Generic memory for events. *Journal of Memory and Language, 24,* 666–678.

15

Go for the skill

DAVID C. RUBIN

There are a few people who think and write so clearly that their work is almost always influential. They can shape a whole field. What they say has to be taken very seriously. Failure to do so can waste a lot of time either because valuable insights are lost or because less-than-valuable insights are followed. Professor Neisser has shown himself to be such a person.

There are some problems that have "garden-path" solutions that are so seductive that psychologists repeatedly take them. Professor Neisser has warned us about many of these, including the reappearance hypothesis and the fact that the physical onset and offset of stimuli are not the psychological onset and offset of stimuli (Neisser, 1967). I think nesting is such a garden path, partly because it contains a kernel of truth and partly because we have been misled by similar concepts in the past. In Gibsonian ecological terms, nesting is a garden path because it makes a structure out of a process.

In what follows, Gibson's use of the word *ecological* is taken specifically to include the following principle: Although we should always start by making a very good description of the environment before wondering how the animal interacts with the environment, we should not copy that description of the environment into the mind. If there is a ringing bell, we should not put an image or other structure to represent the ringing bell in the mind and then study that internal representation (Bransford, McCarrell, Franks, & Nitsch, 1977; Gibson, 1966, 1979; Kolers & Roediger, 1984; Kolers & Smythe, 1984; Kvale, 1977; Skinner, 1974; cf. Shepard, 1984). Although it is theoretically possible to develop a Gibsonian theory of memory that would satisfy this tenet of ecological psychology, Neisser has demonstrated in chapter 14 that such a theory probably cannot be achieved.

From a Gibsonian perspective, Professor Neisser is making a structure out of a process, and when he makes a structure out of a process, he uses a different metaphor, a metaphor that adds much that is not wanted or needed. Mental structures, like other structures, tend (a) to

374

Table 15.1. *Things to put in the mind*

Associations	Nets and nests
Augmented transition networks	Pictures, sometimes moving
Codes, both verbal and imagery	Propositions
Holograms and hierarchies	Schemas, scripts, and similarity spaces
Grammars, story and otherwise	Trees and traces
Maps, MOPs, and mental models	Wax tablets, often brittle

be spatial, (b) to be rigid, (c) to be slow to change, (d) to have boundaries that include and exclude smaller components, and (e) to have specific locations in a more general organization and sometimes even in the brain. None of these properties is necessary, but they nonetheless are part of the metaphor.

In order to state the objection more clearly, two metaphors, or approaches, or ways to look at the world, need to be contrasted. The first is the complex-structure metaphor of which nesting is one example. The second is the skill, or complex-process, metaphor. Anything that can be understood using one metaphor can be understood using the other. A Gibsonian approach, however, strongly favors the latter.

In the complex-structure metaphor, which is the dominant metaphor in cognitive psychology today (Roediger, 1980), structures are devised by the researcher to account for observed behavior, usually by having the structure that the animal perceives in the world copied into an analogous structure in the mind. In the case of nesting, the nesting of events in the world is copied into, and then later explained by, nesting in the mind.

In contrast, in the skill or complex-process metaphor, learning, memory, and perception are accounted for by the animal's developing or tuning or differentiating its abilities, methods, strategies, or expertise. Both metaphors use both structure and process, but they each minimize one and use complexities in the other to explain behavior. In fact, in the skill metaphor, structure is minimized as an explanatory principle to the extent that its existence often seems to be denied completely.

Consider nests and other structures that we might want to put into the mind. Table 15.1 lists some structures that come to my mind. They are all internal copies of external things or relations. Nesting is just one of these structures. I am going to attack nesting only because it is the structure that Professor Neisser chose, but I could take any other structure and make similar arguments. If we want to describe the environment, not what is in the mind, any one of the structures listed in Table 15.1 would be a good description for some levels of some things in the environment.

Each kind of structure has its own properties, and each has its own uses (Rumelhart & Norman, in press). I still have a soft spot for old-fashioned associations. In fact, in a recent and extremely nonecological paper, Michael Friendly and I made a minor perturbation on association theory's *m*, came up with a new variable, produced norms for it, and showed its effects on recall (Rubin & Friendly, 1986). Associations have certain properties. The one we exploited in our paper is that they are directional. That is, the strength of association between node *A* and node *B* need not equal the strength between node *B* and node *A*. Other structures, such as similarity spaces, are not directional, and the distance from node *A* to node *B* in a space must be the same as from node *B* to node *A*. Moreover, if there are three nodes in a similarity space, *A*, *B*, and *C*, the distance from *A* to *B* is always shorter than the distance from *A* to *C* plus the distance from *C* to *B*. This triangle inequality, however, need not hold for associations.

I used to be bothered by all of these structures. I was getting a headache fitting all of them into my finite skull. The prospect of fitting them into an even smaller bird brain was probably part of what kept studies of animal behavior closer to a process metaphor for so long; *learning* is a process, whereas *memory* is a structure, even though both terms have identical operational definitions. Professor Neisser minimized my discomfort, though probably not the bird's, by saying that the reason we have all these structures, and the reason psychologists invent new ones every time they study a new domain, is not because of a lack of elegance; it is merely that the world has many ways in which to be described and many aspects to be described. The trouble is that Gibson's ecological approach does not let us copy any of them into the mind.

Let us return to nests. I think nests are much too rigid, and I choose the word *rigid* because nests, like the modules Professor Neisser also uses, are objects. Consider why nests are too rigid. The evidence comes mostly from Neisser's writings, but is supplemented from other chapters in this book.

First, events can be multiply nested; so this conference is embedded in my sabbatical year, it is embedded in other conferences, it is embedded in trips to Atlanta (Neisser, 1986). All of this is true in the real world and in memory. Moreover, for memory, the same event will be easier to remember in some nestings than in others. Second, mental nests do not map into a physical time line as simply as perceptual nests map onto physical space. We have events such as conferences that are separated, but the trees that are seen at one time nested in a forest are all next to each other (Neisser, 1986). Third, sets of events may be fused together and become one event, as in repisodic memory (Neisser, 1981). Fourth, all nesting cannot be determined at the time of an event; some nesting has to wait until much later (Neisser, 1982). Fifth, nestings may have to be very flexible and change as categories do (Barsalou, 1983). Sixth, we may need separate nestings along many different and not always obvious dimensions, such as reported versus nonreported events (see chapter 13), and thoughts that are beeped versus actions that are beeped (see chapter 3).

The point of all this is that once we commit ourselves to a complex-memory structure, it is not easy to get from the world to that memory structure. Why is it harder to do in memory than in perception? It is because memory lets us escape the tyranny of the present and combine almost any aspects of experiences, including those that are not temporally or physically adjacent (Bartlett, 1932).

What can we do instead of using nesting or other rigid structures? We can use concepts like skill or tuning. That is what an ecological approach, according to Gibson, might do. It wants to change the structures, such as associations, hierarchies, nests, and spaces, into processes such as tuning or skill. Jacoby ended his talk with the thought that memory is not something we search, but something we use. Kolers, Skinner, Bartlett, Neisser (1967), and, most important for our purposes, Gibson tried to avoid copying the animal's environment into one of the structures in Table 15.1. Professor Neisser, to try to do ecological memory in the form that Gibson talks about, should try to avoid it too. It is theoretically possible.

To show the possibility, I need to demonstrate that the explanatory power of a structure can be traded for the explanatory power of a process. Figure 15.1 is a similarity space of animals that can be in the mind. It was formed from the lists of animals that 100 Duke University undergraduates gave in 60 sec. Animals listed near to each other by the undergraduates appear near to each other in Figure 15.1. The method used to form Figure 15.1 is identical with that describe in Rubin and Olson's (1980) study. If we have a complicated structure like Figure 15.1, we can simply put a drop of water on it and let it spread, and we have what is called *spreading activation.* If we put the drop on the node *tiger,* it will spread quickly to *lion* and *elephant* and more slowly to *rabbit.* Similarly, if *tiger* was listed, then the subject would tend to list *lion* and *elephant* near it, often with all three animals occurring together in a rapid burst or cluster of activity. Although spreading activation is one of the simplest (and, in the form portrayed here, one of the stupidest) of all possible processes that we could have, if we have the correct structure, it will describe lots of data. That is, we can have a very stupid process, if we have a very good structure.

Figure 15.2 shows an alternative. We need some paper, a pencil or pen, a real-world Atlanta rat (not a laboratory albino mouse), and a bucket. We write the nodes on pieces of paper, crumple them up into

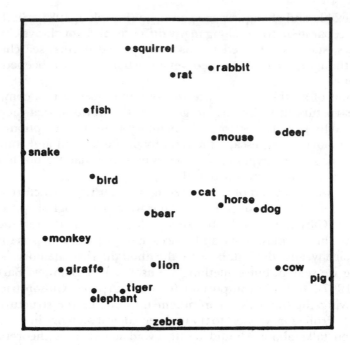

Figure 15.1. A similarity space for the domain of animals.

balls, and throw them into the bucket in a random order. Next we teach the rat, or tune the rat, or develop the rat's skill, to find the right nodes. Teaching and tuning and developing a skill are admittedly currently less specific hypotheses than the structure in Figure 15.1, but unfortunately such process metaphors usually are. In any case, we have a very complicated process and a very stupid structure. The structure is so stupid that we need not talk about it at all. Instead, we can describe the system totally in terms of the rat's tuning and thereby mystify our colleagues who hold to the complex-structure metaphor. Anything that can be done with the similarity space can be done with the bucket. (We can even describe a considerable body of data with a stupid process and a stupid structure [Landauer, 1975], but then we have to be very clever.) We cannot separate the model in Figure 15.1 from the model in Figure 15.2 empirically. They are just different metaphors or approaches.

Which metaphor do we want to use? If we want to remove the object nature of nests and of modules, we choose complicated processes like tuning and say as little as possible about the internal structure.

Consider an actual example of trading structure for process. We had a discussion at the conferences as to whether the autobiographical memory structures presented in Barsalou's chapter 8 were really in the mind

Figure 15.2. A complex-process memory model.

or whether general processes of making a narrative produced the structure Barsalou observed in his summarized-event data. Neisser (1982) raised the same point with respect to the canonical structure of flashbulb memories. We could say that autobiographical memories are stored in a structured way, and we simply start at the beginning and spread until we produce a whole sequence about the occurrences of a summer. Alternatively, we could say that the process of constructing a narrative orders memories that were stored randomly, very much like the semantic nodes were tossed randomly into the bucket in Figure 15.2. Either way will explain the data: the latencies between times, the order of output, and clustering. It may just take a little longer to learn narrative structure or to train a rat than it takes to create a memory structure.

We can say that when people learn, they either have added to their internal structure or have developed a skill. For riding a bicycle, most of us, I think, would prefer to talk about skill, because we would not want to draw a structure such as that in Figure 15.1 for how a 7-year-old maintains balance while going around a curve on a bicycle. But, equivalently, bicycle riding could be described with a complex structure. For catching a ball and for other activities, Bartlett (1932) also preferred skill. After all, his book was named after the complex process of remembering, whereas the book by Ebbinghaus that he criticized was named after the complex structure of memory. Gibsonians would not want to describe complex structures; rather, they would want to say that the behaviors involved become more skilled. We can explain behavior with either a complex structure or a complex process, but if we use a complex process, we get rid of the thing in the mind.

But Professor Neisser uses complex structure. Can he do it otherwise? I do not think so, because I think that he is right about our spatial abilities. Our spatial abilities are so pervasive and so strong that they do not allow for the development of complex-process models. As Neisser (1976) has noted, even the flow diagrams of processing in information-processing models become little boxes. Process ends up being drawn on a blackboard spatially as structures. Even my clever rat had to run around in a spatial bucket because I could not think of, or describe, a process without a rigid, definite structure. Neisser, I, and everyone else I know about work with a spatial metaphor. We just cannot fully utilize a complex-process metaphor. Instead, we tend to change process into structure. That is one reason that Gibson, Kolers, Skinner, and even Bartlett are difficult to understand and seem opaque or even crazy to many people when they stress the complex-process metaphor to the exclusion of mental structures. That is one reason why concepts like tuning or resonance are hard to develop, whereas a concept like semantic network is sufficiently easy to develop that everyone can devise his or her own.

Perhaps approaches that use the mechanisms of mathematics, and thereby remove themselves from normal thought processes, will allow us to develop complex-process models, as opposed to complex-structure models (Grossberg, 1982; McClelland & Rumelhart, 1985). Perhaps we shall stop being so involved with the models we build and with our attempts to distinguish between functionally equivalent metaphors and turn more of our energies to understanding the behaviors that the models and metaphors were initially intended to explain. Time will tell.

For now, however, it appears that Neisser, and the rest of us, simply cannot devise the process model that would advance Gibsonian ecological theory and that current complex-process metaphor solutions, such as tuning and resonance, are too vague. Who could offer an attractive alternative to the complex-structure metaphor? Following Gibson's general approach, I think we should look for an animal that evolved in a constantly changing dense liquid or heavy-gas environment without stable landmarks or directions.

NOTES

The title of this chapter, "Go for the Skill," is a slight change from what Professor Neisser asked me to do in my discussion of his work. I added the *S*. Support for the preparation of this chapter was provided by NSF grant BNS-8410124. I wish to thank Susan Havrilesky for drawing Figure 15.2, Lynn Hasher, Peter Holland, and Wanda Wallace for their comments, and Ulric Neisser for making this chapter possible.

REFERENCES

Barsalou, L. W. (1983). Ad hoc categories. *Memory & Cognition, 11*, 211–227.
Bartlett, F. C. (1932). *Remembering: A study in the experimental and social psychology.* Cambridge University Press.
Bransford, J. D., McCarrell, N. S., Franks, J. J., & Nitsch, K. E. (1977). Toward unexplaining memory. In R. Shaw & J. Bransford (Eds.), *Perceiving, acting, and knowing: Toward an ecological psychology* (pp. 431–466). Hillsdale, NJ: Erlbaum.
Gibson, J. J. (1966). *The senses considered as perceptual systems.* Boston: Houghton Mifflin.
  (1979). *The ecological approach to visual perception.* Boston: Houghton Mifflin.
Grossberg, S. (1982). *Studies of mind and brain: Neural principles of learning, perception, development, cognition, and motor control.* Boston: D. Reidel.
Kolers, P. A., & Roediger, H. L., III (1984). Procedures of mind. *Journal of Verbal Learning and Verbal Behavior, 23*, 425–449.
Kolers, P. A., & Smythe, W. E. (1984). Symbol manipulation: Alternatives to the computational view of mind. *Journal of Verbal Learning and Verbal Behavior, 23*, 289–314.
Kvale, S. (1977). Dialectics and research on remembering. In N. Datan & W. H. Reese (Eds.), *Life-span developmental psychology: Dialectical perspectives on experimental research* (pp. 165–189). New York: Academic Press.
Landauer, T. K. (1975). Memory without organization: Properties of a model with random storage and undirected retrieval. *Cognitive Psychology, 7*, 495–531.
McClelland, J. L., & Rumelhart, D. E. (1985). Distributed memory and the representation of general and specific information. *Journal of Experimental Psychology: General, 114*, 159–188.
Neisser, U. (1967). *Cognitive psychology.* New York: Appleton-Century-Crofts.
  (1976). *Cognition and reality: Principles and implications of cognitive psychology.* San Francisco: Freeman.
  (1981). John Dean's memory: A case study. *Cognition, 9*, 1–22.
  (1982). Snapshots or benchmarks? In U. Neisser (Ed.), *Memory observed: Remembering in natural contexts* (pp. 43–48). San Francisco: Freeman.
  (1986). Nested structure in autobiographical memory. In D. C. Rubin (Ed.), *Autobiographical memory* (pp. 71–81). Cambridge University Press.
  (1987). A sense of where you are: Functions of the spatial module. In P. Ellen & C. Thinus-Blanc (Eds.), *Cognitive processes and spatial orientation in animals and man.* Dordrecht: Martinus Nijhoff.

Roediger, H. L., III (1980). Memory metaphors in cognitive psychology. *Memory & Cognition, 8,* 231–246.

Rubin, D. C., & Friendly, M. (1986). Predicting which words get recalled: Measures of free recall, availability, goodness, emotionality, and pronunciability for 925 nouns. *Memory & Cognition, 14,* 79–94.

Rubin, D. C., & Olson, M. J. (1980). Recall of semantic domains. *Memory & Cognition, 8,* 354–366.

Rumelhart, D. E., & Norman, D. A. (in press). Representation in memory. In R. C. Atkinson, R. J. Herrnstein, G. Lindzey, & R. D. Luce (Eds.), *Handbook of experimental psychology.* New York: Wiley.

Shepard, R. N. (1984). Ecological contraints on internal representation: Resonant kinematics of perceiving, imagining, thinking, and dreaming. *Psychological Review, 91,* 417–447.

Skinner, B. F. (1974). *About behaviorism.* New York: Knopf.

Name index

Subject index

abstract memory, 247
accuracy of memory, 15, 28, 79–81, 365–6; *see also* autobiographical memory, verifiability
action: categories, 61; recall of, 38, 56–9, 62–4; frequency, 64–5; vs. thoughts, 83
action–thought coordination, 132
activity dominance hypothesis, *see* event organization
adaptive hypothesis, *see* functions of memory
adaptive significance of memory, *see* functions of memory
affect: *see* event characteristics, emotion
amnesia, 146, 224; infantile, 17, 244–6, 254, 265, 268, 281, 370; source, 345
analytic vs. nonanalytic processes, 148–9, 162
associations, 376
attributions, 151, 152, 162; *see also* familiarity
autobiographical memory: accuracy of, 93, 120, 121, 315–16; as allegory, 92–3; autobiographical facts, 22; chronological recall, 213–14, 218, 222, 238n; computational theories, 193–5; development, 235, 247, 265, 266; emotion, 78–9; extended-event time lines, 218–26, 235–6, 239n; foil similarity, 96, 115; foils in testing, 93–7, 127, 134–5, 140–2; forgetting of, 81–2, *see also* forgetting; generic memory, 22; hierarchical organization, 213, 219, 364; imagery, 130; inference, 130, 132; methodology, 23–5; narrative styles, 217–18; narrative truth, 315–16; organization by activity, 194, 205–11, 213, 215, 217; organization by locations, 205–11; organization by participants, 205–11; organization by time, 205–11, 238n; personal memory, 22; phenomenal experience, 130, 131, 132; reconstruction, 92, 96, 126, 137, 138, 139,

143; self, 277; self-schema, 23; sharing of, 267–8, 281; specific vs. summarized events, 202–3; summarized events, 204, 222, 224–6, 235–6; for thoughts, 128; *see also* event organization
autobiography, 92; literary, 316–17, 319
awareness of the past, 17–18, 150, 151, 172–3; *see also* unaware uses of memory

ballads, constraints on, 285
ballads, recall of by folksingers: consistency of, 287–92, 303; gist, 290; melody, 290–2; meter, 292, 295, 297; poetic constraints on, 288–92
ballads, recall of by students: causal connectedness, 295–7; imagery value, 294, 296–7; poetic constraints on, 294–5, 297–301; rhythm, 301–3
beeper, 29

clustering, 214–17
comprehension, 195, 198; *see also* event organization; language comprehension
conceptual models, 233
conceptually driven processing, *see* data-driven vs. conceptually driven processing
consistency, 287–92, 303
constructive processes, 14–15, 27–8, 79–81, 342, 366; *see also* accuracy
context, enabling, 312, 313, 314, 319, 320, 321, 325
Copenhagen school, 326–7
copy theories, 26
Crovitz technique, 23–4
cue elaboration, 223
cues: recall accuracy, 52–3; type, 47; *see also* distinctiveness
CYRUS, 196–8, 203–4, 220, 223, 238n

data-driven vs. conceptually driven processing, 159–62